H. Jefferson Powell

THE MORAL TRADITION OF AMERICAN CONSTITUTIONALISM

A Theological Interpretation

Duke University Press Durham and London 1993

Printed in the United States of America
on acid-free paper ∞
Designed by Cherie Holma Westmoreland
Typeset in Bodoni and Caledonia
by Keystone Typesetting, Inc.
Library of Congress Cataloging-in-
Publication Data appear on the last
printed page of this book.

To Stanley Hauerwas, Teacher and Friend

CONTENTS

ACKNOWLEDGMENTS

Behind this book lie many debts. Lorri and Sara, first and foremost, have supported me and helped me keep my work in perspective. I also particularly want to thank Peter Fish, Stanley Fish, Tom Langford, Ken Surin, and Geoffrey Wainwright, who served on my doctoral committees and from whose teaching and criticism I have learned a great deal. Tom Shaffer and Sandy Levinson both took time from busy schedules to give the manuscript a careful reading. I deeply appreciate their comments, even those I was unwise enough not to follow. The Yale Law School supported the research on which the book rests by a Senior Fellowship during the years 1987 to 1989, and I am grateful to the school and to Dean Guido Calabresi for that and much else. It has been a great pleasure to work with the staff at the Duke University Press, and especially with my editor Rachel Toor. They are models of what I think the editors of an academic press should be.

A special thanks must go to Moody Smith, my advisor during my first sojourn in the Graduate Religion Program at Duke. Moody has been a friend and mentor ever since, and without his encouragement, I would not have had the courage to return to graduate school or to complete my doctorate.

The medieval theologian Johannes Eckhart is supposed to have said that "those who write big volumes should have a dog with them to give them life." My dog Psyche was my constant companion during the summer of 1990, when I wrote the first draft of the book. I miss the life and joy she gave me very much.

The person to whom I dedicate this book has taught me, among many other things, that theology is fun and friendship is serious business. And vice versa.

THE MORAL TRADITION OF AMERICAN CONSTITUTIONALISM

INTRODUCTION

When all is said and done, courts are the final interpreters of our laws and our values.[1]

The nations that populate the map of the late twentieth century are built on a variety of divergent foundations. Many, of course, rest on widespread ethnic or linguistic commonality uniting the nation and setting it apart from other countries. Others are the creation of imperial history or fiat. All of them, however, owe much of their external form and internal structure to the political creativity of early modern Europe. Western Europeans of the seventeenth and eighteenth centuries faced potentially catastrophic crises of sectarian violence and moral chaos, crises that appeared to demonstrate the inadequacy of their medieval heritage, the ethical and political order of the *res publica Christianum.* The European response was to create, over the course of a century or so, a novel moral order and an equally novel political form—Enlightenment liberalism and the modern nation-state—and then to impose both that order and that form on the rest of the world.[2] In many circumstances, of course, neither liberal thought nor the presuppositions of the nation-state were especially compatible with preexisting social and cultural structures, with results ranging from the tragic[3] to the comic-opera.[4]

1 Statement in "AIG Issues Forum," *Time*, April 8, 1991, 79 (advertisement).

2 Among the many works dealing with the intellectual and political accomplishments of early modernity, I have found the writings of Alasdair MacIntyre (discussed in chapter 1); Jeffrey Stout, *The Flight from Authority* (Notre Dame: Univ. of Notre Dame Press, 1981); and Anthony Giddens, *The Nation-State and Violence* (Berkeley: Univ. of California Press, 1987), the most helpful.

3 Among many examples, regard the successive (and indeed partly simultaneous) imposition of Marxism and capitalism on Chinese culture, or the attempt to resolve centuries of ethnic and political confusion by dubbing artificial conglomerations such as Nigeria or Yugoslavia nations.

4 I have in mind the proliferation of tiny island-states since 1950, each of

More generally, the course of twentieth-century history puts seriously in question the ability of liberalism and the nation-state to accomplish their original purposes, the creation of order and the control of violence.

Among the populous nation-states of the modern world, the United States arguably is unique. Where other nations arose out of the imposition of liberal political structures on existing *ethnoi* or externally defined geographic areas, the United States is almost purely the product of Enlightenment thought and liberal political action. Created by Western European immigrants to a "new world" where their experience seemed to recapitulate in sober reality the abstractions of social contract and individual autonomy, the political and legal structures of the United States directly translated liberal theory into governmental practice. Substantially freer of the remains of premodern moral orders than their old world cousins, Americans built a society on straightforward liberal principles. The United States is, as its admirers have often proclaimed, a living experiment in the possibility of organizing human life on the principles of reason—"reason" as understood by the writers and politicians of the Enlightenment. On the success of the American experiment, therefore, hangs much of the continuing plausibility of liberalism as a moral and political philosophy.

In the last decade, philosophers and social critics have debated with increasing vehemence the argument that liberalism is morally bankrupt, even as the nation-state seems to be an ever more anachronistic solution to the problems of social cooperation and social violence.[5] Despite the American provenance of much of the debate, however, few writers have taken the political peculiarities of American liberalism into account. Alasdair MacIntyre's generally persua-

---

which finds the trappings of European-style sovereignty necessary to its self-definition. Of course, even here the tragic is never far away. Think, for example, of the stormy political history of such nations as Mauritius.

5 The splintering of the USSR, the increasing importance of the European Community, and the inability of the national government of the United States to resolve or even address any important domestic concerns, all display the increasing irrelevance of the nation-state in its classical modern form. Irrelevance, unfortunately, is not synonymous with insignificance: nation-states remain capable of causing enormous human suffering even as they become impotent to accomplish their original purpose of sustaining order and controlling violence.

sive account of liberalism's moral and political predicament, for example, fails to differentiate the history of liberalism in the United States from the European experience: for MacIntyre, the peculiar moral claims of American liberal politics are simply one more (rather uninteresting) example of liberal propaganda or self-delusion.[6] In addition, despite the Christian identity of some of the debaters (again, MacIntyre is a good example), as yet there have been few distinctively Christian voices in the argument over liberalism's demise. This book is an attempt to evaluate, from a Christian and theological perspective, the current status of the American experiment in liberalism.

The essay begins with a hypothesis that it then seeks to render plausible: although American society and American nationhood originated in a deliberate attempt to embody liberal thought politically, the course of American history diverted liberal thought and action into channels significantly different from those followed in Europe and elsewhere. Former British provincials constituted themselves "Americans" by the deliberate articulation and adoption of explicit, liberal moral principles, such as "All men are created equal and endowed by their Creator with certain unalienable rights" or "We the People . . . do ordain and establish this Constitution." Rather than imposing liberal concepts onto prevenient moral commitments and social forms, Americans attempted to construct moral and social arrangements on the basis of liberal thought. The consequence is a society defined by the (liberal) distinction between the public and the private in which it is a commonplace to describe the courts, a quintessential public institution, as the "final interpreters" of "our values." As de Tocqueville had already noticed a century and a half ago, in the United States all important political questions are ultimately treated as legal questions; since all important moral issues are politically significant (especially including the issue of which moral matters are to be regarded as apolitical), this has come to mean that the law, both as a set of institutions and as a mode of thought, defines the American identity. Moral and political questions in America finally *are* legal questions, whether they concern the authority of the national government to wage war or the authority of a

6 MacIntyre, *After Virtue*, 2d ed. (Notre Dame: Univ. of Notre Dame Press, 1984), 253–54 (hereafter cited as MacIntyre [1984]).

comatose person's family to command the attending physicians to cease their efforts to sustain his or her life.

At the center of American law is the Constitution of the United States, and the decisions of judges interpreting it. The Constitution's centrality is both pragmatic and iconic. It is the "supreme law of the land," and in its name judges, and ultimately the nine justices of the United States Supreme Court, frequently overrule the preferences of presidents, congresses, state officials, and public opinion. The Constitution's centrality, however, extends well beyond the scope of judicial decision; the language of "rights" is the preferred mode of moral discourse in American society as a whole. It is through constitutionalism, as a rhetoric, as a complex of ideas, and as a set of political practices, that American liberalism has shaped American society.[7] Specifically, in MacIntyre's terminology, American constitutionalism[8] is a moral tradition, liberal in its major presuppositions although distinctive in its history and forms.

The assertion that there is or can be a liberal moral tradition is at first sight paradoxical. The goal of Enlightenment liberalism, MacIntyre and others have shown, was to establish "a form of social order in which individuals could emancipate themselves from the contingency and particularity of tradition by appealing to genuinely universal tradition-independent norms."[9] The early liberals identified the particularity of traditions as a primary source of the sectarian violence that threatened European culture (and even survival).[10] By

7 "The leading makers of the American constitution conceived themselves as influenced by political philosophy, which they took in its modern [i.e., Enlightment] form." George P. Grant, *English-Speaking Justice* (Notre Dame: Univ. of Notre Dame Press, 1985), 55. This book argues that the American founders were successful in devising a constitutional order that incorporated substantive Enlightenment commitments.

8 By *constitutionalism* I shall mean the ethos of American constitutional thought as well as its specific workings out in constitutional theory and constitutional adjudication. By *constitutional law* I shall refer to the body of decisions and doctrines employed by American courts in adjudicating constitutional claims. While no sharp line should be drawn between federal and state constitutional law, in general I shall have in view the culture and law symbolized by the federal Constitution.

9 MacIntyre, *Whose Justice? Which Rationality?* (Notre Dame: Univ. of Notre Dame Press, 1988), 335 (hereafter cited as MacIntyre [1988]). See also MacIntyre (1984), 36–50.

10 See Stout, *Flight*, 228–55.

replacing tradition-bound authority with the supposedly neutral canons of reason, they hoped to provide a basis for a stable and humane society consonant with human nature and agreeable to all reasoning persons.[11] By replacing traditional political forms (feudal relationships, the transethnic church) with the nation-state, they hoped to create a political authority that would monopolize the exercise of violence within its geographic sphere,[12] and in turn subject its own violence to the control of reason.

The Enlightenment project was at one and the same time wildly successful and a complete failure. The liberals secured intellectual and institutional dominance, eventually throughout the world, but without achieving either moral consensus or social peace.[13] The ironic result, as MacIntyre recently has acknowledged, was liberalism's emergence as "one more contingently grounded and founded tradition, in conflict with other rival traditions *as such*."[14] The contemporary crisis of liberalism, in MacIntyre's revised analysis, is the crisis of a moral tradition that has lost its way, that has become unable to resolve its dilemmas or reconcile its disputants. Set in the American context, if this analysis of liberalism and its current crisis is correct, we would expect to be able to trace the development of constitutionalism into a moral tradition, and its subsequent decline into a state of intellectual and moral confusion.

With a number of complications and qualifications, the study presented here confirms this expectation. American constitutionalism developed in the nineteenth century into a tradition of enquiry into the moral presuppositions of American liberal society, a tradition that a specific institution, the American judiciary, employed to

11 For the goals of the early liberals, see, e.g., Rogers Smith, *Liberalism and American Constitutional Law* (Cambridge, Mass.: Harvard Univ. Press, 1985).

12 See Giddens, *Violence*, 181–92.

13 The general statement in the text is subject of course to many partial exceptions and qualifications. American society, for example, seems characterized by widespread agreement on the possessive-individualistic strand of liberal moral thought, while American politics legitimately can claim to have secured peace for some of the people, much of the time. Religious and other attacks on possessive individualism, and the myriad failures of American government to constrain violence (its own as well as others') point to the failure of even this most liberal of political orders to fulfill the hopes of the early liberals, and of the American founders themselves.

14 MacIntyre (1988), 346 (emphasis added).

provide a reasoned basis for constraining and directing state violence. Unlike the contemporaneous English and continental legal traditions, which in this period became steadily more explicit in their instrumental subservience to extralegal authority, American constitutionalism successfully established its claim to provide both the ultimate moral language and final moral forum for American moral discussion. Indeed, the moral pretensions and institutional competence of American constitutional institutions appeared to increase dramatically in the first three quarters of the twentieth century, the same period that saw Western liberalism as a whole descend into the intellectual crisis that MacIntyre and others have described.

Many American liberals see the past fifty years or so as a triumphant vindication of liberalism in its American constitutional form.[15] For them, the recent rumblings of concern over the intellectual health of American constitutionalism are the product of adventitious political events (the election of "conservative" presidents who then appoint "conservative" justices)[16] or of selfish opposition to liberal moral principle. Other American liberals, those who think many of the trends of recent jurisprudence are wrong, call for a return to authentic tradition as the solution for constitutional and moral disagreement.[17] This book suggests that neither position is tenable: the

15 This understanding of recent American constitutional history clearly underlies the work of John Rawls, from his famous *A Theory of Justice* (Cambridge, Mass.: Harvard Univ. Press) on. The just social order that *A Theory of Justice* wove behind the "veil of ignorance," which of course Rawls himself now describes as a particular political vision, bears a remarkable and hardly accidental resemblance to the society explicit constitutional theorists such as Ronald Dworkin find in American constitutionalism.

16 There is little or no tradition of genuinely conservative political thought in the United States, if that term is given its European sense of antiliberal, anti-Enlightenment politics. American "liberals" and "conservatives" are equally heirs and children of the Enlightenment, and their (sometimes very real) disagreements are battles over the "true" meaning of liberalism. In this book I will use the word *liberal* as it is used by writers such as MacIntyre and Rogers Smith, to refer to the tradition of thought and action which originates in the Enlightenment and which regards the individual, understood as an autonomous center of will and reason, as logically and morally prior to any community and all moral commitments. On the few occasions it is necessary to take account of contemporary popular political classifications, I will refer to "liberals" and "conservatives" in quotation marks.

17 The best-known of these "conservative" liberals is probably former judge Robert Bork. See Bork, *The Tempting of America* (New York: Free Press, 1990).

American constitutional tradition has worked itself into a conceptual and moral quagmire from which it does not appear to have the resources to escape. Neither a return to the supposedly triumphant progression of the past half-century nor the recovery of an "original understanding" of constitutionalism offers a solution to the problems that bedevil contemporary constitutionalists. Those problems are not the result of poor choices by the voters or of bad faith on the part of the judges, but are the form in which Western liberalism's contemporary crisis finally has manifested itself in that particular strand that is American constitutionalism.

It is my hope that the interpretation of American constitutionalism advanced in this book will be of interest to a variety of different readerships. The critique of liberalism that MacIntyre and others are currently pressing sets fundamental questions against the intellectual and institutional arrangements of Western societies; the counterarguments of the defenders of liberalism raise equally fundamental issues about the nature of moral philosophy and social criticism. This book attempts to contribute directly to this debate by examining sympathetically one of Western liberalism's greatest accomplishments.

The nature and health of constitutional law are topics of great importance to my fellow lawyers, as well as to public officials and American citizens generally. This book presents an account of constitutional law with controversial implications for judicial practice and legal argument, implications that cut across the "liberal"/"conservative" dichotomy that structures so much of contemporary constitutional debate. Even if few legal readers find themselves in agreement with my conclusions as a whole, I believe the unusual perspective from which I have approached a familiar subject may be illuminating.

The proper interpretation of American constitutionalism is a matter of concern not only to intellectual historians, moral philosophers, and lawyers; members of the religious groups that exist within the United States have a vital stake in understanding and responding appropriately to the moral culture of the most powerful modern nation-state. I write from within one such group, the Christian, and the ultimate purpose of this book is to be of service in the Christian community's ethical task of living faithfully in this society. American constitutionalism, with its powerful rhetoric of "justice" and "equality," has tempted Christians from the beginning to treat the American political system as theologically unique, the reflection in the political realm of Christian moral principles.[18] Unlike other systems, the American appears to accord real power to a true forum of principle.[19] Unlike political theories that function primarily as legitimations of the state's use of violence, American constitutionalism claims to privilege the restraint of violence over its exercise, and the dispassionate reason of the judge over the expedient decision of the legislator or executive official. Furthermore, American constitutionalism unquestionably has played an important role at times in checking the abuse of power, a role that Christians have theological[20] reasons for approving.[21] The temptation to ascribe theological value to the institutions and the modes of thought of American constitutionalism is easily understandable, as is the consequent tendency to underwrite uncritical Christian support for the American legal system. The ultimate objective of this book is to challenge any unquestioning theological approval of American constitutionalism and to suggest ways in which Christians involved in the constitutional order (as lawyers, school board members, voters, or victims) can rightly respond to the demands and the pretensions of that order.

This book thus pursues several rather different objectives: the interpretation of American constitutionalism from the perspective of the current debate over Western liberalism, an interest in understanding the history and current situation of constitutional law, the Christian and theological objectives I have just outlined. Those read-

18 See, e.g., William J. Everett, *God's Federal Republic* (New York: Paulist Press, 1988); and Daniel C. Maguire, *A New American Justice* (Garden City, N.Y.: Doubleday, 1980).

19 See Ronald Dworkin, *A Matter of Principle* (Cambridge, Mass.: Harvard Univ. Press, 1982). Maguire describes the United States Supreme Court as "an official philosophical forum." Maguire, *American Justice*, 7.

20 By "theological," I include those aspects of Christian thought and action that are often separated out as moral or ethical. Such a categorization, however sensible in other traditions, seems fundamentally mistaken in a Christian context. The argument that American constitutionalism's claim to constrain and direct violence through reasoned discussion is false is not "merely" a conclusion in some semi-autonomous field of Christian or agapeistic ethics, but is a fundamentally theological assertion: as Caesar always does in the end, the American state lays claim to divine prerogatives, a claim that (as always) is false and idolatrous.

21 The crucial role of the judiciary in the dismantling of legal race segregation in the South is the most obvious example.

ers interested in only a subset of these goals will evaluate my arguments in a different context from that out of which I write, but it is my hope that they will find the essay's application of MacIntyrean social criticism to American constitutionalism as illuminating for their intellectual interests as I have found it for mine.

The argument of the book proceeds in four stages. In the first chapter, I analyze the formal structure of MacIntyre's theory[22] of traditions, practices, and virtues; the last section of the chapter synthesizes the somewhat different substantive accounts of liberalism in *After Virtue* and *Whose Justice? Which Rationality?* The chapter's underlying purpose is to develop conceptual tools adequate to interpret American constitutionalism as a liberal tradition of moral enquiry. Lawyers are not accustomed to regarding constitutionalism as a moral discourse, while much constitutional rhetoric is devoted to denying that constitutional law is legitimately a tradition. Philosophers and theologians, on the other hand, are likely to regard the description of constitutionalism as a moral tradition as an absurdly grandiose claim by self-aggrandizing academic lawyers or, more charitably, as a sort of category error, akin to comparing the tradition of Thomism with the tradition of stamp collecting. By systematizing, and at times correcting, MacIntyre's account of traditions, I hope to render plausible the argument of the second chapter, that the history of American constitutionalism displays the evolution of a particular strand of liberalism into a full-fledged tradition.

The second chapter of the book employs MacIntyre's theoretical tools to present a narrative exposition of American constitutionalism as a moral tradition. The adoption of a narrative form follows from the decision to use MacIntyre's theory: by tracing the historical development of the intellectual, institutional and social aspects of constitutionalism, I establish the validity of treating constitutionalism as a tradition. The course of the tradition's recent history indicates that at present constitutionalism is in an "epistemological crisis" that under-

22 By "theory," all I mean in this context is the pattern of philosophical analysis which MacIntyre presented in *After Virtue* and refined in *Whose Justice? Which Rationality?*. Although chapter 1 indicates some discrete problems and loose ends, I agree with Jeffrey Stout that MacIntyre has created "a vocabulary of moral description and assessment in which a powerful and penetrating critique of our society can be carried out." Stout, *Ethics after Babel* (Boston: Beacon Press, 1988), 266.

cuts its previous claims to rationality. Since the central moral claim of constitutionalism, as with all liberal thought, is that it can constrain and direct violence through reason, constitutionalism's current epistemological problems threaten to undo its claim to moral legitimacy and authority.

In the third chapter of the book, I address the efforts of contemporary constitutional theorists to overcome the crisis of the tradition. Constitutionalism, like liberalism generally, usually has laid claim to neutrality and objectivity. Contemporary constitutional theorists[23] have responded to crisis by explicitly abandoning this claim, and affirming, in a variety of ways, that constitutionalism entails moral commitments specific to a particular community and that, indeed, constitutionalism is the social morality of the American polity. I argue that none of the attempts to deliver constitutionalism from its conceptual troubles succeeds, chiefly because none of the theorists can describe, convincingly or attractively, a moral and rational center to contemporary constitutional thought. Rather than explicating the coherence of shared American moral commitments, contemporary theorists offer little more than a veiled apologia for rule by a liberal oligarchy. Since that oligarchy itself can no longer draw on a healthy tradition of rational enquiry, its decisions are, and will increasingly be, ad hoc responses to political pressure and personal preference.

In the final chapter of the book, I turn to expressly theological considerations. American constitutionalism's substantive moral commitments were always liberal and thus in tension or contradiction with central Christian claims. If the argument in chapters 2 and 3 is persuasive, constitutionalism's ability to fulfill its central promise—to constrain and direct violence through rational discourse—has disappeared even as the moral claims of its apologists have heightened. In particular, the decay of constitutionalism as a rational tradition makes it imperative to determine the appropriate response to the institutional struggle between the courts (with their powerful but essentially unguided pretensions to moral authority) and elected officials (with their democratic pretensions and their vulnerability to

23 Some liberal political theorists have attempted a similar response to the general crisis of liberalism. See, e.g., the later work of John Rawls and Richard Rorty's *Contingency, Irony and Solidarity* (Cambridge, Mass.: Harvard Univ. Press, 1989).

"majoritarian"[24] pressure). Chapter 4 employs John Howard Yoder's theological analysis of secular politics to address that imperative. Two possible answers—an enthusiastic embrace of constitutionalism as the mode of translating theological commitments into secular policy, and the categorical rejection of any use of the language and institutions of constitutionalism—are rejected. The equation of constitutional with theological ethics repeats the ancient Constantinian error of confusing Caesar with God; in addition, Christians who make this error inevitably are blinded to the increasing irrationality and violence of the constitutional "order." A blanket refusal to employ the linguistic and institutional resources of constitutionalism, on the other hand, ignores the real (if limited) possibility of using constitutional argument to enhance the ability of the victim and the outsider to be heard. The Christian lawyer, school board member, voter, or victim must not be deceived by the false claims of American constitutionalism to "establish justice," but he or she need not reject out of hand one means that exists in this society by which the Christian can speak truth to power. I conclude that Christians have a theological basis on which to support and invoke the continued exercise of judicial power on behalf of political minorities because constitutional rhetoric about political speech and political participation rights enhances the ability of the victim and the stranger to be heard. I argue that Christian theological commitments also underwrite strong support for the judicial imposition of procedural regularity on executive and administrative officials, for by doing so courts directly, if only marginally, mitigate the violence and oppressiveness of the state. With respect to most areas of governmental policy, on the other hand, I conclude that Christians have theological reasons to reject the efforts of constitutionalists to substitute policy-making by judges for policy-making by electorally responsible officials. Contemporary American judges do not impose the rule of reason on Caesar, they *are* Caesar. The task of Christians, in the United States as elsewhere, is not to endorse the pretensions of power but to limit the injustice of Caesar.

24 Of course, in contemporary America, elected officials typically are most responsive not to actual (demographic) majorities but to shifting alliances of influential or well-financed pressure groups.

Chapter One

THE CONCEPT OF A MORAL TRADITION

This book is an attempt to interpret and evaluate American constitutionalism on three different levels. I am concerned, first, to understand constitutionalism as a political and intellectual embodiment of Enlightenment liberalism. The derivation of American constitutional law from the political thought of philosophers such as Locke and Montesquieu is of course a commonplace—if a contested one—of intellectual history. What has not yet been done is to examine that intellectual genealogy in the light of the critical rereading of the Enlightenment put forward by contemporary antiliberal philosophers such as Alasdair MacIntyre. That rereading has significant implications for moral and political theory and practice. I am interested in testing the cogency of antiliberal assertions about the history and results of the Enlightenment project through a close examination of the history and current state of American constitutionalism.

This book is also concerned with making sense out of the current situation in federal constitutional law, the law that is articulated in the name of the United States Constitution and that provides a major locus for contemporary American political debate. Most participants and observers, I think, would agree that constitutional discourse is in serious theoretical disarray at the present time, and that this disarray has profound practical consequences for the ongoing process of reaching and criticizing constitutional decisions. Based on my argument that MacIntyre's work provides an illuminating perspective from which to understand constitutionalism as a political tradition, the book advances as well a description and explanation of the disarray in constitutional law that, I hope, will interest all those engaged in its study.

The purpose of this book, finally, is to develop a Christian theological analysis of American constitutionalism. If it is to be genuinely theological, such an analysis ultimately must be practical—oriented toward praxis[1]—and the appropriate practical exposition of Christian faith depends upon the truthful description of the situation in which Christians are acting.[2] The task of truthful description, in turn, often demands that we pay explicit attention to the tools we use in understanding and to the form or genre of our descriptions. In this chapter of the book I address these questions of method.

It is not obvious at first glance that there can be a theological description of American constitutionalism. The outcome of particular constitutional arguments or Supreme Court votes is often of importance to Christians—Christians hardly can be indifferent, for example, to official governmental sponsorship of prayer—but it may not be clear that there is anything theological to be said about the forms of argument or institutional arrangements that lead to those outcomes. This book employs the recent work of Alasdair MacIntyre on moral traditions in order to present a theological interpretation of constitutionalism that can treat its subject as more than a set of outcomes.

MacIntyre's ongoing explication of the notion of moral tradition is itself part of a specific project of social criticism: MacIntyre's attempt to describe and explain the current state of moral discourse in Western culture. MacIntyre's now-famous claim, the so-called catastrophe thesis, is that contemporary moral discussion is endless and unavailing because Western societies lack the sort of shared framework of thought and commitment that is necessary to make moral agreement among disputants possible even in theory. In putting forward this claim, MacIntyre has elaborated an account of "tradi-

1 On the necessity of preserving the theological character of theological ethics, see Stanley Hauerwas, *Against the Nations* (Minneapolis: Winston Press, 1985), 23–50. I accept the arguments of theologians such as George Lindbeck and Dietrich Ritschl that Christian theology is a second-order activity of reflection on and criticism of first-order Christian activities such as worship, witness, and service. See Lindbeck, *The Nature of Doctrine* (Philadelphia: Westminster Press, 1984); Ritschl, *The Logic of Theology*, trans. John Bowden (Philadephia: Fortress Press, 1987). This book's ultimate purpose is to suggest corrections to the contemporary Christian response—in witness and social action—to the American constitutional order.

2 See Stanley Hauerwas, *Christian Existence Today* (Durham, N.C.: Labyrinth Press, 1988), 101–14.

tion" as the framework necessary to rational argument. Christianity is itself a moral tradition (or, to be more exact, a related group of traditions) in MacIntyre's terms, while the dominant modes of thought in Western culture since the Enlightenment have been a self-conscious attempt to escape from or transcend tradition. (MacIntyre's view on the success or failure of this attempt has shifted over time, raising issues discussed below.)

The use of MacIntyre's work enables me both to develop a plausible interpretation of American constitutionalism and to display the logic of subjecting that interpretation to theological criticism. American constitutionalism, I will argue, is one of the specific forms that Enlightenment moral and political thought has assumed in the modern world; put another way, constitutionalism is the product of the Enlightenment's parallel attempts to control irrational and violent action through the institution of the nation-state, and to replace irrational, tradition-dependent moralities with universal norms of reason. However, American constitutionalism became at an early stage a tradition of rational enquiry in MacIntyre's terms. The history of constitutionalism thus supports the conclusion that the outcome of the Enlightenment project was, ironically, the creation of a moral tradition. Identifying constitutionalism as a moral tradition, furthermore, identifies the logic of the theological analysis: Christian theology and American constitutionalism share the intellectual and social structure MacIntyre identifies as characteristic of moral traditions. They both are concerned with the rational exploration of the nature of human community and of the good life, and thus are in a significant sense rivals or competitors.

The task of using MacIntyre's account of traditions in order to develop a description of constitutionalism which I then can analyze theologically requires me to employ more than one genre, and more than one voice over the course of the argument. Chapter 2, which develops the intepretation of constitutionalism as a moral tradition, takes the form of a historical narrative, a choice of genre that follows from my adoption of MacIntyrean interpretive tools. In that chapter, the voice is that of a critical insider, someone sympathetic to constitutionalism's goals and dynamic, but resistant to its dominant forms of self-interpretation.[3] Chapter 3, which discusses contemporary

3 A frequent criticism of MacIntyre's work is that his description of the

constitutionalists' efforts to solve that tradition's intellectual problems, is analytic in form but shares with chapter 2 the perspective of the critical insider. The present chapter and chapter 4, which presents the explicit ethical critique of constitutionalism, both are analytical in style and overtly theological in perspective: they are written in the author's own voice.

PRELIMINARY CONSIDERATIONS

In the introduction I implied that MacIntyre's work can be divided into a "theory" of traditions, practices, and virtues and a substantive account of liberalism. MacIntyre's own work suggests the feasibility of a division into theoretical and substantive elements. His original exposition of the notion of a social practice, for example, is a response to a hypothetical objection that "there are just too many different and incompatible conceptions of a virtue for there to be any real unity to the concept or indeed to the history" of the virtues.[4] Homer, Aristotle, Jane Austen, and Alasdair MacIntyre differ radically over what the substance of the good life for human beings is, the identity of the virtues, and the content of justice. What unites them is not some nonexistent agreement on which "human qualities are genuine virtues and which mere simulacra" (or even vices)[5] but a shared "logical

Enlightenment and of contemporary liberal culture is so unsympathetic as to verge on caricature. See, e.g., Jeffrey Stout, "Virtue Among the Ruins: An Essay on MacIntyre," 26 Neue Zeitschrift für Systematische Theologie und Religionsphilosophie 256 (1984). Whatever the merits of the criticism as applied, its underlying premise—that a MacIntyrean critic ought to strive to understand the tradition he or she is interpreting sympathetically, with something of the insider's concern for the tradition's own commitments and problems—seems correct. MacIntyre's interpretation of ancient Greek ethics is, I believe, a model in this respect: indeed, his interpretation of the Greek ethical tradition is so sympathetic that some critics mistakenly identify his interpretive success as substantive approbation. (Susan Moller Okin, whose criticisms of MacIntyre are discussed below, falls into this error.) On the theoretical issues surrounding what I am calling the necessity of critical sympathy, see MacIntyre (1988), 370–88 (discussing translation).

4 MacIntyre (1988), 181.

5 Id. at 183. MacIntyre suggests that at least one New Testament virtue, humility, would have seemed a vice to Aristotle. Id. at 182.

and conceptual structure."[6] Concepts such as "tradition," "practice," and "virtue" are used by MacIntyre to render visible this conceptual structure, which otherwise lies hidden beneath the manifest differences between, say, Homeric heroes and the inhabitants of Austenian drawing rooms.

The implication of MacIntyre's characterization of liberalism as a tradition in *Whose Justice? Which Rationality?* is that his conceptual apparatus is applicable outside its original role in displaying the unity of the tradition of the virtues. Jeffrey Stout, in particular, has combined strong criticism of MacIntyre's substantive view of liberalism with an enthusiastic endorsement of the methodological usefulness of MacIntyre's theoretical concepts in social criticism.[7] Nevertheless, two possible objections to my proposed procedure should be noted. First, it might be asked whether what I am calling the "theoretical" description of tradition and so on can in fact be separated from MacIntyre's substantive views. The theoretical concepts, after all, clearly derive their structure from the particular Aristotelian tradition they were crafted to describe. Perhaps they are simply inapplicable to a set of human arguments and activities as different from Aristotelian ethics as American constitutionalism. The proper response to this objection is to concede the possibility that it might prove correct. It would be fatally self-contradictory for a MacIntyrean social critic to lay implicit claim to a "neutral" or tradition-independent methodology. The only justification for applying MacIntyre's conceptual tools to American constitutionalism possible is that to be found in execution: does MacIntyre in fact make it possible to give an illuminating and plausible account of constitutionalism?[8]

A second objection to the proposed procedure is related but distinct. MacIntyre's theoretical concepts may work, in the sense that an interpreter employing them will conclude that American constitutionalism looks like a tradition with certain practices which require or call for the exercise of certain virtues, and so on. But, the objection goes, we have predetermined a negative evaluation of

6 Id. at 184.

7 Stout, *Ethics*, 266–67.

8 Stout's use of MacIntyre's theoretical concepts to discuss contemporary medicine seems to me justified by its power and plausibility as an interpretation of medical practice. See Id. at 269–75.

constitutionalism, for the tools we are using to analyze it are designed for and derived from a very different complex of ideas and activities. There are two cogent responses to this objection. Identifying a social reality as a tradition, practice, or virtue is not some sort of ethical compliment: MacIntyre readily admits that what formally are virtues may be (from a viewpoint within another community) substantively vicious[9] and that any practice "may under certain conditions be a source of evil."[10] The theoretical concepts thus are, to some degree, independent of substantive ethical commitments and evaluations; MacIntyre's own treatment of Hume reflects both sympathetic understanding and severe substantive disagreement.[11] Even more fundamentally, the second objection to the proposed method of proceeding is faulty because it assumes the existence of some neutral standpoint from which to describe and evaluate constitutionalism, the very assumption MacIntyre puts in question. To reject out of hand the value of a MacIntyrean inquiry into a given social reality is to refuse to listen to the only means by which MacIntyre's claims can be established—or refuted—in their own terms.[12] The fact that this book's account of constitutionalism is neither "accidentally [n]or by default a partisan narrative with its own deliberate one-sidedness,"[13] does not, by itself, invalidate the argument except for those who are unwilling to consider the possibility that there is no other type of narrative.

The value and feasibility of using MacIntyre's conceptual tools in examining contemporary social activities and institutions can be addressed, finally, by briefly considering an elaborate argument in the

9 MacIntyre (1984), 184 (Aristotle would "not have admired Jesus Christ and he would have been horrified by St. Paul"). In earlier work, MacIntyre himself expressed considerable moral objection to some of Aristotle's views. See MacIntyre, *A Short History of Ethics* (New York: Macmillan, 1966), 79, 83.

10 MacIntyre (1984), 200. MacIntyre expresses indecision about whether there can be genuine practices which "simply *are* evil." Id.

11 MacIntyre (1988), 281–325.

12 MacIntyre is careful to make his case against the existence of neutral, tradition-independent rationality an a posteriori argument: since Enlightenment liberalism is "by far the strongest claimant to provide such a ground which has so far appeared in human history," its failure to do so "provides the strongest reason that we can actually have that there is not such neutral ground." MacIntyre (1988), 346.

13 MacIntyre (1984), 272 (describing *After Virtue*).

negative, that of Susan Moller Okin.[14] Okin denies that MacIntyre's "theory" is of any contemporary value except to further the right-wing politics for which she accuses MacIntyre of being an apologist.[15] The "general and basic problem with [MacIntyre's] way of thinking" is that he is "incapable of dealing with the problem of the effects of *social domination* on beliefs and understandings."[16] Traditions (at least those traditions in which MacIntyre is interested) are invariably reflective of norms of social hierarchy and oppression: they are, in effect, apologies for the status quo. MacIntyre's admirers fail to deal with "the centrality of sexism and elitism" in the Artistotelian, Augustinian, and Thomistic traditions, or, indeed, with the "pervasive elitism . . . and . . . sexism" in MacIntyre's own work.[17] Tradition-dependent theories such as MacIntyre's have no critical distance from the social structures they undergird and so they "*cannot* deal adequately with the problem of domination."[18] Such theories, as a consequence, are intellectually and morally valueless or even reprehensible.

Okin's critique is unfair and illuminating at the same time. She is perhaps inadvertently unfair in that she does not recognize the centrality of conflict and change to MacIntyre's concept of tradition, a matter discussed at length below. On MacIntyre's understanding of tradition it is entirely understandable and even predictable that a fundamental agreement held at one stage in the history of the tradition (e.g., that women are inferior) should later be rejected as repugnant to the tradition. Similarly, MacIntyre's concept of tradition does not maintain that the tradition's commitments are at any given time universally or monolithically held—according to MacIntyre a living tradition is characterized by disagreement and change as much as by consensus. Recognition of the narrative continuity of a tradition (that Jane Austen is Homer's many-times-removed heir, for example) does

14 Susan Moller Okin, *Justice, Gender and the Family* (New York: Basic Books, 1989), chap. 3.

15 Okin notes that "[m]ost of those who discuss [MacIntyre's work] seem far more interested in its methodology than in its political implications." She argues that to do so is to ignore the substantive connections between MacIntyre's thought and reactionary politics. Id. at 44.

16 Id. at 44, 43.

17 Id. at 52, 44.

18 Id. at 72.

not entail admiration or approbation of any of the particular beliefs and practices endorsed earlier in the tradition's history. MacIntyre's "theory" of traditions gives Okin no ground on which to saddle him with the substantive morality of Aristotle or Aquinas.

Okin's critique of MacIntyre is itself inconsistent in a revealing manner. At one point she recognizes that she herself writes from within a tradition (feminism) that itself is a development of or from another tradition (liberalism),[19] but for the most part she simply assumes that her moral commitments provide her with an objective yardstick to measure MacIntyre's success or failure as a moral philosopher. By doing so she ignores the history of how and why the liberal tradition came to reject social hierarchy and male domination, the very history that defines her own viewpoint. She also assumes what is patently not the case, that the liberal egalitarianism she endorses constitutes a rejection of domination rather than the substitution of some forms of domination (that of the state, for example) for others (that of the church or family, for example).[20]

THE MACINTYREAN CONCEPTS

The Concept of Tradition

MacIntyre's most elaborate definition of *tradition* occurs near the beginning of *Whose Justice? Which Rationality?*: "A tradition is an

19 Id. at 61.

20 The statement in the text does not imply, of course, that there are no ethically significant distinctions between different forms of domination from a theological perspective. As chapter 4 will argue in the specific context of American constitutionalism, Christians often have specifically Christian or theological reasons for preferring one set of social institutions or structures to another. See also Hauerwas, *Against the Nations*, 123. The existence of good reasons for preference is not, however, equivalent to the claim that the preferred arrangements are free of the evils one intends to minimize. To make such an equation is, from a theological perspective, to fall into a morally and intellectually serious error. See, e.g., Robert Cover, "Violence and the Word," 95 Yale L.J. 1601, 1608 (1986): in discussing this society's use of the threat of violence to compel convicted criminals to undergo incarceration, Cover wrote that "Very often the balance of terror in this regard is just as I would want it. But I do not wish us to pretend that we talk our prisoners into jail."

argument extended through time in which certain fundamental agreements are defined and redefined in terms of two kinds of conflict: those with critics and enemies external to the tradition . . . and those internal, interpretative debates through which the meaning and rationale of the fundamental agreements come to be expressed and by whose progress a tradition is constituted."[21] MacIntyre provides a shorter definition in *After Virtue*: "A living tradition then is an historically extended, socially embodied argument, and an argument precisely in part about the goods which constitute that tradition."[22] Four elements of these definitions require special attention.

The first element of a MacIntyrean tradition appears tautological: a tradition is historical in nature, "extended in time." By this assertion, however, MacIntyre does not intend to describe as a tradition *any* activity or complex of ideas that just happens to have persisted or recurred over time. The Polynesians whom Captain Cook found employing the term and observing the rules of taboo were acting in a manner that had persisted over time,[23] but they were not thereby participants in a living taboo tradition. The historicity of a MacIntyrean tradition is a matter of both change and continuity, of development on the basis of the tradition's past that leads to reformulations and revisals of that past's agreements and understandings. "For it is central to the conception of such a tradition that the past is never something merely to be discarded, but rather that the present is intelligible only as a commentary upon the past in which the past, if necessary and if possible, is corrected and transcended, yet corrected and transcended in a way that leaves the present open to being in turn corrected and transcended by some yet more adequate future point of view."[24] Captain Cook's Polynesians had at most the fragments of a dead tradition that crumbled away to nothing at the slightest pressure.

MacIntyre's association of historicity with ongoing development and revision is in part a fundamental conceptual point: in order to

21 MacIntyre (1988), 12.
22 MacIntyre (1984), 222.
23 Id. at 111–12.
24 Id. at 146.

describe human actions[25] we must locate them in a history or narrative that renders them intelligible. "Narrative history of a certain kind turns out to be the basic and essential genre for the characterization of human actions."[26] But what is true of individual actions is equally true of those complexes of discourse and action that we might call tradition.

The historicity of traditions in MacIntyre's sense also has to do with the interdependence of reason and tradition. Like other antifoundationalist philosophers,[27] MacIntyre rejects Enlightenment liberalism's attempt to found rationality on some tradition-independent basis. Instead, he claims, "the standards of rational justification themselves emerge from and are part of a history in which they are vindicated by the way in which they transcend the limitations of and provide remedies for the defects of their predecessors within the history of that same tradition."[28] The standards by which arguments and assertions are rationally justified inevitably depend on and are derived from a particular community or "distinctive form of social order."[29] The standards embody the history of that community's arguments. "To justify is to narrate how the argument has gone so far."[30] The Enlightenment *philosophes* believed tradition and reason to be antithetical[31] and strove to replace tradition-dependent modes of argument and enquiry with a contextless rationality-as-such. Their central image of such tradition-free rationality was natural science, and in particular Newtonian physics; however, as MacIntyre points out, the rational superiority to its predecessors and rivals of Newto-

25 Human actions differ in this way from those of other animals. Id. at 209. For humans, "[t]here is no such thing as 'behavior,' to be identified prior to and independently of intentions, beliefs and settings." Id. at 208.

26 Id. at 209.

27 See, e.g., Michael Walzer, *Spheres of Justice* (New York: Basic Books, 1983), 29.

28 MacIntyre (1988), 7.

29 Id. at 321. Cf. id. at 133 ("social context" provides "that setting within which alone rationality can be exercised").

30 Id. at 8.

31 As MacIntyre acknowledges, the *philosophes* in their own context were by no means wholly mistaken. Id. at 7. But it is precisely this insight—that it was their context, their location in a particular history, that justified their critique of their tradition—that the *philosophes* were unable to accept or even to recognize.

nian physics can be demonstrated only by contextual, historically placed argument.[32] Tradition, history and rationality are inextricably intertwined.

The last sentence of the preceding paragraph may be challenged as too sweeping. Some MacIntyrean traditions, the objection goes, are "traditions of rational enquiry,"[33] but they need not all be: as the Enlightenment recognized, there are many sets of human activities, extended over time, that are not concerned with enquiry at all. Not only critical *philosophes*, but even advocates of tradition such as Edmund Burke have defended tradition precisely in opposition to rationality. Perhaps Burke went too far in the other direction, the objection continues, but surely a use of the word *tradition* that excluded Burkean ones would be too narrow and idiosyncratic to commend itself. Finally, MacIntyre himself concedes that traditions of rational enquiry are only a subset of what he would call traditions.[34]

This objection (with apologies to MacIntyre, who seems to grant it) is, I believe, ill-founded. The Enlightenment picture of non- or antirational traditions was itself part of the Enlightenment's critical project as well as of its self-defense. The *philosophes* derided Roman Catholicism, English common law, and Aristotelian science as irrationally tradition-bound precisely because Catholicism, common law, and Aristotelianism were serious intellectual rivals, as well as because they were associated with social and political power that the *philosophes* feared or desired. The Enlightenment description of Catholic theology, for example, as an authoritarian tradition fundamentally antithetical to rational enquiry should be recognized for what it was, part of a bitter polemic (*Ecrasez l'infame!*); as a description, even a hostile one, it was wholly implausible. We can agree with some of the Enlightenment's specific judgments from our various twentieth-century viewpoints (that Newtonian physics is rationally superior to Aristotelian, for example) without adopting the fallacious charge of nonrationality the *philosophes* leveled at their enemies.

The *philosophes* also had in mind non-Western ("primitive") sets

32 MacIntyre (1984), 268. See also Thomas Kuhn, *The Structure of Scientific Revolutions* (Chicago: Univ. of Chicago Press, 1962).

33 MacIntyre (1988), 10.

34 "Not all traditions, of course, have embodied rational enquiry as a constitutive part of themselves." Id. at 7.

of activities as examples of the nonrationality of tradition, but here too that characterization is inappropriate. The concerns and enquiries of, say, the Hindu tradition of ritual, myth, metaphysics, and meditation are not those of the European natural sciences or of Western analytic philosophy. To conclude, however, that the former therefore is non- or irrational is simple (and outrageous) ethnocentricity, a parochialism of precisely the type the *philosophes* were fond of ascribing to their opponents. A set of activities that genuinely lacked (or had lost) its own standards of rationality would be unintelligible even to its participants (recall Captain Cook's Polynesians, who could not even explain to themselves the point of taboo).

The Burkean dichotomy between rationality and tradition was, as MacIntyre stresses, a rhetorical strategy devised for a specific political purpose, the vindication of eighteenth-century England's social and political order.[35] Taken as a theory of tradition, the Burkean exaltation of "wisdom without reflection"[36] is either mistaken or deadly. Burke's description of the specific social arrangement he was defending was simply unsupportable: the constitutional and political order of his England did embody a tradition but scarcely one free of reflection, rational argument, or change,[37] while the laissez-faire economics Burke endorsed reflected a highly sophisticated economic theory developed by such undeniably rational inquirers as Adam Smith. Burke's deprecation of reason made superficial sense only because he equated reason with modes of enquiry and argument characteristic of revolutionary France and further equated those modes of argument with the descent of the Revolution into the Terror.[38] If one actually discovered a Burkean tradition—one devoid

35 Id. at 217–19; MacIntyre (1984), 222.

36 Burke, quoted in MacIntyre (1988), 353.

37 See, e.g., J. G. A. Pocock, *The Ancient Constitution and the Feudal Law*, rev. ed., Cambridge: Cambridge Univ. Press, 1987), for the classic discussion of the rich tradition of rational argument and political practice that made up the English Constitution.

38 Burke's claim that the catastrophic political outcome of the French Revolution was linked to the revolutionaries' embrace of Enlightenment rationality probably was not wholly without merit. The American Revolution, which was led by men who were for the most part as committed as their French counterparts to the Enlightenment's promise of a *novus ordo seclorum*, led to a very different political outcome. This well may have been due in part to the fact that as a group the Americans were not nearly as alienated from their (English) political, legal,

of reflection and argument—it would be "dying or dead,"[39] and increasingly unintelligible to its participants.

MacIntyre's own isolated suggestion that not all MacIntyrean traditions must involve rational enquiry is, I think, a mistake or a slip of the pen. Both his explicit definitions of tradition and his use of the concept throughout *After Virtue* and *Whose Justice? Which Rationality?* reflect the view that ongoing, rational enquiry is a central feature of traditions as MacIntyre understands them. While traditions can "decay, disintegrate and disappear"[40] they do so precisely when their activities of rational enquiry become unable to resolve intellectual or moral problems, or when they become externally corrupted.[41] In becoming less rational, a tradition is ceasing to function as a tradition. The issue, indeed, may be largely a semantic one: MacIntyre sometimes seems to identify rationality with the type of dialectical argument characteristic of certain strands of Western European thought, and it is obvious that such argument is not central to bodies of thought that MacIntyre would certainly want to identify as traditions. But nothing in MacIntyre's theory commits him to a narrow equation of rationality with dialectical argument.

A tradition, then, is historical not merely in the sense of being temporally extended but more fundamentally in that it is constituted by an ongoing argument in which its fundamental agreements are expressed, defined, and revised. It is historical because it has a history, a narrative by which alone it can be understood.

The second characteristic of the MacIntyrean tradition that we must discuss is MacIntyre's assertion that traditions are socially embodied. Historians of ideas and literary critics sometimes use the

---

and religious traditions as were the French. George Grant developed a persuasive argument along these lines in his *English-Speaking Justice*. See also Louis Hartz, *The Liberal Tradition in America* (New York: Harcourt, Brace and World, 1955).

39 MacIntyre (1984), 221–22.

40 Id. at 222.

41 The history of twentieth-century Marxism appears to exemplify both routes to disintegration. Both in theory and in practice Marxist economics has been increasingly unable to resolve problems of production and distribution without extensive borrowings from rival tradition. The politically established versions of Marxism, furthermore, were subjected to massive external corruption and now, it seems, to overt subversion in Eastern Europe and the former Soviet Union. See MacIntyre (1984), 261.

term *tradition* to refer to tendencies or themes in thought and art that they identify across temporally and socially discontinuous settings. The supposed gnostic tradition in Western religion, philosophy, and literature[42] is an example. It is not clear, however, that such tendencies in thought are traditions in any useful sense of that word. No modern thinker, for example, shares any of the overt religious or political concerns that engaged the ancient Gnostics or (except in the most remote manner) the history that created those concerns. Those elements in modern thought that resemble ancient Gnosticism are the product of very different histories[43] and can be understood without more than trivial reference to the original Gnostics.[44] Such parallels are not traditions in MacIntyre's sense.

MacIntyre's insistence on the socially embodied nature of tradition stems from his acceptance of the proposition that language, argument, and understanding are context-dependent. To understand the concepts, agreements, and conflicts that constitute the

42 See the work of literary critic Harold Bloom, e.g., *The Breaking of the Vessels* (Chicago: Univ. of Chicago Press, 1982).

43 No narrative accounting for political theorist Roberto Unger's thought, for example, could plausibly identify Unger's view as the product or descendent of ancient Gnosticism. See Unger, *Passion* (New York: Free Press, 1984); *Politics* (Cambridge: Cambridge Univ. Press, 1987–). This does not imply necessarily that it is meaningless to describe Unger as a gnostic, but only that the description is metaphorical. See Jefferson Powell, "The Gospel according to Roberto: A Theological Polemic," 6 Modern Theology 97 (1989), which identifies Unger's thought as a repristination of ancient Gnosticism.

44 It is of course perfectly possible for a thinker or artist consciously to appropriate particular motifs or ideas from an alien tradition for use in his or her own work, and in such a case knowledge of the source-tradition will be of exegetical or source-critical use in studying the work of the borrower. The third section of "The Dry Salvages" in T. S. Eliot's *Four Quartets* can only be fully interpreted if one recognizes Eliot's conscious use of the Bhagavad Gita. This fact, however, does not make Eliot a participant in the Hindu religious tradition or his poem a contribution to that tradition's ongoing argument. (The proper historical context for Eliot's borrowing is in fact the well-established European literary and artistic custom of orientalizing. See Edward Said, *Orientalism* (New York: Pantheon Books, 1978).) As Augustine recognized long ago, to appropriate successfully the ideas of another tradition for use within one's own is to transform them radically so that they no longer belong to the other tradition. See Augustine, *On Christian Doctrine*, trans. J. F. Shaw (Chicago: Encyclopedia Britannica, 1952), II.27–42. Such borrowings, of course, may be merely superficial (as in the Eliot example) or may involve a profound task of translation, as in Aquinas's use of Aristotle. See MacIntyre (1988), 370–403.

intellectual life of a tradition one must participate in the sociolinguistic context of that tradition. For a tradition to exist or function, there must be (or have been) a body of speakers who make up that context and thus render meaningful such statements as "No, that's not the correct way of doing X." The ability of a Western anthropologist to understand a non-Western culture or of a modern scholar to understand an ancient society rests on the ability to "transfor[m] themselves, so far as is posssible, into native inhabitants" or to become "almost, if not quite, surrogate participants in [ancient] societies."[45]

Another aspect of MacIntyre's claim that traditions must be understood as socially embodied may be more controversial. Modern "conventional academic disciplinary boundaries"[46] assign Plato to the philosophy department, Aristophanes to literature, and the Athenian pottery industry to archaeologists and historians. (Aristotle's polymathic interests result in his departmental dissection along four or five lines.)[47] Interdisciplinary work tends to be done from a standpoint firmly within one of the supposedly transcended disciplines[48]—if it does not itself become simply one more autonomous specialty.[49] Compartmentalizing enquiry in this manner, according to MacIntyre, makes it impossible adequately to comprehend traditions, which always exist both as complexes of ideas and as social interactions and structures.[50] In any living tradition there is so great a degree of reciprocity of presupposition and influence between theory and social embodiment that both must be studied in order to understand either. "A moral philosophy . . . characteristically pre-

45 MacIntyre (1988), 374–75.

46 MacIntyre (1984), 264.

47 Martha Nussbaum has discussed the difficulty she faced as a graduate student in studying Greek philosophy and Greek literature as a unified subject in Nussbaum, *Love's Knowledge* (New York: Oxford Univ. Press, 1990), 10–15.

48 See Arthur Leff, "Law And," 87 Yale L.Rev. 989 (1978).

49 Think, for example, of the fate of American studies (which tends to lapse back into American history) or of women's studies (which tends to become an independent, and therefore compartmentalized, discipline).

50 In discussing emotivism, for example, MacIntyre writes that "it is not clear to me . . . how *any* adequate philosophical hypothesis in this area could escape being also a sociological hypothesis, and *vice versa*. There seems something deeply mistaken in the notion enforced by the conventional curriculum that there are two distinct subjects or disciplines—moral philosophy . . . and the sociology of morals." MacIntyre (1984), 72–73.

supposes a sociology. . . . [I]t also follows that we have not yet fully understood the claims of any moral philosophy until we have spelled out what its social embodiment would be."[51] Conversely, "[f]orms of social institution, organization, and practice are always to a greater or lesser degree socially embodied theories."[52]

The social embodiment of tradition thus is not merely an external prerequisite to its existence (such as, for example, the continued presence of oxygen in Earth's atmosphere) which can be assumed and ignored for the purposes of analysis and critique. MacIntyre's examination of the political and social order of early modern Scotland, for example, is *intrinsic* to his effort to understand the philosophy of the Scottish Enlightenment and of its child and subverter Hume.[53]

The third aspect of MacIntyre's concept of tradition that is of present importance is his characterization of traditions as fundamentally interpretive in nature. Traditions are united by shared "goods"[54] or "fundamental agreements,"[55] but MacIntyre strongly rejects the notion that this implies a static unity of unchanging or unanimous agreement. What enables a tradition to continue and indeed to flourish is its nurturance by "those internal, interpretative debates through the meaning and rationale of the fundamental agreements come to be expressed and by whose progress a tradition is constituted."[56] Broadly speaking the objects of tradition-constitutive

51 Id. at 23. See also MacIntyre (1988), 390: "Philosophical theories give organized expression to concepts and theories already embodied in forms of practice and types of community."

52 MacIntyre (1988), 390.

53 Id. at 209–59. Comprehension of the thought of the Scots philosophers would be equally important to a study of the eighteenth-century Scottish universities and Kirk. Strictly speaking, it would be better not to say that the study of one requires the study of the other but that there is only one subject of study in the first place—the theories-as-embodied-in-social-forms. This subject can be studied for a variety of reasons, some of which might require differences of emphasis. MacIntyre's account of Scots-thought-in-Scots-society appropriately looks somewhat different for this reason from a study of the same subject by someone whose objective was to understand the influence of the Scottish Enlightenment on nineteenth-century British evangelicalism.

54 MacIntyre (1984), 222.

55 MacIntyre (1988), 12.

56 Id. Cf. MacIntyre (1984), 222: a tradition is "an argument precisely in part about the goods which constitute that tradition."

interpretation are all "the beliefs, institutions and practices of some particular community which constitute a given."[57] When challenges to these beliefs and practices, or conflicts over them, arise, participants in the tradition are driven to conscious awareness of it and of their role in carrying the tradition forward.[58] They then seek to interpret, and to revise if necessary, the tradition's express social forms and hitherto implicit theories. "Thus a philosophical theory of the virtues is a theory whose subject-matter is that pre-philosophical theory already implicit in and presupposed by the best contemporary practice of the virtues."[59]

The discovery that the tradition's goods are receiving incompatible interpretations, or that existing ways of thinking are incoherent or unable to resolve new questions, drives the tradition's participants to creative reworkings of the tradition: "the rejection, emendation, and reformulation of beliefs, the revaluation of authorities, the reinterpretation of texts, the emergence of new forms of authority, and the production of new texts."[60] A tradition therefore may change radically over time as its adherents rework or reject older concepts and patterns of activity. The unity of a tradition understood in this manner does not lie in some version of the Vincentian Canon, that which is believed everywhere, by everyone, and all the time. Instead, the tradition's unity and historical identity are displayed by recounting the narrative of how the tradition's adherents have changed their words and their activities. A MacIntyrean tradition finds its identity in its movement.

At the same time he stresses change, MacIntyre gives critical weight to the role of canonical texts in traditions, at least in those "constituted in part by philosophically sophisticated enquiry." "For such a tradition, if it is to flourish at all . . . has to be embodied in a set of texts which function as the authoritative point of departure for tradition-constituted enquiry and which remain as essential points of reference for enquiry and activity, for argument, debate and conflict within that tradition."[61] Thus a major source of disagreement and

57 MacIntyre (1988), 354.

58 Id. at 7–8, 326.

59 MacIntyre (1984), 148.

60 MacIntyre (1988), 355.

61 Id. at 383. This is perhaps an unnecessarily strong claim for MacIntyre to put forward. I see no a priori reason why a tradition might not be "philosophically

debate within a tradition will be "interpretative" in the older, narrow sense of textual exposition.

The final element of MacIntyre's concept of tradition that requires some attention is one which some of his readers probably have found surprising: traditions, rather than being bastions of immobile stability, "embody continuities of conflict."[62] Conflict and the interpretive disagreement over the meaning of the tradition's texts and practices constitute the ongoing life of the tradition. A tradition, in other words, is an *argument*, and arguments proceed by arguing. Participation in a tradition requires involvement in disagreement, for it is in the clash of interpretations that the tradition "progresses," overcomes difficulties and resolves inconsistencies. Understanding a tradition requires one to make sense of its internal conflicts.[63] Furthermore, a tradition may engage in external conflict with "critics and enemies . . . who reject all or at least key parts of [its] fundamental agreements" and with wholly alien communities with which the tradition happens to come into contact.[64]

MacIntyre does not explain fully his use of the language of progress for the processes of change that constitute in his view the ongoing life of a tradition. Progress usually connotes a teleological understanding of change—we make progress toward something.

---

sophisticated" and yet be centered not on canonical texts but on social activities or works of art. (I am assuming that MacIntyre is not using "text" in the currently fashionable extended sense that would permit us to apply it to virtually anything, an assumption that the quotation's context seems to confirm.) The English constitutional tradition was philosophically sophisticated enough to inspire an external interpretation (Montesquieu's *L'Esprit des Lois*) that itself became canonical within the distinct tradition of Western political philosophy. English constitutionalism, nevertheless, was carried forward primarily by debate over English political practice, not over texts such as Magna Carta. In contrast, American constitutionalism plainly is a tradition "embodied in a set of texts," and thus we need not resolve the question of whether MacIntyre's claims about the critical role of texts is too broad.

62 MacIntyre (1984), 222. In *Whose Justice? Which Rationality?* not only the book's title but its opening chapter are intended to put "emphasis upon the necessary place of conflict within traditions." MacIntyre (1988), 11.

63 MacIntyre cites approvingly the Australian philosopher John Anderson who "urged us not to ask of a social institution: 'What end or purpose does it serve?' but rather, 'of what conflicts is it the scene?'" MacIntyre (1984), 163 (citation omitted).

64 MacIntyre (1988), 12.

Since even the most fundamental aspirations and commitments of a tradition are subject to revision on MacIntyre's view, his use of apparently teleological language to describe traditions is unjustified.[65] The language of progress is connected to one of the most important functions that MacIntyre ascribes to conflict within a tradition: conflict leads to the development of a set of characteristic disputes, unresolved questions, and so on, which MacIntyre calls the tradition's *problematic*. The subconcept of the problematic is a useful one in that it clarifies MacIntyre's seemingly paradoxical assertion that a tradition's unity lies less in consensus than in disagreement. What unites participants in a MacIntyrean tradition is as much the problems they think important as the answers they think correct. On the other hand, MacIntyre's description of the problematic as emerging from the tradition's "previous *achievements* in enquiry"[66] raises the same apparent problem of unexplained teleological language as do his references to progress. The problem disappears, however, if one construes mention of progress and achievement as purely descriptive references to a tradition's continuance. A tradition "progresses" or makes "achievements," in other words, if in fact its adherents continue to believe themselves able to respond to questions and problems successfully. Aristotelian science was unable to make further progress, and therefore ultimately died, because its adherents lost confidence in the tradition's capacity to address its own problematic, not because it failed to progress in some teleological sense.[67]

The subconcept of the problematic is important to MacIntyre's description of traditions in that it allows him to explain the continuity of a tradition over time. A second subconcept, that of the *character*, provides a useful tool for identifying the shape of a tradition at a given

65 This is not to say, of course, that from within a given tradition, rational enquiry cannot be seen as aimed at progress toward a telos. MacIntyre, however, has no warrant to identify such a self-understanding as intrinsic to all traditions, and good reasons not to make such a strong claim. Doing so would require MacIntyre to deny traditional status, for example, to most or all Eastern Orthodox theology.

66 Id. at 167 (emphasis added).

67 Newtonian physics triumphed, furthermore, because its adherents—and growing numbers of those educated in the Aristotelian tradition—found the Newtonian narrative of the relationship between the two scientific traditions the more persuasive.

point in time. In any given culture (and, I take it, tradition), MacIntyre asserts that there will be certain special social roles which place "a certain kind of moral constraint on the personality of those who inhabit them in a way in which many other social roles do not."[68] These characters are in a peculiar or exemplary way embodiments of the culture's or the tradition's theoretical and moral commitments.[69] As such, a character provides the members of the culture (or the participants in the tradition) with a cultural and moral ideal. This implies, and MacIntyre explicitly states, that characters will themselves be the objects of conflict and interpretive disagreement, as participants in the tradition argue over how or in what way they embody or define the tradition's commitments. Characters are, in short, "focal points for disagreement."[70]

Continuous argument over a tradition's problematic and focused around its characters is characteristic of a flourishing tradition. But it is possible for a tradition's debates to put in question the tradition itself. "Its hitherto trusted methods of enquiry have become sterile. Conflicts over rival answers to key questions can no longer be settled rationally. Moreover, it may indeed happen that the use of the methods of enquiry and of the forms of argument, by means of which rational progress had been achieved so far, begins to have the effect of increasingly disclosing new inadequacies, hitherto unrecognized incoherences, and new problems for the solution of which there seem to be insufficient or no resources within the established fabric of belief."[71] MacIntyre's term for such a situation is "epistemological crisis," and he regards the resolution of (or failure to resolve) an epistemological crisis as a crucial event in the history of a tradition.[72] A successful resolution of the crisis requires "new and conceptually enriched" solutions to those issues in the preexisting problematic

68 MacIntyre (1984), 27. The constraint arises from the social demand that those who fill the role of characters fuse their role and their personality. Id. at 27–29.

69 "Characters . . . are, so to speak, the moral representatives of their culture and they are so because of the way in which moral and metaphysical ideas and theories assume through them an embodied existence in the social world. Characters are the masks worn by moral philosophies." Id. at 28.

70 Id. at 31.

71 MacIntyre (1988), 361–62.

72 Id. at 361–68; MacIntyre, "Epistemological Crises, Dramatic Narrative, and the Philosophy of Science," 69 *The Monist* 4 (1977).

that had proven intractable. It also demands development of an intelligible explanation of why the resources of the precrisis tradition were inadequate to resolve those issues.[73]

The radical historicity of MacIntyrean traditions renders them unavoidably open to the possibility of the epistemological crisis. Susceptibility to such a crisis raises the possibility that a given tradition will fail to resolve it.[74] If this happens, the tradition is, on the conceptual level, "rationally discredited" and ultimately disintegrates or is replaced by another tradition.[75] Conflict, therefore, not only constitutes the life of a flourishing tradition; it also contains the possibility of the tradition's failure.

MacIntyre's emphasis on the role of conflict and change in the makeup of traditions marks his concept of tradition as an intrinsically political one. Rather than being bloodless explications of abstract patterns of thought, even the most conceptual of traditions are the scenes and vehicles of human argument and struggle. MacIntyre's concept therefore is peculiarly well suited for use in examining American constitutionalism, which is at one and the same time obviously political and yet characterized by ambiguity over the role of politics.[76] To say this is not, however, to claim that the description of constitutionalism as a MacIntyrean tradition is self-evident. Perhaps the most common description of constitutionalism by American

73 MacIntyre (1988), 362.

74 "Every tradition, whether it recognizes the fact or not, confronts the possibility that at some future time it will fall into a state of epistemological crisis, recognizable as such by its own standards of rational justification, which have themselves been vindicated up to that time as the best to emerge from the history of that particular tradition." Id. at 364.

75 Id. at 365–66. MacIntyre's assumption that rational defeat ultimately results in social disintegration obviously raises important questions about his anthropological presuppositions. Those presuppositions need not be explored in this book since the tradition to be examined, American constitutionalism, is a self-consciously rational tradition. By its own terms, such a tradition cannot tolerate rational discrediting without response. For present purposes, we need only make the weak assumption that participants in this type of tradition will find it psychologically and socially necessary to address rational failure in some manner (perhaps, for example, by using physical force to suppress discussion of the failure).

76 MacIntyre's tradition is a very similar concept to William Connolly's concept of politics. See Connolly, *The Terms of Political Discourse*, 2d ed. (Princeton: Princeton Univ. Press, 983), 6.

lawyers treats it as a generative event (the Framing or Founding)[77] in which all constitutional principles were authoritatively set forth, followed by essentially timeless deductive applications of these principles. Interpretive disagreement, according to this popular description, stems from error on someone's part: conflict over the meaning of the Constitution or the proper modes of constitutional argument necessarily signals failure, and change or revision in constitutional commitments is proof of bad faith or apostasy.[78] The narrative description of constitutionalism in chapter 2 will be successful only if my identification of the elements of a MacIntyrean tradition is persuasive and more plausible than the popular description.

The Concept of a Practice

MacIntyre employs the concept of the *practice* to explain concretely the mode by which traditions subsist. "By a 'practice' I am going to mean any coherent and complex form of socially established cooperative human activity through which goods internal to that form of society are realized in the course of trying to achieve those standards of excellence which are appropriate to, and partially definitive of, that form of activity, with the result that human powers to achieve excellence, and human conceptions of the ends and goods involved, are systematically extended."[79] Practices, like the traditions which they embody, are intrinsically historical: they necessarily exist by and through systematic, critical development. "[P]ratices always have histories and . . . at any given moment what a practice is depends on a mode of understanding it which has been transmitted often through many generations."[80]

Not all organized or repetitive human activities are practices. Those that are too uncomplicated or too individualistic do not qual-

77 Or, to be more precise, a set of discrete generative events: the original Founding, the era of the Civil War amendments, perhaps the dates of one or two other important amendments.

78 See Bruce Ackerman, "Constitutional Law/Politics," 99 Yale L.J. 453 (1990), on the extent to which American lawyers deny the existence of change, creativity, or disagreement except as examples of mistake.

79 MacIntyre (1984), 187.

80 Id. at 221. See also id. at 190, 193, 194.

ify.[81] While all practices involve the exercise of "technical skills," not all sets of shared technical skills amount to a practice: some are too narrowly oriented to specific goals or purposes to permit the reevaluation of those goals and purposes and thus cannot be the bearers of a MacIntyrean tradition with its intrinsically argumentative nature.[82]

Two distinctions are crucial to MacIntyre's concept of practice: that between internal and external goods, and that between practices and institutions. MacIntyre uses the example of chess to explain the first contrast. Some of the goods that can be acquired through chess playing are "externally and contingently attached . . . by the accidents of social circumstance"—a grandmaster may win "prestige, status and money." But these goods, though real goods, are not peculiar or internal to chess playing. "There are always alternative ways for achieving such goods and their achievement is never to be had *only* by engaging in some particular kind of practice."[83]

Internal goods are identifiable as such for two reasons. First, they can be specified and achieved only by and within the particular

81 See the useful discussion in Stout, *Ethics*, 268–69. "Every practice requires a certain level or relationship between those who participate in it." MacIntyre (1984), 191.

82 MacIntyre (1984), 193–94. Stout correctly notes that the contrast MacIntyre draws between practices and other sets of activities is "imprecise" and that MacIntyre's brief list of activities that are and those that are not practices (id. at 187–88) is not self-explanatory. Stout seems to be correct as well to suggest that MacIntyre "[p]resumably finds [the activities he denies are practices] insufficiently complex or cooperative, their standards of excellence insufficiently developed, and the ends and goals involved insufficiently capable of systematic extension for them to be grouped with" practices. Stout, *Ethics*, 268.

83 MacIntyre (1984), 188. The last part of this statement is unnecessarily strong. It does not seem impossible a priori that in some societies the sorts of material and social benefits that ordinarily make up the set of external goods might be achievable only through success in achieving the internal good of some practice. Perhaps some periods in imperial Chinese history are an example: competence in the practice of mandarin culture (rhetorical and exegetical expertise in the Confucian classics, bureaucratic skills) may have been the only effective avenues to prestige and material well-being for virtually everyone in that society. See Kung-chuan Hsiao, *A History of Chinese Political Thought* (Princeton: Princeton Univ. Press, 1978). MacIntyre's main point is unaffected: external goods are related to excellence in a practice only because a given society happens to reward excellence with those goods.

practice—in chess such goods include "a certain highly particular kind of analytical skill, strategies, imagination and competitive intensity, a new set of reasons, reasons now not just for winning on a particular occasion, but for trying to excel in whatever way the game of chess demands."[84] Unlike external goods, internal goods can only be obtained by genuine excellence in the activities and skills of the practice. Someone might acquire the reputation and the monetary rewards of a chess grandmaster by cheating (perhaps by using a surreptitious link to a supercomputer or by bribing or threatening his or her opponents) but the player would then have failed to obtain the goods internal to chess playing. The latter are accessible only by the doing.

Second, internal goods are judged by the standards of excellence appropriate and internal to the practice. "Those who lack the relevant experience are incompetent thereby as judges of internal goods."[85] One need understand nothing about chess to evaluate the special benefits pre-*peristroika* Soviet society accorded grandmasters, but to understand why and how they were grandmasters it is necessary oneself to know something of—to have actually participated in—chess playing.[86]

The distinction between internal and external goods explains in part MacIntyre's second distinction, that between practices and institutions. *Institutions*, in MacIntyre's terminology, are those social forms that are necessarily and appropriately directed toward procuring and allocating external goods. The practice of chess playing would decline or die if there did not exist a complex web of chess clubs, national organizers, and so on, all of which require social organization, financial resources, and the exercise of various types of social power. Institutions thus are necessary to sustain practices and their dealings with external goods are not defects but rather intrinsic to the institutions' purposes and to the survival of the practices they support. Every practice is unavoidably involved, through its sup-

84 MacIntyre (1984), 188.

85 Id. at 189.

86 In *Whose Justice? Which Rationality?* MacIntyre, perhaps unfortunately, chose to use a slightly different terminology ("goods of excellence" and "goods of effectiveness") to discuss the internal/external distinction with reference to justice. MacIntyre (1988), 194.

porting institution(s), with external goods. That involvement, however, poses a continuing threat to the practice's health. The "ideals and the creativity of the practice are always vulnerable to the acquisitiveness of the institution [and] the cooperative care for common goods of the practice is always vulnerable to the competitiveness of the institution."[87]

A major task of the second chapter will be to identify the internal and external goods of constitutionalism, and to distinguish its practices from its institutions. Only if constitutionalism involves at least one practice that is characterized by goods internal to that practice will it be plausible to describe constitutionalism as a MacIntyrean tradition.

The Concept of the Virtue

MacIntyre's third major theoretical concept is that of the *virtue*. "A virtue is an acquired human quality the possession and exercise of which tends to enable us to achieve those goods which are internal to practices and the lack of which effectively prevents us from achieving any such goods."[88] The possession and exercise of the relevant virtues are intrinsic to excellence in a given practice. The virtues of analytical concentration and strategic imagination that are necessary means to excellence in chess playing are themselves part of the definition of that excellence.[89] Certain virtues are universal across all practices because forms of them are entailed by the structure of cooperative and complex human activity. "We have to learn to recognize what is due to whom; we have to be prepared to take whatever self-endangering risks are demanded along the way; and we have to listen carefully to what we are told about our own inadequacies and to reply with the same carefulness for the facts. In other words we have to accept as necessary components of any practice with internal goods and standards of excellence the virtues of justice, courage and

87 MacIntyre (1984), 194.

88 Id. at 191.

89 "I call a means internal to a given end when the end cannot be adequately characterized independently of a characterization of the means." So, for example, in Aristotle's ethics, the "exercise of the virtues is itself a crucial component of the good life for man." Id. at 184.

honesty."[90] Justice, courage, and honesty are necessary to the life of practices because they are necessary to sustain any practice and its internal goods against the corrupting power of institutions with their acquisitive and competitive concern for external goods. Without the exercise of justice, courage, and truthfulness by at least some of the participants in the practice, its integrity will be corroded by the lure of external goods and the demands of the sustaining institutions.[91] Thus practices and virtues are tightly connected both conceptually and as a matter of social fact.[92]

The existence of constitutional virtues is inextricably wound up with the existence of one or more constitutional practices, and to argue plausibly for one will involve arguing for the other. In addition, if constitutionalism is a MacIntyrean tradition, it should be possible to find at any given time one or more "characters," social roles or identities that embody the constitutional tradition's commitments and display its virtues.

THE SUBSTANTIVE CRITIQUE OF LIBERALISM

MacIntyre's theory of traditions, practices, and virtues remained essentially unchanged between *After Virtue* and *Whose Justice?*

90 Id. at 191.

91 Id. at 194, 195.

92 "[W]e shall be unable to write a true history of practices and institutions unless that history is also one of the virtues and vices." Id. at 195. MacIntyre's analysis of the relationships between practices, internal and external goods, institutions, and virtues resembles parts of Michael Walzer's argument that a proper theory of justice should concern itself with "domination." By domination Walzer refers to a situation in which social goods of one sort (social good x) are distributed to certain persons "who possess some other good y merely because they possess y and without regard to the meaning of x." Walzer, *Spheres*, 20. Walzer differs from MacIntyre in the ostensible austerity of his formulation: MacIntyre does not insist on there being an intrinsic link between a given external good and the practice excellence in which leads to acquisition of the external good. Taken literally, Walzer's contrary insistence on the avoidance of dominance would seem to render it virtually impossible to justify any distribution of external goods other than the strictest egalitarianism. But see Walzer, *Spheres*, 106–22 (attempting to find some role for markets in a dominance-free society).

Which Rationality?. The latter, while it seldom uses much of the theoretical vocabulary, seems thoroughly in accord with the earlier book's explicit working-out of the theory. MacIntyre's substantive account of liberalism, in contrast, underwent some development and change between the two books. In *After Virtue* MacIntyre appeared to accept as successful modern liberalism's attempt to escape from adherence to tradition as the basis of morality—although the main thesis of that book was that the very success of the attempt had rendered liberal moral discourse incoherent. In *Whose Justice? Which Rationality?* MacIntyre continues to describe flight from tradition as liberalism's ambition but, he now insists, liberalism's failure lies precisely in its own transformation into (one more) tradition. "Liberalism, which began as an appeal to alleged principles of shared rationality against what was felt to be the tyranny of tradition, has itself been transformed into a tradition whose continuities are partly defined by the interminability of the debate over such principles."[93] MacIntyre's accounts of liberalism thus are not identical; it is the claim of this section that they are compatible, and that MacIntyre's more recent characterization of liberalism as a moral tradition is a valuable correction of his original argument, one that strengthens his original objective of explaining and criticizing contemporary liberalism. The narrative argument in chapter 2 provides strong support for this claim by illustrating the transformation of a specific strand of Enlightenment thought (the politics and philosophy of the American Founding) into a specific moral tradition, American constitutionalism.

MacIntyre's treatment of liberalism in *After Virtue* begins with a set of observations about moral discourse in contemporary Western society, his famous catastrophe hypothesis. "The most striking feature of contemporary moral utterance is that so much of it is used to express disagreements, and the most striking feature of the debates in which these disagreements are expressed is their interminable character. I do not mean by this just that such debates go on and on and on—although they do—but also that they apparently can find no terminus. There seems to be no rational way of securing moral agreement in our society."[94] Rather than expressing a shared cultural

93 MacIntyre (1988), 335.
94 MacIntyre (1984), 6.

vision or societal ethos, modern moral discourse is ordinarily and systematically discordant.[95]

In a society guided by a MacIntyrean tradition one would expect argument—plenty of argument—but argument directed toward the goals of better understanding and implementing the tradition's goods. Those goods, always themselves the subject of interpretive dispute and potential revision, would provide the standards by which moral arguments could be resolved and progress identified. But modern Western society lacks any such agreed-upon standards and any "established way of deciding between [moral] claims"; its ostensibly moral discussions are in fact irresolvable clashes between viewpoints that are incommensurable.[96] The result is that Western society is dominated by "emotivism," that is, the dominant social groups act as if "all evaluative judgments . . . are *nothing but* expressions of preference . . . insofar as they are moral or evaluative in character."[97]

Since they start from conceptually incompatible premises and lack shared intellectual or institutional means for resolving moral disagreement,[98] Western liberal individualists can only see disagreement as adversarial struggle, "civil war carried on by other means."[99] "Arguments have come to be understood . . . not as expressions of rationality but as weapons."[100] Morality itself is no longer interpreted as shared rational enquiry into the good life for human beings, but as a set of "expressions of attitudes, preferences and choices which are themselves not governed by criterion, principle or value, since they underlie and are prior to all allegiance to criterion, principle or value."[101] Such attitudes and preferences, the liberal individualist

95 MacIntyre (1988), 1: "[O]ur society is one not of consensus but of division and conflict."

96 MacIntyre (1984), 8.

97 Id. at 11–12. MacIntyre is not, of course, making the claim that modern Westerners are necessarily conscious adherents to the philosophical doctrine of emotivism. Virtually everyone in contemporary Western society *intends to be* nonemotivist; by accepting the limitations liberalism has placed on moral discourse, he or she nonetheless functions as if emotivism were true. See id. at 18, where MacIntyre characterizes his own employment of emotivism as a "cogent theory of use rather than a false theory of meaning."

98 Id. at 8, 138, 152; MacIntyre (1988), 3, 338.

99 MacIntyre (1984), 253.

100 Id. at 5.

101 Id. at 33.

believes, can only be chosen, not adopted as the end result of a process of reasoning.[102] Contemporary moral discussion, as a result, typically ends in the "assertive use of ultimate principles in attempts to close moral debate."[103]

MacIntyre finds the implicit emotivism of modern liberal society displayed across a broad spectrum of social settings. On the "high" intellectual level, philosophical dispute is unending and (as a result) philosophers have largely turned to the search "for a more accurate and informed definition of disagreement rather than for progress toward its resolution."[104] Contemporary political and moral philosophy typically rejects enquiry into human goods and restricts its focus to those rules that constrain the liberal individualist's implementation of his or her values.[105] The institutional arrangements of the liberal state are intentionally designed not to resolve moral disputes rationally through the discovery of the common good but to aggregate and limit individual preferences.[106] The "arenas of public choice are not places of debate, either in terms of one dominant conception of the human good or between rival and conflicting conceptions of the good"; all that they can be, as a result, are "places where bargaining between individuals, each with their own preferences, is conducted."[107] The characters of liberal society, those individual exemplifications of its commitments, incarnate a stark and individualistic emotivism.[108] MacIntyre explains the facial inconsistency of modern moral discourse, which combines an implicit emotivism with a perva-

102 "Unsurprisingly, in a culture dominated by this kind of practical reasoning, the making—and the unmaking—of decisions is a kind of activity which assumes a prominence unknown in other cultures." MacIntyre (1988), 341.

103 MacIntyre (1984), 35.

104 MacIntyre (1988), 3.

105 See, e.g., John Rawls, *Theory of Justice*; Bruce Ackerman, *Social Justice in the Liberal State* (New Haven: Yale Univ. Press, 1980).

106 MacIntyre (1984), 138: liberal society lacks "*any* public, generally shared communal mode either for representing political conflict or for putting our politics to the philosophical question."

107 MacIntyre (1988), 338. Liberalism sees "in the social world nothing but a meeting place for individual wills." MacIntyre (1984), 25.

108 The activities of the Therapist are devoted to enhancing the individual's ability to choose her preferences effectively, the asserted power of the Manager rests on his claim to a technical expertise in implementing whatever ends are independently given him, and the Aesthete simply *is* liberal preference personified. MacIntyre (1984), 25–31.

sive use of ostensibly rational but emotionally charged rhetoric, by a historical thesis. In the earlier stages of Western culture, moral thought and action were embedded in a tradition (actually, as *Whose Justice? Which Rationality?* makes plain, we should speak of a plurality of Western "predecessor cultures") which provided Western morality with standards of rational evaluation. With the emergence of modernity, "the language of morality passes from a state of order to a state of disorder."[109] Various institutional and intellectual changes[110] including the cultural and human disaster of the wars of religion[111] led to the Enlightenment project, a search for nonparticular and tradition-independent rules of conduct.[112] The cultural persistence of fragments of the moral vocabularies of earlier eras[113] accounts for the demand for agreement and the tone of asperity that characterize

109 Id. at 11.

110 MacIntyre makes no attempt to list systematically these changes. Among them we certainly must include the political and religious fracturing of the medieval *res publica Christianum*, the discrediting of Aristotelianism and the decline of Christian orthodoxy, and the conscious subversion of earlier traditions by the advocates of early modern political, social, and economic arrangements.

111 MacIntyre has not adequately answered Stout's claim that he greatly underestimates the importance of sixteenth- and seventeenth-century sectarian strife in the development of liberalism. See Stout, *Ethics*, 222–23. "[M]ight it be that theology got into trouble with the intellectuals largely because it was unable to provide a vocabulary for debating and deciding matters pertaining to the common good without resort to violence." Id. at 222. From the theological perspective I hold, and which therefore informs this book, a central part of the appropriate response to Stout is the claim that most early modern Christians (both Roman Catholics and "magisterial" Reformers) committed a fundamental intratheological error by accepting the legitimacy of employing violence in behalf of Christian truth. See, e.g., John Howard Yoder, *The Priestly Kingdom* (Notre Dame: Univ. of Notre Dame Press, 1984), 22–26, 123–30. Aspects of MacIntyre's work suggest that he would not accept this argument. See, e.g., MacIntyre (1988), 158–62 (discussing the political theology of Pope Gregory VII).

112 "It was a central aspiration of the Enlightenment, an aspiration the formulation of which was itself a great achievement, to provide for debate in the public realm standards and methods of rational justification by which alternative courses of action in every sphere of life could by adjudged just or unjust, rational or irrational, enlightened or unenlightened. So, it was hoped, reason would displace authority and tradition. Rational justification was to appeal to principles undeniable by any rational person and therefore independent of all those social and cultural particularities which the Enlightenment thinkers took to be the mere accidental clothing of reason in particular times and places." MacIntyre (1988), 6.

113 MacIntyre (1984), 10.

contemporary discussions. Freed of the traditional contexts in which they made rational sense, these fragments of moral vocabulary can only be understood in emotivist terms as individual preferences.

At one point in *After Virtue*, MacIntyre briefly discusses the constitutional jurisprudence of the United States Supreme Court. Noting that legal philosophers such as Ronald Dworkin often criticize the Court for its failure to articulate a coherent constitutional law based on American first principles, MacIntyre employs his catastrophe thesis in an ironic defense of the Court: "Even to make such an effort [to devise "a set of consistent principles" behind the Court's decisions] is to miss the point. The Supreme Court . . . play[s] the role of a peacemaking or truce-keeping body by negotiating its way through an impasse of conflict, not by invoking our shared moral first principles. For our society as a whole has none."[114] Here, as generally in *After Virtue*, MacIntyre's claim that contemporary liberal society is unable to engage in shared or public moral discourse rests on his historical conclusion that the Enlightenment project was disastrously successful in its repudiation of tradition. The conceptual incoherence of American constitutional law thus is but one example of the general incoherence of liberal moral discourse. MacIntyre's brief discussion of constitutionalism, however, suffers from the same tendency to "oversimplifying abstractions" and "castigation-by-lumping" that plague *After Virtue*'s description of liberal modernity as a whole.[115] As chapter 2 of this essay will argue, the current impasse in constitutional discussion is not an incidental example of a culturewide and centuries-old problem, but, at least proximately, the result of historical developments in what was until recently a functioning tradition of rational enquiry. In order to comprehend constitutionalism within MacIntyre's account of liberalism, it would be necessary for MacIntyre to recognize the possibility of (a) tradition(s) of liberalism.

In *Whose Justice? Which Rationality?* MacIntyre expressly does just that: he accords the status of a tradition to liberalism itself. What can he mean? Appropriately, MacIntyre comes to this conclusion by

114 Id. at 253.

115 See Jeffrey Stout, "Liberal Society and its Discontents: MacIntyre Homeward Bound," paper delivered at the 1988 annual meeting of the American Political Science Association, Washington, D.C., 1988, 8–9, from which the expressions quoted in the text are taken.

way of a historical narrative. The intellectual, social, and political strife of the early modern period led to the Enlightenment search for tradition-independent moral rules, but that search has yielded over three centuries "no uncontested and incontestable account of what tradition-independent morality consists in."[116] Moral commitments gradually came to be seen as matters of choice and preference, and the task of liberal political philosophy and liberal political arrangements was implicitly defined as the exclusion from the public sphere of all conceptions of the good that might require a reshaping of the society as a whole. From the liberal perspective as it evolved, any claim that an account of the good should be implemented in the public sphere came to be seen as a nonrational and potentially tyrannical assertion of power.

In demanding the exclusion from public discourse of (nonliberal) substantive accounts of the good, liberalism, of course, is enforcing its vision of the good—of human life as the individual and private pursuit of individually chosen goods—and using the power of liberal political arrangements to silence or transform contrary visions.[117] The goal of liberal politics has become the creation and maintenance of a distinction between the public and the private that embodies liberalism's own individualistic presuppositions.[118] Liberalism thereby transforms itself into a tradition with "its own broad conception of the good, which it is engaged in imposing politically, legally, socially, and culturally wherever it has the power to do so."[119]

Liberalism's "historically developed and developing set of social institutions and forms of activity [are] the voice of a tradition."[120] The interminable and irresolvable moral arguments of contemporary society are the intellectual embodiment of this individualistic tradi-

116 MacIntyre (1988), 334.

117 "The culture of liberalism transforms expressions of opinion [including those based on "some nonliberal theory or conception of the human good"] into what its political moral theory had already said that they were." Id. at 343.

118 MacIntyre (1984), 34.

119 MacIntyre (1988), 336. Liberalism's characteristic tolerance of differing views of the good is part of its bifurcation of the social world into the public and the private. As MacIntyre notes, liberal society's "toleration of rival conceptions of the good in the public arena is severely limited." Id. See also Herbert Marcuse, Robert P. Wolff, and Barrington Moore, *The Critique of Pure Tolerance* (London: Cope, 1969).

120 MacIntyre (1988), 345.

tion, their very inclusiveness and unending quality the mode by which they undergird the social forms of liberalism. The legalism so characteristic of liberal societies provides the "order in which conflict resolution takes place without invoking any overall theory of human good."[121] In doing so, liberal legalism becomes the framework within which liberalism's "overriding good"—"the continued sustenance of the liberal social and political order"—can be pursued.[122]

Redescribing liberalism as a tradition creates tension within MacIntyre's portrait of liberalism. For example, the legal order's inability to resolve moral issues in a principled fashion, which was described in elegaic tones in *After Virtue*, becomes essential to the embodiment of liberalism in *Whose Justice? Which Rationality?*. But the redescription gains important analytical and interpretive advantages. First, MacIntyre is able to acknowledge that some of the most important contemporary liberal thinkers have explicitly abandoned any claim to tradition-independent reason or principle, and themselves have redefined the task of liberal moral philosophy as "that of rendering coherent and systematic 'our' intuitions about what is right, just, and good, where 'we' are the inhabitants of a particular social, moral and political tradition, that of liberal individualism."[123] Recognizing that liberalism has become a tradition also would enable MacIntyre to employ his "theory" of traditions, practices, and virtues in the examination of liberal theory and liberal society without inconsistency, although *Whose Justice? Which Rationality?* provides only brief indications of the forms of social embodiment and social hierarchy that a MacIntyrean analysis of the liberal tradition might identify.

Critics of MacIntyre's substantive account of liberalism have attacked the account as unfair: Jeffrey Stout, one of the most penetrating of the critics, has written that MacIntyre's discussion of liberal tradition in *Whose Justice? Which Rationality?* is "utterly unsympathetic caricature at the very point where the narrative most urgently requires detailed and fair-minded exposition if it means to test its author's preconceptions with any rigor at all."[124] The problem, as Stout goes on to note, is in part MacIntyre's failure as yet to examine

121 Id. at 344.
122 Id. at 344–45.
123 Id. at 176; see also id. at 345–46.
124 Stout, "Liberal Society and its Discontents," 8.

liberal thought with the care and specificity he uses in describing the ancient Greeks and the seventeenth-century Scots. But Stout also points to a particular fault as crucial: MacIntyre does not adequately address the particular situation of "dialectical impasse" and religious strife to which the Enlightenment project of early liberalism was a response.[125] "Religious beliefs and conceptions of the good were, in that highly particular context, part of a dialectical impasse that made the attainment of rational agreement on a whole range of issues impossible."[126] Liberal thought and liberal political arrangements, with their typical limitation of the range of moral issues open to public discussion and resolution, were "the arrangements and conventions of people who contracted, in effect, to limit the damage of th[eir] failure ["to achieve agreement on a fully detailed conception of the good"] by settling for a thinner conception of the good that more people could agree to, given the alternatives" of social disorganization and sectarian violence.[127] Liberalism's real moral origins and continuing justification lie not in the various foundationalist theories of ethics of the liberal philosophers, but in its ability to "minimize the unhappy consequences of religious strife"; liberalism, in short, is "pragmatically justified under historical circumstances."[128]

Stout's insistence that acknowledging the historical particularity of liberalism makes the task of criticizing liberalism more complex than MacIntyre seems to admit is a valuable complement to MacIntyre's recognition of liberalism as a tradition.[129] In terms of this book,

125 Stout, *Flight*, 46, 241, 270–71. Stout's concept of "dialectical impasse" closely parallels MacIntyre's "epistemological crisis." See Stout, *Ethics*, 222–26, criticizing MacIntyre for "belittl[ing] what our early-modern ancestors accomplished" by trivializing their success in devising a pragmatic response to religious conflict. Responding to MacIntyre's characterization of liberal politics as "civil war carried on by other means" (MacIntyre [1984], 253), Stout writes that "civil war carried on by other means is preferable to plain old civil war—the kind you get when one fully developed conception of the good, unable to achieve rational consensus, comes crashing down upon another, bringing about rather little good but much bloodshed, tyranny, and terror." Stout, *Ethics*, 224.

126 Stout, *Flight*, 241.

127 Stout, *Ethics*, 225.

128 Id. at 222, 225.

129 Stout's own constructive account of liberalism attempts to combine the pragmatism of Richard Rorty with a critical perspective built out of MacIntyre's concept of practice. See Stout, *Ethics*, 243–92. A complete analysis of Stout's position lies outside the purview of this book; it may be relevant to note one of

Stout provides added content to the claim that American constitutionalism is a liberal tradition of moral enquiry; constitutionalism, chapter 2 argues, arose out of an effort to minimize social strife and has been concerned throughout its history with constraining and directing the violence of the state so that the state in turn can control the violence of the society. From a theological perspective, Stout reinforces the argument MacIntyre makes possible that Christian theology and American constitutionalism are competing traditions. By offering as its goal and justification the achievement of social peace and community—in the actual language of the Constitution, "domestic tranquility" and "a more perfect Union"—constitutionalism implicitly claims for the American constitutional order a justice and "ordered unity in plurality, a genuine *res publica*" that Christianity recognizes only in community constituted by God.[130]

In this chapter, I have attempted to describe the conceptual tools that I use in chapters 2 and 3 in presenting an interpretation of American constitutionalism as a liberal tradition of moral enquiry. With some modifications, Alasdair MacIntyre's richly developed concept of moral traditions provides a theoretical framework adequate to describe constitutionalism's multiple roles as intellectual conversation, political structure, and social activity; at the same time, MacIntyre's framework enables me to bring constitutionalism and Christian theological ethics into juxtaposition as competing moral traditions. MacIntyre's own use of his "theory" as a means of interpreting and criticizing contemporary liberal society, furthermore, suggests the starting point for my interpretation of constitutionalism as a product of the Enlightenment's attempt to ground morality and politics in the universal norms of reason. The attempt, as MacIntyre has asserted and as this book argues, led to the transformation of Enlightenment

---

its central ambiguities. By removing the concept of practice from its original conceptual engagement with the concept of tradition, Stout leaves his "MacIntyrean" social criticism without any obvious basis for moral evaluation other than the principle of avoiding "cruelty." An ethic *can* be constructed with opposition to cruelty as its sole affirmative commitment (see Rorty, *Contingency*), but Stout does not seem willing, as Rorty clearly is, to accept the consequent narrowing of the realm of moral discourse.

130 Rowan Williams, "Politics and the Soul: A Reading of the *City of God*," 19/20 Milltown Studies 55, 60 and generally (1987).

liberalism itself into a tradition or set of traditions. The ultimate purpose, of course, is theological: to provide a truthful description of American constitutionalism that will enable American Christians to live and act appropriately in a world in which constitutionalism is one of the most seductive masks worn by state violence.

Chapter 2

THE MORAL TRADITION OF AMERICAN CONSTITUTIONALISM

Historical accounts of American constitutionalism generally have fallen into one of three forms.[1] Academic lawyers usually have written accounts of the development of constitutional law and judicial doctrine, focusing on the continuities and changes in the Supreme Court's decisions. David Currie's *Constitution in the Supreme Court* is a recent example of the pure form of this "lawyer's legal history."[2] Political historians and scientists tend to address themselves to institutional concerns, tracing the changing role of the Supreme Court, its relationships with other branches of government, and the ebb and flow of power among Congress, President, and states. Charles Warren's great study of *The Supreme Court in United States History*[3] remains the classic example. Finally, writers whose ultimate concern is to make a political argument against the current practices of the Supreme Court sometimes adopt a narrative form for their argument. In the 1930s, for example, federalist Charles Haines narrated the history of a nationalist Supreme Court that had subverted the Constitution's original federalism; in the 1950s, nationalist William Crosskey wrote the story of a faint-hearted

1 By "historical accounts," I mean narrative expositions of American constitutionalism over time. I thus intend to exclude from direct consideration what is perhaps the most common form of "historical" constitutional writing, the search for the "original intent" or the "intention of the framers" of the Constitution. Such work can be done well, with sophisticated appreciation of the context and sources of the framers' thought and purposes, or it can be done poorly, treating the texts acontextually. In either case, however, the writer's concern is deliberately focused on a particular moment in time, usually with the implicit or explicit assumption that what took place after that moment is of secondary importance. In a sense, therefore, even the best of this type of constitutional scholarship tends to be ahistorical.

2 David Currie, *The Constitution in the Supreme Court: 1789–1888* (Chicago: Univ. of Chicago Press, 1985) and *The Constitution in the Supreme Court: 1888–1986* (Chicago: Univ. of Chicago Press, 1990).

3 Charles Warren, *The Supreme Court in United States History* (Boston: Little, Brown, 1926).

Supreme Court's surrender of the nationalist Constitution to the centrifugal forces of federalism.[4]

The present chapter of this book adopts a narrative approach to American constitutionalism for yet another purpose, to argue that constitutionalism is a MacIntyrean tradition of moral enquiry in which are embedded the practices of constitutional adjudication (decision making by the courts) and constitutional theorizing (scholarly commentary and criticism). This tradition is embodied institutionally in the federal judiciary and its exercise of the power of judicial review; it has a secondary institutional location in American law schools, which support the practice of theorizing and serve as media by which theorists influence the courts. This chapter develops the argument by narrating the emergence of a socially embodied, historically extended discourse out of the American Founding's attempt to create a polity based on Enlightenment principles. In particular, chapter 2 traces the development of two major characteristics of this tradition: over time, American constitutionalism came to claim both that it embodies specific moral commitments (a claim that implicitly acknowledges the transformation of liberalism into a particular moral position) and that it is autonomous with respect to moral argument and political preference (a claim that implicitly reinstates the Enlightenment assertion of neutral rationality). The paradoxical consequence has been that constitutionalists usually have wished to claim that constitutionalism both is and is not a morality.[5] In recent years, the chapter concludes, the constitu-

4 Charles Haines, *The American Doctrine of Judicial Supremacy* (Berkeley: Univ. of California Press, 1932); Willaim Crosskey, *Politics and the Constitution* (Chicago: Univ. of Chicago Press, 1953). Occasionally an apologia for the Court will take a similar narrative form. See, e.g., Jennifer Nedelsky, "Confining Democratic Politics: Anti-Federalists, Federalists and the Constitution," 96 Harv. L.Rev. 340 (1982) (persuasively interpreting the official "Holmes Devise" history of the early Marshall Court as an apologetic defense of contemporary mainstream judicial politics).

5 One of the most uncompromising statements of the social-morality interpretation of the Constitution comes from a Christian theological ethicist, Daniel Maguire. Maguire has argued that the Supreme Court, "quite uniquely" in the contemporary world, "fulfills the philosophical function performed by the universities in medieval Europe. It is not merely a case Court—but an official philosophical forum." Maguire, *American Justice*, 7. For Maguire, the Supreme Court's ultimate appeal in support of its judgments is and must be to "moral reasoning." Id. at 51. Compare with this view MacIntyre's: "we lack . . . *any*

tional tradition has found itself forcefully confronted with this paradox and unable to resolve it, an inability that has plunged the tradition into what MacIntyre calls an "epistemological crisis." Chapter 3 examines critically the effort of contemporary constitutional theorists to resolve the crisis by identifying the community of which the Constitution is the shared morality.

The ultimate purpose of the book is, of course, critical and theological; the extended narrative treatment of constitutionalism is, nevertheless, integral to my argument. One of the central lessons of the work of MacIntyre, Stout, and other recent social critics is that the subject matters of ethical reflection and criticism "are nowhere to be found except as embodied in the historical lives of particular social groups and so possessing the distinctive characteristics of historical experience: both identity and change through time, expression in institutionalized practice as well as in discourse, interaction and interrelationship with a variety of forms of activity."[6] Contemporary American constitutionalism does not exist in an Olympian setting removed from the history of how constitutional institutions and constitutional argument came to this point in history.[7] Only by seeing the constitutional practices of adjudication and theory as embedded in the narrative of the constitutional tradition can we understand and properly critique the claims of current theorists or of the current Court.[8] Certain implications flow from the adoption of "philosophi-

---

public, generally communal mode . . . for putting our politics to the philosophical question." MacIntyre (1984), 138.

6 MacIntyre (1984), 265. Christian theologian John Milbank recently noted that "theology has rightly become aware of the (absolute) degree to which it is a contingent historical construct emerging from, and reacting back upon, particular social practices conjoined with particular semiotic and figural codings." Milbank, *Theology and Social Theory: Beyond Secular Reason* (Oxford: Basil Blackwell, 1990), 2. As Milbank's own work makes clear, the same is true of all moral discourses.

7 As Elizabeth Wolgast has observed, "moral philosophy and its debates [occur] not in a vacuum but at a particular place and time, with cultural traditions and practices already in place." Elizabeth A. Wolgast, *A Grammar of Justice* (Ithaca, N.Y.: Cornell Univ. Press, 1987), x.

8 "Once again, the narrative phenomenon of embedding is crucial: the history of a practice in our time is generally and characteristically embedded in and made intelligible in terms of the larger and longer history of the tradition through which the practice in its present form was conveyed to us." MacIntyre (1984), 222.

cal history"[9] as the form of this chapter. The narrative form, if it is to be persuasive, must be what Jeffrey Stout has called "stereoscopic"—focusing at one and the same time on practices *and* institutions, internal *and* external goods, virtues *and* the circumstances that nourish or corrupt them.[10] A narrative of American constitutionalism, properly recounted, will be a story of both conceptual argument and political struggle, neither separating these elements nor collapsing one into the other. The adoption of the narrative form implicitly disputes the many arguments that deny genuine significance to the conceptual and theoretical[11] even as it requires attention to the intimate and reciprocal influence of the internal or intellectual and the external or political. To say this, of course, is to locate this book itself in one or more disputed histories: "the narrative task itself generally involves participation in conflict."[12] Any narrative of American constitutionalism is itself an argument about the meaning of American constitutionalism; such arguments are certain to be contestable and contested. In addition, the ethical and theological interests of the book render its narrative a part of the ongoing history of Christian ethics in America. And that story, too, is one of far-reaching conflict.[13]

Finally, the employment of narrative necessarily requires one to address the question of the narrative's genre, "a question which has to be asked and answered before we can decide how it is to be written."[14] The question of genre is not one of mere style, for as MacIntyre has observed, it is through choosing the proper genre in which to write about a subject that the writer makes crucial determinations about the meaning and truth of that subject.[15] The present narrative belongs to the genre of crisis literature, a genre in which the subject is seen as balanced between opposing disasters without clear indications of how to avert a tragic resolution.[16] In MacIntyre's

9 Id. at 270.

10 Stout, *Ethics*, 279–81.

11 MacIntyre (1984), 272.

12 MacIntyre (1988), 11.

13 See Hauerwas, *Against the Nations*, 26–39.

14 MacIntyre (1984), 212.

15 Id. at 213.

16 The connections between Christian theology and the literature of crisis are strong and long-standing. See, e.g., Karl Barth, *Der Romerbrief* (1919) (discussing the crisis of God's *krisis* on the world).

terminology, this narrative is the story of how a form of Western liberalism became an explicit tradition of moral enquiry and, recently, moved into an epistemological crisis. This story mirrors the one that MacIntyre tells about liberalism generally; by describing in detail the constitutional tradition's rise and decline, I hope to avoid the risk of unsympathetic and therefore implausible caricature. The search of contemporary constitutional theorists for community, which is the subject of the third chapter, is, I shall suggest, the constitutional tradition's attempt to resolve its current crisis.

ANTECEDENTS OF THE CONSTITUTIONAL TRADITION

American constitutionalism was fashioned out of a number of intellectual and institutional sources, sources that from a twentieth-century viewpoint can appear to have been in tension with or antithetical to one another. (The contradictions we perceive often were not evident, of course, to the American founders.)[17] The orthodox scholarly explanation of American constitutionalism's origins throughout most of the twentieth century has been to identify the Constitution as the creation of the Enlightenment, the institutional incarnation of liberalism.[18] While this orthodoxy has been challenged over the past two decades by advocates of the view that civic republicanism was a more vital source of the Constitution, it remains clear that the connections between the Constitution and the Enlightenment were deep.[19] "The

17 American constitutional writers regularly apotheosize the Founders, paying them an honor that dehumanizes them and their accomplishments even while it papers over their considerable disagreements with one another. The use in this book of the term to refer to the social group that wrote and ratified the Constitution is intended to do neither. See Robert Wiebe, *The Opening of America* (New York: Knopf, 1984), discussing the fundamental social unity and the severe political disagreements among politically influential Americans in the Founding era.

18 See, e.g., Hartz, *Liberal Tradition in America*; and Henry F. May, *The Enlightenment in America* (New York: Oxford Univ. Press, 1976).

19 "The leading makers of the American constitution conceived themselves as influenced by political philosophy, which they took in its modern form [of

American Constitution represents perhaps the greatest success of the Enlightenment in turning political life toward [its] goals."[20]

The Enlightenment Origins of American Constitutionalism

Modernity emerged out of the fracturing of medieval culture. As discussed in the introduction to this book, the religious, political, and social crises that confronted Western Europeans of the seventeenth and eighteenth centuries seemed greatly to exceed the cultural resources they had inherited from their medieval ancestors. Of particular importance in the present context is the conclusion reached by early liberals that the intellectual and institutional forms of medieval Christendom were not adequate to ensure a just and peaceful social order—or, indeed, any sort of order at all. At the heart of the Enlightenment was a strongly political agenda, the creation of a social order free of the sectarian violence of the wars of religion because it was free of the moral and intellectual blindness to which the liberals traced that violence. To create such a social order required the development of a new moral anthropology, on the basis of which Enlightenment politicians could construct a novel political form, the nation-state. American constitutionalism was permanently shaped by its origins in the Enlightenment attempt to devise political arrangements that would directly embody its fundamental philosophical commitments to rationalism and individualism.

The logical starting point for Enlightenment thought and early liberal politics was the dethronement of traditional authority in science, education, religion, and politics—in short, throughout corporate and individual life.[21] In place of tradition, which the Enlightenment's protagonists saw as oppressive, unjust, and irrational, they proposed to set reason itself, freed from the shackles of the past and the coercive force of the group.

Standing against the old authorities required a secure point, an Archime-

Enlightenment liberalism]." Grant, *Justice*, 55. See also Smith, *Liberalism*, 13–59.

20 Smith, *Liberalism*, 3.

21 Wolgast, *Grammar*, 1–2.

> dean point from which to strike. So it happened that in a variety of fields—science, theology, political theory, morality—such a point was located in the autonomous, unconnected, rational human individual. Starting with this person and his or her inherent abilities, requirements, and values, one got a neutral and detached perspective on any claim to authority. Thus a new kind of moral, political and epistemological justification came into being, one that derived from the natural, free, rational, and morally autonomous individual. It was an unbinding of the inquiring spirit; it was a new premise for shedding a critical light on old orthodoxies.[22]

This canonization of rational autonomy was, the Enlightenment's protagonists typically argued, grounded in human nature itself, in humanity's capacity for rational self-determination.[23] To be human is to be capable of, and engaged in, the exercise of reason. Those whose autonomous exercise of their individual rationality is compromised by tradition or restricted by social forces are, to that extent, enslaved. They suffer an "indignity to human nature"[24] that Enlightenment thinkers characteristically described as a violation of their "natural" or "human rights." Those who are incapable, wholly or in part, of individually exercising the power of rational self-determination are to that extent less than fully human and not entitled to the full panoply of social and political rights. Candidates for the less-than-fully human category frequently included women, children, the poor, and non-Europeans (particularly, in America, blacks). Thus embedded in the core anthropology of the Enlightenment was what from other standpoints appears to be a moral contradiction: the Enlightenment's picture of humanity provided the moral and political basis for libertarian and egalitarian attacks on social privilege while at the same time it cast an aura of inescapable and unchangeable truth over the prejudices and patterns of social exclusion of the eighteenth-century European intelligentsia.

Human social relations, the Enlightenment thinkers logically concluded, should be governed not by the nonrational and suprain-

22 Id. at 2.

23 Smith, *Liberalism*, 28–30.

24 John Locke, quoted in Maurice Cranston, *John Locke* (London: Longmans, 1957), 225.

dividual norms of tradition but by those "moral precepts [which] derive from an individual conceived without the impact of society."[25] Some Enlightenment figures, for example Kant, identified moral activity with the exercise of reason, while others, Hume or Smith for example, located morality's source in natural tendencies toward sociability and benevolence or in a separate "moral sense." In either case, "the single individual is the ground of moral principles,"[26] and truly moral action is characterized by the individual's exercise of reason.

The Enlightenment's moral and anthropological "atomism," to borrow Elizabeth Wolgast's accurate label, had direct and far-reaching effects on the Enlightenment's theory and practice of politics. While most early liberals believed that human beings were in some fashion naturally social beings, their atomistic premises led them to regard all particular social and political arrangements as artificial, the creation of autonomous individuals associating for reasons they individually found rationally justifiable.[27] The liberal determination to end sectarian violence pointed to the maintenance of civil peace through means other than sectarian repression as a central aspect of any justifiable political order. As it emerged in France, Great Britain, and elsewhere, the modern nation-state clearly reflected the liberal demand for the rationalization of political power. In place of medieval Christendom's complex interweaving of local, urban, feudal, royal, and religious authorities—authorities with "jurisdictions" overlapping in space and subject matter—the nation-state laid claim to a monopolization of political authority within its territory and especially to a monopoly over coercion. At the same time, the nation-state, unlike medieval political forms, was clearly and increasingly distinct

25 Wolgast, *Grammar*, 6.

26 Id.

27 Some early liberals believed that this notion of a "social compact" was, literally and historically, how societies came into being. Others, like their present-day heirs, viewed the ideas of the "state of nature" and the social "contract" as heuristic devices for analyzing and displaying social and political norms in light of their atomistic anthropology. The continuing power of the image of contract in liberal thought is exemplified, of course, in John Rawls, *A Theory of Justice*. "[T]he vision of society as a collection of free calculating individuals puts [Rawls's] book at the heart of modern Liberalism." Grant, *Justice*, 16.

from civil society. Even if individuals are sociable by nature, the nation-state is clearly artificial.

Since there are (or were) no social forms or political structures in the "state of nature," Enlightenment political thought was virtually obligated to be contractual. Only the metaphor of social contract seemed to provide a means of imagining how autonomous, atomistic individuals might associate without compromising their autonomy. Consent, the free choice of the individual to subject himself (it would be misleadingly anachronistic to add "or herself") to social and political arrangements, became absolutely crucial to political legitimacy and to a just organization of power. As Locke wrote, nothing legitimately can put a person "into subjection to any Earthly Power, but only his own Consent."[28] The impossibility or impracticability of obtaining actual consent from all members of a polity posed severe theoretical and practical problems for the early liberals. Eighteenth-century liberals therefore turned toward devising political forms that so clearly protected the "natural rights" of individuals that tacit consent to them could reasonably be postulated: in a rationally organized and just society there would be no rational ground for withholding consent, and to do so would be to show oneself less than fully rational and thus not entitled to fully autonomous choice in the first place.[29] The rhetorical strategy of the American Declaration of Independence, for example, was to assume that the British imperial system originally had been sufficiently protective of the Americans' "unalienable Rights" to merit consent. The bulk of the Declaration then consists of a bill of grievances intended to show that King George III was guilty of "abuses and usurpations evinc[ing] a design to reduce [America] under absolute Despotism." Such "a history of repeated injustices and usurpations," the Declaration argued, justified the Americans in withdrawing their consent and thus delegitimizing the King's authority.

Enlightenment thinkers generally agreed that the origins of government in consent implied that government should be limited in power. For some early liberals including Locke and Jefferson, the

28 Locke, *Concerning Civil Government, Second Essay* (Chicago: Encyclopedia Britannica, 1952), chap. 8, sec. 119.

29 See Grant, *Justice*, 27.

limits on government stemmed from an external, theoretically derived necessity. Certain natural rights are, in Jefferson's language, "unalienable," incapable of being yielded to government.[30] Virtually all early liberals agreed that there were pragmatic objections to granting government unlimited power. To do so would be to disregard, irrationally and imprudently, the darker side of the Enlightenment's anthropology, its assumption that the atomistic individual is prone to disregard the dictates of sociability and natural justice in the pursuit of individual goals. The Enlightenment portrait of men (again, the gendered term is appropriate) as autonomous, rational decision-makers was balanced by this fear of men's individual and irrational pursuit of self-interest. This dualism of reason and unreason owed something, of course, to Christianity,[31] and it was formulated in a variety of sometimes inconsistent ways. Contrast Hume, for whom reason is the servant of the passions, with Kant, for whom reason is, or can be, the master. But in any event the dualism produced in Enlightenment politics the curious spectacle of committed rationalists guided by the conviction that it would be irrational to commit corporate human affairs to the unconstrained governance of reason.

The Enlightenment's political incarnation, the nation-state, thus embodied a seeming paradox. The "formal character of state power as guaranteeing personal security and non-interference in 'private' pursuits . . . demand[ed] that this power be otherwise unlimited and absolutely alone."[32] But the liberal suspicion of human selfishness—a suspicion built into liberal anthropology—demanded some means of controlling the nation-state that did not depend on the virtue of the governors. The Enlightenment's political desideratum, therefore, was to devise a government strong enough to impose civil peace by force if necessary, but possessing built-in safeguards against the

30 Locke wrote that "no Body can transfer to another more power than he has in himself; and no Body has an absolute Arbitrary Power over himself, or over any other, to destroy his own life, or take away the Life or Property of another." Locke, *Civil Government*, chap. 11, sec. 135.

31 See Daniel Boorstin, *The Lost World of Thomas Jefferson* (New York: H. Holt, 1948), 151–66.

32 Milbank, *Social Theory*, 13. Milbank correctly stresses the "fundamentally common origin [of] private property and state sovereignty."

governors' oppressive exercise of choice. "If men were angels, no government would be necessary. If angels were to govern men, neither external nor internal controls would be necessary. In framing a government which is to be administered by men over men, the great difficulty lies in this: you must first enable the government to control the governed; and in the next place oblige it to control itself."[33] The "Enlightenment ideal of holding acts of power up to the critical light of reason"[34] could only be obtained if there were some extra-individual means for compelling individuals to listen to reason. The politics of the so-called Age of Reason were a search for political mechanisms that would not rely on reason.[35]

In response to this dilemma, early liberalism's pessimism about the actual results of human exercises of will and its intensely individualistic premises produced an analytically sharp and politically crucial distinction between the public and private spheres.[36] Unlike much of the Aristotelian tradition, Enlightenment liberalism did not universally insist that human fulfillment involved political activity. The state, rather than being the arena of personal fulfillment and moral education, became something external to the individual and his virtues, interests, and goals. "Liberalism's most distinctive feature is thus its insistence that government should be limited so as to free individuals to undertake private as well as public pursuits of happiness, even if this option erodes public spiritedness in prac-

33 Jacob E. Cooke, ed., *The Federalist* No. 51 (J. Madison) (Middletown, Conn.: Wesleyan Univ. Press, 1961), 349 (hereinafter cited as *The Federalist*). See the important article by Paul Kahn, "Reason and Will in the Origins of American Constitutionalism," 98 Yale L.J. 449 (1989).

34 Robin West, "Disciplines, Subjectivity, and Law," in Austin Sarat and Thomas R. Kearns, eds. *The Fate of Law* (Ann Arbor: Univ. of Michigan Press, 1991), 119.

35 "No longer was politics thought of as rhetoric and persuasion: instead it became technology." Milbank, *Social Theory*, 160. The preference of Enlightenment political theorists and their American heirs for imagery derived from physics and mechanics is striking. Among a myriad of examples, consider this (critical) description of John Adams's political views: "Mr. Adams's *sine qua non* of a good government is three balancing powers, whose repelling qualities are to produce an equilibrium of interests." Centinel No. 1 (1787), in Herbert J. Storing, ed., *The Complete Anti-Federalist* (Chicago: Univ. of Chicago Press, 1981), 2.7.7.

36 See, e.g., Grant, *Justice*, 28–29; Smith, *Liberalism*, 49.

tice."[37] Founding-era American political figures frequently contrasted the richness and fulfillment of their private lives with the barren wasteland of public duty.[38] The tension between these protestations and such figures' obvious desire for public office was not simple hypocrisy: the founders' liberal premises led them sincerely to believe that they *should* find private life their true realm of happiness and public action an onerous duty.[39]

Unable to find individual satisfaction in the public sphere, Enlightenment man was equally unable to seek his own moral education there. One of the most important and distinctive elements of early liberalism in its own time was its "disavowal of the state's traditional concern with human moral fulfillment."[40] Much of the political effort of early liberals from Locke to Jefferson and Madison was directed toward turning "the focus of political life" from moral and religious questions to "matters of material well-being."[41] This emphasis on the public sphere's connection with material goods in turn tended to create a fissure between the (richer) morality of the private sphere, within which natural justice and the social virtues were acknowledged to rule, and the contractual, socially defined rules of public conduct.[42]

As the setting for many of the negative aspects of atomistic individualism, the public sphere tended to be portrayed as restless and aggressive, liable to be controlled by those driven by irrational or selfish goals. The preservation of the private sphere in the face of this threat required the creation and maintenance of one or more political forms: institutional arrangements capable of checking public overreaching; the definition of rights (chiefly those of private property and personal liberty) absolutely immune from legitimate public inva-

37 Smith, *Liberalism*, 14.

38 See Garry Wills, *Cincinnatus: George Washington and the Enlightenment* (Garden City, N.Y.: Doubleday, 1984).

39 On liberalism's reciprocal development of the public realm of the modern state and the intimate realm of the private, see Anthony Giddens, *Modernity and Self-Identity* (Stanford: Stanford Univ. Press, 1991), esp. at 150–52.

40 Smith, *Liberalism*, 31. "[N]o longer did the encouragement of specific virtues form part of the goal to be pursued by the community—once the very essence of 'politics.'" Milbank, *Social Theory*, 160.

41 Smith, *Liberalism*, 24.

42 See Milbank, *Social Theory*, 160.

sion; and the imposition of legal norms on arbitrary governmental action. "Hence [early liberals] carried with them an emphasis on liberty in many forms, on constitutionalism, and on the even-handed rule of law."[43] The Enlightenment's legalism rested on "a confidence, of relatively recent origin, in the capacity of language to confine and control human conduct, to regulate human will and desire by words rather than, always and directly, by the sword. Such confidence ma[de] it possible to imagine that Leviathan might be tamed."[44] However, the pessimism built into Enlightenment anthropology led to an insistence on the impartial or "neutral" administration of law—on "government by law and not by men"—since a "central problem of politics [was] the ways in which distortions of self-interest prevented persons from fairly adjudicating controversies over [individual] rights."[45] For early liberal thought about the administration of government, therefore, the "rule of law" assumed some of the metaphorical primacy that the "social contract" enjoyed in liberal discussions of political legitimacy. Just as the social contract defined the boundary between civil society and the anarchy of the state of nature,[46] so the rule of law marked the limits of reason's control over human conduct.

43 Smith, *Liberalism*, 18.

44 Austin Sarat and Thomas R. Kearns, "A Journey Toward Forgetting: Toward a Jurisprudence of Violence," in Sarat and Kearns, *Fate of Law*, 209, 220.

45 David A. J. Richards, *Foundations of American Constitutionalism* (New York: Oxford Univ. Press, 1989), 31.

46 The social contract was not by any means only an aitiological or historical notion. Founding-era American writers often used the social contract as a tool for interpreting contemporaneous social and political institutions. Rejecting an argument that the Virginia revolutionary convention of 1776 possessed the power to dissolve the prerevolutionary political order but not the power to create a new one, St. George Tucker wrote that the argument led to unacceptable conclusions. "Every man would have been utterly absolved from every social tie, and remitted to a perfect state of nature. . . . [This] could never be presumed. A new organization of the fabric, and a new arrangement of the powers of government, must instantly take place." *Kamper v. Hawkins*, 1 Va.Cas. 20 (1793). In 1803 Tucker expressly noted the hermeneutical nature of "social compact" language: because "the end of civil society [is] in short, a mutual defence against all violence from without . . . each individual *is supposed* to have entered into engagements with each other. . . . And this is, what is ordinarily meant by the original contract

The Enlightenment's general endorsement of the image of law was especially important among English-speaking liberals because it seemed to many of them descriptive of the actual role of law in English history. The political opponents of the early Stuart kings described themselves as defenders of English law as well as of English liberty. In his *Reports*, Sir Edward Coke laid it down as legal doctrine that the law "hath admeasured the prerogative of the King";[47] his later political defense of the autonomy of the House of Commons was couched in terms of fundamental law: "Magna Carta is such a fellow that he will brook no sovereign."[48] The association of law with rights and of rights with a just political and social order was a commonplace of seventeenth-century English political rhetoric. In 1675, for example, William Penn described England's laws as the means by which "its rights are maintained" and "the ancient and undoubted rights of Englishmen, as three great roots, under whose spacious branches the English People have been wont to shelter themselves against the storms of arbitrary government."[49]

The need to constrain governmental choice shaped Enlightenment thought on the practical details of political organization. Because executive officers are prone to act arbitrarily, most early liberals agreed that they should be subject to law administered by neutral magistrates as well as to the overriding will of the legislature. Because the legislature itself is made up of men whose self-interest may or will lead them to transgress the rational and ethical limits on their powers, constitutional arrangements such as balanced govern-

---

of society." Tucker, "View of the Constitution of the United States" (1803), reprinted in Jefferson Powell, *Languages of Power* (Durham, N.C.: Carolina Academic Press, 1991), 154.

47 Quoted in Catherine Drinker Bowen, *The Lion and the Throne* (Boston: Little, Brown, 1957), 291.

48 Id. at 496.

49 Penn, "England's Present Interest Considered," in Philip Kurland and Ralph Lerner, eds., *The Founders' Constitution* (Chicago: Univ. of Chicago Press, 1987), vol. 1, 429. Penn believed that all "those rights and privileges which I call *English*, and which are the proper birth-right of Englishmen" could be "reduced to these three," the right of private property, representation in Parliament, and trial by jury. Id.

ment[50] and separation of powers[51] were necessary. Given the early liberals' general support for parliamentary institutions, their unwillingness to trust the legislature's exercise of reason is striking. As devout a believer in Reason as Jefferson was quite unwilling to trust a legislature that was constrained only by the legislators' deliberations about the common good. Jefferson was, for example, bitterly critical of the Virginia Constitution's de facto concentration of all governmental power in the hands of the legislature, which he regarded as an unwitting betrayal of the purpose of the Revolution. "173 despots would surely be as oppressive as one. . . . An *elective despotism* was not the government we fought for, but one . . . in which the powers of government should be so divided and balanced among several bodies of magistracy, as that no one could transcend their legal limits, without being effectually checked and restrained by the others."[52] Writing a few years later about the federal legislature, Jefferson equated a constitutional "power to do whatever would be for the good of the United States" with a legal commission to engage in tyranny. He refused to place any weight on the legislature's duty to act in accordance with a reasonable judgment about the common good: "as they would be the sole judges of the good or evil, it would be also a power to do whatever evil they please."[53]

The judiciary was no less liable to the influence of bias and passion in the view of the early liberals. Here their solution was twofold: to

50 The notion of *checks and balances*, ultimately derived from Aristotle and Polybius, was that institutions reflecting the one, the few, and the many (in English thought often the monarch, the Lords, and the Commons) should share power. They then would be able, and out of self-interest would be willing, to check each other's tendency to self-aggrandizement. The notion owed much of its popularity in eighteenth-century thought to its susceptibility to reformulation in mechanistic terms. See H. Jefferson Powell, "How Does the Constitution Structure Government," in Burke Marshall, ed., *A Workable Government?* (New York: W. W. Norton, 1987), 22–26.

51 The idea here was to divide governmental powers functionally, for example, by confining the legislature to lawmaking and excluding it from law application. The notions of separation of powers and checks and balances, although often confused by modern lawyers, were quite distinct in origins and eighteenth-century usage. Id. at 26–29.

52 Jefferson, *Notes on the State of Virginia*, ed. William Peden (Chapel Hill: Univ. of North Carolina Press, 1954), 120.

53 Jefferson, Opinion on the Constitutionality of the Bill for Establishing a National Bank (1791), in Powell, *Languages*, 42.

confine judges strictly to adjudication of particular disputes and, more important, to replace the forms of argument of traditional Western European legal systems with a simplified and rationalized code of laws that would require application only, not interpretation. In the most influential work of Enlightenment jurisprudence, Cesare Beccaria's *On Crimes and Punishments*, the most vital reform of traditional criminal law was said to be the elimination of all forms of judicial discretion and interpretation.[54] Continental legal process after Napoleon is marked by its formalism, its style of deductive reasoning from clearly stated premises, and its ostensible rejection of judicial tradition in the form of precedent—all parts of the common Enlightenment program for legal reform.

In the English-speaking countries, the Enlightenment's program of political reform was not usually envisaged as the total elimination of a corrupt *ancien régime*. Instead, the Anglophone liberals tended to interpret traditional English political arrangements as embodying the requirements of Enlightenment rationality.[55] The Baron de Montesquieu's great *L'Esprit des Lois*, for example, portrayed the English parliamentary system as the paradigm of liberal constitutionalism, while liberal criticisms of contemporaneous English practices were described indifferently as defenses of natural rights and as vindications of the ancient English constitution.[56] Colonial American liberals adopted this equation of English tradition and Enlightenment rationality: the Stamp Act Congress of 1765, for example, described English constitutional forms both as "essential to the free-

54 Beccaria contrasted "the constant fixed voice of the law" codified on Enlightenment principles with "the erring instability of interpretation" by judges. Beccaria, *On Crimes and Punishments* (1764), trans. H. Paolucci (Indianapolis: Bobbs-Merrill, 1963), 14–18.

55 Grant's *English-Speaking Justice* brilliantly portrays this peculiarly Anglophone equation of pre-Enlightenment institutions with Enlightenment ideals. Grant, *Justice*, 48–56. The equation was already becoming obsolete in England by the late eighteenth century with the development of ministerial government and the Blackstonian subversion of the classical common law. The American Revolution preserved and indeed reinvigorated anachronistic and "Old-Whiggish" legal and political forms. Modern British lawyers typically view the United States as a "great museum of discarded English legal forms." Lord Hailsham, *Hamlyn Revisited: The British Legal System Today* (London: Stevens, 1983), 38.

56 See John P. Reid, *The Concept of Liberty in the Age of the American Revolution* (Chicago: Univ. of Chicago Press, 1988), 23–27.

dom of a people"—*any* people—and as "the undoubted right of Englishmen." Even as peculiarly English an institution as trial by jury was classed as an "inherent" right.[57]

American constitutionalism's debts to Enlightenment liberalism are manifold and obvious.[58] The American Founders were acknowledged students of Locke[59] and Montesquieu[60] as well as of other liberal writers such as John Trenchard and Thomas Gordon, whose "Cato" essays exercised great influence in late colonial and revolutionary America. "Cato" was expressly and strongly liberal in his political views. Writing in 1721, for example, Trenchard described human nature as radically individualistic: "it is the Ambition of all Men to live agreeably to their own Humours and Discretion."[61] Trenchard's solution to the moral and political problem that results was classically liberal, the establishment of a political order that carefully divided the public sphere of state control from the private realm of individual discretion. "[F]ree countries," he wrote, are those "where Power is fixed on one Side, and Property secured on the Other."[62] The Enlightenment horror of sectarian strife, rein-

57 Resolutions of the Stamp Act Congress (1765), in Melvin I. Urofsky, *Documents of American Constitutional and Legal History* (New York: Knopf, 1989), vol. 1, 43.

58 Early liberalism "supplies some of the most important and characteristic features of American political theory, and the imprint of these ideas is evident and fixed in the Constitution." Wolgast, *Grammar*, 7.

59 Recent attempts to deny Locke any important role in shaping Founding-era thought seem clearly mistaken. See Steven M. Dworetz, *The Unvarnished Doctrine* (Durham, N.C.: Duke Univ. Press, 1990).

60 See Paul K. Conkin, *Self-Evident Truths* (Bloomington: Indiana Univ. Press, 1974), 156.

61 The reader should note that the terms *ambition*, *humours*, and *discretion*, used in conjunction, carried strong connotations of selfishness and arbitrariness in eighteenth-century English. See, e.g., Powell, *Languages*, 29 (discussing the meaning of "discretion" in Founding-era discussions).

62 English liberals from Locke to the American Founders consciously used the term *property* to designate, often simultaneously, both realty in the legal sense and the totality of that which belongs to an individual's *proprium*. See, e.g., Locke, *Civil Government*, chap. 5; James Madison, "Property," (1792) in Marvin Meyers, ed., *The Mind of the Founder*, rev. ed. (Hanover, N.H.: Brandeis Univ. Press, 1981), 186–88. "Cato" emphasized strongly the autonomy of the private sphere: "it is . . . foolish to say, that Government is commissioned to meddle with the private Thoughts and Actions of Men, while they injure neither

forced in the English context by varying and conflicting Protestant memories of persecution, sounded clearly in "Cato:" "Every Man's Religion is his own; nor can the Religion of any Man . . . be the Religion of another Man, unless he also chooses it; which Action utterly excludes all Force, Power, or Government."[63]

The constitutionalism of the Founding era clearly reflected this liberal background. Most late eighteenth-century constitutional instruments expressly acknowledged the liberal objectives of establishing the nation-state and safeguarding the autonomy of the individual. The preamble of the 1780 Massachusetts Constitution, for example, stated that "[t]he end of the institution, maintenance and administration of government, is to secure the existence of the body-politic; to protect it; and to furnish the individuals who compose it, with the power of enjoying, in safety and tranquility, their natural rights."[64] The proponents of the federal Constitution of 1787 relied directly on Enlightenment commonplaces in commending the Constitution's adoption. James Madison, for example, cited the "propensity of mankind to fall into mutual animosities," a propensity fueled powerfully by a "zeal for different opinions concerning religion, concerning Government and many other points" as the source of "faction . . . sown in the nature of man." The Constitution was an appropriate remedy because of "its tendency to break and control the violence of faction."[65] Madison's fellow propagandist Alexander Hamilton ampli-

the Society, nor any of its Members. Every Man is, in Nature and Reason, the Judge and Dispenser of his own domestick Affairs." "Cato" (Trenchard), in Kurland and Lerner, *Founders' Constitution*, 622.

63 The quotations in text from "Cato" (all from essays attributed to Trenchard) are found in id. at 585, 618.

64 The emphasis sometimes lay on the empowerment of government to protect the individual: when Americans devised their federal Constitution, Rep. Daniel Buck told the House of Representatives in 1796 that their first two "great objects" were "first, rules to check the licentious wickedness of individuals, and mark out their separate rights; second, intermediate judges to apply those rules." 5 *Annals of Congress*, 4th Cong., 1st sess. (March 7, 1796) at 431. Just as frequently, Americans stressed the limits their constitutionalism placed on government's ability to do evil. The "utility of a written constitution," Judge William Nelson stated in 1794, lies in its assignment of "limits . . . to those to whom the administration is committed." Kamper v. Hawkins, 1 Va.Cas. 20 (Gen.Ct.).

65 *The Federalist* No. 10 (J. Madison), 59, 58, 56.

fied Madison's argument by stressing that the proposed Constitution's grant to the federal government of express powers of legal coercion would tend to mitigate the role of actual violence in American society by substituting "the Coertion of magistracy" for "the Coertion of arms."[66] A few years after the Constitution's adoption, Cong. Richard Bland Lee justified the new political order in terms of its success in eliminating the violence of the preadoption period[67] and fostering prosperity: "Confidence is restored, and every man is safe under his own vine and his own fig tree, and there is none to make him afraid. To produce this effect, was the intention of the constitution . . . and it has succeeded."[68] The promise of American constitutionalism, at its most fundamental, was to create a realm of peace.[69]

Many of the institutional features of the United States Constitution were directly shaped by the dictates of liberal political thought—the separation and enumeration of limited powers, the constitutional protections for the private sphere (found especially but not exclusively in the Bill of Rights drafted two years after the Constitution's original text), the document's implicit contractarianism. The logically peculiar association of (English) tradition with Enlightenment reason was borrowed almost at once to describe the American constitutions.[70] Equally important for the later history of the constitutional tradition were areas of tension and difficulty which liberalism bequeathed: What form should consent to the American constitutional order take? How are reason and will to be reconciled or balanced in the exercise of governmental power and in constitutional interpretation? What is the relationship between American constitutional argument and the discourse of liberalism from which it stems? How is liberalism's "stress on both liberty and legalism" to be worked out in

66 *The Federalist* No. 15 (A. Hamilton), 95.

67 Lee described "the period which gave birth to our Constitution" as one in which "the ties of confidence between man and man, and, consequently, the ties of morality were broken asunder." 4 *Annals of Congress*, 3d Cong., 1st sess. (Jan. 21, 1794), at 262.

68 Id.

69 Lee's use of biblical imagery to describe the federal Constitution's purpose and effect is striking.

70 See, e.g., Judge Spencer Roane's opinion in Turpin v. Locket, 6 Call. 113 (Va. 1804), in which Roane equated "the dictates of moral justice," "the principles of the [Virginia] constitution," and the "great principles of the revolution."

practice? Many of the deepest issues of the American constitutional tradition's problematic (in MacIntyre's sense) are the product of its liberal origins.

The Civic Republican and Protestant Heritages

As noted earlier, in recent years the usual historical interpretation of the American Constitution as the product of a liberal consensus has been challenged by scholars who insist on the important role played by alternative modes of thought in the Constitution's creation. While some advocates of the civic republican interpretation of the founding view republicanism as antithetical to liberalism,[71] republicanism is better understood as a possible historical complement to liberalism.[72] *Republicanism*, in any event, is a modern term for ideas with diverse origins. J. G. A. Pocock has traced the transmission of Renaissance civic humanism from the Italian city-states of the sixteenth century to England, where it shaped the thought of such writers as James Harrington and Algernon Sydney, and the political practice of opposition politicians including Lord Bolingbroke.[73]

In England, civic republicanism was largely subsumed within the native political tradition modern scholars call the "commonwealth" school of thought. Commonwealth thought originated in the seventeenth century struggles against the Stuart kings that culminated in the Glorious Revolution of 1688.[74] Commonwealth thinkers rested their hope for the preservation of liberty in the exercise of civic virtue by an informed and independent citizenry. Such a citizenry was necessarily limited to those with the natural gifts necessary to wise and courageous action and the economic independence to defy both royal threats and royal bribery. Commonwealth and republican

71 See Dworetz, *Unvarnished Doctrine*, criticizing this view.

72 "The opposition between liberal and republican thought in the context of the framing is, however, largely a false one. Only through a caricature of the tradition can liberalism be thought the antonym to the species of republicanism that operated during the constitutional period." Cass R. Sunstein, "Beyond the Republican Revival," 97 Yale L.J. 1539, 1567 (1988).

73 Pocock, *The Machiavellian Moment* (Princeton: Princeton Univ. Press, 1975).

74 Caroline Robbins, *The Eighteenth Century Commonwealthman* (Cambridge, Mass.: Harvard Univ. Press, 1959).

thought therefore rested on a "profound elitism" with both intellectual and economic components.[75] The "natural inequality of the social classes"[76] that republicans perceived provided them with a republican rationale for the exclusion of women, the poor, and men of other ethnic or racial backgrounds, from the deliberative body of citizens.

In addition to its self-conscious elitism, republicanism in the form the American founders met it was shaped by a deep historical pessimism. Republicans saw free political orders as intrinsically fragile, their political health resting on constant vigilance by the citizenry. Liberty could only survive as long as the citizens were willing to exercise the civic virtues of disinterested public service and, when necessary, armed resistance to tyranny. The 1776 Pennsylvania Bill of Rights, for example, proclaimed that "a frequent recurrence to fundamental principles and a firm adherence to justice, moderation, temperance, industry and frugality, are absolutely necessary to preserve the blessings of liberty and keep a government free."[77] But virtue was constantly threatened by the temptations of "ambition, luxury, and lust" and by the sleepless desire of power for more power. Jefferson, who was deeply influenced by this historical pessimism,[78] expressed its political implications precisely in 1798: "confidence is everywhere the parent of despotism; free government is founded in jealousy, and not in confidence. . . . In questions of power, then, let no more be said of confidence in man, but bind him down from mischief by the chains of the Constitution."[79] The necessity of civic virtue and the inescapability of its corruption were for republican thinkers the conditions of political life, conditions that could be ameliorated—but not eliminated—by the cultivation of virtue by the polity.

75 James Oakes, "From Republicanism to Liberalism: Ideological Change and the Crisis of the Old South," 37 Am.Q. 569 (1985).

76 Linda K. Kerber, "Making Republicanism Useful," 97 Yale L.J. 1663, 1666 (1988).

77 Penn. Bill of Rights article xiv, in Urofsky, *Documents*, 66.

78 See Lance Banning, *The Jeffersonian Persuasion* (Ithaca, N.Y.: Cornell Univ. Press, 1978), for a discussion of the links between commonwealth and republican thought and Jefferson.

79 Kentucky Resolutions of 1798, in Powell, *Languages*, 133.

Seventeenth- and eighteenth-century thinkers interwove liberal republican themes in complex and varying ways. Harrington, for example, defined the central problem of political theory in protoliberal terms: "the main question seems to be how a commonwealth comes to be an empire of laws and not of men; or how the debate or result of a commonwealth is so sure to be according to reason, seeing they who debate and they who resolve be but men."[80] His solution combined "liberal" mechanisms for constraining political choice[81] with an insistence on the necessity of civic virtue.[82] Founding-era Americans readily mixed what modern theorists seek to distinguish. Even those whose commitment to Enlightenment politics was the most undeniable saw no inconsistency in invoking the necessity of civic virtue to free government as well.[83]

The Founders' combination of liberal and republican ideas is

80 Harrington, *Commonwealth of Oceana* (1656), in Kurland and Lerner, *Founders' Constitution*, 340.

81 Id. at 341–42 (stressing the importance of separation of powers and the supremacy of law).

82 Id. at 658–59 (discussing corruption and attributing England's former peace and freedom to rule by "men of country lives [i.e., agrarian virtue], the best stuff of a commonwealth").

83 Madison, for example, wrote that "[a]s there is a degree of depravity in mankind which requires a certain degree of circumspection and distrust: So there are other qualities in human nature, which justify a certain portion of esteem and confidence. Republican government presupposes the existence of these qualities in a higher degree than any other form." *The Federalist* No. 55, 378. The reader will have noted that the combination of a basically liberal politics with some reference to and reliance upon a human capacity for other-directed action could be explained as the persistence of (traces of) pre-Enlightenment, basically Christian moral and anthropological beliefs.

The relationship between Enlightenment liberalism, the "Machiavellian" republican revival of an essentially pagan notion of civic virtue, and Christian and Aristotelian political thought is extremely complicated, and I am not satisfied that Pocock and his followers have stated it correctly. Milbank argues, correctly in my view, that "the eighteenth-century enlightenment was much preoccupied with an attempt to find a new version of antique virtue" while "even the 'civic humanist' tradition is infected by individualism and instrumentalism." Milbank, *Social Theory*, 21. For the purposes of this essay, however, it is not necessary to resolve this important historiographic issue, since, at least as appropriated by early American constitutionalists, liberalism and republicanism were not opposites.

exemplified by the debate in the 1787 Philadelphia convention over governmental concern for public virtue. Late in the convention, George Mason proposed that Congress be given the express power to enact sumptuary laws. Mason was a strong proponent of the centrality of individual rights to political society; indeed, shortly afterwards he refused to sign the Constitution because of its failure to include a bill of rights. Mason's intent in making his sumptuary law proposal was, on the other hand, clearly "republican": he wanted to entrust the national legislature with at least partial responsibility for the shaping of civic virtue.[84] Mason's motion was overwhelmingly defeated, apparently because most of the convention's delegates viewed the Constitution's purpose in liberal terms as the exclusion of national power from the private sphere. But the opponents of Mason's motion shared Mason's belief in the necessity of virtue.[85] The presence of republican themes in the political discourse of Founding-era Americans shows not a rejection of liberalism, but a less-than-perfect satisfaction with the polity and the politics liberalism seemed to demand.[86]

As the constitutional tradition developed, critics of the tradition's apparent course frequently drew upon republican language about corruption and the fragility of liberty. Within the mainstream of the constitutional tradition the language of civic republicanism has been

84 Mason argued in support of his proposal that "[n]o Government can be maintained unless the manners be made consonant to it." James Madison, *Notes of Debates in the Federal Convention of 1787*, ed. Adrienne Koch (Athens, Ohio: Ohio Univ. Press, 1966), 488. Mason's argument was a commonplace. See, e.g., Montesquieu's discussion of the need for sumptuary laws in a republic to protect republican virtue against corruption by "luxury." *The Spirit of Laws*, trans. Thomas Nugent (Chicago: Encyclopedia Britannica, 1952), bk. 7 chaps. 1–2. The significance of Mason's proposal for present purposes lies in the fact that Mason, who was one of the convention's greatest sceptics about a powerful central government, sought to extend the proposed government's authority in such a dramatic fashion.

85 Madison asked in the Virginia ratifying convention "[i]s there no virtue among us? If there be not, we are in a wretched situation. No theoretical checks—no form of government can render us secure." Speech of June 20, 1788, in *The Papers of James Madison*, ed. William Hutchinson (Charlottesville: Univ. of Virginia Press, 1977), vol. 11, 163.

86 James Oakes has argued that eighteenth- and nineteenth-century republicanism "always functioned as an expression of alienation and opposition." Oakes, "Ideological Change," 555.

strikingly absent. Until recently, moreover, even the tradition's critics ordinarily have distinguished a privatized language of "personal" virtue from public questions of political significance.[87]

The civic republican influence on the American constitutional tradition cannot always be clearly distinguished from another source of the tradition—Protestant Christianity. In one sense, of course, American constitutionalism is undeniably but trivially the child of the Reformation: as the creation (for the most part) of English speakers, American political thought and practice were shaped in diffuse and global ways by the overwhelmingly Protestant atmosphere of early modern English-speaking culture. The same is true, however, of the English-language Enlightenment, of the English and Scottish appropriation of civic republicanism, and for that matter of the English common law, the influence of which I shall discuss below. Civic republican pessimism, for example, was shaped by a Calvinist anthropology of humanity as radically fallen and, perhaps, by a lingering and secularized version of Calvinist predestinarianism.[88] American constitutionalism, in turn, rested in part on Calvinist assumptions about human sin and human rationality in its attempt to harness both reason and self-interest in the service of liberty.[89] English liberalism also reflected its Protestant background: the liberal exaltation of the private sphere carried forward in an individualized form the Christian rejection of the classical assumption "that politics itself was inherently redemptive."[90] Protestantism, however,

87 Critics of John Marshall's constitutionalism, for example, typically combined extremely harsh discussion of his political views with glowing concessions about his (individual) virtue. See, e.g., the July 1835 obituary of Marshall written by the radical Jacksonian Democrat William Leggett, reprinted in Lawrence H. White, ed., *Democratick Editorials* (Indianapolis: Liberty Press, 1984), 28–30.

88 John P. Diggins's insightful discussion of Founding-era thought points out that John Adams's views on politics, for example, display "a revealing synthesis of politics and religion: His theory of government derived from Whig and classical ideology while his psychology of political behavior derived from Calvinist theology." Diggins, *The Lost Soul of American Politics* (Chicago: Univ. of Chicago Press, 1984), 71.

89 The classic statement is Richard Hofstadter, *The American Political Tradition* (New York: Alfred A. Knopf, 1948), 3–17. See the important discussion in Diggins, *Lost Soul*, 74–99, esp. at 83: "Much of the reasoning behind the Constitution is steeped in the psychology of temptation and the politics of suspicion."

90 Diggins, *Lost Soul*, 77.

arguably had a direct and particular impact on the formation of the constitutional tradition beyond its background shaping of American culture.

The obvious area of direct Protestant influence lies in the role of New England congregationalism, and its free-church analogues elsewhere, on the formation of a political culture that was simultaneously contractual and protodemocratic. "Congregationalism," Joshua Miller has written, was "the beginning of early American democracy."[91] American congregationalism drew on the radical reformation concept of the church as a gathered community in which "membership must be voluntary."[92] Particularly in New England, the gathered ecclesial community was seen as resting on *covenant*, a form of association brought into existence by the free and active choice of its members to constitute themselves as a community. The notion of covenant differed from traditional patterns of social organization and obligation because its authority over the individual stemmed from the individual's conscious decision. Thomas Hooker, one of the greatest political thinkers of colonial America, wrote that "[t]here can be no necessary tye of mutual accord and fellowship come, but by free engagement, free (I say) in regard of any human constraint."[93]

The Protestant covenant also differed from the social contract or compact of early Enlightenment thought. The covenant, unlike the social contract, was an actual document, subscribed to by its adherents on specific, historical occasions, not a fiction legitimating authority by a dramatic representation of the passive consent of the

91 Miller, *The Rise and Fall of Democracy in Early America, 1630–1789* (University Park: Penn State Univ. Press, 1991), 8. While Miller's discussion focuses on New England Puritanism, the congregationalism of the established Puritan churches of that region was paralleled by dissenting or free-church Protestants elsewhere. The covenant form "was repeated thoughout New England, parts of the central colonies (including the Dutch colonies), and later in the southern piedmont. Wherever dissenting Protestantism went, so too went their church covenants." Donald S. Lutz, *The Origins of American Constitutionalism* (Baton Rouge: Louisiana State Univ. Press, 1988), 25. Professor Lutz's book is a clear and incisive account of the relation between Protestant congregationalism and covenant theology and later American constitutionalism.

92 John Howard Yoder, *The Priestly Kingdom* (Notre Dame, Ind.: Univ. of Notre Dame Press, 1984), 110.

93 Hooker, *A Survey of the Summe of Church-Discipline* (1648), quoted in Miller, *Rise and Fall*, 35.

governed to the exercise of power by the governors.[94] The Protestant covenant went beyond the creation of a domain of social peace policed by political authority to enunciate the self-definition and common commitments of a community with the teleological goal of becoming "a people who follow the Gospels and God's ordinances, and who exist in mutual love and respect."[95] The public realm of such a gathered community, like the *polis* of civic republicanism, was necessarily broader than liberalism's sharp distinction between public and private would permit.[96]

The Protestant concept of the covenant originated in the radical reformation critique of the ecclesiology of the established Catholic and Protestant churches of early modern Europe. In colonial America, it quickly was generalized to serve as the model for the constitution of political communities.[97] Transposed into the political sphere, the covenant provided the rationale for slightly different accounts of political notions—popular sovereignty and the limitation of governmental discretion—that were endorsed by liberalism and civic republicanism as well.[98] If political authority stems from covenant, then it exists only by the choice of those over whom it is exercised, and it can legitimately be wielded only in accordance with the terms of the covenant. In the constitution making of the late eighteenth century, the religious theme of covenant was blended almost inextricably with liberal and republican language.[99] Nevertheless, even at that date it is possible to see distinctively Protestant elements in, for example, the aspirational and self-definitional aspects of the first

94 Miller, *Rise and Fall*, 35.

95 Lutz, *Origins*, 25; see also pp. 28–32.

96 "Unlike modern liberals, the Puritans attributed to the public realm a sense of purpose and mission that required the active support of its citizens." Miller, *Rise and Fall*, 43.

97 See, e.g., Lutz, *Origins*, 25–27. Miller, *Rise and Fall*, 34. Already in the middle of the seventeenth century, Thomas Hooker was treating "the covenant as the basis for all forms of social organization." Clinton Rossiter, *Six Characters in Search of a Republic* (New York: Harcourt, Brace and World, 1964), 23.

98 See Lutz, *Origins*, 28–31; Rossiter, *Six Characters*, 27 (discussing Hooker's thought).

99 Professor Miller rightly stresses, how "gradually and incompletely" originally Protestant and theological concepts and institutions were subsumed by a mostly secular and predominantly liberal "language of contract and individual rights." Miller, *Rise and Fall*, 51.

state bills of rights.[100] Even more importantly, the evangelical fervor generated by the Great Revival around 1800 and the Second Great Awakening of the Jacksonian period played significant roles in fueling the democratic offensive against the elitism of the original constitutional order.[101] Like civic republicanism, Protestantism's primary contribution to the constitutional tradition has been in the role of critic and antagonist.[102]

The Common Law Background to American Constitutional Law

The third major source of the American constitutional tradition, the common law, was at the time of the Constitution's drafting, already itself a centuries-old tradition of moral inquiry. Alone among the emerging nation-states of Western Europe, England's native legal tradition successfully resisted subversion or conquest by the revived Roman law that spread from Italy beginning in the eleventh century. While the practices and concepts of this civil law heavily influenced English equity and admiralty law, captured law teaching in the universities, and dominated Scots law from the Renaissance on, the English common law courts conserved and developed their own peculiar procedures and modes of argument.

The common law was self-consciously particularistic and tradition-dependent. Sir John Davies, attorney general for Ireland under James I, wrote "the classic exposition of the common lawyer's viewpoint."[103] "[T]his law [is] the peculiar invention of this nation, and delivered over from age to age by tradition (for the common law of England is a tradition, and learned by tradition as well as by books)."[104] Those

100 Lutz, *Origins*, 32–33.

101 See Diggins, *Lost Soul*, 169, discussing the "antinomian implications" of evangelical Christianity; Charles Sellers, *The Market Revolution* (New York: Oxford Univ. Press, 1991), 30–31, 157.

102 The most important example being evangelical Christianity's role in the formation of antislavery constitutionalism. See, e.g., Sellers, *Market Revolution*, 401–7.

103 David Wootton, *Divine Right and Democracy* (New York: Penguin Books, 1986), 129.

104 Davies, *Le Premier Report des Cases et Matters en Ley Resolues et Adiudges en les Courts del Roy en Ireland* (1615), preface, in Wootton, *Divine Right*, 133.

steeped in the common law tended to be adverse to adopting the universalizing categories of Roman law, and later of Enlightenment thought at least as it related to law.[105] Classical common lawyers emphatically defended the rationality of the common law—Sir Edward Coke stated that "[r]eason is the life of the law, nay, Common Law itself is nothing else but Reason"[106]—while denying that its reasonableness was the product of its conformity "to some set of transcendent standards of reason or justice (or standards which are distinct from and rationally prior to positive law and custom)."[107] The students of the common law resisted its assimilation to any universal or totalizing discourse. An incident involving one of the greatest of the common lawyers, Sir Thomas More, illustrates the point: "When More was a law student at Bruges, one of the professors there invited any comer to debate him. He would, he said, dispute any question in any science. More asked him whether beasts of the plow, taken in withernam, were capable of being replevied. The professor could not deal with that recondite bit of English common law; Erasmus, who was present, said that the professor retired 'with his withers wrung and More's withernams unwrung.' "[108]

The common lawyers tenaciously defended their traditional categories and concepts—what Davies called the "words of art and form [and] rules and maxims" of the law and Stout has termed a "non-philosophical vernacular" characteristic of flourishing practices[109]—against transformation into tradition-independent terms. The standards of rationality and progress they admitted as applicable to their work were, for the most part, those internal to the common law. When James I (a Scot, not coincidentally) suggested that as the fount of justice the monarch had the competence actually to sit in judgment in court, Chief Justice Coke briskly, if politely, corrected him. "To which it was answered by me [Coke wrote], that true it was that

105 See, e.g., Christopher St. Germain, *Doctor and Student*, ed. T. Plucknett and J. Barter (London: Selden Society, 1974).

106 1 Coke, *The Institutes of the Laws of England* sec. 138.

107 Gerald Postema, "Some Roots of our Notion of Precedent," in Laurence Goldstein, ed., *Precedent in Law* (New York: Oxford Univ. Press, 1987), 16–17.

108 Hauerwas, *Christian Existence*, 207–8. See also William Blackstone, *Commentaries on the Laws of England* (Oxford: Clarendon Press, 1768), vol. 3, 149, note w.

109 Davies, in Wootton, *Divine Right*, 134, 135; Stout, *Ethics*, 272.

God had endowed his Majesty with excellent science and great endowments of Nature. But his Majesty was not learned in the Laws of his Realm of England; and Causes which concern the Life, or Inheritance, or Goods, or Fortunes of his Subjects were not to be decided by natural Reason but by the artificial Reason and Judgment of Law, which requires long Study and Experience before that a man can attain to the cognizance of it."[110] Coke's conceptual point was that justice as understood within the common law tradition could not be ascertained by abstract ratiocination but only through the intimate knowledge of the forms and progress of common law argument acquired by what we might call socialization into the profession. What the student of the classical common law learned through his "long Study and Experience" was not so much sets of rules as "a *capacity to judge* reflectively on the basis of the particular features of cases, features which gain significance in virtue of being read against a larger context of common social life and human 'conversation.'"[111] One learned the common law by becoming a common lawyer—by acquiring the virtues of the common lawyer—and one acquired that identity and those virtues by exposure to and imitation of exemplars.[112]

The common law's most important contribution to American constitutionalism was its proffer of a nonliberal, pre-Enlightenment, tradition-dependent form of rational argument about justice.[113] Classical common law reasoning is well illustrated in a case decided in

110 Prohibitions del Roy, 12 Co. Rep. 63, 64–65 (1608).

111 Postema, in Goldstein, *Precedent*, 21.

112 The late seventeenth-century Chief Justice Sir Matthew Hale wrote that knowledge of the common law "must be gained by the habituating and accustoming and exercising that faculty by reading, study, and observation." Hale, "Reflections . . . on Hobbes His Dialogue of the Lawe," in W. Holdsworth, *A History of English Law*, 7th ed. (London: Methuen, 1956), vol. 1, 503. Compare Stout's argument that the virtues necessary to the practice of medicine are acquired mostly through "imitation of role models." Stout, *Ethics*, 269. The educational literature of the classical common law is replete with examples of the professional wisdom and virtue of earlier common lawyers.

113 Davies wrote, "what is the matter and subject of our profession but justice, the lady and queen of all moral virtues? And what are our professors of the law but her councillors, her secretaries, her interpreters, her servants?" Davies, in Wootton, *Divine Right*, 142.

1344.[114] In that year Adam and Matilda de Flaundres brought a legal action to establish their claim to certain real property. Their claim to the property was based on an alleged grant Matilda's great-grandfather made to his daughter (her grandmother). The defendant in the case, the person then in legal possession of the land, failed to defend his right and Adam and Matilda were on the verge of succeeding in their suit when a Hugh de Langebrugge sought permission to intervene in the case. Hugh claimed that he was entitled to the land upon the current tenant's death and produced a written private deed to that effect. The plaintiffs' lawyer denied Hugh's right to be heard, citing an earlier case in which the court had stated that a person in Hugh's position should not be heard.

In response, Justice William de Sharshulle cast doubt on the authority of the earlier case: "One has heard of that which [Justices] Bereford and Herle did in such a case . . . but nevertheless no precedent is of such force as that which is *resoun*."[115] Sharshulle's comment illustrates an aspect of the common law view of precedent ignored by positivist accounts of law. The earlier case was authority because it was an example of what earlier, distinguished participants in the common law tradition had thought right, not because it was ipso facto binding on later participants. When the plaintiffs' lawyer later raised the earlier case again, he did so explicitly on the basis of the tradition's need for shared understanding. "I think you will do as others have done in the same case, or else we will not know what the law is."

Justice Roger Hillary dismissed this new argument for following the earlier case with the blunt statement that "[l]aw is the will of the justices," probably meaning only to deny the binding nature of the old case rather to anticipate by several centuries a modern positivist theory of law. In any event, Chief Justice John de Stonore interrupted Hillary with a correction: "No, law is *resoun*." And Hugh was permitted to intervene in Adam and Matilda's suit despite the earlier case.

The case of Adam and Matilda illustrates several features of the

114 Flaundres v. Rycheman, 18 & 19 Y.B. Edw. III 374 (C.P. 1344) (L. Pike ed. and trans., 1905).

115 The meaning of this technical law French term is discussed below.

common law tradition of importance for the American constitutional tradition. First, classical common lawyers understood rules differently than did Enlightenment philosophers (or indeed than most modern legal philosophers do). There was a preexisting rule on the question of Hugh's intervention: third parties should not be heard in such cases if their claim of right is based solely on a private charter. But the rule's validity and its application to particular cases was governed by *resoun*. That law French term is, etymologically, cognate to the modern English word "reason"; its use in common law argument often paralleled the modern French expression *avoir raison*—to be in the right. But the term was richer and more complex than its twentieth-century cognates. *Resoun* meant that which is reasonable, that which makes sense. It also and simultaneously meant that which is just, fair, moral. And at times it meant that which is a believable story, an acceptable narrative—people sometimes said "let me display my *resoun*" (i.e., let me tell my story).[116]

For classical common lawyers, rules were discovered in, debated in terms of, and decided with reference to stories of past situations and decisions. A rule of broad generality might emerge from such stories, but its application in future circumstances was always open to further narrative argument. It was not possible, even in theory, to establish in advance a metarule that would determine the proper application of a rule to all the varied circumstances of human life. Even a putatively general rule was limited to cases that a lawyer well schooled in the profession's traditions of argument would agree fell within the *resoun* of the rule. One learned how to be a good legal reasoner by reading and hearing good arguments by lawyers and judges with the virtues of insight, discrimination, judgment, integrity, and so on.

The case of Adam and Matilda also illustrates the classical common law's self-awareness of itself as a tradition of argument. When the plaintiffs' lawyer referred to the earlier case, he was reminding the justices of his and their location in an ongoing narrative of questions answered and disputes adjudicated. His reminder was so much the stronger because he was able to invoke the memory of William de Bereford, a chief justice of the Court of Common Pleas of

116 See *Oxford English Dictionary* (2d ed., 1989), s.v. "reason."

a couple of decades earlier whose wise judgment was proverbial. In suggesting that the court would not follow the earlier decision, Justice Sharshulle implicitly acknowledged Bereford's authority while insisting that the aim of common law argument was not to establish what the rule might be in the abstract so much as to judge what *resoun* would be in the concrete and particular case. In deciding a different case, Sharshulle very well might have relied on Bereford's authority even if the earlier judge had not convinced his contemporaries, for a past lawyer's authority rested primarily on his perceived success in carrying forward the common law's inquiry into the proper resolution of social disputes. A lone dissenter known for his practical wisdom might be seen, in part because of that repute, as the better legal reasoner than the majority judges in the case, just as a rule endorsed by an earlier court could be rejected if it seemed contrary to the later judges' view of *resoun*.

The common law's distinctive modes of rational argument and evaluation[117] were embedded within a broader narrative explaining how the common law had come to take the forms and to play the role it possessed in post-1688 England. That this narrative was substantially mythologized does not of course affect its significance for the common law tradition or its contribution to American constitutionalism. The equation of the common law tradition with "the rights of Englishmen," and of the latter with Enlightenment concepts of individual autonomy and the rule of law, enabled many Americans of the Founding era to make the theoretically improbable assumption that liberal political principles could be explicated in the forms of the common law.

The common law's historical development was intimately con-

117 One theme in MacIntyre's discussion of the social and intellectual background to the Scottish Enlightenment (MacIntyre [1988], 219–37) is the contrast he draws between Scots law and English common law. However, several of the features of Scots law MacIntyre praises were characteristic of the classical common law as well. See, e.g., id. at 223 (Scots law provided "a set of institutionalized means for bringing [political] principles to bear upon the issues of practical life"); id. at 230 (Scots law capable of internal self-correction and progress). MacIntyre's negative view of the common law seems derived from Blackstone, whose famous *Commentaries on the Laws of England* marks the subversion of the common law tradition by Enlightenment concepts of rationality and high Tory concerns for social control. See id. at 228–29.

nected, as one would expect on MacIntyrean grounds, with the rise of common lawyers as a distinct professional class.[118] The common lawyers, at a surprisingly early date, laid claim to special expertise and thereby to special privileges, especially to a monopoly over the rights of audience in and appointment to the royal courts. Even at an early stage the profession was urban and middle-class in nature, and most common lawyers found their social biases reinforced by the values of their profession. As early modern England became increasingly commercialized, lawyers like the social groups from which they usually came became steadily more bourgeois in opinion, opposed to royal overbearing, and supportive of political changes (such as enhancement of the power of the House of Commons) that favored the middle class. A remarkably large number of the leading American revolutionaries were practicing lawyers, and long before the Declaration of Independence American political discussion had taken on a legalistic cast.[119] Edmund Burke, indeed, "attempted to explain the American intellectual climate of resistance in terms of the number of lawyers present in the colonies."[120] While the common law, with its tradition-bound forms of reasoning and its substantive concern for property rights, cannot realistically be seen as an intrinsically radicalizing element in early American society, the institutional myths and predispositions easily lent themselves to the service of the intentionally conservative objectives of the American revolutionaries.

The institutional history of the common law courts, heavily reinterpreted in a Whiggish fashion by eighteenth-century Americans, was of special importance. The common law courts' political struggles with other centers of power (feudal judicatories, the church, Star Chamber, and other prerogative courts) were seen as battles on behalf of the rule of law and English liberty. While the quite different perspective of the courts' historical opponents did not disappear, this reinterpretation of English legal history created a link for many Americans between the activities of courts and the preservation of liberty. The authority of the common law was justified internally by

118 See Wootton, *Divine Right*, 33 (discussing the "rapid rise of the lawyers as a profession" in the late sixteenth and early seventeenth centuries).

119 See Reid, *Concept of Liberty*, 1–10.

120 Shannon C. Stimson, *The American Revolution in the Law* (Princeton: Princeton Univ. Press, 1990), 39.

its own peculiar standards of rational argument; externally, the common law had come to be associated with the growth of English political freedom. Great common lawyers—Lord Coke, John Selden, Lord Hale—were for many late eighteenth-century Americans both heroes in the struggle for liberty and exemplars of common law rationality.[121]

The classical common law tradition was partially subverted in England in the second half of the eighteenth century. Part of the reason, no doubt, was the influence of the Enlightenment's antipathy for tradition-dependent modes of thought, and the shift in the focus of middle-class fear from the king to the working class played a role as well. The actual spade work of demolition was done by two of the most prominent common lawyers of the era: Lord Mansfield and Sir William Blackstone. Mansfield, the Chief Justice of the Court of King's Bench from 1756 to 1788, was one of the towering giants of the common law bench. He was, ironically, not English but Scottish, and he was not overly impressed with common law modes of argument or with the supposed link between the common law and human liberty. Mansfield's own political predilection was toward upholding the exercise of authority by the executive, and his freewheeling treatment of earlier case law and common-law learning in private law cases provoked a long-term reaction in favor of adherence to precedent that ultimately rigidified into a formalistic doctrine of *stare decisis*.[122]

Blackstone was a lackluster barrister who was appointed Vinerian Professor of Law at Oxford in 1758, the first person to hold a university chair in common law. Blackstone's true gifts were rhetorical; the published version of his lectures, the famous *Commentaries on the Laws of England*, was a stylistic masterpiece and a remarkable publishing success, going through almost innumerable editions, abridg-

121 This hagiographical treatment of earlier lawyers, which was to have great and lasting effects on American attitudes toward the law and the Constitution, is almost uniquely English. Despite the great importance of law in Roman thought, for example, great lawyers seldom if ever were lionized in the general culture. For example, Procopius portrayed Tribonian, the great jurist of Justinian's Code, as a corrupt and avaricious judge whose appointment to office was disastrous for the state. Procopius, *The Secret History*, trans. G. A. Williamson (Harmondsworth: Penguin Books, 1966), 141–42.

122 Jim Evans, "Change in the Doctrine of Precedent during the Nineteenth Century," in Goldstein, *Precedent*, 35–72.

ments, and adaptations in England and America up to the end of the nineteenth century. In this country, indeed, the *Commentaries* became by the beginning of the 1800s the core of legal education. Blackstone's success was a mixed blessing, however, for the common law tradition. Blackstone, without really realizing the fact, was like the Scot Mansfield in that he was alienated intellectually from the common law. His method of argument in the *Commentaries*, as a result, was to "[u]se the tools of eighteenth-century analytical 'philosophy,'"[123] which was precisely the intellectual capitulation to universalizing rationality that earlier common lawyers had rejected.

The subversion of the classical common law in England was substantially ignored in America. Lord Mansfield was generally acknowledged as a great judge while his politics were denounced as the result of Scottish and Tory biases.[124] Blackstone's virtues—literary felicity, relative compactness—quickly were recognized in a country with few books and a populace on the move; a long series of American annotators and imitators strove to adapt the *Commentaries* to the American setting.[125] At the same time, most American lawyers tempered their appreciation of Blackstone's pedagogical value with an active recognition and rejection of his politics. This ambivalence toward the author of the *Commentaries* enabled Americans to utilize the book without accepting its substantial distortion of the classical common law.

The contributions of the common law to the American constitutional tradition predated the latter's birth, inasmuch as the common law helped to formulate the colonial Americans' political and revolutionary thinking. The famous Writs of Assistance Case in 1761 will serve as a good example. James Otis, Jr., arguing that the colonial superior court should refuse to issue writs of assistance (basically,

123 Thomas Green, Introduction to William Blackstone, *Commentaries on the Laws of England* (1765–69), photographic reproduction (Chicago: Univ. of Chicago Press, 1979), vol. 1, 5.

124 On Mansfield's ambiguous reputation in the United States, see Edward Dumbauld, *Thomas Jefferson and the Law* (Norman: Univ. of Oklahoma Press, 1978).

125 St. George Tucker, the great legal systematizer of Jeffersonian Republican thought, published an edition of Blackstone with literally hundreds of notes and appendixes intended in large part to counteract Blackstone's "Tory" politics. See Tucker, *Blackstone's Commentaries on the Laws of England* (Philadelphia: Birch and Small, 1803).

unlimited search warrants) to executive officers, made an elaborate common law argument that the writs were not legally authorized. He went on, however, to argue that the same principles of common law provided that even "had this writ been in any book whatever, it would have been illegal. All precedents are under the controul of the principles of the Law. . . . No Acts of Parliament can establish such a writ; though it should be made in the very words of the petition [of the executive officers seeking the writs] it would be void; An Act against the Constitution is void."[126] The notion that the common law's tradition of rational inquiry into justice might at times justify a court in disregarding the dictates of a statute had been broached on occasion by earlier common lawyers, most notably by Lord Coke in Dr. Bonham's Case in 1610. Eighteenth-century English lawyers' loss of faith in their traditional modes of argument led to the eclipse of the idea. In 1766 Blackstone could write that "[t]he power and jurisdiction of Parliament . . . is so transcendent and absolute, that it cannot be confined, either for causes or persons, within any bounds. . . . True it is, that what they do, no authority on earth can undo."[127] In America, in contrast, the concept of the common law as providing a substantive means of examining rationally the justice of positive law played an important role in the formulation of arguments for resistance and later revolution against British authority. John Adams wrote of Otis's argument in the Writs of Assistance Case that it was "the first scene of the first act of opposition to the arbitrary claims of Great Britain. Then and there, the child Independence was born."[128]

The American preservation of the classical common law's tradition-dependent modes of rational inquiry was not limited to those situations where common law argument furthered American political goals: after the Revolution, Americans unreflectively employed common-law argument in their discussion of issues arising under their new, written instruments of fundamental law. A good example is William Cushing's correspondence with John Adams in 1789 concerning the crime of seditious libel. Cushing, then Chief Justice of the Massachusetts Supreme Judicial Court, wrote to ask Adams's advice about whether Massachusetts law should follow Blackstone's

126 L. Wroth and H. Zobel, eds., *Legal Papers of John Adams* (Cambridge, Mass.: Harvard Univ. Press, 1965), vol. 2, 127–28.

127 Blackstone, *Commentaries*, vol. 1, 156.

128 Presser and Zainaldin, *Law and Jurisprudence*, 56.

assertion that truth was no defense against an indictment for libeling a public official. Blackstone's reasoning was that the criminal punishment of seditious libel (unlike the imposition of civil liability for it) was grounded solely in "the tendency of libels to create embarrassments and disturb the public peace." As a consequence, the fact that the libelous assertion was in fact true did not justify the libel; indeed, since a true libel would cause greater disturbance than a false one that the public official could refute, a true libel was a graver crime than a false libel.[129] Cushing's specific question was whether this view, which Blackstone presented as *the* common law rule, was consistent with the state constitution's guaranty of "liberty of the press."

In formulating his question, Cushing alluded to the view held by some American lawyers that Blackstone's rule, as settled law, should govern the proper interpretation of American constitutional protections for press freedom.[130] In traditional common law fashion, however, Cushing declined to treat Blackstone's rule as foreclosing the process of rational inquiry. His analysis began by noting two arguments against the validity of the Blackstonian rule. First, the conclusion that telling the truth made the offense greater was, ethically and rationally, bizarre. In addition, the rule had been questioned in the famous Case of the Seven Bishops (1686) by dissenting Justice Powell. Powell's doubts were of great significance despite the fact that in the *Seven Bishops* decision itself he was outvoted three to one; Cushing pointed out that common lawyers of noted wisdom and virtue (Lord Camden, William Pitt the Elder) regarded Powell as "the only honest man on the bench, at that time."[131]

Cushing conceded that contemporaneous English courts followed Blackstone's rejection of truth as a defense despite Powell's objections, and he went on to present multiple, mutually supporting arguments against the Blackstonian rule. The Massachusetts Consti-

129 Blackstone, *Commentaries*, vol. 4, 150–51.

130 A few years later this argument was the standard justification for the controversial Sedition Act, which was more respectful of free speech than the First Amendment required if the argument were accepted. See, e.g., Harrison Gray Otis, Speech in the House of Representatives (July 10, 1798), 8 *Annals of Congress* 2145 (5th Cong., 2d sess.).

131 Frank Grinnell, "Hitherto Unpublished Correspondence between Chief Justice Cushing and John Adams in 1789," 27 Mass. L.Q. 12–15 (1942).

tution provided, he wrote, that English laws not in use in Massachusetts or repugnant to the state constitution were to be ignored. There were, essentially, no Massachusetts cases from which to decide if the rule was in use in the Commonwealth and on that basis Cushing concluded that the role of truth in seditious libel prosecutions was to be decided "*de novo* upon the reason of the thing and from what may appear most beneficial to society."[132] (Founding-era American lawyers such as Cushing and Adams, whose initiation into the "artificial Reason and Judgment of Law" began with Lord Coke's writings, customarily used the word *reason* in legal contexts as a synonym of the law French *resoun* with all of the latter term's richness.) Invoking "honest Powell" in support, Cushing argued that subsequent punishment for writing the truth was as likely to restrain press freedom as was the prior censorship that even Blackstone agreed would violate "liberty of the press"; furthermore, the text of the constitutional provision made "no such distinction" between prior and subsequent restraints. Cushing also reasoned that on balance truthful criticism of public officials was likely to do more good than harm. On the other hand, he dismissed the possibility of reading the constitutional language as an absolute ban on any governmental interference with speech; part of the purpose of government itself was to protect individual reputation against defamation. Thus the proper interpretation of the constitutional guaranty must balance the government's ethical obligation to protect reputation against its ethical and political obligation to safeguard public discussion of official conduct. The proper balance, Cushing concluded, was to recognize the legitimacy of prosecutions for seditious libel but to treat the truth of the libel as an absolute defense against criminal punishment. In response, Adams endorsed Cushing's reasoning as the best reading of the law and the state constitution.[133]

This exchange between Cushing and Adams is exemplary of the legacy the common law tradition gave to American constitutionalism. Americans socialized into the common law demonstrated self-confidence in the rationality and ethical quality of legal reasoning. They assumed the propriety of critical interaction with earlier arguments and authorities as well as the necessity of paying special

132 Id. at 15.
133 Id. at 16.

attention to the views and actions of figures of outstanding legal intellect and integrity or, in other words, lawyers displaying the virtues of the tradition. They accepted the existence of a creative element in the proper interpretation of legal rules and normative documents—for Cushing and Adams, the best interpretation of the Massachusetts law of press freedom and seditious libel emerged from a process of reasoning that was disciplined without being determinate in a quasi-geometrical fashion. (Still less did they view interpretation as a search for a fixed meaning crystallized beyond change or development in a rule or document.) Implicit also in the Cushing/Adams correspondence was an assertion of institutional competence. Cushing (then a state judge) and Adams (then a private citizen preparing to take up duties as the federal vice president) assumed that it was necessary and appropriate for the state court self-consciously to seek for and apply the rule of law that, in the judges' opinion, best fulfilled the moral and political imperatives of Massachusetts as a polity, and for Cushing as a member of that court to seek the views of Adams, a distinguished lawyer with no official state position at all.

The Practical Political Foreground

The fourth major source of the American constitutional tradition was, of course, the body of pre-1787 political experience. That experience for many Americans supported quite specific institutional arguments. The revolutionary-era state constitutions, for example, generally created extremely weak executives in reaction to colonial dissatisfaction with royal overreaching; the first federal constitution, the Articles of Confederation, provided for no separate executive at all. The consequent weakness of Confederation-era government persuaded many Americans that the reaction to the king had gone too far; most of the Philadelphia framers came to the task of writing the new Constitution with the conviction that a stronger executive was necessary, and the text of the 1787 instrument clearly reflected that conviction. At the same time, the text's vagueness about the exact contents and scope of the president's duties was a product of continuing fears of monarchy. Other aspects of the Articles of Confederation also served as negative examples. Experience under the Articles showed that the federal government could not function without coercive power of its own, especially the power to raise revenue; the Constitution of 1787 empowered the federal government to raise taxes and generally to carry out its tasks by its own coercive power. The Articles' frequent requirement of unanimity in decision, and the stultifying effect this had on federal activity, led to the Constitution's adoption of majoritarian devices for overcoming small but recalcitrant minorities. For many, perhaps for most, of the Constitution's proponents, one of the chief lessons of recent political experience was that popular government is extremely volatile, subject to rapid and radical shifts in course as public opinion is swayed by passion and prejudice. The Constitution in response insulated much of the federal government from popular opinion through such devices as indirect election of the president and Senate. Many of the Constitution's supporters believed that the greater dignity and the remoteness from the mass of the people that would result were the proper remedy for the political instability of the 1780s.[134]

The Constitution also embodied more theoretical or intellectual lessons that its framers believed they had learned. The Constitution was a more pragmatic and less theoretically pure document than the earlier state constitutions or than the Articles of Confederation. Where many of the state instruments announced explicitly that the legislative, executive, and judicial functions of government were to be totally separate (in accordance with good liberal political science), the 1787 Constitution eschewed general pronouncements and outlined a tripartite government in which the functions of government were shared and intermingled in a quite untheoretical manner for reasons of efficiency or safety.[135] The Constitution similarly avoided the Articles' attempt to resolve such theoretical issues as the locus of "sovereignty" in the American Union and the precise demarkation of the scope of federal power. Even the linguistic style of the 1787 instrument reflected a greater command of constitutional rhetoric; for example, the subjunctives of moral exhortation in the earliest state constitutions were replaced by legal imperatives.[136] This very

134 See Michael Kammen, *The Origins of the American Constitution* (New York: Penguin Books, 1986), x–xviii.

135 See Gordon Wood, *The Creation of the American Republic 1776–1787* (Chapel Hill: Univ. of North Carolina Press, 1969).

136 See Robert Ferguson, "'We Do Ordain and Establish': The Constitution as Literary Text," 29 Wm. & Mary L. Rev. 3 (1987).

attempt at precision, of course, made its own special contribution to the constitutional tradition, or more precisely to that tradition's problematic, a central question of which was to be the attempt to reconcile imperative language with conflicting interpretations.

THE EMERGENCE OF THE CONSTITUTIONAL TRADITION

The adoption of the 1787 Constitution and its institutional completion by the First Congress, which fashioned the Bill of Rights and the federal executive and judicial branches, mark a sharp break in the history of American political discourse. With breathtaking speed, Americans of every political persuasion adopted fidelity to the Constitution as the highest political value in their rhetorical arsenals.[137] This canonization of the Constitution was especially noticeable among the opponents of ratification. In the space of five years, almost all staunch "anti-Federalists" moved from vehement denunciation of the Constitution to strenuous insistence that every political action be dictated by devotion to that same Constitution.[138] Much of this constitutional veneration was intellectually vacuous, on par with contemporary American politicians' invocations of the flag.[139] At the

137 This should not be seen as sheer hypocrisy or opportunism. Founding-era Americans united a cheerful confidence that they were establishing, as the new nation's seal proclaimed, a *novus ordo seclorum* with an equally happy belief that they were defending or rediscovering a libertarian tradition of immemorial origins. This curious combination of innovation and conservatism in the American self-image enabled many Americans to interpret political innovations, almost at once, as ancient and reverend forms of community. Jefferson, for example, could describe the Articles of Confederation as "the good, old, and venerable fabrick" of national government six years after the Articles came into effect. Letter of Jefferson to John Adams (Nov. 13, 1787), in Paul Ford, ed., *Writings of Thomas Jefferson* (New York: G.P. Putnam's Sons, 1892–99), vol. 12, 351.

138 See Michael Kammen, *A Machine That Would Go of Itself* (New York: Knopf, 1986), 29.

139 Even thoughtful constitutionalists were not immune from this sort of Fourth-of-July constitutional rhetoric. Madison, for example, wrote a series of newspaper essays in the 1790s criticizing Alexander Hamilton's political programs that derived what little intellectual content they had from warmed-over Commonwealth themes; Madison invoked the Constitution almost as an after-

same time, however, a true MacIntyrean tradition was being fashioned in legislative debates, in the courts, in the executive cabinet, and in legal and political literature.

The incipient constitutional tradition was immediately concerned with textual interpretation, necessarily so since its very existence stemmed from the American polity's adoption of a written Constitution. However, from the beginning Americans engaged in debate they viewed as "constitutional" that went beyond textual exegesis to provide general interpretations of American societal and political beliefs and institutions.[140] The founders "shared a common agenda for public affairs"[141] and employed constitutional argument as the fundamental means for discussing how to define and carry out that agenda. Even as they were engaged in what they sometimes saw as an irresolvable clash of opposing views, the founders were crafting a tradition of rational discussion of their disagreements, one that enabled them to develop intellectual modes and institutional means for resolving disagreements on many (if not all) major political issues. From its inception, therefore, "the basic pattern of American consti-

---

thought, as a means of emphasizing the wickedness of Hamiltonianism. See Madison, "A Candid State of Parties" (1792), in Meyers, *Mind of the Founder*, 188–90. Hamilton's somewhat later proposal that his allies establish a "Christian Constitutional Society" to undermine the popularity of Madison's political party was on a similar level of intellectual vacuity. Hamilton, letter to James Bayard (April 21, 1802), in Marvin Frisch, ed., *Selected Writings and Speeches of Alexander Hamilton* (Washington: American Enterprise Institute, 1985), 510–12.

The tradition of constitutionalism with which I am concerned in this book is related to popular constitutional rhetoric without, I think, being identical with it. The popular tradition of Constitution-worship is best understood in MacIntyrean terms as one of the institutions that undergirds and supports the constitutional tradition proper and the tradition's practices of adjudication and theory. Viewing popular or cultural constitutional rhetoric in this way enables us to analyze fruitfully one of the most important features of those practices, their vulnerability to distortion and corruption by popular pressure and political expediency. To take a recent and controversial example, it is difficult to regard the media campaign against the confirmation of Judge Robert Bork to a seat on the Supreme Court as a constructive contribution to constitutional discussion regardless of one's views on the substantive merits of the nominee.

The history of cultural and popular constitutional rhetoric is brilliantly described in Kammen, *A Machine*.

140 *Turpin*, 6 Call. 113 (Va. 1804) (Roane J), discussing constitutional law question in light of "the effect of the revolution" on American society.

141 Wiebe, *Opening*, 7.

tutionalism [has been] one of *conflict within consensus*,"[142] a paradigm (or so this book argues) of the MacIntyrean tradition as a "continuity of conflict."[143]

The most fundamental conflict in the early constitutional period was over the nature and definition of the constitutional enterprise itself. In terms of constitutional doctrine, the debate was over whether the Constitution should be regarded as a compact or contract among the states[144] (the view of the antinationalist Republicans)[145] or as a grant of authority to the federal government by a unitary American people[146] (the original view of most of the nationalist Federalists).[147] The substantive ethical and political issues were the nature of the American nation-state and the form of the political order's control of violence and instability.

The Republicans interpreted the Constitution, and thus the polity it constituted, in strictly liberal and contractarian terms.[148] The

142 Kammen, *A Machine*, 29.

143 MacIntyre (1984), 222.

144 "[T]he several states composing the United States of America are not united on the principle of unlimited submission to their general government; but . . . by compact, under the style and title of a Constitution for the United States . . . they constituted a general government for special purposes. . . . [T]o this compact each state acceded as a state and is an integral party, its co-states forming, as to itself, the other party." Virginia Resolutions of 1798, in Powell, *Languages*, 130.

145 I ordinarily use "Republican" capitalized to refer to (members of) the political party that originated in opposition to nationalist policies and politicians and existed from the early 1790s up to the mid-1820s, when it fell apart. On a few occasions in the last section of this chapter and in chapter 3, the term is used in its contemporary sense, i.e., belonging to the G.O.P.

146 "[O]ur Government was formed by the people of the United States, in their capacity as such . . . and not by the several States convened in their State capacities." Speech of Rep. George W. Campbell (1803), in Charles Hyneman and George Carey, eds., *A Second Federalist* (New York: Appleton-Century Crofts, 1967), 44.

147 The Federalist party, which existed as a national political force from the early 1790s through the mid-1810s, originally was united by support for a strong national government. After the opposition Republicans obtained lasting control of the presidency and Congress (from 1801 on), some Federalists adopted the Republicans' politically popular description of the Constitution as a state compact.

148 This is not to say, of course, that individual Republicans did not make use from time to time of Commonwealth or civic republican rhetoric about civic

very "foundation of the Constitution," Jefferson informed President Washington in 1791, was "laid on this ground," that the federal government's powers were strictly limited to those explicitly accorded it in the constitutional compact. In thoroughly liberal fashion, Jefferson viewed the national polity as the artificial product of autonomous human wills coming together in contract.[149] The powers granted the federal government were essentially negative. In his first inaugural address as president, Jefferson described the federal government's purposes as limited to preventing violence: it should be "a wise and frugal government, which shall restrain men from injuring one another [and] shall leave them otherwise free to regulate their own pursuits of industry and improvement. . . . This is the sum of good government."[150] The Constitution's definitions of federal power were to be understood as precise legal rules narrowing constraining the exercise of practical reason by officials. As Jefferson wrote earlier, "[t]o take a single step beyond the boundaries thus specially drawn around the powers of Congress is to take possession of a boundless field of power, no longer susceptible of any definition."[151] Similarly, in 1803 St. George Tucker insisted that federal power was limited by the contractual terms written into the constitutional instrument as well as by the natural or antecedent rights which all individuals possessed. As a consequence, he concluded, federal powers were "to

virtue. Strict ideological consistency was not a characteristic of Founding-era Americans.

149 In the early constitutional period, Republican attention focused on the artificial, contractual basis of the federal Union. The Republicans' liberal premises, however, logically pointed to an identical view of the states. See, e.g., the Kentucky Resolutions of 1798, which expressed the Republican "attachment to limited government, whether general or particular." Powell, *Languages*, 133. The Republicans' liberal understanding of the states came to fruition in the next generation, when the Republican opposition to the exercise of governmental power on the state level was so successful that de Tocqueville could describe America as virtually without any government at all. "In spite of anxiously searching for the government, one can find it nowhere, and the truth is that it does not, so to speak, exist at all." Alexis de Tocqueville, letter of Oct. 7, 1831, in de Tocqueville, *Selected Letters on Politics and Society*, ed. Roger Boesche (Berkeley: Univ. of California Press, 1985), 59.

150 Edward Dumbauld, ed., *The Political Writings of Thomas Jefferson* (New York: Macmillan, 1955), 43–44.

151 Jefferson, National Bank Opinion, in Powell, *Languages*, 42.

receive the most strict construction the instrument will bear" where state privileges or individual rights of "personal liberty, or personal security, or of private property" were concerned.[152]

Republican constitutional thought was a quintessential product of Enlightenment liberalism in its modes of reasoning as well as in its substantive account of political society. The Republicans often presented their strict contractarianism as a conclusion derived by deductive logic. Tucker, for example, derived his interpretive rule of strict construction of federal power with regard to state privileges in the following manner. The states originally possessed political sovereignty. Since sovereignty is neither divisible nor transferrable (save by conquest or political suicide), the states must still be sovereign, and the federal Union a mere alliance among these sovereignties. The powers of the federal government thus are merely the delegated authority of an agent. It is a "maxim of political law" that sovereigns do not delegate authority by implication—since power is constitutive of sovereignty one must presume that a sovereign wishes not to delegate any power not expressly mentioned. Therefore, the Constitution's delegations of power to the federal government are to be read narrowly. Q.E.D.[153]

The Republicans' liberal rationalism led them logically to reject any strong reliance on the authority of experience or of precedents. A political or constitutional proposition could only be justified by a chain of reasoning starting from substantive liberal premises (themselves seen, of course, as founded in Reason), not by invoking the prior course of discussion or the views of respected thinkers. If, on proper reasoning, a national bank was unconstitutional in 1791, no argument from subsequent precedent, practice, or experience could change that conclusion; correct reasoning transcends its origins and is external to time and circumstance. The Republicans thus denied the possibility of a tradition of constitutional interpretation in which progress could be made such that an argument plausible at one point in time might come appropriately to be seen as discredited and left behind.[154] Much of the intellectual history of this early Republican-

152 "View of the Constitution," in Powell, *Languages*, 156.

153 Tucker, *Tucker's Blackstone*, vol. 1, appendix, note D, 143.

154 As Peter Porter reminded the House of Representatives in 1811, the Republicans insisted that the normative "Constitution" was the "printed Constitution on his table before him. . . . A Constitution, the injunctions of which, as we

ism consists of the efforts of Republican lawyers to reconcile the strong antitraditionalism of Republican liberalism with the tradition-dependent common-law forms of argument; at least some of the Republicans' difficulty in translating their constitutional politics into constitutional rules of law acceptable to courts came from the judges' unconscious adherence to common-law argument.

The Republicans rejected the authority of institutions as well as the authority of tradition in constitutional discussion. Since Reason is the preserve of no man—and certainly of no institution—any and everyone is potentially a constitutional interpreter and there can be no a priori hierarchy of interpreters. One of the most famous of the early Republican doctrines, appropriately named the Virginia *Syllogism*, illustrated this aspect of their rationalism. When Federalist Justice Samuel Chase insisted that constitutional adjudication was the exclusive prerogative of the federal judiciary, Republican lawyer William Wirt argued that a jury was as capable of reasoning out the Constitution's meaning, and therefore (Wirt said, "the conclusion is certainly syllogistic") entitled to apply its own, not the judges', views.[155]

The Republicans' Federalist opponents were not antiliberal, but their constitutional arguments were shaped to a very great extent by their rejection of the Republicans' contractarianism and extreme rationalism. Federalists of the 1790s consistently spoke of the federal Union not as an artificial league but as a political community, formed by social bonds of language, history, social similarity, and sentiment.[156] The "American people" were for most Federalists a natural grouping in the social universe, and they rejected the Republicans' openness to foreign immigration as contrary to the social fact of American social identity and the political need to exclude the other and the alien.[157]

---

in our best judgments shall understand them and not as they shall be interpreted to us by others, we are solemnly bound, by our oaths to obey." Speech of Jan. 11, 1811, in 22 *Annals of Congress* 627 (11th Cong. 3d sess.).

155 United States v. Callender, 25 Fed. Cas. 239, 253 (C.C.D.Va. 1800).

156 See, e.g., Timothy Stone, Election Sermon (1792), in Charles Hyneman and Donald Lutz, ed., *American Political Writing During the Founding Era* (Indianapolis: Liberty Press, 1983), vol. 2, 839–57.

157 See, for example, Federalist Cong. Theodore Sedgwick's contribution to a 1794 debate over revision of the statute governing naturalization: Sedgwick

The compact theory of the Constitution on which the Republicans built their entire constitutional theory was for the Federalists a perverse misconstruction of the nature of the American nation. While they shared the overall individualism of the Enlightenment, the Federalists argued that individual freedom could truly exist only in a polity that safeguarded the rights of the individual. The Constitution's original advocates, most of whom became Federalists, had argued that it was the weakness of the national government under the Articles of Confederation that had imperiled individual rights in the 1780s.[158] After ratification, the Federalists consistently linked their centralizing interpretation of the Constitution with the protection of individual rights: as Fisher Ames explained to the House of Representatives in 1794, the representative government established by the Constitution "is so far from being a sacrifice of our rights that it is their security; it is the only practicable mode for a great people to exercise or have any rights. It puts them into full possession of them."[159] The Federalist emphasis, in short, was on the connection between "liberal freedom and absolute [state] power."[160]

The Federalists denounced Republican antinationalism as a threat both to the peacefulness of the social order and to the power of the nation to protect individual autonomy. Rejecting the applicability of the compact theory in a 1793 case, Chief Justice John Jay denounced the notion of "state sovereignty" as contrary to truth and to "the cause of liberty." According to Jay, "the value of our free

---

opposed liberal immigration laws because "native" Americans were united by "education, manners, habits, and institutions, religious and civil," while indiscriminately admitted immigrants would, "by the undeviating principles of human nature," form "an union . . . unfriendly not only to the ancient inhabitants but also to social order." 4 *Annals of Congress*, 1007 (3d Cong., 2d sess.).

158 "The sober people of America . . . have seen with regret and indignation that sudden changes and [state] legislative interferences, in cases affecting personal rights, become jobs in the hands of enterprising and influential speculators." *The Federalist* No. 44 (J. Madison), 301. According to the Madison of the Federalist Papers, it was the concentration of power in a central government removed from immediate popular influence that formed "the best security . . . for the rights of every class of citizens." Id., No. 51, 352. Hamilton described the 1787 Constitution, with its expansive delineation of national power, as "in itself, in every rational sense, and to every useful purpose, A BILL OF RIGHTS." Id., No. 84, 581.

159 4 *Annals of Congress*, 924 (3d Cong., 2d sess.).

160 Milbank, *Social Theory*, 19.

republican national government" was that it "places all our citizens on an equal footing" and upholds the principle that "the citizens of America are equal as fellow citizens and as joint tenants in the [nation's] sovereignty."[161]

The Federalist association of individual liberty with the fate of the political community entailed a very different view of governmental power from that held by the Republicans. Rather than being inherently evil and automatically suspect, governmental power was the *form* of freedom itself on the level of the community. Replying to Jefferson's 1791 argument, Hamilton insisted that the Constitution's grants of power should be construed liberally, since the people had granted the power in order to achieve the beneficial purposes of securing the common defense and general welfare.[162] The Republicans' strict constructionism, Fisher Ames argued in Congress shortly before the debate between Jefferson and Hamilton, was a needless and ultimately vain attempt to eliminate the exercise of judgment in political affairs; the purpose of government, Ames insisted, was not to engage in agonized debate over the scope of its commission, but to act for the common good—a notion that was for Ames not merely the chimera or the summation of individual preferences that the Republicans perceived.[163] In 1816, Joseph Story, a Republican justice of nationalist views, described the Constitution's grant of power to the federal government—for Jefferson the measure of liberty's unavoidable but regrettable diminishment—as "this great charter of our liberties."[164]

The Federalists' acceptance of the concepts of a national community and a common good, and their rejection of the Republicans' strict contractarianism, were paralleled by their repudiation of the Republicans' rationalistic model of constitutional argument, in particular the Republicans' assumption that constitutional propositions were deductions from static principles. It was possible, in the Feder-

161 Chisholm v. Georgia, 2 U.S. (2 Dall.) 419, 471–72 (1793).

162 Hamilton, Opinion on the Constitutionality of the Act to Establish a National Bank (1791), in Frisch, *Selected Writings*, 254.

163 Ames argued that the Republicans, in fact, "only set up one construction against another," when in fact the proper course of action was to do whatever "promotes the good of society." Speech of Feb. 3, 1791, in W. B. Allen, ed., *Works of Fisher Ames* (Indianapolis: Liberty Press, 1983), vol. 2, 850–62.

164 Martin v. Hunter's Lessee, 14 U.S. (1 Wheat.) 304, 326 (1816).

alists' view, to progress in constitutional understanding, to interpret more accurately over time the implications and goals of the constitutional polity and text. The Federalists' initial uneasiness with demands for a federal bill of rights rested in large part on their concern that such a textual codification of "the natural rights of man"[165] would serve to freeze constitutional reasoning about those rights at the point it had reached whenever such a bill of rights was drafted. As Edmund Pendleton[166] worried: "May we not, in the progress of things, discover some great and important [rights] which we don't now think of?"[167] To allay such fears, Madison included in the Bill of Rights a provision (our Ninth Amendment) intended to bar the inference that the Bill of Rights forbade progress in the "discovery" of rights.[168] Interpretive progress was, of course, possible with respect to constitutional grants of power as well as in connection with individual rights. In an 1811 senatorial debate, William Crawford rejected the argument that Congress was limited to the powers the founders understood it to have been given: "We are, when acting today, not to inquire what means were necessary and proper twenty years ago . . . but our enquiry must be, what means are necessary and proper today." As Crawford's colleague James Lloyd pointed out, the corollary was that constitutional discussion leads to a progressive, developing body of knowledge: "it is not impossible that hereafter, to provide for all the new cases that may rise under this new state of things, the defined powers may prove only a text and the implied or resulting powers may furnish the sermon to it."[169]

165 Ames, Speech, in Allen, *Works*, vol. 2, 862.

166 Originally a Federalist, Pendleton moved into the emerging Republican party in the mid-1790s out of concern over Hamilton's policies. See Wiebe, *Opening*, 85. Partisan political allegiances, in any event, often were influenced by local political issues and often did not track with precision ideological positions. The infamous Hartford Convention of 1815, for example, was made up almost entirely of New England Federalists but wrote a set of resolutions endorsing a contractarian view of the Constitution, while Justice Story was a Massachusetts Republican who by 1815 was a strong constitutional nationalist.

167 Letter to Richard H. Lee (June 14, 1788), in D. J. Mays, ed., *Letters and Papers of Edmund Pendleton* (Chapel Hill: Univ. of North Carolina Press, 1967), 532–33.

168 The Ninth Amendment states that "[t]he enumeration in the Constitution of certain rights shall not be construed to deny or disparage others retained by the people."

169 Quoted in Hyneman and Carey, *A Second Federalist*, 133.

The Supreme Court's early interpretation of the contracts clause provides a clear example of the progressive, tradition-dependent mode of reasoning the nationalists favored. The clause[170] was included in the 1787 Constitution because of the Philadelphia framers' dislike of state legislation that interfered with contractual relationships between private creditors and debtors,[171] a fact of which the Court's early membership was well aware.[172] But the Court first applied the clause in very different circumstances, where a corrupt state legislature had granted vast amounts of real property to speculators at bargain prices and a subsequent legislature sought to revoke the grants.[173] Speaking for a majority of the Court, Chief Justice John Marshall described the contracts clause and the associated prohibitions of bills of attainder and ex post facto laws as "what may be deemed a bill of rights for the people of each state,"[174] a statement that for a Federalist implied that those clauses were not to be read as a closed set of particular rights. Marshall argued that property grants were a form of contract in that the grantor necessarily made an implicit promise not to reassert the property rights it was granting; he then pointed out that nothing in the Constitution's wording excepted grants generally or grants by legislatures from the protection of the contracts clause. Since the moral evil of legislative interference with "the lives and fortunes of individuals" was the same, whether worked by a bill of attainder, an ex post facto law (both clearly unconstitutional), or a law revoking a prior grant, Marshall concluded that the attempted revocation was unconstitutional. Marshall's wording explicitly linked this conclusion both to "general principles which are common to our free institutions" and to the contracts clause. The fact that the clause's framers only intended to protect private contracts from interference did not limit the Consti-

170 The contracts clause, which is in section ten of Article One of the Constitution, states that "[n]o State shall . . . pass any . . . Law impairing the obligation of Contracts."

171 See Forrest McDonald, *E Pluribus Unum* (Boston: Houghton Mifflin, 1965), 321–25.

172 See Justice William Paterson's opinion in Calder v. Bull, 3 U.S. (3 Dall.) 386 (1798), in which he discussed his failure, as a delegate to the Philadelphia convention, to persuade the convention to write section ten so as to extend the Constitution's prohibition to "retrospective laws in general."

173 Fletcher v. Peck, 10 U.S. (6 Cranch) 87 (1810).

174 Id. at 138.

tution's effect when reasoning from "general principles" revealed that revocation of public grants produced an analogous moral evil.[175]

Almost a decade later, another case came before the Court in which a party invoked the contracts clause.[176] A state legislature had modified unilaterally the prerevolutionary royal charter of Dartmouth College, and the College trustees asserted that this violated the clause. The state defendants argued that the Constitution's makers did not have corporate charters in mind when they wrote the clause. In response, Chief Justice Marshall for the Court squarely rejected the idea that constitutional provisions are limited in meaning to the understanding held by their framers. "It is more than possible, that the preservation of rights of this description [rights under corporate charters] was not particularly in the view of the framers of the constitution, when the clause under consideration was introduced into that instrument. . . . [But to exclude such rights from the scope of the clause, it] is not enough to say, that this particular case was not in the mind of the Convention, when the article was framed, nor of the American people, when it was adopted."[177] Again, Marshall considered the moral and political implications of permitting a state legislature to intervene in settled expectations, and again he concluded for the Court that the protection contemplated by the contracts clause should be extended to a situation not envisaged by the clause's framers.[178] In subsequent cases, the Court continued this process of reasoning, concluding for example that state insolvency laws could interfere with private contractual relationships (despite the framers' explicit concern over such interference) if the law predated the contract.[179]

Perhaps the most famous example of Federalist constitutional reasoning was Chief Justice Marshall's opinion in *M'Culloch v. Maryland*, decided the same year as *Dartmouth College*.[180] *M'Culloch* presented the specific issue of whether a state could tax the federally chartered Bank of the United States. More generally and impor-

175 Id. at 139.
176 Dartmouth College v. Woodward, 17 U.S. (4 Wheat.) 518 (1819).
177 Id. at 644.
178 Id. at 650.
179 Ogden v. Saunders, 25 U.S. (12 Wheat.) 213 (1827).
180 17 U.S. (4 Wheat.) 316 (1819).

tantly, the case raised once more the question of Congress's power to legislate beyond the specific powers enumerated in the text of the Constitution. That issue was hotly debated when the bank was first chartered in 1791—Jefferson and Hamilton's debate over the nature of the Constitution in that year took place in the context of advising President Washington whether to veto the bank bill on constitutional grounds. Marshall began his opinion in 1819 by recalling that both the First Congress and Washington had deliberately considered the issue and had concluded that the Constitution authorized the bank. Marshall made it plain that he was not simply invoking the bare authority of precedent: Congress and president approved the bank act only after "[i]ts principle was completely understood" and after it was criticized "with as much persevering talent as any measure has ever experienced."[181] The constitutionality of the bank "scarcely can be considered as an open question," not simply because a congress and a president had determined the question, but because *that* Congress and *that* president—"minds as pure and as intelligent as this country can boast"—had reached a decision after full and deliberate consideration.

Marshall's invocation of the 1791 decision as authority because of the quality of the reasoning and the virtue of the reasoners was in the classic common-law manner. Continuing in that same manner, he did not rest on prior authority, but went on to consider the reasonability of the earlier conclusion. Marshall began by rejecting the contractarian view of the Constitution: "the government of the Union . . . is emphatically, and truly, a government of the people" and no more artificial or dangerous than the state governments.[182] If, then, the Union is a true political community and the federal government that community's instrument for carrying out the community's common goals, federal power should encompass whatever means are appropriate for achieving those goals. Marshall described the proper approach to evaluating the validity of a congressional choice of means in terms that showed his rejection of the deductive logic of the Republicans. "Let the end be legitimate, let it be within the scope of the constitution, and all means which are appropriate, which are

181 Id. at 402.
182 Id. at 404–5.

plainly adapted to that end, which are not prohibited, but consist with the letter and spirit of the constitution, are constitutional."[183] Terms such as "legitimate," "appropriate," and "spirit of the constitution" were, and were known by both Marshall and his critics, to invite reasoning from and about moral and political values. This type of practical reasoning was, of course, that in which the classical common-law tradition had self-confidently engaged, and which Enlightenment rationalism had led the Republicans to seek to ban from the public sphere.

The bank, therefore, was a constitutional means of pursuing more efficiently the national community's various financial affairs. The state tax, in contrast, was unconstitutional because it was an attempt by a part of the community to act against the will of the whole by interfering with the functioning of an instrumentality of the community. Such an attempt amounted to a denial of the existence of the national community: "[t]he American people have declared their constitution, and the laws made in pursuance thereof, to be supreme."[184]

For the bank's Republican opponents, of course, there was no national community, and the state legislature that enacted the tax represented one of the sovereign principals of which Congress was only the agent. *M'Culloch* consequently was bitterly criticized when it was first decided.[185] For reasons that will be discussed below, however, *M'Culloch* and the common-law approach to constitutional reasoning it exemplified swiftly came to dominate constitutional discussion. Marshall's opinion became a canonical text of scarcely less authority than the 1787 text itself, and constitutionalists were obliged to incorporate it into their own thinking. By the time of the Civil War, the heirs of those who criticized Marshall were employing his mode of reasoning in their own discussions of the powers (surprisingly broad, and unjustifiable on Republican grounds) claimed by the Confederacy's federal government.

The struggle between the Federalist (or nationalist) and the Republican interpretations of the nature of the Union and the Constitu-

183 Id. at 421.

184 Id. at 432.

185 See Gerald Gunther, *John Marshall's Defense of McCulloch v. Maryland* (Stanford: Stanford Univ. Press, 1969).

tion was the most clearly defined and most heated constitutional debate in the formative period of the constitutional tradition. A second intellectual issue—the propriety of drawing directly on moral and philosophical discourse in constitutional argument—attracted less sustained contemporaneous attention despite its obvious importance. The English political tradition, lacking a written constitution, could not and did not recognize any sharp distinction between strictly constitutional-law arguments, and arguments directly based on political theory or moral philosophy. In their "Cato" essays of the 1730s John Trenchard and Thomas Gordon mixed arguments from morality,[186] political theory,[187] history,[188] and law,[189] with no apparent sense that any of these different sources of argument were more or less "constitutional" or authoritative in nature. Indeed, English and prerevolutionary American writers generally displayed little or no awareness that moral, political, historical, and legal arguments could be seen as distinct, at least in discussion of "constitutional" issues.

The first state constitutions reflected this heritage, and often contained provisions that mixed political theory, moral exhortation, and legal rules in what many Americans eventually came to see as an uneasy balance.[190] Eventually a strong tendency toward a dry and imperative legal style in constitution writing became apparent,[191]

186 Trenchard and Gordon defined personal liberty in moral terms as "the Right of every Man" to do as he wishes "so far as by it he does not hurt or controul the Right of Another." "Cato's Letters: Or, Essays on Liberty, Civil and Religious," in Kurland and Lerner, *Founders' Constitution*, 618–20.

187 They defended the right to comment on the actions of public officials on the ground that government is "nothing else but the Attendance of the Trustees of the People upon the Interest, and Affairs of the People." Id. at 618–20.

188 See id. at 46–47 (discussing history of free speech in the Roman Republic and in Tudor and Stuart England).

189 See id. at 621–22 (discussing the relationship between "the undoubted Right of the Subject" and the king's "legal Prerogative").

190 A good example is the religious liberty clause of the 1776 Virginia Declaration of Rights: "That religion, or the duty which we owe to our Creator, and the manner of discharging it, can be directed only by reason and conviction, not by force or violence; and therefore all men are equally entitled to the free exercise of religion, according to the dictates of conscience; and that it is the mutual duty of all to practise Christian forbearance, love, and charity towards each other." Article 16.

191 See generally Ferguson, "Constitution as Literary Text."

and the Constitution of 1787 and the federal Bill of Rights were couched almost entirely in recognizably legal terms.[192] The move toward legalism in constitution writing was accompanied by an increasing emphasis on the unique role of constitutional texts in American constitutionalism. In a 1794 judicial opinion, St. George Tucker expressed the increasingly prevalent opinion that the world had known no true constitutionalism prior to the American Revolution because before that time there had been no written constitutions. For Tucker, the textuality of an American constitution was what made it "not an ideal thing, but a real existence: it can be produced in a visible form."[193]

English constitutionalism, of course, had canonical texts of varying sorts and degrees of importance—for example, Magna Carta, the 1688 Bill of Rights, the Habeas Corpus Act—but none was uniquely authoritative. The American constitutional instruments obviously possessed greater centrality, and at an early point some Americans recognized and adopted the possibility of distinguishing constitutional "interpretation" in the sense of textual exegesis from other sorts of political argument. Debate over this possibility broke into the open with the Supreme Court's decision in *Calder v. Bull* in 1798.[194] *Calder* was a challenge to the Connecticut legislature's grant

192 To the 1776 Virginia provision concerning religious liberty quoted above compare the religion clauses of the First Amendment (drafted in 1789): "Congress shall make no law respecting an establishment of religion, or prohibiting the free exercise thereof." The earlier text's assertion of the political value of religious freedom and its moral exhortations to "forbearance, love and charity" are absent from the later, and the indicative and subjunctive moods have been replaced by the imperative. For another example, compare Article Ten of the Virginia Declaration of Rights (general warrants "are grievous and *ought* not to be granted") with the Fourth Amendment ("The right of the people to be secure . . . *shall* not be violated, and *no* [general] warrants shall issue") (emphases added). The point is not that an earlier and expansive view of constitutional rights was replaced by a narrower understanding—for the Federalists at least, adherence to the common-law mode of reasoning ensured that the imperatives of the later texts would be interpreted expansively. The change to which I am pointing was from an earlier view of "constitutional" discourse that saw it as a mélange of political, moral, historical, legal, and even theological (see Locke's seldom-read *First* Essay Concerning Civil Government!) argument to a later view of constitutional discourse as constitutional-law debate, however broadly or narrowly "law" was understood.

193 Kamper v. Hawkins, 1 Va.Cas. 20 (Gen.Ct. 1794).

194 Calder v. Bull, 3 U.S. (3 Dall.) 386 (1798).

of a new trial to the losers in an inheritance dispute in the state's lower courts; the losers had forfeited the right to appeal to the state's highest court through tardiness. After the new trial unsurprisingly came to a different verdict, the prevailing parties in the first round of litigation challenged the legislature's action as a violation of the federal Constitution's prohibition of ex post facto laws. The justices unanimously agreed that the ex post facto clause was limited to criminal statutes, and that as a consequence the legislative action was constitutional, but two members of the Court entered into a vigorous (if unnecessary) debate over the nature of constitutional discussion. Samuel Chase went out of his way to stress that constitutional argument was not limited to interpretation of the constitutional text: "I cannot subscribe to the omnipotence of a state legislature, or that it is absolute and without controul; although its authority should not be expressly restrained by the Constitution, or fundamental law."[195] After listing a variety of legislative actions he assumed everyone would view as immoral and unjust, Chase concluded that "[t]o maintain that our federal, or state, Legislature possesses such powers, if they had not been expressly restrained, would, in my opinion, be a political heresy, altogether inadmissible in our free republican governments." Chase expressly based this conclusion on the liberal principle that governmental authority is derived from consent to the social contract, and that consent to certain government actions could never be inferred. Chase rejected the Calders' claim because he concluded that the legislature's grant of a new trial to the Bulls, in the peculiar circumstances of the case, was not an immoral or unjust act.[196]

Justice James Iredell took sharp issue with Chase's willingness to treat liberal moral and political propositions as directly relevant to a question of constitutional law. Iredell asserted that no court could pronounce a law "void," if the law were within "the general scope of [the] constitutional power" of the legislature, "merely because it is in [the court's] judgment, contrary to the principles of natural justice."[197] In large part, Iredell was expressing a corollary of the emphasis on the textuality of the Constitution, but behind his position,

195 Id. at 387–88.
196 Id. at 394.
197 Id. at 399.

as behind Chase's, lay the influence of liberalism. In Iredell's case, however, the dominant liberal motif was the Enlightenment's attempted expulsion of "thick" accounts of the moral good from the public sphere. "The ideas of natural justice are regulated by no fixed standard; the ablest and purest men have differed upon the subject; and all that the court could properly say, in such an event, would be, that the legislature, possessed of an equal right of opinion, had passed an act which, in the opinion of the judges, was inconsistent with the abstract principles of natural justice."[198]

The disagreement between Chase and Iredell superficially resembles that between Republican rationalism and Federalist (common law) traditionalism, but it was in reality a dispute along very different lines. Chase and Iredell were initiating a debate, which has continued to the present and is of central significance to this book, over the autonomy of constitutional discourse as a distinct tradition of rational inquiry. Iredell's purpose was to defend the particularity of constitutional argument against Chase's apparent assimilation of constitutional to political or philosophical discourse, not to restrict constitutionalists to the rigid deductive logic of the Republicans.[199] For Chase, American constitutionalism was simply one setting in which liberal political thought was to be debated and implemented, not different in kind from the grand jury charges and sentencing homilies in which Chase frequently put forward his vision of the moral order of the Republic.[200] For Iredell, in contrast, American constitutionalism was fundamentally shaped by the centrality of a uniquely authoritative legal text. Constitutional discourse was open to moral and prudential considerations, just as the classical common law had always incorporated such matters in legal discussion—in *Calder* Iredell carefully examined the "policy" and "reason" of the ex post facto clause.[201] But constitutional argument was not identical to or indistiguishable from liberal political philosophy. It was legal and exeget-

198 Id.

199 Iredell was in fact a Federalist, and in other circumstances he clearly evinced adherence to the Federalists' preferred common-law modes of argument. See, e.g., G. McRee, ed., *Life and Correspondence of James Iredell*, 558 (1857) (reprinting a 1799 grand jury charge).

200 See Stephen Presser's remarkable study, *The Original Misunderstanding* (Durham, N.C.: Carolina Academic Press, 1991).

201 3 U.S. at 400.

ical in a fashion that gave it autonomous standards of rationality that structured discussion and set limits on the questions and issues constitutionalism could address.[202]

In the decades following *Calder*, constitutionalists continued the debate between Chase and Iredell over the question of constitutionalism as an autonomous intellectual discipline distinct from political philosophy. In 1802 the Republican leadership in Congress proposed a bill to abolish sixteen federal judgeships established by the prior Federalist-controlled Congress. Because the bill would deprive the (Federalist) incumbents of their offices notwithstanding the Constitution's guaranty of judicial tenure "during good behavior," debate over the bill centered on its constitutionality. The debate included both sophisticated discussions of the nature and importance of judicial independence and separation of powers in a liberal society, and legal wrangling over the proper construction of the Constitution. While the debate obviously was fueled by partisan considerations, many participants displayed genuine concern over the proper approach to constitutional matters. Republican Vice President Aaron Burr, for example, corresponded privately with several friends over the view he should take (as president of the Senate) of the bill. Burr wrote Barnabus Bidwell that he was persuaded that as a strictly legal matter the bill was reconcilable with the Constitution: "[t]he Constitutional right & power of Abolishing one Judiciary System & establishing another, cannot be doubted." But Burr remained unsure "whether it would be constitutionally Moral." Bidwell replied, in effect, that the *constitutional* question was, simply, the legal one, and that consequently Burr's legal opinion (which Bidwell shared) was the answer to Burr's constitutional question. The morality of the bill was, for Bidwell, an aspect of "the expediency of the measure."[203] Similar private discussions about the proper understanding of constitutional argument took place among Republican leaders over the constitutionality of the Louisiana Purchase.[204]

202 Id. at 400 (constitutional argument cannot address all conceivable forms of the abuse of political power).

203 M. Kline and J. Ryan, ed., *Political Correspondence and Public Papers of Aaron Burr* (Princeton: Princeton Univ. Press, 1983), vol. 2, 659–60, 675–76.

204 Secretary of the Treasury Albert Gallatin argued that the absence from the Constitution's text of authorization for the purchase did not render the purchase unconstitutional since the Union and its government had an "inherent

The debate over the autonomy of constitutional discourse continued on the Supreme Court as well. Chief Justice Marshall often used arguments from political theory, particularly early in his service on the Court. In 1803, for example, Marshall argued that the federal government was obligated to provide a remedy "for the violation of a vested legal right" because "the very essence of civil liberty certainly consists in the right of every individual to claim the protection of the laws whenever he receives an injury." Marshall rested this axiom of liberal legalism solely on its inherent reasonableness, without reference to the Constitution's text.[205] Seven years later, Marshall provided alternative sources for the Court's decision that a state could not revoke its grants: the contracts clause read in common law fashion, and "the nature of society and of government."[206] Justice William Johnson disagreed with Marshall's expansive interpretation of the contracts clause; Johnson would have based the Court's constitutional conclusion solely on "general principle, or the reason and nature of things; a principle which will impose laws even on the Deity."[207]

From the middle of the second decade of the nineteenth century, however, the justices' employment of explicitly philosophical arguments rapidly diminished. In the cases involving vested rights, for example, the Court came to treat the argument as one over the correct interpretation of the contracts clause rather than as an exploration of "general principles" or "the nature of government."[208] At the same time, as discussed above, the Court and constitutionalists generally were clearly rejecting the Republicans' rationalism in favor

---

right to acquire territory." Memorandum to Thomas Jefferson, in Urofsky, *Documents*, 187. President Jefferson, in contrast, maintained that legitimate constitutional argument was limited to interpretation of the constitutional text, and that political theory arguments about the inherent nature and powers of government were irrelevant and pernicious. "Our peculiar security is in possession of a written Constitution. Let us not make it a blank paper by construction." Letter to Wilson C. Nicholas, in Dumbauld, *Political Writings*, 144.

205 Marbury v. Madison, 5 U.S. (1 Cranch) 137, 163 (1803).

206 10 U.S. at 135.

207 Id. at 143.

208 "[T]he Court subsumed higher-law principles into . . . textual bases after Fletcher v. Peck, and Marshall's 'general principles' language turned out to be a dead end." William Wiecek, *Liberty under Law* (Baltimore: Johns Hopkins Univ. Press, 1988), 44.

of the common law's tradition-dependent forms of argument. The Supreme Court, here as so often, was both cause and effect: the justices were reflecting the emergence of a consensus that constitutional discourse was a distinct form of inquiry even as their example was contributing to the development of that consensus. The American constitutional tradition emerged from its formative period a somewhat paradoxical bricolage of liberal political morality discussed and developed through the tradition-dependent and nonliberal modes of argument of the classical common law.[209] Agreement on the autonomy of constitutional discussion and on the use of common-law modes of argument was the crucial intellectual precondition for the emergence of American constitutionalism as a self-conscious tradition of rational inquiry in the MacIntyrean sense.

The early intellectual development of constitutionalism was interrelated with social developments. During the first few decades, the nascent tradition's most important and most unique practice evolved, that of constitutional adjudication. This practice, now commonly known as *judicial review*, is the power of courts to disregard and declare void legislative acts that in the courts' judgment violate the Constitution. Judicial review is unquestionably the most original aspect of the developed American political order; the practice of constitutional adjudication is what gives American constitutionalism its social importance and its characteristic form.

Sir William Blackstone, writing in the 1760s, stated what was by then the received wisdom of the British political system. He repeated language found in earlier law books that the "law of nature . . . is of course superior in obligation to any other [and] no human laws are of any validity, if contrary to this."[210] But Blackstone, and English legal opinion of his day generally, rejected any claim that judges could enforce this law of nature (or reason) in the teeth of positive law. If Parliament, he wrote, should "positively enact a thing to be done that is unreasonable, I know of no power that can controul it."

209 "American constitutional interpretation in the Supreme Court seems a central case of common law methodology." Frederick Schauer, "Is the Common Law Law?," 77 Colum. L.Rev. 455, 477 n. 41 (1989).

210 Blackstone, *Commentaries*, vol. 1, 41. The classic account of the fortunes of this sort of talk in English-speaking law is Edward Corwin, *The Higher Law Background of American Constitutional Law* (Ithaca, N.Y.: Great Seal Books, 1929).

For a court to attempt to do so would be "to set the judicial power above that of the legislature, which would be subversive of all government."[211] In the British system, therefore, the legislature was truly sovereign, wielding its powers "absolutely and without controul."[212] The conclusions about justice reached through legal reasoning were subordinate to the political power of Parliament because Parliament, as a matter of political theory, was supreme.

In this area, as with the common-law mode of reasoning, late colonial and revolutionary-era Americans appropriated an anachronistic form of English thought. Seventeenth-century common lawyers, including some of the most famous, were believed to have held views contrary to that of Blackstone. In the most famous example, Lord Coke declared in a 1610 case that "in many cases, the common law will controul Acts of Parliament, and sometimes adjudge them to be utterly void: for when an Act of Parliament is against common right and reason, or repugnant, or impossible to be performed, the common law will controul it and adjudge such Act to be void."[213] What Coke and the authors of similar statements actually meant by them is unclear, but late colonial American lawyers took them to have asserted a judicial power to disregard or invalidate unreasonable and unconstitutional statutes. In the Writs of Assistance Case, for example, James Otis stated that "an act against the Constitution is void; an act against natural equity is void: and . . . the executive courts must pass such acts into disuse."[214] This view of the powers and responsibilities of courts flowed together with the American propensity to invoke the terms of their colonial charters against conflicting parliamentary enactments,[215] and the intermingling provided the background for the development of the practice of judicial review as a means of enforcing the new American state constitutions.

In the 1780s lawyers invoked the legitimacy of constitutional adjudication leading to judicial invalidation of legislation hesitantly and against opposition, but "by 1787, some eight or nine cases in eight states may have claimed for judges the power to hold statutes

211 Blackstone, *Commentaries*, vol. 1, 91.

212 Id. at 160.

213 Dr. Bonham's Case, 8 Coke Rep. 118a (C.P. 1610).

214 Wroth and Zobel, *Legal Papers of John Adams*, vol. 2, 127–28.

215 See, e.g., the Virginia House of Burgesses' 1765 Stamp Act Resolutions, in Urofsky, *Documents*, 41.

unconstitutional."[216] Much of the literature supporting the adoption of the federal Constitution assumed the legitimacy of constitutional adjudication,[217] and in the 1790s the propriety of some sort of judicial review became generally accepted.[218] Early Supreme Court decisions engaged in the practice without much elaboration,[219] and the most sophisticated discussion took place in a state court case, *Kamper v. Hawkins*, examining the constitutionality of a Virginia statute under that state's constitution.[220]

The *Kamper* court's members unanimously agreed that the statute, which gave unusual powers to the state district courts, violated their interpretation of the state constitution, and that as a consequence the district courts should not obey it. But the judges disagreed sharply over the exact nature of constitutional adjudication. One judge believed that the only power of judicial review a court could undertake was to protect the judge's conscience; where the judge thought the legislature had attempted to authorize or compel him to exercise a power not sanctioned by the constitution, and only in that circumstance, the judge was entitled to disregard a statute.

Two *Kamper* judges held a view of constitutional adjudication that assimilated it to the ordinary duty of a court to resolve disputes brought before it. That duty, as a matter of course, required the judge to decide which legal rule applied to the dispute and to choose between conflicting rules. Where one such rule was the Constitution, they concluded, the judge was required to follow it even if that entailed disregarding a statute. Constitutional adjudication, viewed in this manner, did not involve the assertion of a special institutional role for the courts, and one of the judges asserting it specifically disavowed any claim that the courts were "the champions of the people, or of the Constitution, bound to sound the alarm, and to execute an opposition to the legislature." The unacknowledged weakness of this "judicial process" position was its implicit assump-

216 Wiecek, *Liberty*, 14.

217 See, e.g., *The Federalist* No. 78 (A. Hamilton).

218 See Sylvia Snowiss, *Judicial Review and the Law of the Constitution* (New Haven: Yale Univ. Press, 1990), 2–3.

219 See, e.g., Calder v. Bull (1798), supra, evaluating the constitutionality of a state statute; and Hylton v. United States, 3 U.S. (3 Dall.) 171 (1796), reviewing the constitutionality of a federal law.

220 1 Va.Cas. 20 (Gen.Ct. 1793).

tion that the cases of genuine conflict between statutes and the Constitution would be clearly or uncontroversially identifiable: the most its proponents could say was that "the violation must be plain and clear."

Two of the *Kamper* judges went on to play personally significant roles in American constitutional history. St. George Tucker, who was professor of law at the College of William and Mary as well as a judge, published an enormously influential annotated edition of Blackstone's *Commentaries* that included a 150-page appendix presenting Tucker's interpretation of the United States Constitution, while Spenser Roane became the leading Republican jurist of the 1810s. In *Kamper*, Tucker and Roane set forth an understanding of constitutional adjudication that accorded that practice, and the courts institutionally entitled to undertake it, a unique and central place in American constitutionalism. As Roane put it, where a litigant alleges that the legislature has violated the Constitution, the case ceases to be an ordinary legal dispute and "the controversy is between the legislature on one hand, and the whole people . . . (through the medium of one individual) on the other." A constitutional decision by a court is not merely a means of saving the judges' consciences or of resolving a particular dispute; "they are bound to decide, and they do actually decide on behalf of the people."

For Tucker and Roane, both Republicans committed to the Republican belief in a multiplicity of constitutional voices, constitutional decisions by the courts enjoyed a special position. As Tucker wrote, the Constitution as supreme law "must be resorted to on every occasion, where it becomes necessary to expound what the law is. This exposition it is the duty and office of the judiciary to make. . . . Now since it is the province of the legislature to make, and of the executive to enforce obedience to the laws, the duty of expounding must be exclusively vested in the judiciary." As a consequence, the courts were not obliged to defer to the constitutional opinions of the legislature in all but "clear and plain" cases of unconstitutional legislation. Instead, the judiciary was obliged to follow and enforce its own reading of the Constitution, interpreted in classical common law fashion.[221]

Chief Justice Marshall gave the Supreme Court's first elaborate

221 All quotations from *Kamper* are in Powell, *Languages*, 74–88.

discussion of constitutional adjudication in a case decided a decade after *Kamper*, in his famous opinion in *Marbury v. Madison*.[222] Marshall described judicial review in terms almost identical to those used by the "judicial process" judges in *Kamper*. Since it is "the very essence of [the] judicial duty" to "determine which of [two] conflicting rules governs the case" before the court, a judge confronted with a conflict between the Constitution and a statute had no choice but to apply one and disobey the other; the Constitution's status as supreme law would invariably resolve that conflict against the statute. But Marshall wholeheartedly endorsed Tucker's and Roane's view that courts involved in constitutional adjudication should enjoy a unique place in constitutional discourse. In a deliberate echo of Tucker's *Kamper* opinion, Marshall stated that "it is emphatically the province and duty of the judicial department to say what the law is." Since the Constitution is law, for Marshall it was "emphatically the province and duty" of the courts to determine what the law of the Constitution is, a task that Marshall like Tucker and Roane approached in the traditional common-law mode. The obvious conclusion, which Marshall never stated explicitly in *Marbury*, but which friends and critics alike perceived,[223] was that the judiciary's constitutional interpretations should enjoy unique and probably final authority for all constitutional discourse.

The attempt by Tucker, Roane, Marshall, and others to claim a central role for the practice of constitutional adjudication in the emerging constitutional tradition had to compete for a time with claims for special status for legislative, executive, and academic interpretation. The tradition itself might be said to have begun in Congress during the debates of the first session of the First Congress over whether the Constitution gave the president unilateral removal power over officers appointed with the Senate's approval. The 1791 debate in the House of Representatives over the constitutionality of the national bank bill produced elaborate and well-reasoned discussions of the nature of the Constitution, the modes of constitutional argument, and the proper interpretation of various constitutional provisions. The same pattern of sustained congressional deliberation

222 5 U.S. (1 Cranch) 137 (1803).

223 See, e.g., Jefferson's letter to George Hay (June 2, 1807), in Powell, *Languages*, 216–17, for Jefferson's perceptive critique of this aspect of *Marbury*.

on constitutional matters recurred throughout the first decades following ratification.[224] Beginning with the struggle over the admission of Missouri as a slave state in 1819 and the rise of the "second party system" in the 1820s, however, congressional interpretation of the Constitution was increasingly overshadowed by partisan politics and regional conflict over slavery. By 1840 the generally nationalist Whigs in Congress had committed themselves to supporting the Supreme Court as the primary and final forum for constitutional discussion, whereas the constitutional views of Democratic congressmen were in thrall to their party's political need to defend Southern interests at all costs.[225] While constitutional discussion never wholly disappeared from the legislature, by the time of the Civil War the Congress no longer made the pretense of being a particularly important or particularly expert forum for the sustained consideration of constitutional questions. In MacIntyrean terms, the practice of congressional constitutional interpretation had become moribund.

The executive branch's claim to a major role in constitutional discussion followed a path roughly similar to that of congressional constitutionalism. President Washington regarded the exercise of the power to approve or veto legislation as a practice parallel to adjudication; he consulted cabinet members and friends in Congress on the constitutionality of bills presented for his signature and on one occasion vetoed a bill as unconstitutional. While considering whether to approve the 1791 bank bill, Washington requested opinions in writing from Secretary of State Jefferson, Secretary of the Treasury Hamilton, and Attorney General Edmund Randolph. Jefferson's memorandum in response portrayed the veto power as the specific institutionalization of a constitutional practice: "The negative of the President is the shield provided by the Constitution to protect against the invasions of the legislature." In typically liberal fashion, Jefferson identified "ambition, or interest" as primary sources of legislative error; he treated the president—or perhaps President Washington—as sufficiently

224 See especially the debates over federal subsidies to industry (1792); relief for disaster victims in Savannah (1794); implementation of the Jay Treaty (1796); adoption of the Alien and Sedition Acts (1798); and repeal of the "Midnight Judges" Act (1802); rechartering the national bank (1811, 1815, 1816); and internal improvements (1817, 1818).

225 See generally William Freehling, *The Road to Disunion* (New York: Oxford Univ. Press, 1990).

disinterested to interpret the Constitution in accordance with reason.[226]

As president, Jefferson himself was actively involved in constitutional discussion, personally and through correspondence, with his cabinet, members of Congress, state officials, and private citizens.[227] Jefferson's primary theme was the right of different actors to independent judgment. While Jefferson's relations with the congressional leadership avoided the presentation of any legislation he felt obliged to veto, Jefferson engaged in an active struggle with the federal courts throughout his two terms in office, both over substantive constitutional questions and over the respective places of presidential and judicial interpretation of the Constitution. During the 1807 treason trial of Aaron Burr, for example, Jefferson instructed the prosecutor to dispute the assertion in *Marbury* that the exposition of constitutional law was the "province and duty" of the courts in any special or unique manner. While Jefferson did not dispute the right of judges to interpret the Constitution in carrying out their duties, he saw no reason why judicial opinions should control the constitutional views of other actors. "In the cases of [those prosecuted under the 1798 Sedition Act], the judges determined the sedition act was valid under the Constitution, and exercised their regular powers of sentencing them to fine & imprisonment. But the executive [i.e., Jefferson] determined the sedition act was a nullity under the Constitution, and exercised his regular power of prohibiting the execution of the sentence."[228] Jefferson regarded *Marbury* as a judicial attempt to monopolize constitutional discussion on institutional grounds, an attempt he found offensive to Enlightenment assumptions about rational argument as well as to the liberal political requirement of separation of powers.

In accordance with the logic of his vision of constitutional discourse as a chorus of sometimes discordant voices, Jefferson did not hesitate publicly to disagree with the courts, denying the power of courts to subpoena the president, and instructing the attorney general to refute in the newspapers a judicial opinion contrary to Jeffer-

226 National Bank Opinion, in Powell, *Languages*, 43.

227 See Dumas Malone, *Jefferson the President: First Term* (Boston: Little, Brown, 1976), 110–13.

228 Letter to George Hay (June 2, 1807), in Powell, *Languages*, 217.

son's views of the law.[229] Later Republican presidents shared his opinion that the president should play a prominent role in constitutional discussion, but combined it with an institutional concern to render the federal government efficient that Jefferson seems to have lacked or rejected. Madison, Jefferson's immediate successor, vigorously communicated his constitutional views to Congress; unlike Jefferson, Madison exercised the veto power several times on constitutional grounds. On the other hand, Madison quietly abandoned Jefferson's claim to the right to disregard judicial orders the president thought unconstitutional or contrary to law.[230] Madison's most important exercise of presidential interpretation was his concurrence with Congress in establishing a second Bank of the United States. In justifying his action, Madison revealed the ascendancy that classical common-law modes of argument were gaining over the rationalistic logic the Republicans originally favored. Representative Madison had fought the first bank bill in 1791, and President Madison explained that his opinion of the best interpretation of the "bare text" of the Constitution remained unchanged. But, Madison went on, the constitutional tradition as a whole, speaking through considered legislative decision, judicial approbation, and presidential and state acquiescence, had concluded that the Constitution did authorize congressional chartering of a bank. It was no longer appropriate, therefore, for Madison to use his institutional power as president to impose his personal exegesis of the constitutional text; the Constitution's public meaning, the meaning he was duty-bound to obey, was the meaning that had emerged from the ongoing process of constitutional discussion.[231]

The place of presidential interpretation became the subject of intense controversy after the election of Andrew Jackson in 1828. In 1830 Jackson vetoed an internal improvements bill, probably in large measure because of partisan political considerations. But Jackson's veto message rested his opposition on constitutional grounds and implicitly contradicted the constitutional views of the Supreme Court. Two years later Jackson made his disregard for the Court's

229 See William Goldsmith, *The Growth of Presidential Power* (New York: Chelsea House, 1974), vol. 1, 558–61.

230 See Powell, *Languages*, 253–56.

231 Letter to Charles Jared Ingersoll (June 25, 1831), in Powell, *Languages*, 293–94.

decisions express when he vetoed a bill renewing the charter of the second national bank and did so on constitutional grounds. To the argument that the bank's constitutionality was incontrovertible after the Supreme Court's decision in its favor in *M'Culloch*, Jackson replied: "Mere precedent is a dangerous source of authority, and should not be regarded as deciding questions of constitutional power, except where the acquiescence of the people and the States can be considered as well settled."[232] Jackson thus did not disagree that constitutional interpretation was progressive in nature; his quarrel was with according the Supreme Court as an institution a special role.[233]

Jackson's Whig opponents assailed his vetoes as infringements on what they regarded as the special institutional role of the Supreme Court,[234] and however politically expedient that argument initially may have been, it gradually became a genuine article of Whig political belief. Jackson's own Democratic party, ironically, came to share the Whigs' opposition to the veto as a locus of constitutional discussion in the 1840s; the Supreme Court's proslavery decisions of the 1840s and 1850s served Democratic political interests, as did the ability of Democratic politicians to defend proslavery decisions through deference to the Court as the authoritative interpreter of the Constitution.[235] Although presidents since that time have on occasion cited the Constitution in vetoing legislation, the veto power itself has not remained the established intrepretive practice that Jefferson and Madison wished it to be.

The rise to dominance of the practice of constitutional adjudication and the correlative eclipse of congressional and presidential interpretation were the product of a group of factors, especially including the exigencies of political partisanship and the divisive influence of the slavery issue. But the triumph of adjudication as *the* primary practice within the constitutional tradition resulted in and was partly the result of the rise to power of the legal profession as well. Throughout the first half of the nineteenth century, the profes-

232 Jackson, Veto Message (1832), in Urofsky, *Documents*, 236.

233 Id. at 236–37, 241–42.

234 See, e.g., Irving H. Bartlett, *Daniel Webster* (New York: W. W. Norton, 1978), 130–31.

235 See Michael F. Holt, *The Political Crisis of the 1850s* (New York: W. W. Norton, 1978), 202–3.

sion was the locus of a struggle between the efforts of a well-educated and well-off elite to "raise the standards" of the bar, and the contrary endeavors of populists and radical Jacksonians to democratize and demystify the law.[236] As de Tocqueville noted in the 1830s, the elite lawyers tended to prevail in the long run,[237] and a key element in their argument was the equation they drew between constitutional discussion—the trump card of American politics—and lawyers' discourse.

The professionalization of constitutional interpretation can be traced in the development of constitutional theory in the early Republic. Constitutional theorizing emerged almost at once as an elite activity requiring the intellectual and financial resources of the upper class, and by that token closed to those without the education and leisure of that upper class. The earliest examples of constitutional theory, however, were not narrowly legal or professional in character. St. George Tucker's 1803 annotations on Blackstone, for example, wove complicated patterns of relationship between constitutional exegesis, liberal moral philosophy, and contemporaneous international law (this last itself the complex and rationalistic product of the interaction of Enlightenment morality and civil law principles).[238] Other early theorists examined constitutionalism within the context of historical investigation and economic theory.[239] By the 1820s, however, books on constitutional theory displayed an increasing concern to focus on issues of direct professional relevance for lawyers and judges. William Rawle's 1825 treatise combined a genuine interest in locating American constitutionalism within the political history of Western civilization with an acceptance of the primacy of legal argument and Supreme Court decisions in constitutional discussion; James Kent's almost-simultaneous (1826) volume on federal constitutional law was concerned almost entirely with judicial precedent.[240] With the publication of Justice Joseph Story's three-

236 See Perry Miller, *The Legal Mind in America* (Garden City, N.Y.: Doubleday, 1962).

237 *Democracy in America*, trans. G. Lawrence (Garden City, N.Y.: Doubleday, 1969), 266–67.

238 See Conkin, *Self-Evident Truths*, 24–26.

239 See, e.g., John Taylor, *An Enquiry into the Principles and Policy of the Government of the United States* (1814).

240 Rawle, *A View of the Constitution* (1825); Kent, *Commentaries on American Law*, vol. 1 (1826).

volume treatise in 1833, constitutional theory had clearly become an activity internal to the legal profession. Story cast constitutional issues and arguments in exclusively technical legal terms, even repudiating implicitly his own earlier flirtation with extralegal constitutional argument.[241] While the elite legal profession's capture of constitutional theory and discussion was identified and criticized by some acute observers, most notably Hugh Swinton Legaré,[242] it was never successfully resisted. Constitutional theory, like institutionalized constitutional interpretation, had become the business of lawyers, and more particularly of the elite bar that dominated the Supreme Court, the academy, and the most remunerative and socially significant areas of legal practice.

By Chief Justice Marshall's death in 1836, the constitutional tradition, in a form recognizable to late twentieth-century Americans, was firmly established. The practices of constitutional adjudication and constitutional theory had emerged and been shaped by the elite bar, and the political authority of judicial decisions in the name of the Constitution was generally accepted throughout society. But the tradition and the practices contained within themselves unresolved tensions. The common law vision of discourse as tradition-dependent had prevailed over the competing Enlightenment preference for rationalistic logic, but most of the substantive values and commitments of the constitutional tradition were thoroughly liberal: individualism, society as an artificial social compact, human relationships as the intersection of autonomous rights-bearers, the supremacy of the national empire over local communities. The internal goods of constitutional adjudication had been identified: respect for text and prior decisions, logical coherence and adherence to the norms of ordinary legal argument, freedom from partisan politics.[243] The Supreme Court's central and authoritative institutional role in constitu-

241 Story, *Commentaries on the Constitution* (Boston: Hilliard and Gray, 1833). See H. Jefferson Powell, "Joseph Story's Commentaries on the Constitution: A Belated Review," 94 Yale L.J. 1285 (1985).

242 See M. Legaré, ed., *Writings of Hugh Swinton Legaré* (New York: D. Appleton, 1845), 102 (book review of Kent's *Commentaries* originally published in 1828).

243 The very anger with which many Americans greeted judicial decisions that appeared partisan revealed the importance of this norm. See G. Edward White, *The Marshall Court and Cultural Change* (New York: Macmillan, 1988), 927–64.

tional discussion was generally accepted, without many Americans noting the difficulty this created for the justices: they were expected to undertake the deeply moral and political task of applying shared social values to the resolution of disputes, but to do so within the confines of professional (i.e., technical and disinterested) legal argument.

By 1836, it was also clear what the tradition's central MacIntyrean character was: neither the lawgiver (as in classical thought) nor the virtuous citizen (as in commonwealth and Jeffersonian thought) but the Great Judge. John Marshall successfully disentangled the Supreme Court from involvement in party politics and based its claim to constitutional authority on its self-conscious disavowal of nonlegal modes of decision making. "The source of judicial authority, then, was in the process of judicial reasoning";[244] after Marshall, American constitutionalism and a common-law tradition of moral reasoning seemed inextricably linked. Marshall's intellectual prowess and his personal humility and virtue were legendary, even in his lifetime and among his enemies; over time after his death, criticism of Marshall became almost unthinkable, and the image he had created of the Great Judge became central to constitutional discussion.

The constitutional tradition's problematic had also emerged by 1836. Questions of national power and state autonomy were most prominent, since the tradition's rejection of Republican contractualism had not entailed a wholesale rejection of liberalism's fears of overweening national power. Liberal political theory's concern to safeguard individual autonomy in the form of property rights had shaped the constitutional doctrine of vested rights, but Supreme Court decisions displayed a countervailing, if not yet fully articulated, solicitude for legislative power to act in the public interest. The deepest and most troubling problem for the tradition, of course, was the status of slavery. As a serious threat to the political survival of the Union, slavery posed an external threat to the continued existence of the constitutional tradition, but it also presented constitutionalists with a set of purely internal problems. Slavery was difficult to reconcile with the Enlightenment libertarianism that permeated

244 G. Edward White, *The American Judicial Tradition*, 2d ed. (New York: Oxford Univ. Press, 1988), 34. White's discussion of Marshall's rule in the evolution of the constitutional tradition is illuminating. See id. at 7–34.

American constitutionalism, but at the same time restrictions on slavery contradicted the tradition's insistence on respecting property rights. Largely because of the slavery issue, individual legal arguments and judicial decisions in the antebellum period are often marked by conflict between the pursuit of the internal goods of the tradition (logical argument, textual fidelity, and so on) and the external goods of maintaining the Union and the institutional power and prestige of the courts. In the case of *The Antelope*,[245] for example, the Supreme Court was confronted with the legality of the international slave trade, an activity that American legal opinion almost unanimously agreed was contrary to natural justice, and that was forbidden to American citizens. (The putative slaveowners in the case were Spanish and Portuguese.) The Court sidestepped the issue by announcing that the trade violated "the law of nature" (liberal moral principles) but was not contrary to any judicially enforceable law. By doing so, the Court avoided a potentially damaging clash with politically potent proslavery forces, but at the cost of issuing an opinion patently dictated by expediency rather than by legal reasoning.[246] Secreted within the noble image of the Great Judge there was already a trace of his negative counterpart, the Crafty Judicial Politician.

THE CRISIS OF SLAVERY, SECESSION, AND RECONSTRUCTION

The quarter-century between John Marshall's death and South Carolina's secession from the Union was, for the most part, a time of consolidation for the constitutional tradition. While the Court under the leadership of Marshall's successor Roger Brooke Taney was a shade less nationalistic than the Marshall Court had been, in general the Taney-era justices upheld and even extended Marshall's substantive legal doctrines.[247] The Taney Court's adherence to Marshall's

245 23 U.S. (10 Wheat.) 66 (1825).

246 See John Noonan, *The Antelope* (Berkeley: Univ. of California Press, 1977).

247 Only one of the post-Marshall justices, Peter V. Daniel, proved to be a

use of common law, tradition-dependent modes of reasoning was even more complete, and the justices as well as the elite bar generally resisted the attempts of pro- and antislavery activists to import moral or political philosophy directly into constitutional argument. *Prigg v. Pennsylvania*[248] was paradigmatic of Taney Court conservatism. *Prigg* involved the constitutionality of a free-state statute that had the purpose and effect of interfering with the federally guaranteed right of slaveowners to reclaim fugitive slaves. Writing the official opinion of the Court, the antislavery New England Justice Story invoked traditional "rule[s] of interpretation" and "the principles of the common law"[249] in concluding that the Constitution's fugitive slave clause ousted state law entirely from the regulation of the interstate recapture of fugitives. The question for Story was one of constitutional text and structure—"whether the power of legislation upon this subject is exclusive in the national government"[250]—not of the political morality of slavery. Story himself believed his opinion a subtle victory for free-state critics of the federal fugitive slave because the opinion attempted to absolve free-states from cooperation with slavecatchers,[251] but that view was a private reflection on the extralegal consequences of an ostensibly legally derived decision.[252]

If Taney had died in 1856, he would have enjoyed an undisputed

---

true advocate of states'-rights Jeffersonianism and Daniel's views isolated him intellectually on the Court. See John P. French, *Justice Daniel Dissenting* (Cambridge, Mass.: Harvard Univ. Press, 1964). On the Taney Court's continuation of the Marshall Court's work, see Carl Swisher, *The Taney Period* (New York: Macmillan, 1974).

248 41 U.S. (16 Pet.) 539 (1842).

249 Id. at 610, 613.

250 Id. at 622.

251 Chief Justice Taney may have held a similar view: his concurring opinion concluded that "on the contrary, it is enjoined upon [the states] as a duty to protect and support the owner when he is endeavoring to obtain possession of his property." Id. at 627. Taney, like Story, couched his arguments in terms of the "true" "rule[s] of construction" to be applied to the constitutional text. Id. at 629.

252 Story's son and biographer reported that his father "repeatedly and earnestly spoke of [*Prigg*] to his family and his intimate friends, as being 'a triumph of freedom.'" William W. Story, *Life and Letters of Joseph Story* (Boston: Little, Brown, 1851), vol. 2, 392. But the younger Story also wrote that the frequent criticism of *Prigg* "as if it had been decided on moral grounds" was wholly mistaken. "[I]n fact, the question was purely legal, and not ethical. [Justice Story] merely stated the *law* as he honestly believed it to be." Id. at 391.

claim to being a worthy inheritor of the character of the Great Judge. Unfortunately for Taney's historical reputation, he lived to decide the infamous case of *Dred Scott v. Sandford.*[253] *Dred Scott* presented the question of whether a black person could sue for his freedom in federal court. The asserted basis for federal jurisdiction was Scott's claim that he and his alleged master were citizens of different states; Scott's substantive claim to freedom rested on the fact that a former master had taken him to live for several years in Illinois territory, an area forever free under the Northwest Ordinance and the Missouri Compromise. Scott's arguments on both issues were strong; in particular, the majority legal view even in slave-state courts was that residence in a free state or territory freed the slave. Nevertheless, the Court held that Scott was not and could never be a citizen because of his race—a remarkable view clearly contrary to previous understanding—and that as a result the federal courts could not hear his case. Taney did not stop at that point, although legal tradition said that a court without jurisdiction should announce the fact and nothing more; instead, he went on to state that Congress had no power to exclude slavery from any federal territory. Not only was Scott not a free individual, but the national legislature was powerless to restrict slavery.

Dred Scott was a Pyrrhic victory for proslavery politics. Rather than settling the constitutional question of slavery permanently in the South's favor, the case substantially damaged the Court's esteem in the North and prompted such conservative Northern lawyers as Abraham Lincoln to reconsider the Court's institutional role in constitutional discourse. From the perspective of this book, *Dred Scott* showed that the primary institutional locus of the constitutional tradition had been corrupted by concern over the external political goods of national stability and union. Taney's opinion for the Court patently sacrificed the internal goods of intelligible continuity with past discussion and even of historical and legal honesty in a vain effort to end political strife over slavery. Taney's pre–*Dred Scott* stature as an exemplification of the Great Judge meant that his and his colleagues' failure posed a serious threat to the continued coherence of constitutionalism as a tradition of rational inquiry.

The tradition's survival was, ironically, the product of the actions

253 60 U.S. (19 How.) 393 (1857).

of that group of Americans who approved of *Dred Scott*, the slaveholders of the South. The election of the antislavery "Republican"[254] Abraham Lincoln to the presidency in 1860 precipitated the withdrawal of most of the slaveholding Southern states from the Union. With only one partial exception, these states justified their actions on the old radical-Jeffersonian ground that as parties to the constitutional compact, they were entitled by Northern aggression to declare the contract at an end and secede from its structures.[255] The Confederacy thus originated in a curiously legal or at least "legalistic" action; it was the creation not of a revolution but, as its creators contended, of the exercise of a strict constitutional right. Indeed, the ordinances of secession adopted by Virginia, the Carolinas, and Georgia claimed only to repeal the ordinances by which they had originally consented to the Constitution.

Secession and the ensuing Civil War were, of course, most immediately a political and military crisis, but they also can usefully be seen as posing an epistemological crisis for the constitutional tradition. Legal opinion even in the North was originally divided over whether the federal government could do anything other than protest secession. Many early constitutional theorists had endorsed the actual legality of secession,[256] and President James Buchanan's attorney general advised him in late 1860 that although secession was technically illegal the federal government had no legal means to stop it.[257] Even though Northern public and legal opinion soon rallied behind President Lincoln's decision to resist disunion by force, the

254 In the middle of the 1850s a coalition of "Conscience Whigs" and antislavery Democrats formed a new political party that almost immediately eclipsed the Whig organization and soon put the Democratic party on the defensive throughout much of the North. The coalition adopted the old Jeffersonian label "Republican" as a deliberate claim that it was the true bearer of the original Jeffersonians' liberal commitments to individual rights. See, e.g., Abraham Lincoln, Public Letter (1859), in Richard N. Current, ed., *The Political Thought of Abraham Lincoln* (Indianapolis: Bobbs-Merrill, 1967), 22–24.

255 The convention that purported to take Kentucky out of the Union adopted both an ordinance of secession and a declaration of independence, thus covering all the theoretical bases.

256 Rawle, a strong nationalist, conceded the right of a state to leave the Union in his widely read 1825 treatise. The treatise was for many years the official constitutional-law text at West Point.

257 Jeremiah S. Black, Opinion of Nov. 20, 1860, 9 Op.A.G. 517.

Civil War saw a continuous debate over the constitutionality of various governmental actions.[258]

President Lincoln, a slim majority of Supreme Court justices, and many elite lawyers sought to justify the stern measures and vast expansion of the national government by arguments continuous with prewar constitutionalism, although with mixed intellectual success. Other Northerners took more radical positions, attacking the constitutional tradition as unworkable, morally bankrupt, and tainted with *Dred Scott.* Radical constitutionalists such as Timothy Ferrar and William Whiting developed what modern scholars have labeled the *adequacy theory* of the Constitution.[259] The Constitution, the adequacy theorists argued, was intended to create a national government capable of achieving the Preamble's goals of forming a Union, establishing justice, promoting the general welfare, and so on. To debate whether the text of the constitutional instrument or existing judicial precedent authorized or permitted the national government to do something necessary to achieve its goals was to substitute lawyers' quibbles for statesmanship; the real Constitution was always "adequate" to the government's and the nation's needs. Some adequacy theorists, indeed, simply rejected any role at all for constitutionalism in the sense of a text-centered form of reasoning.[260]

Adequacy theory obviously was less a theory of constitutional interpretation in the tradition's sense than a proposal to replace the tradition with something quite different, and its appeal to courts and to the elite bar was (unsurprisingly) limited. The theory had its most direct influence during the war by providing an unfailing justification for the government's actions. Whiting, for example, was employed by the War Department to write a military manual on the government's powers that went through forty-three editions by 1871.[261] Adequacy theory's more fundamental intellectual legacy was its contribution to the final resolution of the original constitutional dispute

258 See, e.g., James G. Randall, *Constitutional Problems under Lincoln*, rev. ed. (Urbana: Univ. of Illinois Press, 1951); Arthur E. Bester, Jr., "The American Civil War as a Constitutional Crisis," 69 Am. Hist. Rev. 327 (1964).

259 Harold Hyman and William Wiecek, *Equal Justice under Law* (New York: Harper and Row, 1982), 234–35, 246–47.

260 See Sidney Fisher, *The Trial of the Constitution* (1862).

261 Whiting, *War Powers Under the Constitution of the United States* (43d ed. 1871).

over the nature of the American nation-state. Jeffersonian contractarianism and Federalist nationalism coexisted uneasily throughout the antebellum period; few constitutionalists of the period between 1800 and 1860 were consistent in their invocation of either. The Lincoln administration's response to secession, however, could not be justified without making a straightforward equation between the federal Union and the liberal nation-state, and adequacy theory drew that equation.

President Lincoln himself often made arguments that were reminiscent both of Jeffersonian and of early nationalist thought, and his initial justification for attempting to subdue the secessionists rested on the identification of the United States as a unitary nation-state that was soon picked up by adequacy theorists.[262] Lincoln's own constitutional thinking, however, posed an essential challenge to much of the substance of the developed constitutional tradition. Lincoln's constitutionalism was decisively shaped by his participation in the political struggle against the expansion of slavery during the decade before secession. Lincoln rested his own politics squarely on the Declaration of Independence and its assertion that "all men are created equal and endowed by their Creator with certain unalienable rights."[263] He saw that principle as the fundamental premise of the American Republic, the "axiom"[264] from which both the Constitution and the American political order were (or should be) derived.[265] The product of Lincoln's public arguments and theoret-

262 See Lincoln, Message to the Special Session of Congress, July 4, 1861, in Current, *Political Thought*.

263 Lincoln "spent a good part of the 1850s repeatedly relating all the most sensitive issues of the day to the Declaration's supreme principle. If all men are created equal, they cannot be property. They cannot be ruled by owner-monarchs. . . . Their equality cannot be denied." Garry Wills, *Lincoln at Gettysburg* (New York: Simon and Schuster, 1992), 120.

264 In 1860 Lincoln wrote a public letter on Jefferson's birthday praising Jefferson for having "the coolness, forecast, and capacity to introduce into a merely revolutionary document, an abstract truth, applicable to all men and all times." "The principles of Jefferson," Lincoln explained, "are the definitions and axioms of freedom." Letter to Henry L. Pierce and others, April 6, 1859, in Current, *Political Thought*, 123–24.

265 "Lincoln distinguished between the Declaration as the statement of a permanent ideal and the Constitution as an early and provisional embodiment of that ideal, to be tested against it, kept in motion toward it." Wills, *Lincoln at Gettysburg*, 101.

ical reflections was a constitutional vision profoundly egalitarian in its assumptions and its direction of movement.

In 1855 Lincoln still conceived of "equality" in essentially liberal and libertarian terms: attacking Know-Nothing nativism in that year, he wrote that a Know-Nothing republic would rewrite the Declaration to read "'all men are created equal, except negroes, and foreigners, and catholics.' When it comes to this I should prefer emigrating to some country where they make no pretence of loving liberty—to Russia, for instance, where despotism can be taken pure, and without the base alloy of hypocracy [*sic*]."[266] But Lincoln's reflections on the "tension that exists within the principle of democratic self-governance itself"[267] drove him gradually away from the traditional liberal pairing of the sovereign individual and the sovereign nation-state (even when the latter was redefined as a majoritarian democracy). Robert Burt's recent study of Lincoln's constitutionalism illuminatingly describes "the central lesson of Lincoln's tension: that the principle of democracy contains an inherent contradiction between the concepts of equal self-determination and majority rule and can therefore provide no univocal guidance for the resolution of social conflict or even for determining which institutions should address it."[268] After he became president, Lincoln increasingly sought to base his fundamental decisions on a deepened, substantive principle of equality rather than on the formal, juridical equality of liberal (and constitutional) thought that tolerated the enslavement of blacks, the disfranchisement of women—and the conquest of the Southern "rebels." Lincoln's war aim was "not to subjugate the South but to restore the Union as a political relationship among equals";[269] his experience during the war pushed him toward a racial egalitarianism that would transcend the rampant racism of his culture.[270]

266 Letter to Joshua F. Speed, Aug. 24, 1855, in Current, *Political Thought*, 83.

267 Robert A. Burt, *The Constitution in Conflict* (Cambridge, Mass.: Harvard Univ. Press, 1992), 80.

268 Id. at 81.

269 Id. at 89.

270 Robert Burt traces the change in Lincoln's racial thinking to the fact that blacks "joined Lincoln to fight and die for the Union" and thus had come to be in "an independent, mutual relationship" demanding fully equal "claims for his respect." Id. at 94–95.

"By the end of the war Lincoln clearly viewed the black soldiers in the same

Lincoln's egalitarianism proposed a profound rethinking of the Enlightenment individualism of the constitutional tradition[271] and implicitly challenged the tradition's focus on a hierarchically preeminent Supreme Court in control of the tradition's central practice.[272] He also flatly rejected the tradition's self-identification as an autonomous discourse quite distinct from morality or religion. Lincoln freely and powerfully reinfused directly ethical and theological language into his constitutional arguments and political speeches.[273]

The assassin's bullet abruptly terminated Lincoln's rethinking of American constitutionalism, but his challenge to the tradition continued, shifted now to Congress. It was the Radical Republican leadership there who proposed a full-scale intellectual and moral response to the post-*Dred Scott* crisis of constitutionalism. The congressional Radicals combined a Marshallian insistence on the breadth and supremacy of national power and national institutions (radicalized under the influence of adequacy theory) with egalitarian themes derived

---

way that he had always viewed white Southerners. This was, moreover, the same way that Lincoln demanded white Southerners see him—as a participant in a voluntarily entered relationship that could not subsequently be abandoned for unilaterally determined self-interest. This was the bedrock axiom for which Lincoln fought the Civil War—not equality as an abstract principle but equality that had come to life in active association, where burdens and benefits had been shared and accordingly must be equally accounted for." Id. at 95–96.

271 See Wills, *Lincoln at Gettysburg*, 146–47.

272 Most famously, in his first inaugural address, Lincoln denied that the constitutional "policy of the government, upon vital questions, affecting the whole people, is to be irrevocably fixed by decisons of the Supreme Court, the instant they are made, in ordinary litigation between parties." To treat the practice of constitutional adjudication by courts as the primary vehicle for the constitutional tradition's ongoing life would be, for Lincoln, a denial of the popular and egalitarian nature he saw in the tradition: "the people will have ceased, to be their own rulers, having, to that extent, practically resigned their government, into the hands of that eminent tribunal." See Current, *Political Thought*, 175–76. Lincoln did not question the legal finality of a judicial determination; fundamentally, he was denying the practical restriction of the tradition's community to elite lawyers and judges and attempting to reopen the tradition to "the people" as *their* mode of rational enquiry into the moral demands of their life together.

273 "Lincoln brought back into American political discourse the spiritual concepts of 'good' and 'evil.'" Diggins, *Lost Soul*, 298. Diggins links Herman Melville with Lincoln in this "Christianiz[ation of] the American political imagination." Id.

most immediately from the prewar antislavery movement.[274] Although the Radicals sometimes insisted that the original Constitution and Bill of Rights, properly interpreted, invalidated slavery and mandated racial justice,[275] they generally conceded that formal amendments were necessary to render secure the emancipation and legal rights of Southern blacks. As a result, they successfully pushed for the passage of three amendments intended radically to reshape the federal structure and the intellectual bounds of federal constitutionalism.[276]

The Thirteenth Amendment confirmed and completed the Emancipation Proclamation by entirely outlawing slavery. To the Radicals, the abolition of slavery was not the mere elimination of a legal category of property or the transfer of the freedmen from one legal status to another; indeed, the Radical understanding of the amendment could not be put in narrowly legal terms at all. The abolition of slavery, they argued, entailed that "the ex-slaves immediately and automatically ascended to all the rights, privileges and responsibilities of full citizenship."[277] Emancipation, in other words, was a fundamental reworking of the social order, and such measures as the Freedmen's Bureau Act (which attempted to provide educational, vocational, and economic opportunity for the freedmen) were as much a corollary of the amendment as the 1866 Civil Rights Act (which imposed a legal prohibition on state laws relegating blacks to secondary legal status).

The immediate effects of the Thirteenth Amendment fell far short of the Radicals' goals. Southern white resistance, as well as conservative and elite-bar interpretations of the amendment as the mere legal elimination of the property relationship of slavery[278] prompted the Radicals to a new round of constitution making. The Radicals saw the Fourteenth Amendment as the technical legal confirmation of the

274 See William Wiecek, *The Sources of Antislavery Constitutionalism in America* (Ithaca, N.Y.: Cornell Univ. Press, 1977). The exact extent to which the Radicals were directly influenced by Lincoln, who of course was also an heir of prewar antislavery thought, is unclear.

275 See William Nelson, *The Fourteenth Amendment* (Cambridge, Mass.: Harvard Univ. Press, 1988), 64–90.

276 See Hyman and Wiecek, *Equal Justice*, 386–438.

277 Wiecek, *Liberty*, 93.

278 See Hyman and Wiecek, *Equal Justice*, 390.

Thirteenth Amendment's reworking of society.[279] Section one of the amendment explicitly overruled *Dred Scott*'s denial of the possibility of black citizenship and used familiar constitutional/legal language to ensure that state law recognized that citizenship. Section two of the amendment spelled out the Radicals' belief that citizenship implied political power by imposing a legal sanction on states denying blacks the right to vote. The clumsiness of this mode of turning into law the Thirteenth Amendment's political implications led a few years later to the third and final Radical constitutional amendment, the Fifteenth, which embodied a blanket legal rule forbidding racial distinctions in voting rights. Both the Fourteenth and the Fifteenth Amendments were accompanied by legislation intended to further legalize and thus protect the social and political revolution the Radicals believed followed upon the abolition of slavery.

It is a commonplace of American history that Reconstruction was largely a failure. Within twenty years of the adoption of the Thirteenth Amendment, Southern whites had retaken control of every Southern state government from biracial Radical administrations, the Radicals had lost cohesion and control of Congress, and the Supreme Court had reasserted its traditional institutional supremacy by invalidating various pieces of Radical legislation. Southern white resistance, Northern white racism, and a general white unwillingness to exert national power indefinitely in behalf of the freedmen eroded the Radicals' political strength, and indeed, the "radicalism" of many former Radicals. As C. Vann Woodward has noted, by the 1880s it was "quite common" to find former Radicals "mouthing the shibboleths of white supremacy regarding the Negro's innate inferiority, shiftlessness, and hopeless unfitness for all participation in the white man's civilization."[280]

What usually goes unnoticed is that the Radicals tried—and failed—to rework the intellectual nature of the constitutional tradition as well.[281] Radical Reconstruction was truly revolutionary, on

279 Id. at 386–438.

280 Woodward, *The Strange Career of Jim Crow*, 3d rev. ed. (New Haven: Yale Univ. Press, 1974), 70.

281 Interpreting "the meaning of Reconstruction" is a fair-sized cottage industry, chiefly because so much legal and rhetorical advantage in current disputes is believed to lie with those who can marshal the "original intent" of Reconstruction on their side. Any discussion that is less than a full-dress original

the intellectual plane of the constitutional tradition as well as in the overtly political and social spheres. In response to the constitutional tradition's manifest failure to resolve the moral and intellectual conundrum of slavery, and the apparent corruption of its primary institution, the courts, the Radicals proposed—and for a few years acted upon—a dramatic reshaping of the meaning of constitutionalism in the United States. They explicitly challenged and rejected the tradition's legalization of constitutional discourse, and expressly reintroduced liberal moral and political philosophy into constitutional discussion. They rejected the authority of precedent (although not the relevance of experience) and denied the finality of Supreme Court decisions. Unsurprisingly, they attempted to reinvigorate Congress as the primary institutional locus of constitutional discussion. By empowering Congress to legislate in an indeterminate but clearly vast new area of civil and political life (all three amendments gave Congress the power to legislate to effectuate their purposes), the Radicals sought to recast constitutionalism from a legal discussion about the location and distribution of political power into an explicitly moral discourse about the requirements of political and social justice. The Radical solution to the crisis into which slavery had brought the constitutional tradition was to rework that tradition from the ground up.

The Radicals' intellectual redefinition of constitutionalism failed for a variety of reasons. Clearly the white racism that undermined Radicalism's political power from without and within played a major role in discrediting Radicalism's intellectual program. The conservatism and political self-interest of the elite bench and bar were another important factor. Elite lawyers overwhelmingly refused to

---

interpretation, as a consequence, necessarily relies on historical scholarship that is hotly contested. In this book I have accepted as correct the view of the Reconstruction that is, in broad terms, shared by such works as Eric Foner, *Reconstruction: America's Unfinished Revolution* (New York: Harper and Row, 1988), Hyman and Wiecek, *Equal Justice*, and Nelson, *Fourteenth Amendment*, i.e., the "liberal" interpretation. The book's overall narrative would not have fundamentally changed, however, if I had adopted the "conservative" interpretation, since I accept—and the "liberal" scholars unhappily concede—that by the end of Reconstruction constitutionalism had been reconstituted on terms scarcely changed, except for the elimination of slavery, from the era of *Dred Scott*. The "conservative" interpretation of Reconstruction simply ascribes this repristination of antebellum thought to the Radicals themselves.

accept the Radicals' delegalization of constitutional discourse and their attempt to change its focus from questions of institutional power to issues of social justice. The federal courts, and especially the Supreme Court, reflected and enforced this rejection of Radicalism by insisting on treating the Radicals' constitutional amendments as particularized legal rules that worked specific and quite narrow changes in prewar constitutional doctrine. (An ironic result was that the Court's adherence to the modes of constitutional argument that produced *Dred Scott*, modes now employed to cabin in and de-radicalize the new amendments, rehabilitated the Court's reputation among elite lawyers and their business allies.) The Radicals themselves contributed to the failure of their proposed constitutional revolution by their increasing reliance on traditional legal modes of argument and, especially, by their use of technical legal language in the Fourteenth and Fifteenth Amendments, language that lent itself to reinterpretation in conservative directions.

In the 1869 case of *Texas v. White*, the Supreme Court formally accepted adequacy theory's identification of the federal Union as *the* American nation-state, although the Court did so in terms that may have given some of the Radical leaders pause.[282] The Court's rejection of Radical constitutionalism became apparent in its first major confrontation with the Radicals' amendments. In the *Slaughterhouse Cases*,[283] the Court held that the Thirteenth and Fourteenth Amendments were discrete legal prohibitions of slavery and expressly racist legislation rather than general charters of equality and social justice; the Court also rejected the argument that the amendments fundamentally changed the relationship between the nation and the states. The Court understood what it was doing: Justice Samuel Miller's opinion for the majority accurately summarized Radical constitutionalism only to reject it as unthinkable.

> Was it the purpose of the fourteenth amendment . . . to transfer the security and protection of all the civil rights which we have mentioned, from the States to the Federal government? And where it is declared that Congress shall power to enforce [the amendment], was it intended to

282 While the Court agreed with the adequacy theorists that the Union was "indestructible," it ascribed the same status to states in language reminiscent of antebellum "dual sovereignty" rhetoric. 74 U.S. (7 Wall.) 700, 725 (1869).

283 83 U.S. (16 Wall.) 36 (1873).

> bring within the power of Congress the entire domain of civil rights heretofore belonging exclusively to the States? . . . [S]uch a construction . . . would constitute this court a perpetual censor upon all legislation of the States, on the civil rights of their own citizens, with authority to nullify such as it did not approve as consistent with those rights. . . . [T]hese consequences are so serious, so far-reaching and pervading, so great a departure from the structure and spirit of our institutions [that w]e are convinced that no such results were intended by the Congress which proposed these amendments, nor by the legislatures of the States which ratified them.[284]

The *Slaughterhouse* decision was, to be sure, a narrow five-to-four vote, but the four justices who dissented in that case were, as it turned out, Radicalism's highwater mark in convincing the Supreme Court to rethink prewar constitutionalism. After *Slaughterhouse*, overwhelming majorities of the Court consistently endorsed the *Slaughterhouse* conclusion that the Radicals' constitutional amendments could not possibly be "intended" to transform constitutionalism into the Radicals' vision. The Radicals' desire to extend national power was gradually whittled down by the Court into little more than an expansion of the Court's own jurisdiction; the Court reasserted (and Congress eventually acquiesced in) the prewar institutional primacy of the judiciary;[285] the Radicals' understanding of constitutionalism as an inquiry into the forms of social justice was transmogrified into a new version of the older tradition's concern with the distribution of institutional power.[286]

In 1883 the Court decided the *Civil Rights Cases*,[287] a decision seen at the time and ever since as the official judicial interment of Reconstruction.[288] The decision ruled unconstitutional the last major piece of Radical legislation, the 1875 Civil Rights Act, which forbade

284 Id. at 77–78.

285 The last great effort of the Radicals to assert congressional leadership in the articulation of a constitutionalism of "rights" was the "Blaine amendment," a proposed constitutional amendment that would have extended the First Amendment's prohibitions on religious establishments and interference with religious "free exercise." Despite support from President Grant, the weakened Radical leadership could not even pass the amendment through Congress.

286 See Nelson, *Fourteenth Amendment*, 181–200.

287 109 U.S. 3 (1883).

288 See Hyman and Wiecek, *Equal Justice*, 500.

racial discrimination in public transport and public conveniences. Eight justices joined in an opinion stating that the Thirteenth Amendment's abolition of slavery simply did not affect racial discrimination—slavery was a specific legal category, not the core of an overall social structure of racial hierarchy. The majority justices also held that the Fourteenth Amendment addressed only formalized legal rules that discriminated invidiously on the basis of race; in their view the amendment authorized neither the courts nor Congress to interfere with "private" (the Court's word was "individual") discrimination or with state support for "private" acts of racism.[289] Only one member of the Court (ironically, the only former slaveholder) recognized and accepted the amendments' origins in the Radicals' desire to eliminate social injustice.[290] The Supreme Court's infamous validation of Jim Crow thirteen years later in *Plessy v. Ferguson*[291] merely restated the fact of the absorption of the Radicals' amendments into traditional legal/constitutional discourse; the Court insisted on reading the amendments against the background assumption that constitutionalism's concern is with the distribution of public power and the protection of the private affairs of the liberal individualist against public intrusion, not with the meaning of social morality and justice. The prewar constitutional tradition had survived the crisis brought on by slavery not by accepting the Radicals' new vision, but by a gentlemen's agreement to inter and forget slavery, and otherwise to continue constitutional discussion as if *Dred Scott* and the Civil War had never happened.

THE MIDDLE YEARS OF THE CONSTITUTIONAL TRADITION

The surprising reemergence of the pre–Civil War constitutional tradition from the crisis of slavery was largely the product, I have argued, of external factors: white racism, the weaknesses of the Radicals as a political force, the opposition of the elite and conserva-

289 Id. at 16–17, 24.
290 Id. at 26 (Harlan J dissenting).
291 163 U.S. 537 (1896).

tive bar to Radical egalitarianism coupled with the desire of bar and bench to maintain (or regain) prewar power and privilege. At least one internal factor should be noted as well. The prewar constitutional tradition reemerged in part because in the end it proved able to explain and accommodate the undeniable political and legal changes that survived the wreck of Reconstruction. The destruction of antebellum chattel slavery was an event of cataclysmic social import, involving among other legal consequences the extinction of billions of dollars worth of vested private property. That event, which the Radicals saw as a social revolution, the defenders of the antebellum tradition interpreted as the use of an ordinary means of lawmaking (the amendment process) to eliminate an anomaly in the liberal individualism of American law. The incredible expansion of federal governmental power during the war and Reconstruction, for the Radicals the People's assertion of their rightful sovereignty, became for traditionalists a set of discrete answers to prewar questions about the relative authority of federal and state authority. These amendments and answers left undisturbed both the forms of argument and the substantive structure of discussion of the tradition. For the majority of those active in constitutional discussion after about 1880, the constitutional tradition of John Marshall—and of Roger Taney—had always contained the solutions to the problems that nearly led to its collapse. What had been lacking was the will to address the issue of slavery legally, and the refusal of Marshall and Taney's fellow-Southerners to acknowledge the implications of the national supremacy Marshall and Taney supported.

Antebellum constitutional discussion had revolved around federal/state relations at their most fundamental level, and around the degree of protection courts should afford vested rights. In the tradition's middle years, the two themes coalesced, and the most common and most fruitful source of discussion and disagreement came to concern the relative powers of federal courts and state legislatures over questions of economic liberty. Despite the best efforts of conservative politicians and lawyers, neither the federal nor the state governments returned to their prewar minimalist forms. The genie of governmental power, once released, remained available for state intervention in a wide range of health, safety, and economic issues that antebellum legislatures had left almost untouched. The massive industrialization of the society that simultaneously occurred created novel problems and social tensions, and the near-universality of white male suffrage ensured that the concerns of the poor and working classes would enjoy at least fitful legislative attention. Out of the complex interplay between populist and reformist politics, conservative political and legal defensive maneuvers, and the tendency of government to grow larger by inertia was born the modern American bureaucratic and regulatory state.[292] The Civil War settled the formal question of the "location" of the nation-state in the American political order; the development of a federal regulatory bureaucracy during the war, and its growth afterwards, far more than official constitutional doctrine, marked the federal government's substantive approximation to the modern nation-state. "Surveillance as the mobilizing of administrative power . . . is the primary means of the concentration of authoritative resources involved in the formation of the nation-state."[293]

The threat to concentrated wealth posed by the growth of regulatory power in a polity governed in part through mass politics did not go unnoticed. The elite bench and bar of the late nineteenth century overwhelmingly shared the American upper classes' fear of "socialism"—democratic and populist legislation with regulatory or redistributive economic effects.[294] The liberal individualism underlying American law could easily be interpreted to support or require the laissez-faire economics and social Darwinism of social theorists such as the Englishman Herbert Spencer and the American William Graham Sumner. First constitutional theorists, and then courts adjudicating constitutional cases, borrowed laissez-faire theory to provide the intellectual underpinning for constitutional arguments that would put constraints on regulatory and redistributive legislation.

The initial and primary legal battleground was in the states, with scholars and judges challenging social legislation passed by reformist legislators as infringements on the constitutional rights of property and liberty. The constitutional theorists Thomas Cooley[295] and Chris-

292 See William Nelson, *The Roots of American Bureaucracy, 1830–1900* (Cambridge, Mass.: Harvard Univ. Press, 1982).

293 Giddens, *Violence*, 181.

294 See Arnold Paul, *Conservative Crisis and the Rule of Law* (Ithaca, N.Y.: Cornell Univ. Press, 1960).

295 Cooley, *Constitutional Limitations on the Legislative Powers* (1868). This famous and widely influential treatise was reissued in many later editions.

topher Tiedemann[296] argued that state legislative power (the "police power") was subject to strict and searching constitutional scrutiny by the courts.[297] While Cooley, Tiedemann, and other theorists of the period were conscious of, and honest about, the social and economic theories underlying their constitutional arguments, in accordance with the constitutional tradition they shaped those arguments as interpretations of the language of the state and federal constitutions. The theorists and their judicial disciples regarded the Fourteenth Amendment's prohibition on deprivations of "liberty" or "property" except by "due process of law," and its requirement that states afford all "persons" (a term quickly construed to include artificial persons such as business corporations) "equal protection," as adequate textual bases for judicial protection of liberal individualism against "paternalistic" legislation. From the 1880s through the end of the 1930s, state and federal courts cited such arguments in invalidating social legislation deemed to infringe freedom of contract or the individual's autonomous use of his or her (in reality, usually a corporate "its") property.

In a curious fashion, this use of the Fourteenth Amendment echoed the concern of the amendment's Radical creators for social justice, although of course, the justice envisaged by the Radicals and that sought by Gilded Era theorists and courts was quite different in substance. From the perspective of constitutional history, however, the most important aspect of this doctrine of economic *substantive due process*[298] was its demonstration that laissez-faire constitutional-

296 Tiedemann, *Treatise on the Limitations of the Police Power* (1886).

297 Cooley and Tiedemann were initially concerned primarily with state constitutional limitations on social legislation. Their arguments, however, were transferred, easily and quickly, to federal constitutional adjudication in the name of the Fourteenth Amendment. See, e.g., Ritchie v. People, 155 Ill. 98 (1895) (invalidating a state law limiting maximum hours of female employees as a violation both of Fourteenth Amendment and state constitutional principles of freedom of contract).

298 This term is the conventional modern label for interpretations of the due process clauses that treat the word *liberty* as authorizing courts to invalidate legislation because, in the courts' view, the legislation infringes (or infringes too much) individual liberty. Both the effort of courts in the 1885–1937 period to protect "freedom of contract" and the contemporary judicial protection of rights to contraception and abortion are substantive due process doctrines. See Frank Strong, *Substantive Due Process of Law* (Durham, N.C.: Carolina Academic Press, 1986).

ism was not a repudiation of post-Civil War nationalism. Laissez-faire judges and theorists were not opposed to the centralized power of the nation-state; indeed, they viewed that power, properly distributed and directed, as central to the protection of individual autonomy. Substantive due process represented a fundamental constitutional choice to locate ultimate power over social and business regulation in a centralized judicial system.

Constitutional doctrine was not, to be sure, the only clear indication of the connection between laissez-faire individualism and the courts as the agents of centralized state power. Perhaps the most dramatic illustration of the connection occurred in 1892, when the Supreme Court upheld the use of the equity power of the federal courts to justify the military suppression of labor unrest and the subsequent punishment, without jury trial, of labor leader Eugene V. Debs.[299] The Court explained its decision, which was on the doctrinal level a startling innovation, by direct analogy to the national government's use of force to conquer the Confederacy. To a majority of the elite bench and bar at the end of the nineteenth century, the preservation of individual autonomy from "socialism" and the assertion of centralized and ultimately coercive power by the courts were mutually supporting and central elements of the American polity.

Late nineteenth-century laissez-faire constitutionalism, however innovative in scope and detail, was a recognizable development of the tradition's basic liberalism. The modes of legal argument of the period were, however increasingly more liberal than (common-law) traditional. By the end of the century, many judicial opinions were cast in a style of formalistic deductive reasoning reminiscent of Enlightenment rationalism.[300] The rise of formalism was associated with an institutional development of the greatest importance for the history of the constitutional tradition. From about 1880 on, law schools associated with universities achieved an ever-greater influence on the professional training of American lawyers, and especially of elite

299 In re Debs, 158 U.S. 564 (1895).

300 Sheer political expediency played a role at times, no doubt, in judicial use of formalistic reasoning. It obviously was more attractive to present the invalidation of a popular piece of legislation as a conclusion of deductive logic than as an exercise of practical judgment.

lawyers.[301] Led by the Harvard Law School, these new-style educational bodies created a new mode of legal instruction (the case method), a new genre of legal literature (the law review), a new subprofession of elite lawyers (the purely academic lawyer), and a new image of legal reasoning (as a scientific enterprise parallel in intellectual rigor and ambition to the recognized sciences). The professors and graduates of the new schools expected judicial opinions to meet their new standards of "scientific" accuracy; from their very inception, both the case method and the law review served largely as vehicles for professorial criticism of judicial shortcomings. The judiciary, in turn, proved receptive to (or at least sensitive to) academic criticism and over time was itself largely populated by products of the new schools. Judicial formalism as a rhetorical style seems to have been, in large measure, a means of achieving the objectivity and precision the "scientific" image of law demanded. The new law schools, by the early twentieth century, clearly had become institutions in the MacIntyrean sense.

The Supreme Court accepted the twin innovations of substantive due process and stylistic formalism more or less simultaneously. Formalism was a rhetorically powerful means of expressing the Court's determination to treat the Reconstruction-era amendments as discrete legal rules. Already in the 1883 *Civil Rights Cases* the Court employed formalistic distinctions between positive and negative state action in order to limit the effect of the amendments, and its subsequent refusal to interfere with Jim Crow or with the disfranchisement of black voters in the 1890s and 1900s was expressed in rigorously formalistic terms: for example, the Court upheld the 1890 Mississippi Constitution, which was adopted for the express purpose of eliminating black voting, on the ground that its words, read in a context-free manner, contained no racial reference.[302]

The Court at first approached substantive due process gingerly. The Court's initial rejection of the Radicals' social-justice understanding of the Reconstruction amendments (the *Slaughterhouse*

301 See Robert Stevens, *Law School* (Chapel Hill: Univ. of North Carolina Press, 1983), 73–84.

302 Williams v. Mississippi, 170 U.S. 213 (1898). Professor Wiecek writes of "the rationalizations, fictions, and formalism that marked the opinions of [the Court] in race-related cases" in this period. Wiecek, *Liberty*, 101.

Cases) was in a case criticizing legislation for interfering with economic liberty, not racial equality, and for a few years it appeared that the Court would limit the due process clause to purely procedural matters.[303] In the 1880s, however, the Court clearly accepted the legitimacy of substantive due process as a mode of constitutional argument,[304] and by the end of the decade the justices were ready to begin an active career of determining the proper line between liberty and legislation. "Between 1890 and 1934, the Supreme Court struck down some two hundred statutory and administrative regulations, mostly under the due process clause of the Fourteenth Amendment."[305]

As a development in the intellectual history of the constitutional tradition, economic substantive due process was no more bizarre or illegitimate than many earlier doctrines of unimpeachable validity. The doctrine required courts to exercise practical judgment in determining the morally proper bounds of governmental interference with the market's social and economic effects, but such overtly moral and political decision making was characteristic of constitutional adjudication almost from the beginning. The Marshall Court, for example, had indicated that the commerce clause (which on its face is solely a grant of power to Congress) put judicially enforceable limits on a state's ability to interfere with interstate commerce even in the absence of congressional legislation; the Taney Court put this hint into effect and ultimately held in *Cooley v. Board of Wardens* that state legislation affecting commerce was subject to a judicial determination of whether the legislation interfered with important national concerns.[306] The doctrine of *Cooley* expressly required the Court to engage in policy judgments about which areas of commerce must be under exclusive national control and about the degree of state intrusion permissible in areas of concurrent control. Such explicit exercises of practical judgment were, of course, familiar to lawyers trained in the classical common-law tradition.

303 See, e.g., Munn v. Illinois, 94 U.S. 113 (1877) (refusing to reexamine judicially a legislative determination of the proper balance between economic freedom and regulation in the public interest).

304 See, e.g., *Railroad Commission Cases*, 116 U.S. 307 (1886).

305 Paul Brest and Sanford Levinson, *Processes of Constitutional Decisionmaking*, 2d ed. (Boston: Little, Brown, 1983), 234.

306 Cooley v. Board of Wardens, 53 U.S. (12 How.) 299 (1851).

Despite its traditional antecedents, almost from its inception economic substantive due process was the object of severe criticism. In particular, critics pointed to the perceived lack of consistency in the doctrine's application.[307] While most of the justices in this period accepted the doctrine as a valid mode of constitutional argument, and accepted further the doctrine's theoretical underpinning in laissez-faire economics, many observers, especially among the new "scientific" lawyers of the academy, doubted that the Court's decisions were coherent. The "science" of law, as they understood it, required that legal decisions meet the demands of a formal, quasi-deductive logic, a requirement that the practical judgments of substantive due process could not satisfy even in theory. The sinuous path of the Supreme Court's decisions were, from this viewpoint, a sign of intellectual failure rather than the inevitable result of applying practical judgment to changing circumstances.

The Court's seeming inability to apply economic substantive due process consistently stemmed from two major sources. One was the presence of differing and sometimes starkly inconsistent views among the Court's members. Some justices offered general criticisms of the doctrine's laissez-faire underpinnings on occasion (e.g., John Marshall Harlan) or frequently (e.g., Oliver Wendell Holmes, Jr.). Other justices combined sympathy for the economics of the doctrine with a considerable sense of deference to the legislative process (e.g., Chief Justice William Howard Taft). Still others—most

307 The problem may be illustrated by the Court's dealings with state and federal legislation regulating employment relationships. The basic constitutional question was whether the challenged legislation bore a reasonable relation to a goal within the legislature's legitimate jurisdiction *and* did not interfere unreasonably with individual liberty and property. The Court's answers were complex, to say the least. In 1897 the Court announced in sweeping terms that the due process clauses protect freedom in negotiating and carrying out employment contracts against legislative interference. The following year, however, the Court upheld a statute imposing a maximum-hours limitation on mineworkers' contracts. The Court subsequently struck down a substantially identical law concerning bakery workers, and in later decisions alternately sustained and invalidated minimum-wage legislation statutes intended to prohibit certain types of employment relationship. The Court's employment decisions were never fully rationalized, and indeed at times the Court's opinions simply ignored existing precedent without even the pretense of explanation. "The cases that involved the rights of individuals and organized workers, like so many other matters of the time, divided into two inconsistent streams of precedent." Wiecek, *Liberty*, 125.

notably the "Four Horsemen" of the 1920s and early 1930s—applied substantive due process with rigor. The shifting patterns of voting that resulted were sufficient on their own to create decisional and doctrinal confusion.

The other major source of inconsistency was the sheer volume of state and (increasingly over time) federal regulatory legislation. The Court was physically unable to review more than a fraction of this mass of new law, and chance played a significant role in which cases the justices heard (and thus in the factual peculiarities and competency of lawyering in those cases). In any event, a rigorous, across the board application of the concept of freedom of contract in a market economy would have compelled the Court, in essence, to rule the modern business of government unconstitutional. Not even the most doctrinaire supporters of the doctrine on the Court wished to contemplate the wholesale uprooting of the bureaucratic state, and no doubt none of the justices thought that an attempt to do so would go unchallenged. But the admission that *some* governmental limitation of contractual freedom was legitimate necessarily meant that the Court's decisions would display a pattern of alternating acceptance and invalidation.

Lochner v. New York,[308] the case that subsequently gave a name to this era of constitutional discussion, was paradigmatic of economic substantive due process debate. *Lochner* involved a challenge to a state statute limiting employment of bakery workers to ten hours per day and sixty hours per week; the defendant Lochner was convicted of permitting or requiring his employees to work in excess of the weekly limit, but a bare majority of the Supreme Court reversed the conviction on substantive due process grounds.

Justice Rufus Peckham's opinion for the Court began by defining the Court's task in substantive due process cases as reaching a judgment that properly struck the balance between the "general right to make contract[s]" freely and the state's "power to prevent the individual from making certain kinds of contract . . . in the legitimate exercise of its police power." According to Peckham, therefore, the specfic legal question before the Court was whether the statute in *Lochner* was "fair, reasonable and appropriate . . . or . . . an unreasonable, unnecessary and arbitrary . . . interference with the right of

308 198 U.S. 45 (1905).

the individual." Peckham carefully took note of a seven-year-old case in which the Court upheld a maximum-hours regulation of mine-workers' contracts, and pointed out that the Court's decision had rested on "the kind of employment . . . and the character of the employes" involved in mining. Unlike miners, however, bakers were "in no sense wards of the State." Furthermore, unlike labor in a mine, "the trade of a baker . . . is not an unhealthy one to that degree which would authorize the legislature to interfere." Both conclusions obviously involved the exercise of practical judgment; Peckham could have pointed out that similar exercises of practical judgment lay at the heart of common-law reasoning by analogy and thus were well within the modes of inquiry sanctioned by the constitutional tradition.

Having concluded that the nature of bakery employment did not make the challenged statute a "reasonable [or] appropriate" health and safety measure, Peckham drew the conclusion that it was an impermissible intrusion into the freedom of Lochner and his employees to make contracts. Only then did he note that in the majority's opinion the statute was bad economics as well as bad law: "It seems to us that the real object and purpose were simply to regulate the hours of labor between the master and his employes," or in other words, to favor labor over capital.[309]

There were two dissenting opinions in *Lochner*. Justice Harlan attacked Peckham's opinion in the opinion's own terms. Harlan took note of the existence of empirical evidence that baking was an extremely dangerous occupation, and of the respectability "among civilized peoples" of the view that laborers' working hours should be limited in the interest of their health. Harlan made it clear that he was not thereby contradicting the liberal-individualistic premises of substantive due process: legislative concern for workers' health stemmed from the public interest in their "capacity to serve the State, and to provide for those dependent upon them."[310] Given the legitimacy of the legislative concerns, and the existence of evidence supporting the reasonability of its choice of means, Harlan rejected the majority's reasoning and its conclusion.

Harlan's dissent shared with Peckham's majority opinion a robust

309 Id. at 53–64.
310 Id. at 72.

confidence in the capacity of common-law reasoning to reach appropriate conclusions about the proper scope of constitutional liberty. Harlan's disagreement was with the cogency of Peckham's reasoning, not with his form of argument. Justice Holmes's dissent, in contrast, put forward a more radical critique. Holmes did not reject the legitimacy of giving judicially enforceable meaning to the word *liberty* in the due process clauses—to do so would have been to bring into question the whole structure of traditional constitutional argument—but he attacked economic substantive due process as a direct importation of a specific philosophical theory, a form of argument that the constitutional tradition had rejected early on. "The Fourteenth Amendment does not enact Mr. Herbert Spencer's Social Statics." The legitimate way to give substantive meaning to liberty, according to Holmes, was to respect the autonomy of the tradition and to develop reasonable extensions of the "fundamental principles [of liberty] as they have been understood by the traditions of our people and our law."[311]

Holmes's dissent was, in MacIntyrean terms, an accusation of external corruption; in Holmes's view, the majority had sacrificed the internal goods of legitimate argument and respect for the autonomy of constitutional inquiry out of a desire to advance their personal economic and political beliefs (beliefs, coincidentally, that Holmes himself basically shared). Holmes's primary historical importance, however, was even more fundamental: he both contributed to and was the patron saint of a theory of constitutional interpretation, initially conceived as a rejection of substantive due process, that has shaped the remainder of American constitutional history.

This theory, which I shall label the "Modern Theory" of constitutional interpretation, had its intellectual roots in several sources. One was the presence of an antiformalist strain in legal scholarship. Holmes himself was an early contributor; his *The Common Law* (1881) presented a thoroughly antiformalist history of common-law reasoning that was coeval with the emergence of legal formalism. The Harvard Law School, the nursery of formalism, played an increasingly antiformalist role under the leadership of Roscoe Pound (from 1916), who called for a "sociological" jurisprudence. Other important figures included New York Judge Benjamin Cardozo,

311 Id. at 75–76.

whose famous lectures on *The Nature of the Judicial Process* (1920) described judicial decision making as a form of practical reasoning aimed at reaching conscious policy choices; contracts scholars Samuel Williston of Harvard and Arthur Corbin of Yale; and the National Conference of Commissioners on Uniform State Laws, which from 1906 on promulgated proposed state laws that were "not designed to provide rules for decision" to be applied deductively, so much as "to provide access to the prevailing academic wisdom" on legal questions.[312]

Antiformalism by itself need not have posed a threat to substantive due process: the majority opinion in *Lochner* was not notably formalistic in style, and its underlying structure of practical judgment and reasoning by (dis)analogy was recognizably a form of the tradition's thoroughly nonformalistic common-law modes of argument. The importance of antiformalism for the history of the constitutional tradition lay in the growing importance of the notion of *democracy* in American thought. Beginning with late nineteenth-century political scientists such as Professor Woodrow Wilson of Princeton,[313] American intellectuals laid increasing stress on the democratic nature of the American Republic, meaning by this that political power was exercised (primarily? only?) by officials electorally responsible to the citizenry. Although the most thoroughgoing political analogue to this intellectual development, the Populist movement of the 1880s and early 1890s, ultimately collapsed, many of its themes were picked up by successful mainstream politicians (Professor Wilson, it should be remembered, eventually became President Wilson). Antiformalism, by insisting on the element of policy choice and practical judgment in judicial decision making, rendered constitutional law democratically suspect. Whereas judicial decisions involving the common law per se or statutory interpretation were subject to easy correction by the electorally responsible legislature, federal court constitutional adjudication resulted in the displacement of democratic decisions by unelected judges. Substantive due process was the primary target of democratic critics of the courts, but the implications of the democratic challenge were

312 Grant Gilmore, *The Ages of American Law* (New Haven: Yale Univ. Press, 1971), 71.

313 See, e.g., Wilson, *Congressional Government* (1885).

sweeping: all of constitutional law as traditionally understood seemed to rest on an antidemocratic method of decision making. Democracy, understood as a political system in which the only public moral rules are those sanctioned by the people through the aggregative method of majoritarian and representative legislation, seemed to leave no room for the exercise of practical judgment by unelected judges acting within a nonpositivist tradition of moral inquiry.

The Modern Theory of constitutional interpretation was crafted by opponents of substantive due process for the twin purposes of discrediting that doctrine while establishing the democratic legitimacy of some form of constitutional adjudication. The major themes of the Modern Theory were clearly articulated in its earliest formulation, James B. Thayer's article on "The Origin and Scope of the American Doctrine of Constitutional Law." Thayer was a faculty member at the Harvard Law School, the first scientific professor there to teach constitutional law (originally considered too "unscientific" to be a proper subject of study), and the editor of the first casebook on constitutional law, which served as a widely influential advertisement for Thayer's constitutional views.[314] Thayer originally delivered "The Origin and Scope" as a lecture at the World Exposition in Chicago in 1893; the accident of the lecture's original international provenance may have played a role in its concern to maintain the centrality of democracy in American law. The lecture was immediately published in the Harvard Law Review and subsequently as a separate pamphlet by a major legal publisher with great marketing success.[315] "The Origin and Scope" vigorously reasserted the constitutional tradition's claim to intellectual autonomy, but Thayer added a new element to the claim by insisting that constitutional discussion should be free of even the indirect influence of moral and political philosophy. Thayer went on to define the central issue in the tradition's problematic as the reconciliation of constitutional adjudication with the majoritarian and democratic presuppositions Thayer ascribed to the American political and legal systems. Thayer concluded that this reconciliation could only be accomplished by requiring judges to defer to legislative decisions except where there was no

314 Thayer, *Cases on Constitutional Law* (1895).
315 Kammen, *A Machine*, 178–79.

reasonable doubt that the legislature had violated a constitutional norm.

Thayer portrayed the view of constitutional interpretation outlined in "The Origin and Scope" as the original and traditional understanding of American constitutionalism, one that had been obscured in recent years by politically motivated and intellectually corrupt judges and treatise writers. In fact, however, while various pieces of Thayer's theory were borrowed from the tradition, the theory as a whole was a thoroughly modern innovation. Not even the early Jeffersonian critics of Marshall had argued that the primary intellectual issue in constitutional discussion was the reconciliation of constitutional conclusions with electoral accountability and majoritarianism. (Jefferson himself, for example, enthusiastically agreed with the idea of constitutional interpreters overruling "democratic" choices; he simply thought Marshall was a corrupt interpreter.) Although it was true that courts sometimes had asserted a commitment to uphold statutes in the absence of undeniable constitutional mistake, such a clear error rule was inconsistent with the Marshallian principle that it is "emphatically, the province and duty of the judicial department, to say what the law is" (*Marbury*).[316] Furthermore, the modes of common-law reasoning that the tradition had accepted and practiced were fundamentally inconsistent with Thayer's understanding of constitutional interpretation. For Thayer, constitutionalism was not a progressive inquiry into implications and applications of those moral, political, and legal principles embodied in the constitutional text, but a last-resort means of safeguarding static legal rules frozen into that text.[317] Thayer's views also implied a role for constitutional scholarship different from the traditional one; rather than exploring the past development and future extension of constitutional discussion, Thayer saw the primary task of the scholar and theorist as the identification and criticism of judicial usurpation of democratic choice.

Opponents of liberty of contract jurisprudence soon recognized in the constitutional theory of "The Origin and Scope" a powerful intellectual tool for criticizing substantive due process. By Thayer's

316 Snowiss, *Judicial Review*, 173–74.
317 7 Harv. L. Rev. 179 (1893).

logic, decisions such as *Lochner* were clearly illegitimate—the legislation at issue in *Lochner*, for example, could not easily be said to involve a "clear error," and the majority opinion had expressly noted the intellectual connections between its legal conclusions and laissez-faire political economics. Since Thayer had claimed for his theory both democratic and constitutional-traditional credentials, Thayerite critics of substantive due process could argue—and, no doubt, believe—that *Lochner* and its kindred were antidemocratic *and* anticonstitutional innovations. Such an argument obviously had great appeal to the practicing bar, with its instinctive conservatism, and to public at large, with its reverence for "Democracy."

Despite its claims to a historical pedigree, Modern Theory constitutionalism was in fact a proposal for radical reform in the constitutional tradition's practices and self-understanding. Constitutional theorizing, only now finding a consistent institutional basis in the new law schools, was to be transformed from the constructive exploration and extension of the tradition's present achievements to the essentially negative task of policing the courts' intrusions on democracy. Constitutional adjudication, the tradition's central practice, was rendered intrinsically problematic even as its central activity—the application of common-law modes of reasoning to the resolution of moral-political questions—was labeled "anti-democratic" and illegitimate. The Modern Theory was, in fact, not so much a democratic as a radically liberal argument; starting from the premise that the only legitimate public moral choices are those derived from representative government's aggregation of individual choices, Modern Theory left no space for tradition-dependent modes of making public moral decisions.

By the late twenties, the Modern Theory dominated academic opinion and legal instruction at the elite law schools and enjoyed in a popularized form wide support among practicing lawyers and the politically active public.[318] In large part, this was the product of the

318 I here relegate to a footnote an important factor in the legal history of the period: the rise of Legal Realism. The Legal Realists were a group of academic lawyers who began articulating in the 1920s a radically antiformalist account of American law. In its most extreme form, Legal Realism denied that legal reasoning played any significant role in judicial decision making whatsoever. Court decisions, instead, were determined by the judges' policy choices (explicit or not) or even by their subconscious psychological makeup. See Jerome Frank, *Law*

decline in intellectual popularity of the laissez-faire liberalism on which *Lochner* rested.[319] A second factor was the emergence of Justice Holmes as a professional and public hero. Holmes was an unlikely subject for democratic apotheosis: an aloof Boston aristocrat, Holmes had little sympathy for political reform or even for democracy as a moral ideal. However, Holmes was a master of the English language; as such he was increasingly well known to the bar (for his pithy opinions) while his occasional public addresses (usually patriotic—Holmes was a Civil War hero) attracted wider attention. His resistance to economic substantive due process enabled his admirers to (mis)describe him as the democrat among the justices; his adherence to free speech libertarianism after the First World War confirmed his reputation in the academy. In the twenties, Holmes had acquired a phalanx of admirers who lost no opportunity to stress to the bar and to the public that Holmes was the epitome of the truly American judge.[320] In particular, Holmes was lionized in the law schools; to law professors aware of and embarrassed by their marginality in the intellectual life of the university, Holmes seemed living proof that the study of law could be carried out on the highest level of intellectual sophistication. And the professors' enthusiasm for Holmes naturally affected the views of the increasingly large segment of the elite bar that had attended a university law school.

In MacIntyrean terms, Holmes had become the constitutional tradition's primary character, the second Great Judge. His admirers explained his dislike for *Lochner* as a noble adherence to the democratic premises of the Modern Theory. By coopting Holmes—or rather the image they had created of Holmes—the proponents of the Modern Theory had successfully captured one of the primary means

---

and the Modern Mind (New York: Brentano's, 1930). Realism owed much to earlier antiformalists such as Holmes and Cardozo, but went far beyond them in its radical dismissal of the forms of traditional common-law legal argument. See William Twining, *Karl Llewelyn and the Realist Movement* (Norman: Univ. of Oklahoma Press, 1973). While Legal Realism's impact on the subsequent course of American law was significant, it does not seem to me to have added much to the specifically constitutional discussion not already articulated by Thayer and others.

319 On the effect of this decline on the law of contract, see Grant Gilmore, *The Death of Contract* (New Haven: Yale Univ. Press, 1974).

320 See John Dewey's paean, "Justice Holmes and the Liberal Mind," 53 New Republic 210 (1928).

by which a tradition defines itself. In doing so they not only widened Modern Theory's popularity, but also substantively affected the general understanding of the constitutional tradition's past. The public-image-Holmes was, as John Marshall's successor as a Great Judge, an implicit repudiation of Marshall and of the common-law modes of moral inquiry Marshall symbolized. Explicit repudiation was not far behind.[321]

Modern Theory was not unchallenged in the 1920s and early 1930s. A majority of judges and a powerful segment of the elite bar and the business community remained committed to the legitimacy of economic substantive due process. The issue divided the constitutional institutions of court and law school, and produced increasingly shrill denunciations by both sides of their opponents' views. A MacIntyrean tradition in which a large body of discussants have concluded that the tradition's primary institutional locus has abandoned concern for the tradition's internal goods, and in which the defenders of that institution hold the same view of its critics, is a tradition in crisis. Unsurprisingly, therefore, constitutional discussion was increasingly riven by dogmatic defenses and criticisms of the Court. The Great Depression and President Franklin D. Roosevelt's New Deal provided the final impetus for a major intellectual and institutional confrontation.

The depression spurred government, both on the state and the federal levels, to a variety of innovative responses. Some of these responses transferred power from courts and private decision-makers to administrators employing "policy science" approaches to social problems. Many involved unprecedented public intervention into the market and into private property rights. Virtually all resulted in a great expansion in the size of government and the scope of its activities,[322] or, put in other terms, a radical contraction of the

321 Perhaps the most dramatic attack on the traditional evaluation of Marshall and of early constitutionalism generally was Vernon Parrington, *Main Currents in American History* (New York: Harcourt, Brace and World, 1927), vol. 2, 19–26. Holmes himself subtly contributed to the demotion of Marshall, see Holmes, "Chief Justice Marshall," in Holmes, *Collected Legal Papers* (New York: Harcourt, Brace and Howe, 1920), 266–71, although Holmes's own constitutional views were by no means the pure incarnation of Modern Theory commitments portrayed by his admirers.

322 See William Leuchtenburg, *Franklin D. Roosevelt and the New Deal* (New York: Harper and Row, 1963).

"private" sphere and a corresponding and dramatic increase in the power of the nation-state. The Court's initial constitutional response to these innovations was restrained: it upheld state regulation of prices and creditors' rights while sustaining congressional power to void private contractual provisions requiring payment in specie.[323] "But beginning in the spring of 1935, the Court invalidated federal and state economic regulation in a string of decisions."[324] By the time of Roosevelt's reelection in November 1936, an outside observer well might have concluded that a majority of the Court had created a "regulatory no man's land" shielded by constitutional adjudication from "all federal and state efforts to cope with the economic difficulties of the Depression."[325] For many critics internal to the tradition, the Court's decisions confirmed their fear of a radically antidemocratic institution illegitimately imposing its members' political preferences on the Republic.

With the great electoral victory of 1936 behind him, President Roosevelt proposed the famous "Court-packing plan," which would have given him enough new appointments to the Court to outvote the antidemocratic majority.[326] Whether Roosevelt's proposal, which the president unveiled in February 1937, influenced the Court's subsequent actions remains unclear, but in any event the Court permanently interred the plan within weeks by abruptly changing its course. On March 29, in *West Coast Hotel Co. v. Parrish*, the Court sustained a minimum wage law indistinguishable from one it had invalidated the previous year.[327] Two weeks later the Court upheld a comprehensive federal labor relations statute in *N.L.R.B. v. Jones & Laughlin Steel Corp.*[328] Subsequent decisions confirmed that the Court had abandoned any intent to interfere substantially with the New Deal or with parallel legislation in the states; after March 1937 the Court regularly sustained social and economic legislation against constitutional challenge. Roosevelt's extraordinary opportunity to choose new justices—he made eight appointments between 1937

323 See, e.g., Home Bldg. & Loan Assoc. v. Blaisdell, 290 U.S. 328 (1934).

324 Wiecek, *Liberty*, 136.

325 Id. at 137.

326 See William Leuchtenberg, "The Origins of Franklin D. Roosevelt's 'Court-Packing' Plan," 1966 Sup.Ct.Rev. 347.

327 300 U.S. 379 (1937).

328 301 U.S. 1 (1937).

and 1941—and his care in selecting nominees ensured that the "switch in time that saved nine" would be permanent.

THE CONSTITUTIONAL TRADITION IN THE MODERN ERA

The Supreme Court resolved the constitutional crisis of the 1930s by significantly redirecting the constitutional tradition. The Court's adoption of judicial deference to legislative choice in 1937 represented a major adjustment in the Court's institutional relationship to Congress, the state legislatures, and administrative agencies. The Court surrendered its leading role as the most important centralizing agent of national power—a role it had played since the Gilded Age of the late 1800s—to Congress, and accepted the consequent transformation of the moral and political bases for the assertion of centralizing power.[329] The Court's role with respect to state government and the greatly expanded federal bureaucracy became primarily that of guarding congressional prerogatives against intrusion from the states or corruption by the agencies.[330]

329 In the *Lochner* era, the assertion of the coercive power of the nation-state typically took the form of judicial interference with local "democratic" decisions, interference justified by the exercise of practical judgment about the moral/constitutional legitimacy of the decisions. After 1937 the courts acknowledged that assertions of national power typically would be actions mandated by Congress and justified on the positivist ground that Congress had mandated them.

330 After 1937 the courts abandoned their *Lochner*-style moral examinations of state legislative decisions, but the federal judiciary remained actively involved in policing state interference with congressional statutes (the preemption doctrine) and with the national common market (the "dormant" commerce clause). Judicial supervision of the agencies was recentered on compelling bureaucrats to act in accordance with congressional legislation (administrative law). Preemption and some administrative law was sheerly positivistic: the enforcement of the congressional will. Decisions under the dormant commerce clause, and some questions involving bureaucratic action, often took more traditional common-law forms, although here too an effort was made to bring judicial action into line with Modern Theory premises about democracy. See, e.g., Justice Harlan Fiske Stone's attempt to reconceptualize the dormant commerce clause as protecting the nation-state's democratic process in *South Carolina Highway Dept. v. Barnwell Bros.*, 303 U.S. 177 (1938).

The Court explained and justified the readjustment in its institutional relationships by a wholesale and increasingly enthusiastic adoption of the Modern Theory as constitutional orthodoxy. The Court now regularly insisted on the primacy of democratic decision making and treated judicial review as an extraordinary exception to the general conduct of judicial business.[331] Upholding a federal ban on the interstate shipment of "filled milk," the Court stated in 1938 that it would "presume the existence of facts supporting the legislative judgment" unless there were affirmative proof that "preclude[s] the assumption that [the statute] rests upon some rational basis."[332] Rejecting a 1941 due process challenge to a state limitation on the fees a business might set for its services, the Court squarely overruled a directly relevant precedent, and explained that it was "not concerned . . . with the wisdom, need or appropriateness" of legislation.[333] Some constitutionalists, most notably Justice Felix Frankfurter (appointed in 1939), took the Modern Theory to its logical (or extreme, depending on one's viewpoint) conclusion and "abandoned activism in favor of deference to legislatures in virtually all matters."[334]

A majority of the Court's members, however, were unwilling to abandon (in effect) the time-honored practice of constitutional adjudication altogether. These justices were driven by strong institutional imperatives.[335] This unwillingness was not mere nostalgia; the abolition of constitutional adjudication would have ended the Court's role as a bearer of the tradition. The Frankfurterian posture of ex-

331 One important side effect probably was an elevation in the stature of law schools as the institutional loci of constitutional theory understood as the means of ensuring judicial fidelity to democracy.

332 United States v. Carolene Products Co., 304 U.S. 144, 152 (1938). Compare the *Lochner* Court's willingness to reevaluate and reject the legislature's reading of the evidence—or the Marshall Court's willingness to exercise its own practical judgment as to which types of legislative regulation comport with the contracts clause's protection of vested rights.

333 Olson v. Nebraska, 313 U.S. 236, 246 (1941), overruling Ribnik v. McBride, 277 U.S. 350 (1928).

334 Smith, *Liberalism*, 81.

335 The federal judiciary, and the Supreme Court in particular, are institutions "structured in terms of power and status, and [which] distribute . . . power and status as rewards. Nor could they do otherwise if they are to sustain not only themselves, but also the practices of which they are the bearers." MacIntyre (1984), 194.

treme deference would have sharply reduced the Court's power and prestige, and as a corollary the prestige of the elite academic lawyers who made their livings by analyzing and criticizing the Court's constitutional decisions. The shared if implicit project of these justices and constitutional scholars became the search for modes of constitutional argument that could satisfy Modern Theory's requirements of philosophical neutrality and deference to all but clearly demonstrable legislative error, and thus avoid the reduction of constitutional discussion to the politically powerless status of academic philosophy.

Frankfurter's judicial deference was not only unappealing for institutional reasons; it was additionally an overreaction to the political impetus behind the triumph of Modern Theory. Most of the pre-1937 academic proponents of Modern Theory assumed that the theory was consistent with the practice of constitutional adjudication under Marshall, indeed that Modern Theory *was* Marshall's understanding of constitutionalism. While historical research rendered the latter assumption intellectually untenable by the late thirties,[336] neither the professoriate nor the Court wished to reject the Marshallian jurisprudence that seemed to be the foundation for Rooseveltian nationalism. Perhaps of even greater importance was the role of public opinion. Public reaction to the Court-packing plan showed that popular anger at the Court stemmed from the belief that its anti–New Deal decisions were antidemocratic and therefore anticonstitutional, *not* from a rejection of a countermajoritarian role for the Court in the protection of "constitutional rights."[337] Hidden amid the mass of substantive due process decisions of the *Lochner* era, indeed, were cases that appeared positively democratic in the 1940s. Constitutionalists turned to those cases in their search for a continued role for constitutional adjudication.

During World War II, governmental propaganda and American public opinion alike identified freedom of speech, press, and religion as among the chief moral and political values the Western Allies were defending against fascism. As it happened, the *Lochner* era Court, almost unintentionally, had laid the groundwork for a constitutional law protecting those freedoms. At the beginning of the twentieth century, the Court unanimously had agreed that the First Amend-

336 See, e.g., Haines, *Judicial Supremacy*.
337 Leuchtenberg, *New Deal*, 233–39.

ment's guarantees provided only limited protection against federal interference, and none at all against state regulation.[338] When Congress enacted and the Wilson administration enforced statutes punishing criticism of American participation in World War I, the Court upheld an initial round of convictions in opinions written by Holmes in the spring of 1919.[339] The decisions met a withering stream of academic criticism, and in the fall of 1919 Holmes wrote the first of a series of famous dissents[340] in which he and Justice Louis Brandeis argued that the national value of free speech required special judicial solicitude for speech and press freedom.[341]

Holmes's actual grounds for disagreement with the Court's majority often were narrow,[342] but his rhetoric provided a sweeping justification for the claim that freedom of speech was central to the constitutional tradition. "When men have realized that time has upset many fighting faiths, they may come to believe even more than they believe the very foundations of their own conduct that the ultimate good desired is better reached by free trade in ideas. . . . That at any rate is the theory of our Constitution."[343] Holmes rejected the contention that constitutional free speech was limited to the narrow view held by eighteenth-century Anglo-American law by invoking the progressive nature of constitutional discussion; the tradition, Holmes argued, had progressed beyond that original understanding of "freedom of speech."[344]

The relationship between Holmesian free speech jurisprudence and the Modern Theory of constitutional interpretation was uncer-

338 See, e.g., Patterson v. Colorado, 205 U.S. 454 (1908) (opinion of the Court by Holmes J).

339 See, e.g., Schenck v. United States, 249 U.S. 47 (1919).

340 Abrams v. United States, 250 U.S. 616 (1919).

341 On the debate over the origins of Holmes's First Amendment jurisprudence, see Sheldon M. Novick, "Justice Holmes and the Art of Biography," 33 William & Mary L.Rev. 1219, 1228–1231 (1992).

342 In *Abrams*, for example, Holmes argued that the pamphlets for which the defendant was being punished were so feeble that no rational person could believe them a threat to national security. Id. at 626, 628.

343 Id. at 630.

344 "I had conceived that the United States through many years had shown its repentance for the Sedition Act of 1798 [a federal statute upheld by the courts but allowed to expire by the Jeffersonian Republicans who believed it violated the first amendment]." Id. at 630.

tain at first. Holmes himself, of course, was not a true adherent of the Modern Theory, as his dissent in *Lochner* showed, and he portrayed his position as one justified primarily by the importance of free expression in the constitutional tradition. When he and Louis Brandeis persuaded their colleagues to agree in 1925 that the Constitution protected freedom of speech against state as well as federal interference, indeed, they did so as an interpretation of the word *liberty* in the Fourteenth Amendment—in other words as a form of (noneconomic) substantive due process.[345] However, most of the leading advocates of Modern Theory were, in addition, free speech "liberals" as well, and found it almost impossible not to applaud as Holmes and Brandeis succeeded in marshalling majorities to protect freedom of speech and press beginning in 1927.[346] By the time the Court abandoned economic substantive due process a decade later, there was a growing body of decisions sustaining free expression claims, and those cases survived the 1937 "switch in time" as a living (and indeed actively expanding) body of law.[347]

The *Lochner* era also produced a small body of decisions concerning racial justice that post-1937 constitutionalists did not wish to jettison. Once again, this was the consequence, in part, of external circumstance: American propaganda during the Second World War made much of the evils of Nazi racism, and in the postwar period national officials, including members of the Court, were conscious of the international embarrassment American racism caused the self-anointed defender of democracy.[348] The *Lochner* precedents were more a collection of individual rulings than a coherent body of antiracist law. The Court had never repudiated the formalist logic that had led it to overturn Radical Reconstruction legislation and uphold Jim

345 Gitlow v. New York, 268 U.S. 652, 666 (1925). The concession was in principle only; the Court in fact upheld the conviction despite the free speech claim.

346 See Fiske v. Kansas, 274 U.S. 380 (1927).

347 The Court's decision in *Pierce v. Society of Sisters*, 268 U.S. 510 (1925), striking down a statute forbidding parents to send their children to parochial school, was understood by the Court at that time as a straightforward substantive due process decision involving no First Amendment issues. (Holmes, indeed, dissented.) It was available, however, after 1937 for reinterpretation as a First Amendment decision that at least touched on religious freedom.

348 See Mary Dudziak, "Desegregation as a Cold War Imperative," 41 Stan. L. Rev. 61 (1988).

Crow, but over time it had slowly built up decisions implicitly pointing in a different direction. In 1911, for example, the Court threw out a Deep South law that turned farm labor contracts into virtual deeds of peonage, and in 1917 the justices struck down statutorily required residential segregation.[349] *Nixon v. Herndon* (1927) merely invalidated an unusually incautious and brazen attempt to eliminate black political power, a Texas statute explicitly restricting Democratic party primary elections to white voters, but its sequel, *Nixon v. Condon* (1932), involved a strikingly aggressive (and thoroughly nonformalistic) form of analysis: the Court refused to permit Texas to circumvent *Herndon* by delegating the power to determine who could vote in the Democratic party primary to the official party organization, a nominally private corporation that (of course) had immediately exercised the power to exclude blacks from participation.[350] The Court's spasmodic interventions in the area of criminal procedure also frequently involved, as a factual matter, the protection of black defendants against racially biased police or trial procedures.[351]

In the areas of freedom of expression and religion, racial justice, and fair criminal procedure, then, post-1937 justices and scholars generally wanted to continue the *Lochner* era's development of a progressive constitutional law. Their problem was reconciling continuing inquiry and adjudication in these areas with the tenets of the Modern Theory, since the questions involved seemed to involve the substitution of judicial for democratic judgment in a manner similar to that of *Lochner*. Since almost no one at the time, for example, claimed that government could *never* curtail or limit free speech, it

349 Bailey v. Alabama, 219 U.S. 219 (1911); Buchanan v. Worley, 245 U.S. 60 (1917). Both decisions, of course, were perfectly explicable in substantive due process terms: the statute overturned in *Bailey* imposed contract terms on black tenant farmers and their white employers, while the law at issue in *Buchanan* denied homeowners the right to contract to sell to whomever they wished.

350 *Herndon*, 273 U.S. 536 (1927); *Condon*, 286 U.S. 73 (1932).

351 See, e.g., Moore v. Dempsey, 261 U.S. 86 (1923); Powell v. Alabama, 287 U.S. 45 (1932). Not all constitutional criminal procedure cases of the period were race-related: the Court occasionally displayed an unwillingness to permit federal authorities to act in flagrantly unfair or oppressive ways. See, e.g., *Weeks v. United States*, 232 U.S. 383 (1914), holding that evidence seized by federal marshals in violation of the Fourth Amendment could not be used in a federal criminal prosecution.

was implausible that First Amendment decisions did not require the courts to exercise practical judgment in modes in tension with the Modern Theory.[352] (The criminal procedure cases sometimes posed different questions; in them, the Court often was dealing not with legislative decisions but with misconduct by individual executive or judicial officials.)

One theoretical solution to the problem was simply to employ economic substantive due process methodology to other ends. This was, essentially, Holmes's approach to the First Amendment issue: simply define the threatened interest as "fundamental" (in *Lochner*, economic liberty; in the First Amendment area, liberty of expression) and then insist on the legitimacy of a judicial remeasuring of the appropriateness of the balance the legislature had struck between the fundamental right and the public good. This retooling of *Lochner*-esque reasoning was, in fact, the Court's first answer to the problem. Within months of the "switch in time," the great anti-*Lochner* jurist Benjamin Cardozo (who was appointed to succeed Holmes on the Supreme Court) announced in *Palko v. Connecticut* that while the due process clause would no longer extend fundamental-rights status to freedom of contract, the Court would continue actively to protect "immunities [it deemed] implicit in the concept of ordered liberty." Cardozo gave as examples the First Amendment rights of speech, press, and religion, and the right of a criminal defendant to counsel.[353] *Palko* made it clear that the Supreme Court would continue to engage in traditional common-law reasoning in adjudicating claims based on some liberal autonomy rights, although not when the rights asserted were economic in character. In the 1940s, the justices sometimes described the rights entitled to continued judicial inquiry and defense as having a "preferred position,"[354] but the label stated a fact without explaining its justification. The obvious defect of the *Palko* approach was that by itself it was no less antidemocratic than

352 It was implausible to argue that there was "no state of facts either known or which could reasonably be assumed" (*Carolene Products Co.*, 304 U.S. at 154) to support a legislative judgment that, say, antiwar pamphleteering endangered the public safety more than a statute forbidding it infringed the appropriately defined rights of the individual. Similar arguments were easily available to criticize continued judicial development of the other areas as well.

353 Palko v. Connecticut, 302 U.S. 419, 324–25 (1937).

354 See, e.g., Murdock v. Pennsylvania, 319 U.S. 105 (1943).

Lochner and gave no greater assurance that the Court was not simply following its moral or political preferences in defiance of democratic authority: the *Lochner* justices, after all, had thought their decisions based on a reasoned inquiry into the "immunities implicit in the concept of ordered liberty."[355]

Supporters of "preferred position" jurisprudence were unable to distinguish it convincingly from *Lochner*, leaving it presumptively illegitimate under the Modern Theory. On the Court, Frankfurter continually criticized it as intellectually vacuous,[356] a sheerly negative critique that ultimately eliminated the rhetoric but not the theoretical problem since the other justices were not willing to accept Frankfurter's posture of extreme deference. A more positive approach was developed by Justice Hugo Black, who joined the Court in 1937. Within a decade, Black had settled upon a reinvigorated focus on the constitutional text as the proper alternative to what he sometimes scorned as the "natural law/due process" jurisprudence of *Lochner*.[357] According to Black, the Court could satisfy the democratic dictates of Modern Theory by deferring to the legislature except where a statute infringed one of the rights specifically defined in the first eight amendments of the Constitution. Because Black believed that the framers of the Fourteenth Amendment had intended that text to "incorporate" the first eight amendments, his approach allowed judges to continue to protect freedom of speech, the right to counsel, and so on against state as well as federal interference.[358] Judges were entitled to follow their own judgment in

355 As Professor Smith has pointed out, *Palko* "fundamentally perpetuated the *Lochner* higher law approach." Smith, *Liberalism*, 81. The "preferred position" jurists of the next decade, he writes, simply asserted the fundamental nature of First Amendment and criminal procedure rights "without much discussion." Id. at 82.

356 Frankfurter, somewhat inconsistently, approved of Cardozo's terminology of "implicit in the concept of ordered liberty," probably because it recalled language used by his idol Holmes. See, e.g., Rochin v. California, 342 U.S. 165 (1952). Frankfurter rendered this theoretical inconsistency harmless by failing to find very many "immunities" that actually were implicit in "ordered liberty."

357 See Adamson v. California, 332 U.S. 46, 74 (1947) (Black J dissenting).

358 In 1948 four justices including Black urged the adoption of Black's "incorporation" thesis about the relationship of the Bill of Rights to the Fourteenth Amendment, but he never secured the necessary fifth vote. Id. Indeed, even the 1948 vote was illusory: two of Black's fellow-dissenters in *Adamson* wrote separately to indicate that they would not only enforce all rights enumer-

applying textually defined rights because those rights were themselves the product of a democratic adoption (or ratification) process. Black denied that his textualism gave judges excessive latitude in judgment by insisting that the Court not extend textual rights beyond the texts' original meaning, interpreted broadly but also formalistically.[359]

Black's fundamental failure, however, did not lie in inadequate politicking among his colleagues: his textualism was as vulnerable to Modern Theory criticism as *Lochner* or *Palko*, albeit in a somewhat more subtle manner. Adherence to the Modern Theory did not require the adherent to deny the possibility of reasoned judgments about whether a statute violates the Constitution; the burden of the Modern Theory was merely that where reasonable people could differ over the question, judges should defer on democratic principle to the legislature. Black argued, correctly, that reasonable people could disagree over whether the legislature had infringed economic liberty "inappropriately" or "unreasonably," and concluded that *Lochner* was therefore wrong. He was never able to satisfy most other constitutionalists that exactly the same argument did not apply to his interpretations of the text of the Bill of Rights. Critics such as Frankfurter consistently demanded an explanation of why Black should not defer to legislative judgments about the compatibility of

---

ated in the Bill of Rights through the Fourteenth Amendment, but also whatever other "immunities" they found implicit in "ordered liberty." Id. at 133 (Murphy J dissenting). Since the whole point of Black's textualism was to avoid the judicial freedom licensed by "ordered liberty" rhetoric, this position made no sense at all except as an assertion of judicial aggressiveness.

359 What I mean by this last statement can best be shown by illustration: Black viewed the (textually enumerated) right of freedoms of speech and press broadly in the sense that he extended them to everything that seemed to him to be "speech" or an exercise of "the press," whether it was a Communist Party discussion or a piece of pornography. See, e.g., Dennis v. United States, 341 U.S. 494, 579 (1951) (Black J dissenting from affirmance of conviction of Communist party members); Ginzburg v. United States, 383 U.S. 463, 476 (1966) (Black J dissenting from affirmance of conviction of pornographer). On the other hand, Black's definition of "speech" and "the press" was strikingly formalistic: he consistently refused to extend First Amendment protection to most symbolic behavior no matter how analogous to the literal speaking or printing of words. See, e.g., Street v. New York, 394 U.S. 576, 609 (1969) (Black J dissenting from First Amendment decision protecting flag-burning as expression).

their enactments with the Constitution's language.[360] Black's response—that courts should enforce the text up to the limits of its meaning and not beyond—depended on the plausibility of his belief in clear textual meanings, and even his admirers sometimes found it difficult to define the boundaries of the text's plain meaning except as whatever Justice Black said they were.[361] An additional problem with Black's view was that it denied the legitimacy of common-law arguments extending the scope of a textual provision by analogy, with disturbing results: delegitimation of much settled constitutional principle and arbitrariness in results.[362]

The most intellectually fruitful attempt to reconcile the repudiation of *Lochner* with continued judicial activism in some areas attracted little attention at first; indeed, its creator, Justice Harlan F. Stone, initially proposed it in a footnote to a 1938 opinion.[363] In its text, the *Carolene Products* opinion rejected a due process challenge to a piece of federal social legislation by invoking a strong version of Modern Theory judicial deference; the famous footnote four ultimately provided the theoretical agenda for justifying nondeferential adjudication for the next several decades.[364] The "activist"[365] jurisprudence of the Warren Court was, often explicitly, an attempt to work out the practical implications of footnote four; the contempo-

360 See Gerald T. Dunne, *Hugo Black and the Judicial Revolution* (New York: Simon and Schuster, 1977), 250–73, 354–72.

361 See G. Edward White, *The American Judicial Tradition*, 2d ed. (Oxford: Oxford Univ. Press, 1988), 331–34.

362 Black, for example, believed that a police-compelled stomach pump was a "search" within the meaning of the Fourth Amendment, but denied the relevance of the amendment to a wiretap of a telephone conversation that did not require a physical intrusion. Compare Rochin v. California, 342 U.S. 165 (1952) with Katz v. United States, 389 U.S. 347 (1967).

363 *Carolene Products Co.*, 304 U.S. at 152 n. 4.

364 "Since the constitutional revolution of 1937, American public law has been dominated by a paradigm that first appeared in a 1938 case of no importance, United States v. Carolene Products Co. . . . *Carolene Products*' footnote 4 contained concepts that have dominated constitutional development for the past half century." Wiecek, *Liberty*, 156.

365 The term *judicial activism* is tainted, perhaps fatally, with critical overtones. In this book, nonetheless, I use it solely in its literal sense: in my usage an activist Court simply means a Court that engages in a great deal of constitutional adjudication resulting in a considerable body of decisions invalidating decisions by elected officials.

rary crisis in constitutionalism flows directly from the perception that it is impossible to explain important parts of contemporary constitutional law—most centrally, *Roe v. Wade*—within the framework Stone provided.

Footnote four states:

> There may be narrower scope for operation of the presumption of constitutionality when legislation appears on its face to be within a specific prohibition of the Constitution, such as those of the first ten amendments, which are deemed equally specific when held to be embraced within the Fourteenth. See Stromberg v. California; Lovell v. Griffin.
>
> It is unnecessary to consider now whether legislation which restricts those political processes which can ordinarily be expected to bring about repeal of undesirable legislation, is to be subjected to more exacting judicial scrutiny under the general prohibitions of the Fourteenth Amendment than are most other types of legislation. On restrictions upon the right to vote, see Nixon v. Herndon; Nixon v. Condon; on restraints upon the dissemination of information, see Near v. Minnesota ex rel. Olson; Grosjean v. American Press Co.; Lovell v. Griffin, supra; on interferences with political organizations, see Stromberg v. California, supra; Fiske v. Kansas; Whitney v. California; Herndon v. Lowry; and see Holmes, J., in Gitlow v. New York; as to prohibition of peaceable assembly, see De Jonge v. Oregon.
>
> Nor need we enquire whether similar considerations enter into the review of statutes directed at particular religious, Pierce v. Society of Sisters, or national, Meyer v. Nebraska, or racial minorities, Nixon v. Herndon, supra; Nixon v. Condon, supra; whether prejudice against discrete and insular minorities may be a special condition, which tends seriously to curtail the operation of those political processes ordinarily to be relied upon to protect minorities, and which may call for a correspondingly more searching judicial inquiry. Compare McCulloch v. Maryland; South Carolina v. Barnwell Bros, and cases cited.[366]

The intellectual heart of the footnote consists of its second and third paragraphs. Both paragraphs proceed from the Modern Theory premise actually stated in the text of the *Carolene Products* opinion: the American political/legal system is democratic, and the results of democratic deliberation produced by electorally responsible legisla-

366 304 U.S. at 152 n.4 (citations omitted).

tors are entitled to a presumption that they accord with the popular will, and thus with the constitutional framework which exists to serve that will. But paragraphs two and three did not interpret the Modern Theory as being a kind of "democratic relativism" whereby whatever a majority decides is right by definition,[367] nor did they assert that American constitutionalism's only fundamental value is a commitment to the forms of majoritarian decision making. Instead, Stone intended to sketch out two types of situations in which it is unreasonable to assume that the political process has safeguarded substantive constitutional commitments.

The first group of situations, paragraph two, in which Stone rejected deference involves legislative interference with the democratic process itself. Stone gave as examples restrictions on voting rights and on the freedom of the press. Such restrictions, he suggested, clearly interfere with the democratic process by making it more difficult "to bring about the repeal of undesirable legislation." The underlying premise was that part of what renders democracy an attractive moral and political ideal is its self-correcting nature: an informed and enfranchised citizenry can put pressure on wayward politicians or vote them out of office. Legislation that makes it more difficult to challenge those in power thus does not share (or share fully) in the moral foundation of democracy even if enacted by an elected legislature.

Paragraph three outlined a second set of situations in which democracy might go awry, those in which "prejudice against discrete and insular minorities . . . tends seriously to curtail the operation of those political processes ordinarily to be relied upon to protect minorities." Stone gave as examples legislation directed at or disadvantaging religious, national, and racial minorities. The underlying premise again had to do with the moral foundation of democracy: democratic government is responsible and responsive to all members of the society. Stone assumed that the nature of democratic politics usually makes it impossible for those in power to harm particular groups of citizens too seriously or for too long a time. It is

367 I have borrowed Rogers Smith's useful term, although not his interpretation of footnote four. See Smith, *Liberalism*, 81. The present chief justice expressed a true democratic relativism in an article written while he was an associate justice. See William Rehnquist, "The Notion of a Living Constitution," 54 Tex. L. Rev. 693 (1976).

difficult to craft legislation that isolates and harms those the politicians might wish to harm without affecting the politicians' own supporters; in addition, in a complex and heterogeneous society such as the United States political alliances ordinarily will be fluid and shifting, making today's enemies tomorrow's allies. For these reasons, it is possible to assume that an elected legislature will be responsive to all of its constituents, at least over time. Social prejudice against a minority defined by some permanent characteristic such as race, however, can be sufficiently virulent that nonminority citizens may be unwilling (often or ever) to make alliances with them, while the nature of the characteristic renders it possible to design legislation harmful to them that does not disadvantage the majority. Such legislation, again, does not fully share the moral characteristics that make democracy admirable.

Because legislation falling within the situations envisaged in paragraphs two and three is not enacted under the conditions that render democracy an attractive political system, Stone did not think democracy could serve as the ground for judicial deference to the legislature. Instead, such legislation should be subject to a "more exacting" or "more searching" judicial examinination of its reasonability and compatibility with constitutional principles. Paragraphs two and three thus supplied a rationale for nondeferential constitutional adjudication in precisely those areas of *Lochner*-era precedent that most of the justices wished to preserve and extend—First Amendment freedoms, racial justice, and (because of the factual links to racism) criminal procedure.[368]

Some of footnote four's subsequent admirers have interpreted Stone's constitutionalism as concerned only with the "proper" functioning of the political process, but the text need not be read in this manner. Footnote four can as easily be seen as a statement of the moral and political commitments that Modern Theory ascribed to American democracy that attempts to connect them to the additional moral and political commitments embedded in the constitutional

368 As Smith notes, paragraphs two and three authorized "heightened protection" of "criminal rights . . . as well, since they were frequently claimed by blacks and other minority litigants." Smith, *Liberalism*, 81. The universalizing principle of Anglo-American law ordinarily would require that criminal procedure rights accorded to a black defendant (because of his or her minority status) be applied to white defendants as well.

tradition. This latter interpretation of the text finds an interesting echo in the footnote's case citations. In paragraph two the footnote cites several cases that clearly rested on a substantive rather than a process basis. The rationale of *Herndon* and *Condon*, the two "white primary" cases, for example, was not solely that black participation in Democratic party primaries would bring about pressure to change "undesirable legislation" such as Jim Crow; the cases clearly embodied the conclusion that American constitutionalism was substantively committed to ensuring the active political participation of all those nominally entitled to vote. The footnote also cites *Whitney v. California*,[369] which was known chiefly for Justice Brandeis's concurrence. In that opinion, Brandeis explicated freedom of speech as instrumental to "the final end of the State [which is] to make men free to develop their faculties": "the function of [free] speech [is] to free men from the bondage of irrational fears."[370] Stone's citation of *Whitney* was an implicit recognition of Brandeis's liberal individualism as one of the tradition's substantive commitments.[371] More fundamentally, of course, the vision of democracy that underlay and made sense of paragraphs two and three was itself a substantive moral argument about when theoretically "democratic" processes are and are not worthy of respect.

On its surface, paragraph one offered a different and even inconsistent rationale for limiting Modern Theory deference.[372] The suggestion of a "narrower scope" for the usual "presumption of constitutionality when legislation appears on its face to be within a specific prohibition of the Constitution" did not in itself answer any of the criticisms of textualism that Black would later encounter. Paragraph one, nevertheless, can be read as an integral and intellectually con-

369 274 U.S. 357 (1927).

370 Id. at 375.

371 Paragraph three also contained case citations difficult to explain on a pure-process interpretation of Stone's meaning. He cited Marshall's great opinion in *M'Culloch*, for example, a case in which no "discrete and insular" minority was even remotely involved. Stone's point presumably was that the legislation at issue in *M'Culloch* (a state statute taxing the national bank) had been enacted by a legislature free politically to ignore the constitutional commitments to national unity and to equality of financial burdens among the states.

372 Indeed, paragraph one was added to the original draft of the footnote at the request of Chief Justice Charles Evans Hughes. See Louis Lusky, "Footnote Redux: A Carolene Products Reminiscence," 82 Colo. L. Rev. 1093 (1982).

sistent part of the Modern Theory. Again, the case citations serve as a shorthand means of expressing part of the argument. Paragraph one cites only two cases as examples of legislation that "on its face" was "within a specific prohibition of the Constitution." Both cases were free speech cases, and on that basis were also cited in paragraph two. What makes their placement in paragraph one interesting is the fact that neither involved legislation that plausibly could be regarded as a literal transgression of the First Amendment's *text*:[373] *Stromberg v. California*[374] struck down a prohibition on the entirely silent display of a red flag, while *Lovell v. Griffith*[375] involved no direct limitation of expression at all, but only a licensing scheme. In contrast, *Near v. Minnesota*,[376] which footnote four cites in paragraph two, invalidated a statute that was arguably a literal "abridg[ment of] the freedom . . . of the press." By citing *Stromberg* and *Lovell*, but not *Near*, in paragraph one, the footnote implicitly rejects the suggestion that the paragraph assumed or depended upon a "plain meaning" view of language. The enumerated "prohibitions" of the Constitution were signposts of the substantive moral-political commitments of American constitutionalism, commitments that were parts of the moral foundation that made *American* democracy politically attractive. Legislation infringing one of those commitments to that extent does not share the characteristics that make *American* democracy morally admirable, and judges therefore need not presume its constitutionality out of respect for (*American*) democracy. Paragraph one, in other words, can be read as footnote four's explicit acknowledgment that the footnote proposes a theory of *American* democratic constitutionalism rather than of constitutionalism or democracy in the abstract.[377]

373 Since both cases involved state and not congressional restrictions on expressive freedom, in a sense neither was *literally* an intrusion on the first amendment ("Congress shall make no law, etc."), but as Stone indicated in the footnote, he viewed the Fourteenth Amendment's free speech component as a straightforward application of the First Amendment's prohibitions to state authority.

374 283 U.S. 359 (1931).

375 303 U.S. 444 (1938).

376 283 U.S. 697 (1931).

377 Footnote four's importance as a canonical text of Modern Theory constitutionalism greatly overshadows in importance whatever specific ideas Justice

Over the sixteen years following *Carolene Products*, the lion's share of theoretical attention was given to the loud and at times heated debate between Frankfurter and the admirers of extreme deference and "ordered liberty" jurisprudence, on the one hand, and Black and his textualist disciples, on the other. Constitutional adjudication, however, progressed for the most part along the lines laid out in footnote four.[378] The Court almost invariably upheld federal and state social and economic legislation but at the same time continued the process of developing the implications of the constitutional commitments to expressive and religious freedom. Most importantly and impressively, the NAACP and other civil rights groups repeatedly pushed the justices and other national officials to conclude that this racial exclusion or that racial segregation was inconsistent with American constitutionalism.[379] The legal-political strategy of the black civil rights leadership since the 1930s had been one of the piecemeal dismantling of Jim Crow and other forms of legalized racism through the creation and case-by-case expansion of specific legal rules. By the early 1950s, the black strategists believed the time had arrived for a frontal assault on the emotional bastion of legal racism, segregated public schools in the South.[380] This "high-risk gamble"[381] paid off: in *Brown v. Board of Education* (1954),[382] a

Stone had in mind when he included it in his opinion. My interpretation treats the footnote as an occasion for a synthetic restatement of Modern Theory thinking. See also J. M. Balkin's brilliant article, The Footnote, 83 Northwestern L. Rev. 275 (1989).

378 Stone's personal contribution was minor; appointed chief justice in 1941, the burdens of that responsibility and the intervention of the Second World War occupied most of his energy until his untimely death in 1946.

379 The period, of course, did not move consistently in one political direction only. It witnessed the Court's approval of the explicitly race-based relocation of Japanese-Americans (*Korematsu v. United States*, 323 U.S. 214 [1944]) and its timid retreat from a vigorous defense of political and expressive freedom during the McCarthy era (see, e.g., *Dennis*, 341 U.S. 494 [1951]). Both incidents displayed the tradition's vulnerability to the external corruption of its overshadowing institutional focus, the Supreme Court, by the external goods of political expediency and national self-assertion.

380 See Mark Tushnet, *Segregated Schools and Legal Strategy: The NAACP's Campaign Against Segregated Education, 1925–1950* (Chapel Hill: Univ. of North Carolina Press, 1987).

381 Wiecek, *Liberty*, 158.

382 347 U.S. 483 (1954).

unanimous Supreme Court held de jure grade school segregation unconstitutional.

The legal, political, and social consequences of *Brown* make up much of the subsequent history of the United States. Most of that story, including especially the long and unhappy tale of white resistance, will be silently passed over. In the context of this book, our interest is in *Brown*'s effects on the history of constitutionalism as a tradition of rational discussion, although of course those effects cannot be understood fully without some awareness of their external context. In particular, it became clear almost at once that discussion of *Brown*'s meaning and intellectual significance was inextricably tied up with the institutional concerns of judges and other individuals dealing with the legal effect of the decision.[383]

Brown's greatest long-term intellectual impact arose from the difficulty constitutionalists had identifying the constitutional principles on which it rested. In one sense, the principle of *Brown* was straightforward and widely accepted: outside the white South the decision was generally regarded as morally correct from the beginning. The problem, of course, was that the constitutional tradition's long-standing insistence on the autonomy of constitutional discourse made direct reliance on the case's "moral goodness" unacceptable to most constitutionalists. Chief Justice Earl Warren's opinion for the Court did not ease the problem. The opinion initially hinted that the original meaning of the Fourteenth Amendment was significant to the Court's decision, but then described the historical evidence as inconclusive; Warren closed his historical discussion with what amounted to a dismissal of the relevance of history.[384] Warren then discussed the importance of public education to "our democratic society," but this in itself did not explain why equally funded and maintained but segregated schools would not satisfy the Fourteenth

383 See, for example, *Brown v. Board of Education* (known as *Brown II*), 349 U.S. 294 (1955), which ordered desegregation not immediately but "with all deliberate speed." *Brown II* and later decisions concerning remedies raised a host of intellectual questions about the relationship of courts to other governmental entities and the intelligibility of a scheme of constitutional rights that included both the right of blacks to desegregated education and the right of whites to some degree of free choice.

384 "[I]n approaching this problem, we cannot turn the clock to 1868 when the Amendment was adopted or even to 1894 when Plessy v. Ferguson [the decision upholding legal segregation] was written." 347 U.S. at 492.

Amendment's demand for "equal protection."[385] Warren's answer appeared to be that school segregation inflicted psychological harm on black children, an assertion he supported with a footnote reference to a variety of social-science studies.[386] Critics of *Brown*, many of them supporters of desegregation, challenged the use of contestable empirical data to resolve a great constitutional issue.

The weaknesses many observers perceived in the *Brown* opinion were to a certain degree the result of Warren's deliberate attempt to announce the end of segregated schools with as little melodrama as possible.[387] On the opinion's face, however, one thing was clear: *Brown* was a case about segregation in public schools, and the Court's reasoning, however weak or unclear, concerned the significance of segregation in that specific setting. Warren carefully avoided any general discussion of Jim Crow laws, or a declaration that *Plessy* (the original "separate but equal" decision) was overruled. The Court's summation of its argument was carefully limited: "We conclude that in the field of public education the doctrine of 'separate but equal' has no place."[388] Nonetheless, after *Brown* the Court unanimously invalidated *all* instances of de jure segregation, of whatever sort, brought before it, and did so without further reasoning or explanation beyond a citation to *Brown*.[389] The Court, obviously, intended to treat *Brown* as having overruled *Plessy*, but it had given no justification for doing so. *Brown*, then, appeared to stand for a conclusion that its reasoning did not even purport to reach.

The Court's failure to explain its expansion of *Brown* into a total invalidation of segregation came at a time when the American legal profession had absorbed the lessons of antiformalism and Legal Realism and reached a broad consensus that although legal decision

385 Id. at 493. In 1950 no state with segregated schools in fact supported black education at the same funding level as white schools. In response to the legal threat posed by the several lawsuits that ultimately became *Brown v. Board of Education*, several Southern states were approaching equality of funding by 1954. See Richard Kluger, *Simple Justice* (New York: Knopf, 1975), 673–76, discussing the efforts of the white South Carolina government to equalize spending in response to the *Brown* litigation.

386 347 U.S. at 494 n. 11.

387 See Brest and Levinson, *Processes*, 431–32.

388 347 U.S. at 495.

389 See, e.g., Holmes v. City of Atlanta, 350 U.S. 879 (1955) (desegregating municipal golf courses).

making is not deductive ("scientific" in the late nineteenth-century sense), it is—or ought to be—reasoned. Former Realists like Karl Llewelyn who in the thirties were radical sceptics about the influence of legal argument on judges' decisions were by the sixties devout believers in the autonomy and rationality of legal reasoning.[390] Most academic lawyers were in agreement on the criteria identifying legitimate legal decisions; a court's exercise of its legal jurisdiction was legitimate only if it could and did offer a reasoned and rationally persuasive justification for the decision, employing the agreed-upon modes of legal argument. The most influential teaching book of the era, *The Legal Process* by Henry Hart and Albert Sacks, was one long indoctrination in this viewpoint; although never officially published, the book shaped academic views, and derivatively those of the bench and bar, for a generation. Hart and Sacks portrayed the heart of Anglo-American law as the common-law process of resolving novel legal questions by the rational reconciliation and extension of the relevant authorities, legislative, judicial, and scholarly. From the standpoint of "legal process" thought, the Court's apparent failure in *Brown* to undertake its duty of reasoned explanation was at best a dereliction of duty and, perhaps, an implicit confession that *Brown* could not be justified in legal terms. Despite *Brown*'s moral attractiveness, as they pondered the Court's behavior, some of the most distinguished constitutionalists of the period came to believe that the Court had revived the old antidemocratic error of *Lochner*—the substitution by judicial fiat of judges' political preferences for the decisions of democratic legislatures.[391]

The immediate problem of justifying *Brown* as a blanket invalidation of segregation was solved by the early 1960s, with the articulation by scholars of a satisfactory legal rationale: the actual and unmistakable purpose of de jure segregation had been to relegate black Americans to second-class citizenship, a purpose that even the *Plessy* Court had conceded was unconstitutional.[392] Perhaps in part because the intellectual problem with its activism in *Brown* seemed resolved,

390 See, for example, Llewelyn's paean to legal reasoning, *The Common Law Tradition: Deciding Appeals* (Boston: Little, Brown, 1960).

391 See, e.g., Herbert Wechsler, "Toward Neutral Principles of Constitutional Law," 73 Harv. L. Rev. 1 (1959).

392 See, e.g., Charles Black, "The Lawfulness of the Segregation Decisions," 69 Yale L.J. 421 (1960).

the Warren Court embarked, beginning around 1961, on a remarkable campaign of aggressive constitutional adjudication, reminiscent of the *Lochner* era in the Court's willingness to overrule democratic choices in the name of the Constitution. Without accepting Justice Black's argument that the Fourteenth Amendment directly applied all of the provisions of the first eight amendments to the states, the Court achieved much the same result by a case-by-case process of holding individual Bill of Rights requirements "incorporated" into the meaning of the due process clause.[393] Since the Court was simultaneously working a significant expansion-by-analogy of the meaning of most Bill of Rights provisions,[394] the result was a vast expansion in the sphere of judicial institutional control over legislative and executive action.

The Warren Court's constitutional activism raised questions of legitimacy within the terms of post-1937 Modern Theory constitutionalism. Most if not all of the Court's most innovative decisions, to be sure, arguably fell within one of the situations permitting nondeferential review set forth in paragraphs two and three of Justice Stone's footnote four; the Court's equal protection jurisprudence, in particular, was a sustained effort to work out the rational implications of the footnote. Much of the elite bar and most academic lawyers, furthermore, believed the Court's decisions, as a whole, were morally desirable and faithful in a deep sense to the democratic ideals that Modern Theory ascribed to the constitutional tradition. The justices, furthermore, apparently had learned a lesson from the legal-process critique of *Brown*; most of the major 1960s decisions were announced by opinions that employed traditional common-law modes of argument. On the other hand, the Court's decisions were undeniably a significant (and escalating) expansion of the institutional power of the unelected federal judiciary, and thus a constriction of the scope of majoritarian decision making that (at least in scope) was difficult to reconcile with the Modern Theory. Critics of the Court charged that it was involved in the imposition of the justices' own political views, without legal justification and in de-

393 See, e.g., Duncan v. Louisiana, 391 U.S. 145 (1968).

394 See, e.g., Gideon v. Wainwright, 372 U.S. 335 (1963) (the constitutional right to assistance of counsel requires the state to provide indigent felony defendants with publicly remunerated defense counsel).

fiance of the democratic process. Perhaps as fundamental to many critics was the very feature of the Warren Court's jurisprudence that its admirers found most compelling: regardless of the presence or persuasiveness of the legal reasoning the Court offered to support its decisions, the motive force behind its activism often seemed moral and political. The Court had become, in fact, the most visible and most powerful agent of social reform in the Republic. Even if one approved of the directions the Court was driving society, for constitutionalists reared to regard the detached, Olympian Holmes as the Great Judge, the moral fervor of the Warren Court could be disturbing. Indeed, the resulting debate could be characterized with only modest exaggeration as a discussion over whether Chief Justice Warren was the present exemplification of the tradition's Great Judge or its antithesis.[395]

The intellectual agenda for this debate was defined by Professor Alexander Bickel of the Yale Law School in his book *The Least Dangerous Branch*, published in 1962. Bickel was a self-conscious traditionalist who thought *Brown* and its progeny were both innovative and an admirable development in the American constitutional tradition. At the same time he accepted the democratic premises of the Modern Theory. The "root difficulty" in constitutional adjudication for Bickel thus was the fact that it is "a counter-majoritarian form in our system."[396] As such, Bickel thought that constitutional adjudication could be legitimate only if it served a function that was necessary to a democratic society, that no other institution could fill adequately, and that was "peculiarly suited to the competences of the

395 Warren was not the intellectual leader of the Court that bore his name. Although the fact was not generally recognized at the time, it has since become clear that Justice William Brennan provided much of the intellectual energy and the intra-Court political skill that gave the Warren Court its coherence. See Owen Fiss, "A Life Lived Twice," 100 Yale L.J. 1117 (1991). Nevertheless, it was Warren's obvious and deeply held vision of the Court as a moral force, not Brennan's skillful craftsmanship, that came to symbolize the Court's activism and the questions it raises for the constitutional tradition. Warren was famous for his habit in constitutional cases of interrupting technical legal argument with the questions "But is it fair? Is it just?" Much of constitutional theory since the sixties has been an attempt to decide whether this habit showed Warren to be the embodiment of the tradition's meaning or of its corruption.

396 Bickel, *The Least Dangerous Branch* (New Haven: Yale Univ. Press, 1962), 16.

courts."[397] Bickel believed that he had found such a function in the need to combine principle with expediency. "No good society can be unprincipled; and no viable society can be principle-ridden."[398] While elected officials necessarily are responsive to the demands of expediency, Bickel did not think them well-suited institutionally or (often) personally to addressing questions of principle. Judges, in contrast, "have, or should have, the leisure, the training, and the insulation to follow the ways of the scholar in pursuing the ends of government."[399] Through their professional immersion in "the tradition of our society" and their institutional insulation from political pressure, federal judges possess the capacity to interpret "the evolving morality of our tradition" and to recall a temporarily wayward democracy to that morality.[400]

Identifying the constitutional task of courts as one of vindicating an "evolving morality" could on its face seem to invite the *Lochner* error of the replacement of democratic decisions by the judges' subjective preferences. Bickel believed this risk was acceptably minimal, however: judges acting in good faith are constrained intellectually, internally by their own professionalization, and externally by their obligation to submit the reasoning behind their decisions to criticism by other constitutionalists. Judges are constrained institutionally, furthermore, both by the limits on the remedial powers of the courts and by the ultimate amenability to democratic correction of their decisions.[401] Bickel also argued for the legitimacy of judges' taking expediency into account by avoiding unnecessary confrontation with the majoritarian branches of government through the use of technical and procedural means for declining to decide cases on their merits.

Bickel's reformulation of the central issue in the constitutional tradition's problematic—the countermajoritarian difficulty and the

397 Id. at 24.

398 Id. at 64.

399 Id. at 25–26. Bickel's argument about judges' competences was constructed with the life-tenured and highly educated federal judiciary in mind. State judges often are elected officials subject to many of the same political pressures that Bickel thought rendered legislators and executive officers unreliable interpreters of principle.

400 Id. at 236.

401 Id. at 258.

difficulty of securing judicial virtue against the vice of subjective choice—has been widely accepted. His solution to the problem, which was essentially a reaffirmation of the tradition's self-confidence as a form of rational inquiry tempered by a strong emphasis on prudence,[402] met with less success.[403] Describing the judicial task as one of interpreting morality to society sounded to many constitutionalists like an open invitation for a return to the *Lochner* error of exalting the choices of judges over those of society. Bickel's failure to resolve this issue was not, at first, of great practical significance. The Supreme Court in the sixties enjoyed a favorable institutional environment. From 1963 to 1969 "liberal" Democrats who generally shared the Court's egalitarian views controlled the elected branches of the federal government, while throughout the period many influential academic constitutionalists approved the Court's results if not always its reasoning.[404] There was little contact between the scholarly criticism of the Court (focused on the Bickelian questions), and political opposition to the Court, which was directed by specific groups against specific decisions. Richard Nixon successfully campaigned for president in 1968 on a "law and order" platform calling for curbs on the Supreme Court's criminal procedure decisions, but little change in the Court's basic approach to constitutional adjudication seemed to result from his subsequent appointment of four justices between 1969 and 1971.[405]

402 See Anthony Kronman, "Alexander Bickel's Philosophy of Prudence," 94 Yale L.J. 1567 (1985).

403 Indeed, before his premature death in 1974, Bickel himself came to doubt the ability of the Supreme Court to interpret and apply the "tradition of our society" without in actual fact imposing the justices' private political preferences on the democratic process. See Bickel, *The Supreme Court and the Idea of Progress* (New Haven: Yale Univ. Press, 1969), arguing that the Warren Court had "remembered the future and invented the past."

404 See, e.g., Charles Black, "The Unfinished Business of the Warren Court," 46 Wash.L.Rev. 3 (1970). Black, one of Bickel's colleagues at Yale, was paradigmatic of professorial opinion in the sixties. Black acknowledged the countermajoritarian difficulty, but having offered his own solution for it (Congress's control over federal court jurisdiction meant that a majoritarian body always could shelter democratic choices from judicial interference) Black in effect called on the Court to continue on the task of elaborating and enforcing "liberal" and egalitarian values without further worry over the difficulty.

405 Outside the area of criminal procedure, where the Court became marginally more "conservative" after Warren retired in 1969, an impartial observer

The American constitutional tradition appeared to be flourishing in the early 1970s. Intellectually, it enjoyed a broad range of agreed-upon propositions, and a lively debate over the theoretical framework for those propositions. President Nixon's inability to bend the Court in a "conservative" direction seemed to show the health of the tradition's central institution by proving the Supreme Court's ability to resist external pressure and pursue internal goods. The Supreme Court, however, was about to embark on a new round of substantive due process decisions that, like *Lochner*, would test the compatibility of constitutionalism as a tradition of moral inquiry with the democratic presuppositions of the Modern Theory.

THE CRISIS OF *EISENSTADT* AND ITS AFTERMATH

The immediate intellectual history of the new substantive due process begins with the Court's 1965 decision in *Griswold v. Connecticut.*[406] *Griswold* was a challenge to an 1879 statute criminalizing the use, recommendation, or provision of any contraceptive drug or device. The statute was a dead letter and could not have passed the state legislature in 1965; its survival on the statute book was due to Roman Catholic opposition to its repeal.[407] Indeed, a great majority

---

would have noted no major changes in the Court's jurisprudence before the mid-1980s. See Vincent Blasi, ed., *The Burger Court: The Counter-Revolution That Wasn't* (New Haven: Yale Univ. Press, 1983). The immediate reason was personal: two of Nixon's appointees turned out to hold views of the judicial role indistinguishable from that of Earl Warren, and the new chief justice, Warren Burger, was a weak leader who was unable or unwilling to challenge Justice Brennan's political skills. The underlying reason probably had to do with the nature of Nixon's, and most of the popular, criticism of the Court. Most popular criticism of the Court was narrowly aimed at specific results, and often reflected no deep-seated concern at all over the Court's basic understanding of its role. Even assuming Nixon's attack on the Court was not purely expedient, it seems clear that it was quite limited; Nixon wanted the Court to ease up a bit, not to reverse course. When a later administration *did* seek a substantive change in the Court's actions, it had no difficulty in finding justices who would do so.

406 381 U.S. 419 (1965).

407 See Dudziak, "Just Say No: Birth Control in the Connecticut Supreme Court Before *Griswold v. Connecticut*," 75 Iowa L.Rev. 915 (1990).

of Americans (including apparently all of the justices) in 1965 thought the statute "an uncommonly silly law."[408] The question of its constitutionality, however, might have seemed settled in its favor; the law did not affect a "discrete and insular minority," it did not interfere with free speech or other political rights, and it did not seem in any obvious way to fall within the criminal procedure or other enumerated guarantees of the Bill of Rights. *Griswold*, in short, appeared to be a straightforward substantive due process case, intellectually identical to *Lochner* except that the "liberty" at issue was related only peripherally to freedom of contract; the Warren Court had only recently reiterated in strong terms its repudiation of *Lochner* and its adherence to a Modern Theory view of constitutionalism.[409] The Court, however, ruled the statute unconstitutional by a seven-to-two majority.

The official opinion of the Court in *Griswold* did not concede that the decision revived *Lochner* or violated the premises of Modern Theory. Justice William O. Douglas began with a vigorous denial of any such intention, and Douglas never explicitly described the basis of the Court's decision as the due process clause. Instead, Douglas located the constitutional principle at issue in the "penumbras, formed by emanations from [the] guarantees" of the Bill of Rights.[410] This rather odd expression earned Douglas's opinion much criticism. However, rhetoric aside, Douglas's point seems to have been a thoroughly traditional common-law argument, extending recognized legal norms by combination and analogy: if (as all agree) the First Amendment protects privacy in one's associations, the Fourth Amendment one's person and home against unreasonable searches, and so on, then by analogy the Constitution protects a married couple from governmental intrusion into the intimacies of their marriage. The special character of the marriage relationship, which state law abundantly recognizes, is sufficiently analogous to the special nature of one's body, home, associations, etc., to warrant analogous constitutional protection. The analogy, of course, is not necessarily

408 *Griswold*, 381 U.S. at 527 (Stewart J dissenting).

409 Ferguson v. Skrupa, 372 U.S. 726 (1963).

410 381 U.S. at 484–85. Douglas cited the First, Third, Fourth, Fifth and Ninth Amendments. The language of "penumbras" originated with Holmes. See, e.g., Springer v. Government of the Philippine Islands, 277 U.S. 189, 209–210 (1928) (Holmes, J., dissenting).

persuasive but in form it is wholly traditional and quite distinct from a "preferred position" strategy of determining on extratextual grounds that a certain interest is a fundamental constitutional right.

The initial problem with Douglas's attempt to avoid *Lochner* while deciding *Griswold* against the validity of the statute was that only one of his colleagues, Justice Tom Clark, thought his effort entirely successful. Five of the justices in the majority joined separate concurrences that rested the decision in whole or in part on substantive due process grounds. The dissenters thus found it easy to portray *Griswold* not only as poorly reasoned but, much more seriously, as a subversion of the 1937 repudiation of *Lochner*.[411]

If later decisions had read *Griswold* in the terms of Douglas's opinion, the case might have had no great theoretical significance. *Griswold*, as Douglas portrayed it, easily could have read as one of the line of cases, variously decided under the rubric of the First and the Fourth Amendments, that were extending the Fourth Amendment's concern with the sanctity of the home.[412] The Court, however, soon read *Griswold* in a different fashion.

In *Eisenstadt v. Baird*,[413] the new Burger Court struck down a state statute that criminalized the distribution of contraceptive drugs or devices to unmarried persons. In terms of legal doctrine, *Eisenstadt* was an equal protection decision. The majority held that the statute's differentiation between married persons (to whom one could legally distribute contraceptives) and unmarried persons (to whom one could not) bore no rational relationship to the statute's supposed purposes.[414] The case's theoretical significance lay in the

411 Id. at 514–15 (Black J dissenting).

412 See, e.g., Stanley v. Georgia, 394 U.S. 557 (1969).

413 405 U.S. 438 (1972). Only two of the new Nixon appointees were eligible to vote in *Eisenstadt*, and they divided over its proper resolution.

414 As a technical matter, the equal protection clause comes into play only when the validity of a statutory distinction is at issue. Since *all* statutes employ distinctions, for present purposes there are no relevant differences between equal protection and due process doctrine. (In the *Lochner* era, the Court used either clause indifferently—and often both simultaneously—to protect economic liberty.) Even after repudiating *Lochner*, the Court had always conceded that both the due process and the equal protection clauses imposed the minimal substantive requirement that the prohibition (due process) or the distinction (equal protection) a statute employed to reach its goal be rationally related to that goal. Given the post-1937 Court's willingness to *presume* legislative knowledge and purpose, this "rationality review" standard was virtually impossible to fail.

Court's rejection of the state's argument that the differentiation was rationally related to the moral distinction the state had chosen to draw between sexual activity within and without marriage.

Writing for the Court, Justice William Brennan reasoned that *Griswold* had undermined the state's argument. Brennan acknowledged that the Douglas opinion in *Griswold* appeared to rest the decision on the special nature of the marital relationship, but he treated that language as mere rhetoric: "If the right of privacy means anything, it is the right of the *individual*, married or single, to be free from unwanted governmental intrusion into matters so fundamentally affecting a person as the decision whether to bear or beget a child."[415] *Griswold*, as Brennan for the Court now read it, was not an attempt to extend textually enumerated constitutional prohibitions to cover an analogous situation; it was instead a judicial recognition of an individual interest so fundamental that a court could vindicate it even in the absence of any textual basis more definite than the word *liberty*. Indeed, Brennan's reading of *Griswold* turned Douglas's reasoning on its head. Douglas had argued that the decision in *Griswold* was consistent with the special nature of the marital relationship that the state itself recognized in law. For Brennan, a statutory attempt to accord marriage such a special status would be an unconstitutional discrimination if it conflicted with the judicially recognized individual right of privacy.

Eisenstadt was an intellectual milestone in constitutional history. As a matter of constitutional theory, it clearly marked the reemergence of substantive due process as a mode of constitutional argument that the Court considered legitimate.[416] The Court rejected the state's proffered moral basis for the statute not because the text of the Constitution invalidated that moral viewpoint, and not because the statute interfered with the political process or disadvantaged a minority group, but solely because the Court believed the state's moral choice was an unreasonable intrusion into individual matters the

415 Id. at 453 (emphasis added).

416 Douglas continued to insist that *Griswold* was based on the text of the Bill of Rights. Id. at 455 n. 4 (Douglas J concurring). Justice Potter Stewart, on the other hand, had dissented in *Griswold*, but joined the majority in *Eisenstadt* because he concluded that *Griswold* had reversed the post-1937 repudiation of substantive due process. See *Roe v. Wade*, 410 U.S. 113, 167–68 (Stewart J concurring).

Court considered "fundamental." Such substantive judgments about moral-political matters clearly are not foreign to common-law reasoning, but post-1937 constitutionalists had not expected the Court to impose them on majoritarian legislation unless some special reason existed for declining to give deference to the product of the democratic political process. *Eisenstadt*, and Brennan's opinion in *Eisenstadt*, clearly lay outside the area of nondeferential review footnote four had outlined. Further expansion of the *Eisenstadt* approach to constitutional adjudication implicitly would revive the old *Lochner*/Modern Theory debate.

On a broader cultural and intellectual level, *Eisenstadt* revealed the Court's journey away from the political morality of footnote four to the identification of a radically individualistic liberalism as the moral content of American constitutionalism. Footnote four, and the New Deal and Warren Court decisions that followed it, rested on an understanding of the American polity that, although statist and "rights" oriented, identified the incorporation of the disadvantaged into an enriched political community itself constituted in part by other communities (religious, familial, and so on) as a central moral objective of the Constitution. *Eisenstadt*, in contrast, denied the legitimacy of any moral content to American political organization beyond the protection of the atomistic individual against intrusion. George Grant's analysis of *Roe v. Wade* is more accurately a description of *Eisenstadt*: "The decision then speaks modern liberalism in its pure contractual form: right prior to good; a foundational contract protecting individual rights; the neutrality of the state concerning moral 'values'; social pluralism supported by and supporting this neutrality."[417] As a matter of logic, *Eisenstadt* achieved what *Roe v. Wade* publicized, the reduction of the American constitutional universe to the rights-bearing individual and the "federal" nation-state.[418]

417 Grant, *English-Speaking Justice*, 70.

418 *Eisenstadt* also repudiated (in logic) any remaining "federal" element to the moral order of American constitutionalism. Despite their nationalism on issues of economic regulation, the New Deal justices had generally agreed that the states were the proper centers for the political formulation of shared moral standards. While the Warren Court's race cases necessarily involved a denial of state autonomy in addressing moral questions involving race relations, the Court was careful to do so without rejecting the states' role as the primary setting for

The implications of *Eisenstadt* became unmistakable the following year when the Supreme Court by a seven-to-two vote held that the due process clause places severe restrictions on the democratic process's ability to regulate or forbid abortions.[419] Writing for the Court, Justice Harry Blackmun found no difficulty in concluding that the decision to have an abortion fell with the fundamental right of privacy recognized in *Eisenstadt*: "This right of privacy . . . founded in the Fourteenth Amendment's concept of personal liberty . . . is broad enough to encompass a woman's decision whether or not to terminate her pregnancy."[420] Blackmun acknowledged, however, that the state had presented one justification for its highly restrictive abortion statute potentially strong enough to override even this fundamental right: the state's argument that the legislature had acted to protect the life of (unborn) human beings. Blackmun conceded that if a fetus is a legal "person," not only would laws protecting fetuses be constitutional, but laws permitting abortion presumably would violate both the equal protection and the due process clauses. Blackmun rejected the state's argument on two grounds. He concluded, first, that it was historically implausible that the Constitution's references to "persons" originally were understood to include the unborn.[421] Blackmun then asserted that the Court was not competent to determine as a legal matter "the difficult question of when life begins," and that as a consequence it could not accept the state's

---

public moral debate. See, e.g., Loving V. Virginia, 388 U.S. 1 (1967) (striking down antimiscegenation statute). *Eisenstadt* flatly denied the states' power in an area traditionally held to be wholly beyond the national government's particular moral-political concerns.

419 The actual holding in *Roe* was that a woman's fundamental right of privacy essentially excludes state interference with a decision to abort before the fetus is viable, but that after that point the state may regulate or even prohibit abortion except for the purpose of saving the woman's life. The famous "trimester analysis" stemmed from the Court's decision to use three-month periods as administratively convenient rough approximations to the facts of fetal development and medical technology; the main consequence was that the Court identified the middle three months as a period when the state could regulate abortion in the interests of the mother's health although not to protect the fetus from a decision to abort.

420 410 U.S. at 153. This sentence is the entirety of the Court's reasoning on this point.

421 Id. at 156–58.

assertion that "life" begins at conception.[422] Only two justices dissented.[423]

Roe soon became the most controversial single Supreme Court decision since *Brown*, perhaps since *Dred Scott*. The "political hurricane"[424] the decision provoked drew from several sources—religious objections to abortion, a more diffuse sense that *Roe* was an act of judicial arrogance, a still more general fear that cases such as *Roe* were an endorsement of an overly individualistic view of American life.

The political resistance to *Roe* is, in and of itself, an important part of recent constitutional history. *Roe* quickly generated significant external pressure on the Court and on the federal judiciary as a whole. That pressure almost certainly played a part in Chief Justice Burger's migration from support for *Roe* to an open willingness to overrule it,[425] and probably influenced the acquiescence of a majority of the Court in legislation hostile to abortion when the justices would not have countenanced analogous interference with other "fundamental" rights.[426]

The controversy over *Roe* was not merely institutional or external, however; *Roe* unveiled the meaning of *Eisenstadt*, that the constitutional tradition had entered a full-scale epistemological crisis. *Eisenstadt* was unmistakably inconsistent with the Modern Theory premises on which all of modern constitutional discussion had been based. As Justice Stewart's concurrence in *Roe* candidly admitted, *Eisenstadt* and *Roe* "can be rationally understood only" as deci-

422 Id. at 159.

423 Even these dissents were of little theoretical significance. Justice William Rehnquist expressly conceded that the due process clause provided substantive protection to the privacy interest at stake; his disagreement with the majority was solely with the point at which the Court had struck the balance between the woman's right and the state's power. Id. at 173 (Rehnquist J dissenting). Justice Byron White's dissent on its face appeared to reject any form of substantive due process (id. at 221 [White J dissenting]), but this apparently uncompromising refusal to return to *Lochner* was undercut by the fact that White concurred in the judgments in both *Griswold* and *Eisenstadt*.

424 Wiecek, *Liberty*, 179.

425 See Thornburgh v. American College of Obstetrics, 476 U.S. 747, 782 (1986) (Burger CJ dissenting).

426 See Maher v. Roe, 432 U.S. 464 (1977) (upholding funding discrimination).

sions in the "long line" of substantive due process cases.[427] *Eisenstadt* and *Roe* thus made it plain that the Burger Court's objection to *Lochner* was not that the mode of judicial decision making in *Lochner* violated the democratic principles of American constitutionalism by imposing judicial values on democratic choices, but only that the *Lochner* justices "generally chose the 'wrong' values for protection."[428] Morality, in the intellectual universe presupposed by *Eisenstadt*, is a matter of choice, of selecting "values" according to criteria that themselves are the product of the assertion of the individual choosing will.

Roe itself also seemed to display a rejection of or disdain for constitutionalism understood as a tradition of rational inquiry. Justice Blackmun's statement that the Court was not competent to determine when "life" begins and that therefore the Court could not accept the state's judgment on the issue turned *all* of twentieth-century constitutional reasoning (*Lochner* included) on its head. The question before the Court of whether a fetus is a legal "person" for Fourteenth Amendment purposes obviously was within the Court's competence; by definition, all "legal" questions are. (It is "emphatically the province and duty" of the Court "to say what the law is," as John Marshall would have said.) Furthermore, in the past the Court had addressed the very question of the definition of "personhood," in the context of determining whether a corporation (a legal "person" under state law) is a "person" for constitutional purposes.[429] If, on the other hand, what Blackmun meant was that the question involved issues of fact or policy that lay beyond judicial purview, then the unmistakable conclusion both the *Lochner* Court and the New Deal justices would have drawn was that the Court should defer to the legislative process.

Eisenstadt and *Roe* have evoked a variety of responses among constitutional lawyers and scholars. Some simply have attempted to dismiss *Roe* as an individual bad decision, a mistake.[430] (*Eisenstadt* often escapes such criticism, a deep irony given its much greater

427 Id. at 168 (Stewart J concurring).

428 Ira Lupu, "Untangling the Strands of the Fourteenth Amendment," 77 Mich. L. Rev. 981, 989 (1979).

429 See Santa Clara Co. v. Southern Pacific R.R., 118 U.S. 394 (1886).

430 See, e.g., John H. Ely, "The Wages of Crying Wolf: A Comment on *Roe v. Wade*," 82 Yale L.J. 920, 935–36 (1973).

intellectual importance.) Others have explained the cases as the Court's pursuit of middle-class values at the expense of legal consistency.[431] There is general agreement, however, that the reemergence of substantive due process marks a turning point in constitutional history. If the revived doctrine is to be upheld, the basic terms of constitutional discussion must be rethought; if the doctrine is to be rejected, the tendencies in pre-*Eisenstadt* constitutional discussion that led to it must be identified and overcome. In either event, it is clear that the Modern Theory that served as the framework for constitutional discussion for most of a century must be revised or replaced. The next chapter turns to the attempts to do just that.

431 See Thomas Gray, "Eros, Civilization and the Burger Court," 43 Law & Contemp. Probs. 83 (1980).

Chapter Three

CONSTITUTIONALISM AS THE AMERICAN SOCIAL MORALITY

The contemporary epistemological crisis of the constitutional tradition has resulted in a variety of responses. One is to deny the possibility of coherent constitutional discussion, and to admit that constitutional adjudication is, as MacIntyre has asserted, a purely pragmatic maintenance of the balance between various political forces.[1] Most constitutional scholars, however, have been unwilling to give up the concept of constitutionalism as a tradition of rational inquiry, and the period since 1980 has seen the articulation of a great variety of theoretical responses to the the tradition's intellectual dilemma.

Philip Bobbitt, in one of the most creative contributions to constitutional literature of the period, has brought the philosophy of the later Wittgenstein to bear on American constitutionalism. Bobbitt argues that the tradition's problems can only be addressed successfully from an internal perspective and that, indeed, much of the sense of crisis comes from mistaken attempts to address intratradition concerns from extratradition perspectives. Such attempts, according to Bobbitt, "share . . . a fundamental epistemological mistake. Each of these perspectives assumes that law-statements are statements about the world (like the statements of science) and thus must be verified by a correspondence with facts about the world."[2] But law-statements are not reducible to propositions about "the world";[3] instead, the law is a conceptual activity of making choices that must be explained using the shared "modalities" of legal argument, modalities that derive their force not from some external

1 See, e.g., Brest, "The Fundamental Rights Controversy," 90 Yale L.J. 1063 (1981). This is the essential position of Harvard professor Laurence Tribe, the greatest contemporary constitutional doctrinalist. See Tribe, *Constitutional Choices* (Cambridge, Mass.: Harvard Univ. Press, 1985).

2 Bobbitt, *Constitutional Interpretation* (Oxford: Basil Blackwell, 1991), xii.

3 By statements about "the world," Bobbitt intends to include statements about history and morality.

correspondence but from their role in defining the very activity of constitutional interpretation. Bobbitt repudiates "the notion that law takes place within a framework that is independent of the structure of legal argument. [He] rejects the view that a set of legal presuppositions exists that are discoverable in the absence of legal argument, upon which legal argument is supposed to depend."[4] "It follows . . . that constitutional law needs no 'foundation.'"[5] Legal arguments, rather than being propositions about the world, "are moves within a serious game, movements as practiced as any classical ballet and yet no less contingent."[6] The question of whether a given interpretation is "legitimate" that so occupies post-*Eisenstadt* debate is answered according to Bobbitt by determining whether the interpretation is articulated using the accepted modalities: "The working of the arguments maintains legitimacy."[7]

Bobbitt's Wittgensteinian interpretation of constitutionalism sharply distinguishes the question of legitimacy, which can only be addressed within the tradition's argumentative "game," from the question of the justice of the American constitutional order. The Constitution, he insists, is "agnostic" about moral "values" other than those implicit in the tradition's commitment to debate and reasoned explanation,[8] but this agnosticism is precisely the means by which the tradition makes it possible to achieve justice (as measured by some extraconstitutional "moral analysis").[9] Because the modalities that make up constitutional argument are irreducible to one another, conflict in the answers indicated by different modalities can be re-

4 Bobbitt, *Constitutional Fate* (New York: Oxford Univ. Press, 1982), 245.

5 Id. at 237.

6 Bobbitt, *Constitutional Interpretation*, 34. In another clear echo of Wittgenstein, Bobbitt describes the various "modalities" of argument recognized within the constitutional tradition as "a legal grammar that we [participants in the tradition] all share and that we all have mastered prior to our being able to ask what the reasons are for a court having power to review legislation." *Constitutional Fate*, 6.

7 Bobbitt, *Constitutional Fate*, 181. "[T]he very functioning of the argumentative modes works to insure that there is consensus among those persons operating within the conventions." Id. at 245.

8 Bobbitt, *Constitutional Interpretation*, 169, 182, 184–85.

9 Id. at 169–70. "How do we determine that a decision is just? We measure it against our values. Our values justify our practices." Id. at 166. I will not discuss Bobbitt's implicit view of moral "value" and "choice."

solved only by a "recursion to conscience."[10] The modalities thus provide a means through which extraconstitutional justice may be pursued. "The multiplicity of modes [of argument] gives us a way to measure a possible legal world against our sense of rightness, going back and forth between a proposed interpretation and its world, and ourselves."[11] The attempt to find an extratradition "foundation" for legitimate constitutional argument, Bobbitt concludes, undermines the tradition's justifiability by canonizing some "particular decision process" in the place of the conscientious exercise of choice among "possible worlds" that the "incommensurate modalities give us."[12]

Bobbitt's response to the contemporary crisis of constitutionalism is in many ways a deeply traditional one; he rejects the fear that the system is morally awry by placing its moral justification outside constitutionalism. But Bobbitt's traditionalism is a heterodox voice in contemporary constitutional debate.[13] Most participants in that debate agree on a different, and profoundly untraditional starting point: they modify or reject the tradition's long-standing claim to autonomy—to being distinct from philosophy, morality, or extralegal politics—and instead explicitly identify constitutionalism as a form of the broader category of moral discourse. In this chapter I analyze a variety of recent works in constitutional scholarship that make this identification.

Interest in explicitly treating constitutionalism as a species of moral reasoning cuts across the spectrum of substantive constitutional and political viewpoints: there are, for example, social morality constitutionalists who accept the legitimacy of modern substantive due process as well as ones who reject it. Theorists who adopt the social morality approach nevertheless usually share certain fundamental presuppositions that guide their work. First, they take it to be an axiomatic truth that *Brown v. Board of Education* was correctly decided, not just in the sense that its result was morally admirable in some sense external to constitutionalism, but that it was *constitutionally* correct, a proper exercise within the practice of constitutional adjudication. Second, the social morality theorists share the

10 Id. at 184.

11 Id. at 158.

12 Id. at 184, 157.

13 See Bobbitt, *Constitutional Fate*, 244–45, for Bobbitt's recognition of this fact.

presupposition that *Roe v. Wade* is problematic, and that its existence demands an explanation. This presupposition stems from the persistence of Modern Theory concerns; the substantive due process decisions make it plain that judges make explicit political and moral choices when they engage in constitutional adjudication, and contemporary constitutionalists generally share the view that this fact makes the countermajoritarian difficulty unavoidable. The common task the social morality theorists are attempting is to identify the legitimate sources of those political and moral choices. By doing so, the theorists hope to provide standards for the rational evaluation of constitutional arguments and decisions. Finally, the participants in the social morality approach share the assumption that the federal courts—and especially the Supreme Court—will and should continue to engage in constitutional adjudication. That practice is so central to the constitutional tradition that to propose to abolish it seems to most American constitutionalists a rejection of constitutionalism *tout court*.

THE MORALITY OF THE POLITICAL PROCESS

The contemporary search for a theoretical response to the post-*Eisenstadt* crisis in constitutionalism began in earnest with the publication of John Hart Ely's *Democracy and Distrust* in 1980. Ely, a law professor now at Stanford University, saw his task as the reconciliation of Warren Court activism with Modern Theory democratic presuppositions;[14] substantive due process, and *Roe* in particular, in Ely's view, are not an extension but a betrayal of the Warren Court's legacy. Ely shares Bickel's opinion that the countermajoritarian difficulty can only be resolved if constitutional adjudication serves some function that American democracy requires but cannot fill through the usual majoritarian processes. Ely, however, rejects Bickel's proposal that this function has to do with an "evolving morality" that is

14 John Hart Ely, *Democracy and Distrust* (Cambridge, Mass.: Harvard Univ. Press, 1980) is dedicated "[t]o Earl Warren: you don't need many heroes if you choose them carefully."

embodied in, or connected to, constitutionalism. *All* theories that permit courts to trump democratic decisions on the basis of the judges' moral views are inconsistent with democracy both in principle and in practice. Morality-based constitutional adjudication contradicts democratic principles by its explicit assumption that an unelected judicial elite is better able to make moral judgments than the people acting through majoritarian political processes. Morality-based constitutionalism in practice simply produces the *Lochner-Roe* sequence; constitutional law imposes whatever moral preferences a majority of the justices share and changes when those preferences shift.[15]

Endorsing morality as the basis of constitutional discussion, in Ely's view, is also inconsistent with the text of the Constitution. The Constitution's text is overwhelmingly concerned with process. Virtually all of the 1787 instrument deals with structuring the institutions of national government, all of which are majoritarian, or subject to majoritarian control. Virtually all of the amendments adopted after 1791 have concerned process, some (e.g., the Twelfth) addressing problems in the original structure and others (e.g., the Fifteenth) extending the range of persons entitled to participate. Ely concedes, of course, that some constitutional provisions appear to express substantive moral concerns, but he argues that even in these texts the real purpose addresses process. The First Amendment, for example, safeguards the freedom of discussion necessary to democratic politics while excluding from the process and its outcomes the substantively moral concerns of religious faith. The Thirteenth Amendment's prohibition of slavery, again, corrects the defect in the original structure that permitted a group of Americans to be excluded altogether from the political process. Even the criminal procedure guarantees of the Bill of Rights at least partially reflect a desire to limit the power of unelected judges.[16] While Ely admits that a few provisions are irreducibly substantive and moral in character (e.g., the Eighth Amendment's ban on "cruel and unusual punishments"),[17] they are for him the rare exceptions that prove the rule.[18]

Ely, however, shares the classical liberal distrust of the outcomes

15 Id. at 63–70.
16 Id. at 172–73.
17 Id. at 97.
18 Id. at 101.

of majoritarian processes that plays a role in the liberal veneration of rights. The very authority that Ely accords the community can be captured by a group, or used to abuse the unpopular and the politically unsuccessful. The unique judicial function, the legitimate arena for constitutional adjudication, lies in the protection of the democratic process from capture or abuse. Judges are entitled to overturn specific political outcomes if those outcomes stem from a defect in the process, such as the systematic exclusion of a racial minority from participation. Judges are entitled to overturn specific political outcomes if those outcomes have the purpose and effect of creating a defect in the process, such as a restriction on free political discussion.[19] If neither condition is present, then judges must enforce whatever legal rules the process produces. The abortion statute in *Roe v. Wade*, in Ely's view, was not the consequence of the exclusion of any members of the community from democratic politics (women could vote), nor did it limit or distort those politics (proponents of abortion rights remained free to take political action to overturn the statute). *Roe* therefore is a paradigm of the judicial usurpation of the community's prerogative of making moral choices.[20]

Ely's representation-reinforcing[21] theory of constitutional adjudication closely tracks the argument Justice Stone outlined in his famous *Carolene Products* footnote. In his own terms, furthermore, Ely achieves his goal of reconciling American democracy with the jurisprudence of the Warren Court. Most of the Warren Court's innovative constitutional decisions addressed what Ely describes as defects in the democratic process; the criminal procedure decisions, which are an apparent exception, often were concerned factually with the impact of criminal law on those excluded from full participation in the process.

Ely's highly sophisticated argument is, of course, a failure if

19 Id. at 105–34. The relationship Ely perceives between these theoretically defined occasions for constitutional adjudication and the text of the Constitution is not always clear, as he does not want judges to act without textual warrant and he does not seem to want to exclude the possibility of judges enforcing a substantive moral-political rule if that rule is adequately specified in the constitutional text. See id. at 94–98. Ely's implicit solution to this problem is to assume that all or virtually all of the text concerns process, and that all situations involving a defect in the process fall under some textual provision.

20 Id. at 2–3.

21 Id. at 181.

construed as an attempt to avoid moral commitments, for at the heart of Ely's argument is a vision of what the nation created by the Constitution is and is about. Ely's United States exists on the basis of an explicit agreement to abide by the results of the democratic processes the Constitution creates, in return for the constitutional promise that all members of the community can participate in those processes. (The abolition of slavery and the guarantee of the franchise to blacks, women, those too poor to pay a poll tax, and 18 to 20-year-olds are for Ely simple corrections of irrational limitations on membership in the community.) Unlike classical liberalism, Ely freely recognizes the legitimacy of community decisions on moral issues and of community imposition of those decisions on individuals—in a sense, for Ely there are no individual rights in the sense of a sphere of personal autonomy legally secure from community invasion. The one fundamental moral commitment that constitutes the American community is the commitment to a democratic process in which all participate without hindrance, and the only real "right" is the right so to participate. Ely's theory thus exemplifies in a particularly clear fashion the intrinsic connection between the liberal individual as rights-bearer and the nation-state as rights-protector.

Ely's theory suffers from a variety of internal problems the most general of which is that he has achieved apparent coherence by a set of intellectual slights of hand. Only by a strained and implausible reading of the text can the written Constitution be transformed into an almost purely process-oriented outline of government. The attempt to do so, furthermore, necessarily ignores or discounts the abundant historical evidence that many of the genuinely process-centered elements of the Constitution originally had substantive purposes beyond the creation of a democratic process. The interlocking system of federal and state authority, for example, was devised in large part to provide protection for property rights *against* the redistributive threat posed by democratic legislation,[22] while the Reconstruction amendments' transfer of power to Congress was driven by the assumption that the national legislature would provide protection for substantive individual rights.

Despite his apparent concern for constitutional history, Ely's theory is also faulty from the standpoint of constitutionalists con-

22 See, e.g., *The Federalist* No. 10 (J. Madison), 56–65.

cerned to preserve the continuity of the tradition. Ely's description of process-perfection as the authentic heart of the constitutional tradition is reminiscent of Thayer's similar claim for Modern Theory in that both arguments ignore the history of substantive rights adjudication that begins with John Marshall. Ely, again like Thayer, fails to take account of the importance of common-law modes of argument (which depend on the expansion of substantive principles by analogical reasoning) throughout the life of the tradition. In the end, the picture of the national community Ely draws owes more to his own theoretically derived picture of democracy than to the particularities of American history.

Perhaps the most fundamental problem with Ely's constitutional theory is that it cannot deliver what it demands and promises, a mode of discussion whereby constitutionalists can identify legitimate occasions for judicial intervention without inviting the judges to make substantive political and moral choices. The identification of "defects" in the democratic system, which for Ely is the core of the courts' legitimate constitutional task and supplies the only proper basis for constitutional adjudication, necessarily involves substantive moral and political choices. Is the exclusion of resident aliens from the franchise an unobjectionable definition of the community, or a defect in the openness of the political process? Are laws interfering with the ability of Native Americans legally to use peyote for religious purposes an exercise of the community's authority to make substantive moral judgments and enforce them on its members, or an attack on a discrete and insular minority that judges should overturn? Should a court invalidate an antipornography ordinance on the ground that it restricts the free expression of ideas necessary to democratic governance? What about an ordinance banning lectures commending a new sexual ethic? (And if the answers to the last two questions are different, why?) Ely's "process" theory can be put into practice only by the continuous exercise of substantive judgments which the theory ostensibly forbids judges to make.

Professor Bruce Ackerman of Yale, a critic of Ely,[23] has developed an alternative theory of constitutionalism based on a conception of the national political process. Unlike Ely, Ackerman's theory endorses the legitimacy of judicial involvement with substantive moral

23 See Ackerman, "Beyond *Carolene Products*," 98 Harv. L. Rev. 713 (1985).

and political choices. Judges should do so, in Ackerman's view, when the history of the constitutional tradition indicates that at some point in the past "the People" chose to constitutionalize the moral or political issue at stake. By an imaginative, detailed, and quite innovative retelling of American constitutional history, Ackerman seeks to show that *Brown* and *Griswold* are legitimate implementations of the moral-political choices the People have made in prior acts of "higher lawmaking."[24]

Ackerman acknowledges that the contemporary period has been characterized by a crisis in constitutional thought, although he blames the crisis on the failure of theory to explicate a basically healthy practice of constitutional adjudication. Ackerman identifies the social origin of the crisis in "a breach between theory and practice" generated by the intellectual confusion—or, perhaps, the *trahison des clercs*—of the contemporary American intelligentsia. "[M]ost people," Ackerman argues, possess "a rough-and-ready grasp of the animating constitutional ideals of American democracy" based on their experience of "the basic rhythms of American constitutional life" (elections, court decisions, state/federal interaction, and so on); practicing lawyers and judges are similarly familiar with the "distinctive principles of American democracy" that are the source of their day-to-day administration of public law.[25] The contemporary crisis is artificial, created by those Ackerman scornfully calls " 'sophisticated' constitutionalists" and "the leading lights of the nation's universities."[26] These misguided intellectuals, in Ackerman's opinion, have long lost touch with the historically shaped and particularistic nature of the American constitutional tradition; as a result, they have lost their ability to explain, understand, or participate in the tradition's practices on its terms.[27] This intellectual alienation of the elite from its own constitutional identity and history has driven the elite to look elsewhere for the tools with which to inter-

24 See Ackerman, *We the People: Foundations*, vol. 1 (Cambridge, Mass.: Harvard Univ. Press, 1991); "Discovering the Constitution," 93 Yale L.J. 1013 (1984); "Constitutional Politics/Constitutional Law," 99 Yale L.J. 453 (1989).

25 Ackerman, *Foundations*, 4.

26 Ackerman, "Constitutional Politics/Constitutional Law," 99 Yale L.J. at 454. Ackerman, a distinguished scholar at one of the most elite of law schools, gives no sign of seeing any irony in his attack on "sophisticated" intellectuals.

27 Ackerman, *Foundations*, at 3–5.

pret constitutionalism: "sophisticated constitutional thought has increasingly sought to elaborate the genius of American institutions with the use of themes generated elsewhere," chiefly themes borrowed from European political and moral philosophy. Since such borrowings were not "designed with American history in mind" their alien concerns and universalistic pretensions render them quite inapposite for understanding the historically defined American constitutional tradition.[28] The intellectual elite therefore can make little sense of the course of modern constitutional law.[29]

If the intellectual elite bears most of the responsibility for creating the contemporary crisis, the lawyers and judges whom Ackerman praises have played a (much less damaging) negative role by their inability to explain fully their judgments about the constitutional tradition's meaning. The practical constitutionalists quite rightly have sought to express the "patterns of constitutional law that emerge over decades and generations" through a "professional narrative" of the tradition's development.[30] Unfortunately the flaws in the prevailing "received narrative" have rendered it unsuccessful in addressing the intellectual issues raised by contemporary constitutional law.[31]

As Ackerman unfolds the official or received constitutional narrative, its main plot line is structured by the sharp distinction it draws between the Founding—the creation and implementation of the Constitution in the late 1780s—and all subsequent constitutional history. The Founding was truly "jurisgenerative"[32] in the sense that it involved the creation "from scratch" of a new constitutional order embodying novel politico-legal principles, and was adopted through procedures that were in fact illegal under existing law (the Articles of Confederation). Like the Revolution that preceded it, the Founding was in the truest sense the creation of law by the American People in

28 Ackerman, "Constitutional Politics/Constitutional Law," at 455, 454.

29 Compare Ackerman's reference to the "modern lawyers and judges" who have been "far too sensible [and] astute in their practical judgments" to fall into the errors of "academic commentators who have been keeping score by the wrong scorecard on the side-lines." Id. at 461.

30 Ackerman, *Foundations*, 4–5.

31 Ackerman, "Constitutional Politics/Constitutional Law," at 456, 459.

32 Id. at 456, quoting Robert Cover, "Nomos and Narrative," 97 Harv.L. Rev. 4, 11 (1983).

their direct and sovereign character. No act of jurisgenesis since can make a similar claim: "modern Americans tell themselves stories that assert the deep continuity of two centuries of constitutional practice" since the Founding.[33] Although the received narrative recognizes (correctly) that the Founding can be classified with two subsequent events—Reconstruction and the confrontation between the Supreme Court and the New Deal in the 1930s—as turning points, "the stories lawyers tell about each of the three turning points do not invite them to reflect upon the common features of these great transformative exercises."[34]

When contemporary lawyers come to speak of the Reconstruction-era amendments, Ackerman asserts, they use different language. "[W]hile the professional narrative insists that Reconstruction was *substantively creative*, it supposes that it was *procedurally unoriginal*."[35] The Radicals, after all, changed the Constitution by using the formal amendment process created by the Founders. The received narrative uses yet a third means of characterizing the 1937 repudiation of *Lochner*, one which fails to see any substantive originality. Instead, Ackerman writes, contemporary lawyers invoke a "myth of rediscovery"; the New Deal justices merely were returning to the constitutional views of John Marshall which the *Lochner* era had obscured.[36]

Ackerman faults the received professional account of constitutional history on two grounds: it is historically wrong, and its effect on the theoretical understanding of constitutionalism is pernicious. The received narrative's historical errors are products of its excessive formalism, which, for example, leads lawyers to think that the constitution making of 1865–70 differed from that of 1935–37 *because* the former added text to the printed Constitution and the latter did not.[37] Such a formalistic account misses the historical reality that the 1860s Radicals were as procedurally creative as the original Founders: the "formal" ratification of the Reconstruction amendments was achieved, in fact, only by the exertion of extralegal political pressure on the presidency, the ex-Confederate states, and the Supreme

33 Ackerman, *Foundations*, 34.
34 Id. at 41.
35 Id. at 42.
36 Id. at 43.
37 Ackerman, "Constitutional Politics/Constitutional Law," 491.

Court. The Radicals were successful in doing so only because they mobilized the national political processes on their side in the election of 1866, and so were able to claim "a mandate from the People to destroy the autonomy of dissenting institutions." The 1866 election, and the subsequent acquiescence of the "dissenting institutions" in the Radicals' lawmaking marked the occurrence of a "constitutional moment" in which the People spoke directly to adopt the Radicals' constitutional agenda. Unless they are understood in Ackerman's manner as the product of the People's extraordinary reassumption of direct lawmaking power, the formal Reconstruction-era amendments, obtained by coercion and fraud, would have to be deemed illegitimate.

Ackerman interprets the constitutional history of the mid-1930s as a similar instance of (formally illegal) higher lawmaking: the Republic reached a constitutional impasse (the anti-New Deal decisions) followed by a political mobilization of the People (Roosevelt's electoral victory in 1936) which made possible the exertion of extreme pressure on the dissenting institution (the Court), and led to the general acceptance of a genuinely new constitutional vision. The New Deal legitimation of a powerful activist and centralized government was substantively creative rather than a mere restatement of Marshall's views *and* it was procedurally creative—the New Deal constitutionalists found it unnecessary to invoke the amendment process even formally.

The theoretical purpose of Ackerman's proposed correction of the received narrative is to establish the validity of his own normative account of American constitutionalism. The constitutional tradition recognizes "two different levels of decision" that legitimately "may be made in a democracy. The first is a decision by the American People; the second by their government." Decisions by the People require an extraordinary political mobilization that, after fair opportunities for debate, can persuade a supermajority of Americans to support a transformation of the constitutional order. A proposed change in constitutional principles that successfully negotiates this "specially onerous lawmaking path" is entitled to a special kind of legitimacy because it can claim rightly "that its initiative represents the constitutional judgment of We the People."[38] The ordinary deci-

38 Ackerman, *Foundations*, 9.

sions of government, in contrast, enjoy only a derivative legitimacy based on their enactment through processes approved by the People in a previous exercise of higher lawmaking.[39] Ackerman labels this two-track theory of democratic decision making *dualist democracy*. Dualist democracy requires some institutional means of preserving the decisions of the People against the lesser authority of ordinary democratic politics, and thus constitutional adjudication plays "an absolutely essential part" in American demcracy *qua* democracy.[40] "Rather than threatening democracy . . . the courts serve democracy by protecting the hard-won principles of a mobilized citizenry against erosion by political elites who have failed to gain broad and deep popular support for their innovations."[41]

The theoretical confusion that grips current academics, and that increasingly unsettles the bench and bar, stems in part from the fact that the "dominant opinion among serious constitutionalists today" is what Ackerman calls *monistic democracy*.[42] Monistic democrats believe that democracy "requires the grant of plenary lawmaking authority to the winners of the last general election," providing that the rules for free and fair elections and open political debate are observed.[43] That belief entails the conclusion that "any institutional check upon the electoral victors is presumptively anti-democratic," a conclusion that renders almost any form of constitutional adjudication fatally inconsistent with (monistic) democratic principles.

Ackerman believes that the dominance of monistic democracy is simply an error, the consequence of forgetting the dualistic nature of American democracy and replacing it with "(an idealized version of) British parliamentary practice." Monistic democrats equate "democracy" *tout court* with their own pet version, and so cannot see the "profoundly democratic point" to the dualistic-democratic practice of judicial review.[44]

39 Ackerman, "Constitutional Politics/Constitutional Law," 461–62; *Foundations*, 6–7.

40 Ackerman, "Constitutional Politics/Constitutional Law" at 465.

41 Ackerman, *Foundations*, 10.

42 Id. at 7–10. Ackerman's monistic democracy corresponds to what I have labelled the democratic premises of Modern Theory.

43 Id. at 8. The resemblances to Ely and Stone as well as to Thayer will be obvious.

44 Id. at 8, 9.

Ackerman identifies a second intellectually popular but erroneous interpretation of constitutionalism, that of the "rights foundationalists." These constitutionalists deny, sometimes unwittingly, the "primacy of popular sovereignty" in the American order. For them, the primary purpose of constitutionalism is not to embody and carry forward the People's higher lawmaking actions, but to protect "[w]hatever rights are Right." Put in other words, rights foundationalists deny the autonomy of constitutional discourse. Rights theorists disagree, to be sure, on which rights are fundamental, but they all agree on the importance of subordinating democracy to the protection of fundamental rights. It therefore is crucial for a rights theorist to specify which rights are, in fact, "Right." The difficulty that accompanies the effort to distinguish conflicting claims to fundamentality typically drives rights theorists "to recur to great philosophers like Kant and Locke in an effort to understand the Constitution," a move Ackerman calls the foundationalist's "turn to the Great Books."[45] Rights foundationalists thus come to resemble monistic democrats in that their constitutional theories are driven by ideas borrowed from non-American sources.[46] Monistic democrats are puzzled by the practice of constitutional adjudication and rights foundationalists are dismissive of democracy; they share a commitment to a fundamentally ahistorical and universalizing approach to constitutionalism that leaves them unable to interpret American dualistic democracy.

Dualistic democrats, in contrast, can make sense of the constitutional tradition and its practice of constitutional adjudication. The dualist insists that "the Constitution is best understood as a historically rooted tradition of theory and practice."[47] That tradition operates both by common-law "patterns of concrete decisions built up by courts and other practical decisionmakers over decades, generations, centuries,"[48] and by the jurisgenerative impact of "constitutional politics."[49] Constitutional adjudication, as practiced (generally) and as understood by the theory of dualistic democracy, is democratic

45 *Foundations*, 11–12.

46 Rights foundationalists add the additional sin of elitism. Ackerman, "Constitutional Politics/Constitutional Law," 465–67.

47 *Foundations*, 22.

48 Id. at 17.

49 Id. at 18.

and legitimate because it respects the historicity of the tradition but is also capable of creatively synthesizing the various revolutionary exercises of higher lawmaking power by the People. Integral to this dualist understanding of constitutionalism is a confidence that constitutional interpretation can be "a disciplined activity with its own criteria of good and bad arguments, its own claim to integrity" rather than "a political con game." "Dualism presupposes the possibility of interpretation."[50]

Ackerman illustrates the interpretive power of dualistic theory by discussing *Griswold.* The Court's decision, he writes, was an appropriate "synthetic interpretation" of the relationship between the People's 1787 "affirmation of individual liberty" and their 1937 "affirmation of activist government." The original founders associated liberty primarily "with the rhetoric of contract and private property," an association that gave rise to *Lochner*. But in 1937 the People disavowed freedom of contract by legitimating a socially and economically activist state. The *Griswold* Court correctly decided that the 1937 decision was not a Popular rejection of the underlying commitment to individual liberty, and that as a result the People's rejection of constitutional protection for the liberty of "market actors" did not apply to "more intimate relationships."[51] *Griswold* was "nothing less than a brilliant *interpretive* proposal. Granted, when the Founders thought about personal freedom they used the language of property and contract; given the New Deal repudiation of this language, doesn't the language of privacy provide *us* with the most meaningful way of preserving these Founding affirmations of liberty in an activist welfare state?"[52]

Ackerman's dualist-democratic theory of the Constitution is creative and at times brilliant in detail. It suffers from a series of faults, however, that render it unpersuasive. The plausibility of the notion of the *constitutional moment*—the event of extralegal higher lawmaking that constitutes a decision by the People—is crucial to Ackerman's theory. But the concept is unworkable. In order to be useful, the concept must apply to any historical event that meets the criteria

50 Id. at 60.

51 Id. at 150–58; "Constitutional Politics/Constitutional Law," 536–42. While Ackerman carefully avoids comment on *Roe*, his defense of *Griswold* seems equally applicable to the question of abortion rights.

52 Ackerman, *Foundations*, 159.

Ackerman sets out. Ackerman, however, does not want to invest any and every temporarily successful constitutional doctrine with the mantle of higher lawmaking; he quite clearly wants to legitimate *Brown* and *Griswold*, but not *Bowers v. Hardwick*.[53] The only constitutional moments Ackerman wishes to acknowledge in addition to the Founding are the Reconstruction and the New Deal, perhaps not coincidentally periods of rapid constitutional change in directions Ackerman favors. But Ackerman's theoretical tool, wielded by someone without his preferences, can as persuasively identify a longer or different list of moments when the People spoke. The Jeffersonian Republicans, for example, explicitly understood their electoral triumph in 1800 as a constitutional "revolution" in which the People pronounced in favor of Jeffersonian constitutional views and authorized the victors to bring dissenting institutions (e.g., the Federalist judiciary) to heel. Given the considerable plausibility of the Jeffersonian claim to have wrought a major substantive change in the content of constitutional discussion,[54] 1800 seems an eminently suitable candidate for constitutional momenthood, if one for which Ackerman would have faint political enthusiasm.[55] Much more ominously for Ackerman, the modern Republican party's capture of the presidency in the 1980s—with its avowed and activist constitutional agenda, its presidential landslides, its dismantling of some of the social welfare apparatus of the activist national government, and its inexorable transformation of "dissenting institutions" such as the Supreme Court and the Democratic party—seems almost a paradigm of Ackermanian higher lawmaking. Ackerman's attempt to avoid this result

53 478 U.S. 186 (1986). *Bowers*, the decision that refused to extend the *Roe* privacy right to protect the intimate relations of adult homosexuals, was the Court's first theoretically important decision to reflect the impact of President Ronald Reagan's attempt to use the power of appointment to undercut substantive due process and the jurisprudence of the Warren Court.

54 See Powell, *Languages*, chaps. 5–11, passim, tracing the broad impact of the "revolution of 1800" on the development of American constitutionalism.

55 Ackerman acknowledges the Jeffersonian "revolution of 1800" as an "important example of successful constitutional politics" (*Foundations*, 196), but insists that we should not "read too much into" the Jeffersonian attempt to make their electoral victories a plebiscite on their anticentralizing constitutional views. Id. at 73. For Ackerman, it was the Marshall Court properly and successfully exercising its "preservationist function" that was representing the constitutional will of the People. Id. at 62, 71–72.

has been to identify the Senate's rejection of Robert Bork's appointment to the Supreme Court as the People's rejection of Reaganist constitutional thought,[56] a response that seems both formalist in the extreme (the Senate subsequently has gone on to confirm three Republican nominees to the Court each of whom seems as Reaganist as Bork) and trivial. Taking Ackerman seriously may lead to rejecting the results Ackerman wishes to commend.

A second problem with Ackerman's theory is its naive and thoroughgoing positivism. The justification of judicial review as the preservation of legal rules ordained by the People against contradiction by ordinary government actions is convincing only if there is good reason to believe that judges' interpretations of the People's rules are systematically more likely to be correct than the interpretations implicit in elected-branch decisions. Ackerman makes no attempt to explain why that should be so beyond whatever inferences may be drawn from his praise for common-law reasoning, and his own examples of good constitutional argument do not seem very comforting.[57] Indeed, Ackerman's rejection of the amendment process as the sole legitimate means of officially changing the substantive rules actually eliminates one of the main traditional arguments in favor of allowing courts to trump legislatures.

Ackerman's positivism shares with all positivist theories of law the additional problem of explaining the source of obligation to the law. Unlike Ely, who proposes a sort of social contract as the moral basis of constitutionalism (America as a community is constituted by an implicit bargain whereby each citizen gives the power of coercion to the community in return for the community's guarantee of equal political participation rights), Ackerman's higher lawmaking compels obedience (the judges to the rules the People have declared, ordinary government officials to the judges, the rest of us to the ordinary

56 Id. at 50–52. See also Ackerman, "Transformative Appointments," 101 Harv. L.J. 1164 (1988).

57 Ackerman's "synthetic" explanations of *Brown* and *Griswold* are dazzling rhetorical justifications of those decisions; Ackerman does not explain how other constitutional lawyers, or in particular busy judges with dockets to manage, can adopt and employ his *method* of interpretation. As with some other constitutional theorists, the implicit message of Ackerman's work is that the theorists themselves must supply the constitutional arguments and conclusions for lawyers and judges whose training and duties preclude the ability to make substantive contributions to constitutional discussion.

officials *except* when we are engaged in higher lawmaking) simply because the People have spoken (again, according to the judges).[58] Ackerman's praise for the common-law mode of reasoning is in fact limited to the common law's use of analogy and precedent in discussion; the classical common law's goal of discerning and applying substantive standards of justice and reasonability through the forms of law is wholly absent. Ackerman's constitutional tradition is a tradition of rational inquiry into the commands of a politically unlimited sovereign, commands that he concedes are sometimes imperfect or immoral.[59]

Perhaps the most fundamental problem with Ackerman's theory is that it is a positivism of the sovereign's will that puts a myth in the sovereign's place. The entire edifice rests on the almost literal force he gives to the traditional rhetoric of popular sovereignty. The language of popular sovereignty, of course, has played a central role in American political history. The American revolutionaries justified their highly illegal defiance of their quite unmythical sovereign as an act of the people,[60] and the early constitutional tradition invoked popular sovereignty to explain the authority of constitutional texts and the supremacy of national over local power. Ackerman however seems to vest this language with an astonishing literalness. Capitalized references to "We the People,"[61] the "will of the People" or of "We the People of the United States,"[62] "the American People,"[63] and (most frequent of all) "the People,"[64] are ubiquitous in Acker-

58 Ackerman, "Constitutional Politics/Constitutional Law," 469–71.

59 Id. at 455. Whatever criteria Ackerman uses in making such a judgment cannot include constitutional or legal principles, since those principles, in his view, are the creatures of the sovereign and subject to its plenary control. See Ackerman's discussion of a hypothetical amendment establishing a national religion. *Foundations*, 14–15.

60 See the opening and closing of the Declaration of Independence ("When . . . it becomes necessary for one people to dissolve the political bands which have connected them with another . . . We . . . in the name, and by the authority of the good people . . . ").

61 E.g., Ackerman, *Foundations*, 7; "Constitutional Politics/Constitutional Law," 458.

62 E.g., Ackerman, *Foundations*, 23;"Constitutional Politics/Constitutional Law," 465.

63 Ackerman, "Constitutional Politics/Constitutional Law," 471.

64 E.g., Ackerman, *Foundations*, 6; "Constitutional Politics/Constitutional Law," 490.

man's constitutional theory writings. Nor is this a mere linguistic tic. The notion of dualistic democracy is predicated on the claim that at certain times in American history the people as a collectivity deliberated and chose the constitutional rules under which they willed to be governed.

The problem here is both historical and normative. The 1787 Constitution was, it is true, ratified by a process that was remarkably open and "democratic" for the time—but "the people" who participated excluded white women and children, Native Americans, slaves (among whom the vast majority of blacks were counted), and even significant numbers of adult white males. The process was, in addition, one that culminated in decisions by representative assemblies several of which probably ignored the known views of a majority of their constituents.[65] The processes by which the Reconstruction-era amendments were adopted were even more convoluted, as Ackerman's own narrative makes clear.[66] And the "switch in time" that repudiated *Lochner* may not have been caused primarily by Roosevelt's political successes at all; public and congressional opinion was running strongly against the Court-packing plan before the Court announced its change of mind, and (as discussed above) the internal critique of *Lochner* had been going on long before the New Deal. Only the first of Ackerman's constitutional moments even purported to involve the voting public as a group in any part of the direct constitutional discussion, and none of them came anywhere near the national referendum that Ackerman's rhetoric suggests.

Ackerman's constitutionalism rests, in the end, on a simple ontological mistake; he posits the existence of a People that acts in identifiable ways and speaks in comprehensible tones. The entire elaborate theory is an extended account of the activities of this entity, but the narrative does not provide a plausible description of its

65 Ackerman simply ignores the logical and theoretical problems inherent in his equation of majoritarian and representative decisionmaking with the "will" or "decision" of the collectivity.

66 The Thirteenth Amendment, the only Reconstruction amendment about which it is clear that even a simple majority of Americans were in favor, was declared ratified by counting the actions of the legislatures the ex-Confederate states elected in the summer and fall of 1865. Almost simultaneously, Congress refused to seat the senators those assemblies chose on the grounds that the "legislatures" involved were not elected by democratic means and enjoyed no legitimate authority.

central character. Ackerman's national community is a political myth treated as a historical reality.

NEOREPUBLICAN MORALITY

The attempt to base constitutionalism on the morality of the political process is related to but distinct from a second strand in contemporary theory, the civic or neorepublican school. The original source of inspiration for neorepublican constitutional theory was the historical scholarship of the 1970s that challenged the Lockean consensus on the liberal origins of American political thought.[67] Other intellectual currents subsequently fed into the so-called republican revival in constitutional thought. Antiliberal political theory played a role,[68] and a 1980s backlash against the political success of public choice theorists clearly was significant. Cass Sunstein of the University of Chicago School of Law, for example, came to neorepublican constitutionalism by way of reaction to the impact of public choice (and Chicago School economics) on Sunstein's primary area of scholarship, administrative law.[69] Much of American administrative law involves the delegation to agencies of the power to interpret and implement very general statutory language "in the public interest."[70] From the dawn of the American administrative agency, interpretation "in the public interest" had been understood to involve a determination of what policies would most benefit national society viewed as a whole; lying behind the legal doctrine was a view of legislation as a quest for the true common good and not as the chance outcome of clashes and compromises between warring interest groups. Public choice and law-and-economics scholars beginning in the 1970s began a sustained intellectual assault on the assumption that any such

67 See Cass Sunstein, "Beyond the Republican Revival," 97 Yale L.Rev. 1539 (1988).

68 See, e.g., Frank Michaelman, "Law's Republic," 97 Yale L.Rev. 1493, 1494 n. 4 (1988).

69 See, e.g., Cass Sunstein, "Interest Groups in American Public Law," 38 Stan. L. Rev. 29 (1985).

70 See generally Peter Strauss, *An Introduction to Administrative Justice in the United States* (Durham, N.C.: Carolina Academic Press, 1989).

common good exists. Instead, they argued, majoritarian legislative decisions always embody the aggregation and brokering of the disparate preferences of politically influential groups. The only legitimate goal of the administrative interpretation of statutory law therefore is to identify and enforce the set of bargains that produced the final statutory text.[71]

Against the public choice elimination of the concept of the common good, Sunstein has argued that political decisions can transform, not just embody, private preferences, and that American courts should employ their institutional powers to shape legislative outcomes in nonaggregative "public-regarding" directions.[72] Sunstein does not deny the aggregative and interest-group nature of the legislative process; instead, his argument is that courts are entitled to use their powers (including the practice of constitutional adjudication) to impose "republican" interpretations on the law. Public-regarding republican values for Sunstein are essentially those derived from New Deal/Great Society social welfare thought, and the libertarian and egalitarian themes associated with the Warren and early Burger Courts.

The most carefully developed of the neorepublican theories is

71 The public choice argument may require illustration. Assume Congress enacts a clean water act. The statute contains very general language about guaranteeing "safe drinking water for all Americans" and orders the Environmental Protection Agency to implement it "in the public interest." The statute also contains a variety of particular provisions indicating specific requirements and exceptions. Under the older view, the EPA appropriately would have interpreted the specific provisions in the light of its (the agency's) view of how best to achieve clean water for all, with the likely result that exceptions would be construed narrowly and requirements broadly. The public choice theorists insist that the notion of a "public interest" separate from the aggregation of private preferences is a myth: the statute is simply the result of the efforts (in most cases, partly successful and partly not) of proenvironmentalists to impose strict standards, industry supporters to avoid regulation, and so on. The older view, according to public choice theory, simply permitted the agency to rewrite the statutory bargain so that some groups ended up with more of a victory than they had the legislative strength to achieve through the political process. On the application of public choice theory to law, see Daniel A. Farber and Philip P. Frickey, *Law and Public Choice* (Chicago: Univ. of Chicago Press, 1991).

72 See, e.g., Sunstein, *After the Rights Revolution* (Cambridge, Mass.: Harvard Univ. Press, 1990).

that of Harvard Professor Frank Michaelman.[73] Michaelman's basic objective has been to show that notions of civic virtue support an activist role for the Supreme Court in protecting a substantive ideal of individual freedom and equality against legislative intrusion. The "republican" image of society[74] is one in which citizens empowered to exercise their own moral judgments come together to make decisions informed by common deliberation, mutual sensitivity, and equal respect. The resulting laws deserve obedience because of their unselfish and virtuous origins and (presumably) content. Constitutional adjudication is justified by its ability to correct the failures of deliberation into which the actual majoritarian process sometimes falls, and thus to ensure that the moral content of the law is admirable and deserving of obedience. On the level of legal doctrine, therefore, Michaelman strongly supports the Court's continued use of substantive due process to impose civic virtue on a sometimes unvirtuous public.

The underlying problem that made the revival of substantive due process into a full-blown epistemological crisis, according to Michaelman, is American constitutionalism's vulnerability to the temptation of what he calls *authoritarianism.* The Court, constitutionalists, and governmental officials alike are inclined toward accepting "alienated authority,"[75] the pronouncement of and obedience to political and moral norms solely because they are the "formally enacted preferences" of a past legislature or constitutional process or stem from "the received teachings of an historically dominant . . . orthodoxy."[76] Michaelman traces the origins of this constitutional tendency to authoritarianism to classical liberalism's scepticism about the ability of individuals to "communicate persuasively to one another [their] diverse . . . experiences of needs and regrets, values and

73 See, e.g., Michaelman, "Law's Republic," supra; "Traces of Self-Government," 100 Harv. L. Rev. 4 (1986); "Possession versus Distribution in the Constitutional Idea of Property," 72 Iowa L. Rev. 1319 (1988).

74 Like Sunstein, Michaelman believes that neorepublicanism stands in the tradition of early modern civic-virtue thought, although he concedes, as does Sunstein, that the specific libertarian and egalitarian values of neorepublican virtue differ from those consciously held in the eighteenth century.

75 Michaelman, "Law's Republic," 97 Yale L. J. at 1517.

76 Id. at 1496.

interests, and, more broadly, interpretations of the world."[77] This liberal scepticism leads directly to a market interpretation of politics, in which the public sphere is seen as the means "through which variously interested and motivated individuals and groups seek to maximize their own particular preferences."[78] Michaelman thus has a clear interpretation of the current constitutional crisis; having forgotten its civic-virtue justification, pluralist liberals cannot understand constitutional adjudication as anything other than the introduction of yet another set of private preferences, ones that happen to enjoy extraordinary institutional authority.

Contemporary liberal constitutionalism is rapidly disintegrating, according to Michaelman. The emerging "conservative" majority on the Court and its supporters have responded by advocating "an excessively detached and passive judicial stance toward constitutional law" that avoids imposing their own preferences at the cost of essentially abandoning the practice of constitutional adjudication.[79] The advocates of a continued active role for the Court, on the other hand, cannot reconcile their desire for the Court to enforce libertarian and egalitarian values with allegiance to democratic decision making.

Michaelman chooses Ackerman as the paradigm of authoritarian constitutional thought. For Ackerman, Michaelman points out, the Court cannot enforce any substantive moral or political principle unless there has been "an actual . . . event of jurisgenerative popular politics."[80] The Court thus has no independent role in the determination of constitutional principles but is merely "the agent of our constitutional past," the enforcer of alienated authority. For neorepublicanism, in contrast, the Court is the vehicle of a continuing and evolving conversation about the nature of the common good and individual liberty, and constitutional adjudication is one of the primary means by which deliberation about those matters is structured.[81] The dialectic between personal opinion, legislative enactment and judicial decision creates the possibility of "personal self-revision under social-

77 Id. at 1507.
78 Id. at 1508.
79 Id. at 1496.
80 Id. at 1519–20.
81 Id. at 1502.

dialogic stimulation,"[82] through which "private-regarding 'men' become public-regarding citizens and thus members of a people."[83]

Neorepublican theory requires two social prerequisites. First, the polity must be a true social community rather than a mere conglomeration of individuals.[84] The community, furthermore, must share a tradition of moral discourse, not merely (as authoritarian liberals such as Ackerman assume) "extraordinary and episodic" flights into higher lawmaking.[85] The neorepublican constitutional tradition Michaelman believes he can trace back through American history allows at least the working hypothesis that the United States meets both criteria.

Michaelman's neorepublicanism is an ambitious attempt to dissolve the countermajoritarian difficulty and thus overcome the current epistemological crisis; it is, I believe, clearly unsuccessful. Michaelman, like his intellectual opponent Ackerman, must posit the existence of a national community which he is unable to locate in social reality. Ackerman does so by taking literally the rhetoric of popular sovereignty, Michaelman by admitting that the necessary community may not exist, and then ignoring the problem.[86] The problem with this procedure is that Michaelman does not purport to be writing a *Utopia* but rather an interpretation of an existing political-legal system. To bracket the question of whether the interpretation fits the system is to undermine the entire enterprise. Michaelman's studious refusal to address the plausibility of his neorepublican account of American constitutionalism makes his theory an escape from, not the resolution of, the tradition's problems.

Michaelman's theory suffers from a second flaw: Michaelman blames the constitutional crisis on pluralist liberalism but fails in the end to break with pluralist liberalism himself. Surprisingly for a self-described advocate of civic virtue, Michaelman expressly accepts liberalism's goal of avoiding public discussion about questions of the human good. Indeed, the way to commend a political perspective or proposal in Michaelman's republic is to show its value in unmistak-

82 Id. at 1504.
83 Id. at 1502.
84 Id. at 1506.
85 Id. at 1514, 1521 n. 112.
86 Id. at 1506.

ably utilitarian terms.[87] Neorepublicanism shares liberalism's rejection of any attempt to articulate a common moral vision—other than the morality of tolerance—through politics and law. Such an attempt would amount to "static, parochial . . . coercive communitarianism"; if defined in terms of traditional Christian moral commitments, it would be "frightening" and "moral majoritarian."[88] The fault in the Court's decision upholding a sodomy law (*Bowers v. Hardwick*) lay in the Court's willingness to permit the state "to give expression and effect to a legislative majority's moral" views.[89]

Michaelman is equally liberal in his failure to note that he himself has a moral-political agenda, albeit not articulated as such, that he believes government can and should pursue. Michaelman defines human nature as constituted by an endless self-critical search for wider perspectives[90] from which he derives a series of moral imperatives that neorepublicanism is intended to implement. Michaelman reinterprets the American rhetoric of popular sovereignty along these lines as demanding a government based on "respect for the human capacity for self-renewal."[91] Authoritarian jurisprudence is a mistake because past decisions of the community interfere with the ongoing self-transformation of individuals.[92] Neorepublicanism is committed to what Michaelman calls "the modern context" of "equality of respect, liberation from ascriptive social roles, and [the] indissolvable plurality of perspectives" while it is hostile toward anything smacking of "organicist culture," unifying interpretations of "social experience and normative perspectives," and "social-role constraint."[93] Neorepublican civic virtue is almost indistinguishable from the duty of indifference to others that is the primary virtue of radical libertarianism.

Michaelman's allegiance to liberal individualism is matched by his endorsement of liberal egalitarianism. The moral necessity of individual and corporate self-criticism requires some means of ensuring that "a new slant on the world penetrate[s] the dominant con-

87 Id. at 1504.
88 Id. at 1495.
89 Id. at 1496, 1533.
90 Id. at 1528.
91 Id. at 1500–1501, 1528.
92 See, e.g., id. at 1532–36.
93 Id. at 1526, 1506.

sciousness." It is the role of neorepublican constitutional law to fill that role by constantly pressuring dominant social groups to open their minds and broaden their horizons.[94] Constitutionalism must do so, furthermore, whether its participants like it or not. Despite his talk about a politics of "dialogic self-modulation,"[95] Michaelman's theory in fact has little respect or even tolerance for democratic politics. Neorepublican constitutional law must serve as "the institutionalized discipline that render[s] legislative politics trustworthy" by measuring the results of the political process against the "transcendental" or "metaphysical" standards of neorepublicanism.[96] The goal is so to shape and correct legislative decision making that "everyone" subject to the law "can regard himself or herself as actually agreeing that [the laws in question] warrant being promulgated" as compulsory.[97]

Michaelman concedes the common-sense observation that current American law cannot meet this "validity condition,"[98] and even that he is unable to assert "unconditionally that republican constitutionalism is possible for us."[99] These are, however, only theoretical embarrassments, for the requirement of universal assent can be satisfied in practice by employing a variant on John Rawls's famous "veil of ignorance" argument.[100] A law is valid if it can be imagined that all Americans, "arguing sincerely on behalf of one another or of everyone" would regard it as deserving legal enactment.[101] I have deliberately cast this summary sentence in the passive voice in order to reflect Michaelman's reluctance to specify outright *who* is to do the imagining and under what actual conditions of discussion. The answer, although not express, is clear: the justices of the Supreme

94 Id. at 1529–30.

95 E.g., id. at 1527.

96 Id. at 1501, 1510–13. Michaelman is explicitly using the distinction the later Rawls has drawn between political (tradition-dependent) and metaphysical (classically liberal context-free) political theories. Neorepublicanism rests on what Michaelman calls a "historicized" version of a metaphysical philosophy of human nature and society.

97 Id. at 1526.

98 Id. at 1526–28.

99 Id. at 1527.

100 See id. at 1511–12 for an explicit reference to the veil of ignorance heuristic.

101 Id. at 1512–13.

Court, following the "institutionalized discipline" of neorepublican constitutional law, are ideally situated to carry out the task of imagining what the ideal content of the law must be.[102] "Why *ought* the Supreme Court not be an organ of politics, if that is what it takes to secure liberty and justice. . . . Why *ought* popular-majoritarian preference rather than judicial argument ultimately determine the question of law?"[103] Michaelman states at one point that "[a]ctual democracy is not all there is to political freedom."[104] This is, however, an understatement; according to neorepublicanism, "actual democracy" is a perennial threat to freedom, and government by a judiciary properly embued with late twentieth-century libertarian and egalitarian views is the very image of a free political order. Michaelman resolves the constitutional crisis by declaring false one of the central themes—the primacy of democratic decision making—of modern constitutional discussion.

AMERICAN SOCIAL MORALITY AS A CIVIC RELIGION

Some contemporary constitutional theorists believe that the current epistemological crisis can be overcome by explicating the "religious" nature of the American polity. These theories of civic-religious constitutionalism take a variety of forms, and their proponents often disagree sharply about the substantive implications.[105] This section focuses on the work of Michael J. Perry, a law professor at North-

102 Id. at 1537.
103 Id. at 1498.
104 Id. at 1537.
105 See, e.g., the symposium on "Religious Dimensions of American Constitutionalism" recently published in 39 Emory L.J. 1–215 (1990). The range of substantive legal opinion found within civic-religious constitutionalism can be illustrated by comparing the work of Richard J. Neuhaus and Michael J. Perry. Neuhaus and Perry define the religious nature of American constitutionalism in almost identical terms; compare Neuhaus, "The Moral Delegitimatization of Law," 4 Notre Dame J. of Law, Ethics & Public Policy 51, 52–53 (1989), with Perry, *The Constitution, the Courts, and Human Rights* (New Haven: Yale Univ. Press, 1982), 97. They nonetheless disagree radically over the moral content of constitutional law.

western University and a Roman Catholic, whose version of civic-religious constitutional theory is the most elaborate and most discussed. The lengthiest statement of Perry's specifically constitutional views was published in his 1982 book on *The Constitution, the Courts, and Human Rights*. Perry wrote the book as an explicit response to the crisis in constitutional theory and out of the conviction that the controversy "is both coherent and resolvable."[106]

Perry agrees with most other constitutionalists in viewing the crisis as primarily a debate about the legitimacy in a democracy of the type of decisions *Brown* and *Roe* exemplify, but he draws a distinction to clarify what is at stake. *Interpretive* judicial review involves the judicial enforcement against contemporary legislatures of the "complex of value judgments the framers wrote into the text of the Constitution." Almost everyone (Perry was writing before Michaelman began publishing on neorepublicanism) agrees that interpretive review is legitimate.[107] *Noninterpretive* judicial review is "constitutional policy-making (by the judiciary) that goes *beyond* the value judgments established by the framers of the written Constitution (extraconstitutional policymaking)."[108] Perry directs his attention almost entirely to noninterpretive review of "human rights issues"[109] both because the current crisis revolves around cases such as *Eisenstadt* and because he thinks that "[v]irtually all of modern constitutional decisionmaking by the Court" of any importance is noninterpretive in nature.[110] Indeed, Perry believes that the tradition is in crisis because the recognition that essentially all modern constitu-

106 Perry, *Rights*, xii.

107 Id. at 11.

108 Id. at ix. Perry notes the existence of a third category, "contraconstitutional policymaking," which would be judicial policymaking that went "*against* the framers' value judgments." Perry dismisses the issues contraconstitutional judicial review would raise with the claim that "virtually no constitutional doctrine . . . established by the modern Supreme Court represents a value judgment contrary to any of the framers' value judgments." Id. This argument seems to beg the question. Contemporary proponents of judicial restraint such as Robert Bork argue that what Perry calls "extraconstitutional" judicial policymaking is actually contrary to the founders' value judgments because it takes from the democratic branches authority the founders thought those branches ought to wield.

109 Id. at 61. Perry defines these as "issues concerning the nature and extent of the fundamental rights of individuals vis-à-vis government."

110 Id. at 2.

tional law is noninterpretive carries the implication that if noninterpretive review cannot be justified, modern constitutional law is a failure.[111]

The intellectual problem with justifying noninterpretive review is for Perry the familiar countermajoritarian difficulty. Americans are "philosophically committed" to "the political principle that governmental policymaking . . . ought to be subject to control by persons accountable to the electorate." This principle is "axiomatic" in American culture: "it is judicial review, not that principle, that requires justification."[112] Perry rejects the value of any attempt to dissolve the countermajoritarian difficulty by redefining democracy to include judicial review. Such attempts contradict the generally assumed cultural notion of democracy and the best theoretical definitions of it, both of which treat it as a procedural concept.[113] On the other hand, Perry also rejects definitions of democracy that gauge an institution's democratic credentials solely by how perfectly it reflects current public opinion. The American commitment to democracy has been to representative, not plebiscitary democracy. "What is crucial is electoral accountability, not degree of responsiveness to majority sentiments."[114] Nonetheless, even as so defined this commitment renders constitutional adjudication facially illegitimate.[115]

What renders the countermajoritarian difficulty solvable is the fact that the American social commitment to democracy is axiomatic but not exclusive. Americans are historically and culturally committed to a second and "coequal principle": "electorally accountable policymaking is constrained by the value judgments embodied in the constitutional text."[116] Interpretive judicial review is the institutional means the American polity evolved to give substance to the value judgments the text constitutionalizes.

Perry defends interpretive review against arguments that it necessarily involves a mindless literalism or that it is impossible to

111 Perry repeatedly emphasizes that unless some justification for noninterpretive review is found, the modern practice of constitutional adjudication and its conclusions—including *Brown v. Board of Education*—must be discarded. See, e.g., id. at 2–3, 11, 63, 130.

112 Id. at 9.

113 Id. at 3–4.

114 Id. at 31.

115 Id. at 7.

116 Id. at 24, 12.

discern and apply the Founders' value judgments in a coherent manner; as far as it goes, interpretive review is in Perry's view an appropriate mode of constitutional adjudication.[117] But, and this is crucial to Perry's argument, the legitimacy of interpretive review is not self-evident. The text itself does not command or authorize interpretive review, nor is there convincing evidence that the Founders intended to constitutionalize "any theory of the proper scope of judicial review."[118] Interpretive review is legitimated, instead, by a functional justification:[119] interpretive review is legitimate because the Founders sought to make their constitutionalized value judgments "limits on federal law [with] the force of law." "Because the limits are a part of the supreme law, some institution must enforce them. Otherwise the limits are not legal norms in any meaningful sense, but are, at most, political [or] moral norms."[120] The federal judiciary is the institution "with the greatest institutional capacity to enforce the legal norms of the Constitution in an disinterested way."[121]

Interpretive judicial review, then, is legitimate; Perry on the other hand rejects *interpretivism*, the claim that "*only* interpretive judicial review is legitimate."[122] Perry's response to interpretivism is to argue for the moral unacceptability of limiting constitutional adjudication to interpretive review. The intellectually consistent interpretivist, Perry insists, "must oppose" *Brown v. Board of Education* and many other morally and politically attractive decisions "because [the governmental actions struck down] were present to the minds of the framers but the framers chose not to ban them."[123] The problem is quite general with respect to the "power limiting constitutional provisions": those provisions "typically represent and embody . . . discrete, determinate value judgments about what sorts of political

117 Id. at 32, 61–75.

118 Id. at 74.

119 By a functional justification, Perry means "a justification based on the essential function the practice serves" in American government. Id. at 13.

120 Id. at 14, 15. Perry, of course, is assuming without arguing one side of a fundamental dispute in the philosophy of law: is the existence of an enforcement mechanism essential to a norm being "legal" instead of "merely" political or moral?

121 Id. at 15–16.

122 Id. at 11 (emphasis added).

123 Id. at 33.

practices" the Founders wished to ban,[124] and so necessarily cannot serve to uphold a long list of free speech and equal protection decisions that Perry believe enjoy near-universal approval.[125]

Perry hopes by this point to have caught the reader between the Scylla of theoretical incoherence and the Charybdis of abandoning *Brown*, the one person/one vote principle, and the entirety of the modern First Amendment. He offers his theory of noninterpretive review as the way out. Interpretivism suffers from the defect of its virtue; by binding constitutional adjudication to the Founders' value judgments, interpretivism limits constitutional law to the level of moral insight the Founders achieved. But "the Constitution established by the framers does not ordain a perfectly just society,"[126] and so interpretivism writes moral imperfection into the fundamental law. Perry hopes the reader will therefore agree that it is morally desirable to find a justification for a form of judicial review that is not limited to the Founders' level of insight.[127]

The justification for the noninterpretive review that Perry offers to meet this moral desideratum parallels the justification he provided for interpretive review. Noninterpretive review cannot be legitimated on the basis of the text or of the Founders' intentions,[128] so we must seek a functional justification. Noninterpretive review's function, unsurprisingly, "is the elaboration and enforcement by the Court of values, pertaining to human rights, not constitutionalized by the framers; it is the function of deciding what rights, beyond those specified by the framers, individuals should and shall have against government."[129]

At the parallel point in his argument for the legitimacy of interpretive review, Perry invoked the American social commitment to constraining democratic choices by values embodied in the constitutional text. In order to justify noninterpretive review, Perry de-

124 Id. at 71. Perry thinks that the Constitution's grants of power to the federal government, in contrast, are intentionally "indeterminate in scope." Id. at 41.

125 Id. at 117.

126 Id. at 88.

127 "I prefer to let the framers sleep. Just as the framers, in their day, judged by their lights, so must we, in our day, judge by ours." Id. at 75.

128 Id. at 20, 24, 92.

129 Id. at 93.

scribes "a particular conception of the American polity that seems to constitute a basic, irreducible feature of the American people's understanding of themselves," a conception that Perry says can be described as religious.[130]

Perry's use of the language of (civic) religion is meant to refer to a specific set of ideas. The American people[131] have understood themselves as "chosen," placed somehow under the obligation to realize in their political life a higher law than their own collective will. This sense of chosenness was originally expressed in straightforwardly biblical terms, but it has persisted over time even as "the cultural cast of the metaphors" has become less and less biblical in tone. "The American people still see themselves as a nation standing under transcendent judgment: They understand . . . that morality is not arbitrary, that justice cannot be reduced to the sum of the preferences of the collectivity."[132] A corollary to this religious self-understanding has been an acceptance of the idea of *prophecy*, the task of which is to call the nation to judgment "in the here and now" when the people "fail in their responsibility."[133] American prophecy, in Perry's view, has not served a purely backward-looking, restorative role, but plays a role in moral evolution as well. The American people are committed to a continuing recognition that "we are fallible and we must struggle incessantly to achieve a better—a broader and deeper—understanding." Prophecy's role with respect to this aspect of the American religious self-consciousness is to drive political practice into harmony with an "evolving, deepening moral understanding."[134]

Perry is somewhat reluctant to stake the persuasiveness of his entire constitutional theory on acceptance of his argument about the "religious" self-consciousness of the American people.[135] However,

130 Id. at 97.

131 Perry is careful not to rely on a mythical "We the People." By "the people" he simply means the "great bulk of those who have been responsible for establishing, developing and maintaining" the American political system. Id. at 97. Perry does not address the fact that this "great bulk" has been over time a quite small oligarchy among the total group of persons living within the United States.

132 Id. at 97, 98.

133 Id. at 98.

134 Id. at 99.

135 See id. at 99–100.

the argument plays an essential role in the theory, bridging the gap between the polity's social commitments and the function of protecting human rights not addressed by the Founders. Electorally responsible officials inevitably will deal with moral questions that "challenge and unsettle conventional ways of understanding the moral universe," and neither their own political judgments nor interpretive review are adequate means of addressing the resulting problems. The officials' inevitable concern with their own political fortunes virtually ensures that they will deal with unsettling or novel questions by "reference to the established moral conventions of the greater part of their particular constituencies."[136] The Founders' value choices (and therefore interpretive review) are more likely to be part of the conventional understanding than to provide innovative means of addressing new issues. Unless then some other institution can serve the function of engaging in an "ongoing, vigorous reevaluation of established moral conventions," the American people's religious commitment to moral evolution will not be fulfilled. Noninterpretive review by a judiciary free of electoral accountability is that institution; in Perry's civil-religious language, noninterpretive review is the institutionalization of prophecy.[137]

Justifying noninterpretive review does not by itself inform the judges how they should engage in it once the traditional legal methods of interpretive review become useless, and so Perry examines what "source of values . . . can serve as a reservoir of decisional norms for human rights cases."[138] Perry rejects as unworkable two

136 Id. at 100, 120–21.

137 Id. at 101, 98. Perry briefly explores another way of justifying noninterpretive review that leaves aside the language of civil religion and even the notion of moral evolution. "[A]s a society we seem to be open to the possibility that there are right answers to political-moral problems." If so, he assumes, our openness to this possibility justifies noninterpretive review as a search for those "right" answers. Still uneasy about the plausibility of this pared-down version of his claim about American social commitments, Perry offers one final move that abandons altogether any claim about those commitments: "even if evidence [is] slight that we are open to that possibility [of moral right answers], we *should be* open to it." Id. at 102 (emphasis in original). At this point, Perry has saved his theory from one of its chief weaknesses—the unconvincing nature of his argument about American religion—at the expense of reducing the theory to the simple assertion that judges should impose their views of the right moral answers because they think those views are correct.

138 Id. at 93.

obvious suggestions, the American moral and political tradition and the current consensus of Americans. Those who invoke either tradition or consensus as a source of noninterpretive review are guilty of "a serious failure to face the unsentimental truth about the severely fragmented character of concrete American traditions and values."[139] Even with respect to the shared social commitment to democracy there is no general "consensus as to *the sort of* democratic process that ought to prevail in America."[140]

Perry concludes that there is only one "source of values" to which judges sensibly can turn in making noninterpretive decisions—the "right answers to political-moral problems."[141] Judges are to decide human rights cases explicitly on the basis of what they think is right.[142] The American people's religious self-understanding with its belief in moral evolution assumes that there are such right answers, since one could not otherwise speak of moral *evolution* in a teleological fashion.[143] Furthermore, noninterpretive review makes sense only on the assumption that there are right answers discoverable by reasoned argument. The lack of any agreement on which philosophical or religious approach is the correct one to use in looking for the right answers is not a problem. The right answers, Perry asserts, will "frequently represent . . . a point at which *a variety* of philosophical and religious systems of moral thought and belief converge." What matters is not that judges determine the right (or best) argument on a moral question, but that they come to the right *conclusion*.[144]

Simply recommending orthopraxy rather than orthodoxy does not, of course, do anything to explain how a judge is to reason toward the right answer or how anyone could tell when the judge has found it. Perry's answer is to provide discrete pieces of advice to the judge. The judge should consult what he or she "personally regard[s as] the

139 Id. at 94.
140 Id. at 79.
141 Id. at 102.
142 Id. at 102.
143 From the standpoint of evolutionary biology, Perry's use of the metaphor of moral evolution is almost perverse: the biological theory of evolution is not teleological. This observation is not purely rhetorical, for Perry's (mis)use of the metaphor stems from one of the most important underlying assumptions of Perry's 1982 book, his unexamined liberal and foundationalist understanding of morality.
144 Id. at 109–10.

most relevant and fruitful moral thought."[145] He or she should "give weight, which is not to say *conclusive* weight," to moral views that are widely shared, and thus permit a "subtle, dialectical interplay between Court and polity."[146] The judge should reach conclusions only after "a very deliberate search for right answers."[147]

The almost off-hand character of Perry's suggestions about how courts should engage in noninterpretive review is intentional. Perry does not believe there is or could be any generalizable mode of moral reasoning or any definable set of moral principles to which judges should be bound. In "the exercise of noninterpretive review . . . the determinative norms derive—again not in an unselfconscious way—from the judges' own moral vision."[148] In deciding human rights cases, judges act explicitly as individual legislators, adopting the moral answers that each of them believes are right.[149] There was nothing wrong methodologically with the *Lochner* Court's imposition of the justices' moral beliefs on legislatures—Perry thinks *Brown* did precisely the same thing. The difference between *Lochner* and *Brown* is that the former gave a wrong answer, and the latter a right one, to the respective moral questions at issue.[150]

Perry then addresses a final problem: how do the American social commitments to democracy, to constitutional constraints, and to a religious self-consciousness of obligation to seek moral right answers interrelate? Perry's implicit assumption seems to be that the commitment to democracy enjoys a certain kind of lexical priority over the other two. The relationship between democracy and the existence of constitutional constraints (and their enforcement through intrepretive review) ultimately is ordered by the formal amendment process, by which the people democratically can change the content of the constitutional text. Perry reconciles democracy and the American religious self-consciousness through another legal argument, the existence of virtually plenary congressional (democratic) control over

145 Id. at 110.

146 Id. at 124, 113.

147 Id. at 123.

148 Id. at 123.

149 "The problem of how to proceed, when dealing with a difficult human rights issue, is not different for the justice than it is for the legislator." Id. at 111.

150 Id. at 125.

the jurisdiction of the federal courts. While Congress (probably)[151] cannot reverse a Supreme Court human rights decision, it can silence the Court.[152]

Perry's 1982 theory of noninterpretive review has attracted great attention, but the theory is not ultimately convincing. The structure of the argument depends on the sharp contrast Perry draws between interpretive and noninterpretive review, but this dichotomy is a false one, at least in the very strong form he adopts. Interpretivism (the claim that interpretive review is the only legitimate kind) need not be construed so narrowly. Perry's historical claim that the text's human rights provisions were intended to bar only quite specific and narrow governmental practices is controvertible. Among many apparent exceptions to Perry's assertion one might cite the cruel and unusual punishment clause; the Ninth Amendment, which on its face appears to refer to an open-ended set of rights; and section one of the Fourteenth Amendment. More generally, there is substantial evidence that the Founders intended to constrain government by a broad range of unwritten principles.[153] Perry, in addition, does not acknowledge the concept of a tradition of rational inquiry in which novel interpretations of the tradition's texts are rational extensions of the earlier understanding of the texts. For Perry, apparently, moral decisions either follow narrowly past understanding or they repudiate it (however sympathetically and deliberately).[154] Perry eliminates interpretivism from serious consideration as a means of protecting human rights by arguments a serious interpretivist need not accept.

Perry's 1982 theory is also flawed by his description of the moral reasoning he thinks courts should employ in noninterpretive review. Perry's account of the judges' moral stance is stringently individualistic. Each judge must come to his or her own decisions, determined

151 Perry equivocates over the power of Congress to reverse *Roe* by statute. Id. at 135–37.

152 Id. at 128. Since the question of federal court jurisdiction is one of structure rather than of human rights, the only legitimate basis on which the Court could review a jurisdiction-stripping statute would be interpretive, and Perry believes that the founders clearly intended to give Congress almost unlimited power to determine the scope of the courts' jurisdiction. Id. at 133.

153 See Suzanna Sherry, "The Founders' Unwritten Constitution," 54 U.Chicago L.Rev. 1127 (1987).

154 Perry, *Rights*, 95–96.

only by individual conscience and unconstrained by any legal, philosophical, or social context. While Perry believes in the existence of discoverable moral right answers, he does not believe in the existence of generally articulable criteria for their discovery or recognition. We are never told, for example, how Perry knows that *Lochner* was wrong and *Brown* right or, for that matter, how the justices knew. Perry urges judges to consult a variety of moral perspectives, but on principle he provides no guidance on what the judge should look for. The only moral principles in Perry's theory are the inviolability of the individual judicial conscience and the openness to reversal of all previous moral decisions. The theory of noninterpretive review is a restatement of moral intuitionism, with the exercise and implementation of intuition limited to federal judges. The result is that Perry's moral theory is functionally emotivist.[155]

The notion of religion Perry employs also causes problems. Perry stresses that he is not using the term *religious* in a "sectarian, theistic, or otherwise metaphysical sense," but this statement (which is italicized in the book) oversimplifies the manner in which Perry in fact uses the word. His affirmative definition is rooted, he says, in the word's "etymological sense." The term is shorthand for that which refers to "a binding vision—a vision that serves as a source of unalienated self-understanding, of 'meaning in the sense of existential orientation or rootedness.'"[156] Given Perry's criticism of the notion of an American tradition as unrealistic, he is unwilling to think of the American civil religion in social terms; he instead adopts an "experiential-expressive" interpretation of religion[157] that leads straight into his radically individualistic understanding of moral decision making. At the same time, Perry's experiential-expressive rhetoric, with its abstract and universalizing tone, conceals from him and from the incautious reader how particular (how sectarian, if you will) Perry's own moral judgments are.[158]

155 Not, of course, that Perry means to be an emotivist; the point is that his use of moral judgments is functionally emotivistic. See, e.g., MacIntyre (1984), 269, discussing emotivism as "an empirical thesis about the use and function of moral judgments."

156 Perry, *Rights*, 97.

157 See Lindbeck, *Doctrine*, 31–32.

158 Perry's opinions as to the right moral answers are almost always clear—and almost always are those one would predict an academic lawyer teaching in an elite law school would hold. The one exception, Perry's uncertainty about abor-

Perry's 1982 book contains various indications that his ultimate moral stance, one he shares with much of the upper-middle classes in recent Western society, is shaped by liberal individualism, the popular appropriation of psychoanalysis, and some forms of existentialist literature and philosophy. However, the book explicitly uses the moral vocabulary of the *therapeutic* account of human life—"alienation," "authenticity," "growth," "openness"—only on occasion.[159] In contrast, Perry's allegiance to the therapeutic account and to its libertarian and egalitarian preferences dominates his 1988 sequel, *Morality, Politics and Law*.[160]

Much of Perry's 1988 book addresses issues that are not directly relevant to this essay,[161] and other parts restate arguments made in the 1982 book.[162] Nonetheless, *Morality, Politics and Law* does add (or qualify) several aspects of Perry's constitutional theory. First, as just mentioned, the new book greatly expands the explicit role of therapeutic rhetoric. Discussing the notion of "naturalist" moral knowledge he develops in the book, Perry explains that personal "growth" is fundamental to the moral life.[163] Naturalist moral knowledge is "knowledge of how to live so as to flourish . . . to live the most deeply satisfying lives of which we are capable." Perry identifies Aristotle as the original naturalist moral philosopher and states that on the naturalist account moral knowledge is always particularistic and antifoundationalist.[164] "[B]asic moral beliefs," by which Perry means primarily beliefs about what lives are "most deeply satisfying," are, he writes, "less the property of individuals than of communities."[165] Perry remains firmly committed, however, to the radical

tion, seems clearly connected to his Catholicism. None of this is a ground for criticism, of course, and I in fact admire many of Perry's moral views. The point is that Perry's moral language, like liberal moral discourse generally, expresses very specific ethical commitments as universal rational principles.

159 See MacIntyre (1984), 30–31, on the role of the therapist in contemporary Western society.

160 Perry, *Morality, Politics and Law* (Oxford: Oxford Univ. Press, 1988).

161 See, e.g., his attack on Rawls and Dworkin, Perry, *Morality*, 55–73. Perry's moral views make the attack an intramural disagreement among liberals.

162 E.g., his discussion of interpretivism/noninterpretivism, now relabeled "originalism/nonoriginalism." Id. at 122–45.

163 Id. at 20–21.

164 Id. at 11, 228 n. 4.

165 Id. at 29.

individualism of the 1982 book.[166] The telos of individuals is "radical growth," which may involve "disintegration of personality as well as, hopefully, reintegration."[167] The purpose of politics is therapeutic, a part of the search for self-knowledge: "we come to know who we truly are—we come to know our authentic selves."[168]

Perry's naturalism is an important monument to the resistance of modern liberal culture to nonliberal criticism. Perry's intention is to be a radical critic of "the liberal political-philosophical project," and references to nonliberals such as MacIntyre and Stanley Hauerwas are ubiquitous in the book. But the assumptions of the 1988 volume are as thoroughly liberal as those of the 1982 book. Perry's psychologized Aristotelianism exemplifies the capacity of liberalism to transform opponents into images of itself.

Another feature of Perry's later book important for our purposes is his revised view of tradition as a meaningful source of constitutional argument.[169] In 1982 Perry saw himself as a philosophical liberal and did not need tradition in order to talk about moral "right" answers: Perryesque judges in 1982 were to seek the answers that are (metaphysically) right, period. Perry's subsequent adoption of naturalism makes this view untenable; Perry now believes that meaningful moral discussion must begin from "whatever 'shared understanding'—whatever shared particular beliefs—can be located among the interlocutors."[170] Naturalism thereby creates a serious problem for Perry because he continues to believe that American moral culture is deeply pluralistic, marked by "the reality of deep, pervasive, persistent moral dissensus."[171] The problem is resolved by asserting the existence of a Rawlsian overlapping consensus. In 1982 Perry saw the

166 See, among many examples, his discussion of the primacy of individual "integrity" and conscientious "choice" in moral life (id. at 101), and his utilitarian justification for social relationships in terms of their value to the individual (id. at 22–23).

167 Id. at 31–32.

168 Id. at 153.

169 Perry's repudiation of "rights-talk" (id. at 185–88) is superficially a striking change, but his unwavering individualism dictates that his theory continue to relate individuals to the community through the enforcement of individual interests in autonomy. As a consequence, Perry's rejection of the term *rights* is of no normative significance.

170 Id. at 36.

171 Id. at 3, 54.

dissensus as *too* deep, *too* radical to permit the identification of any general agreements beyond the most superficial. In 1988 he suggests that even in "a large, morally pluralistic society like our own," the members of the differing groups "might share enough basic beliefs that moral reasoning is often a realistic possibility for them."[172] Despite the careful qualifications of this opening statement, the rest of Perry's argument depends upon the assumption that such a level of basic agreement does in fact exist and that judges usefully can consult it in making noninterpretive ("nonoriginalist") decisions.[173]

Perry introduces a significant modification in 1988 to his account of the relationship of democracy to constitutional adjudication. While he still thinks that electorally accountable decision making is generally viewed as legitimate, he now thinks that "it is *not* axiomatic that that value is lexically prior to all other values."[174] Perry therefore no longer recognizes the existence of a countermajoritarian difficulty. Judicial policy-making is no more problematic than policy-making by elected officials.[175] Indeed, *Morality, Politics and Law* makes it plain that Perry thinks judicial policy-making is in fact *less* problematic than are the products of the electoral political process.

Perry explains his preference for judicial policy-making through another dichotomy, this one between "a deliberative, transformative politics" and "a politics that is merely manipulative and self-serv-

172 Id. at 51.

173 See, e.g., id. at 87. Perry's 1988 discussion of *Roe v. Wade* demonstrates his new approach. Perry now thinks that the Court should have invalidated the statute actually at issue in *Roe*—which criminalized all abortions except to save the life of the mother—but should not have adopted the broad trimester analysis. His reasoning is that American public opinion, across a broad spectrum, accepts the morality of abortion in cases of a serious threat to the woman's life, rape, incest and to avoid the birth of "a genetically defective child whose life would be short and painful." Perry speculates that a ruling that limited the right to an abortion to these situations would have not have been "very controversial." The trimester analysis was also a mistake because it was an attempt "to preempt discourse" about the morality of abortion; instead, the Court should see its role as one of helping to "shape the ensuing political debate" by compelling legislators and others to think and argue over the moral questions involved. Id. at 175–77. The discussion of *Roe* exemplifies the limits of Perry's new concept of overlapping agreement; it is shallow—essentially a suggestion to discern American "tradition" by opinion poll—and its conclusions are likely to be much more controversial than Perry seems to recognize.

174 Id. at 164.

175 Id. at 160–69.

ing."[176] Politics will be "merely manipulative and self-serving if citizens and others treat as a given, a fixed point . . . what they want (their 'preferences') and, therefore, who they are." Politics on that basis can *only* be manipulation. Good politics, on the other hand, is that in which "the questions of what we ought to want and, therefore, who we ought to be are open, not closed."[177] Manipulative politics enables participants, at best, to maximize their preferences; "deliberative, transformative politics," which has as "a principal constituent" moral discourse, empowers participants to know and to change who they are.[178]

Perry is deeply skeptical about the likelihood that legislation, policy-making by elected officials, will be anything other than manipulative in American society.[179] His chapter on legislation, significantly titled "[t]he problem of legislative coercion," has as its major theme the dangers inherent in legislative decisions with a moral component.[180] Perry summarizes his view of legislation as demanding "a strong reluctance on coercive legislative strategies and, so, for a tolerant legislative agenda." There ought to be "a sensible, discriminating awareness about—even a presumption against—the use of coercive state power."[181]

No such presumption should limit the judiciary. "[C]onstitutional adjudication, at its best, is a species of deliberative, transformative politics."[182] Perry is deeply *un*skeptical about the courts' "institutional capacity to engage in the pursuit of political-moral knowledge."[183] Judges can and should engage in an unabashed search for moral good, acting both "as representatives of the political community" and as the "disturbing and even prophetic" "interlocutors of the political community and its elected representatives."[184] Constitu-

176 Id. at 4.

177 Id. at 151–52.

178 Id. at 153.

179 See, e.g., id. at 96–97 (strongly intimating that legislative moral decisions will be oppressive and moral-majoritarian).

180 See, e.g., id. at 98–99 (legislators should be acutely conscious of their fallibility). Perry does not expressly acknowledge that *all* legislation has such a moral component.

181 Id. at 102.

182 Id. at 121.

183 Id. at 147.

184 Id. at 159.

tional adjudication so understood is the "occasion for moral discourse and growth" in American society.[185]

Perry's reevaluation of tradition as a source of American constitutional argument leads him to rework somewhat his account of the role of the constitutional text. The text, the 1988 book argues, both has an original meaning and "is also a symbol of fundamental aspirations of the political tradition."[186] The formal task of noninterpretive or nonoriginalist review is to identify the aspirations symbolized in the text, to decide which are worthwhile, and to enforce the worthwhile ones in accordance with each judge's "*own beliefs* as to what the aspiration requires."[187] Perry now asserts that judges should enforce "only aspirations signified by the text," but this is a purely formal restraint: as Perry himself suggests, it is difficult to conceive of any political "aspiration" that could not be found symbolized in Perry's "text."[188]

The 1982 version of Perry's constitutional theory urged judges to act as the prophets of the American civil-religious commitment to moral growth, subject externally to congressional control of their opportunities to speak and internally to their awareness of the primacy of democracy (and thus of the exceptional nature of judicial policy-making). The 1988 version of the theory has repudiated the primacy of democracy and so needs neither the external nor the internal constraint of the 1982 account. The epistemological crisis of the constitutional tradition that Perry set out to resolve has disappeared into a Platonic Republic with, perhaps, a "majoritarian difficulty" caused by the continuing existence of elected officials. The constitutional community of which Perry writes[189] consists, as a prag-

185 Id. at 142.

186 In this respect, Perry sees the Constitution's role in American life as strictly parallel to the part he thinks sacred texts play in religions. Id. at 133, 136–40.

187 Id. at 134–35, 149. As in 1982, Perry declines on principle to provide criteria for determining which aspirations are worthwhile and which are not, other than the empty injunction that the judges should consult their own consciences.

188 Id. at 134. On the purely formal and quite unconstraining nature of Perry's new "textualism," see also Perry, "The Authority of Text, Tradition and Reason: A Theory of Constitutional Interpretation," 58 So. Calif. L. Rev. 551 (1985).

189 "For many—most?—of us, the constitutional community is a splendid achievement." Perry, *Morality*, 158.

matic matter, of the justices of the Supreme Court and the elite lawyers and scholars who make up the contemporary Court's cultural and institutional milieu.[190] Perry's constitutionalism is a celebration of rule by a radically individualistic moral elite—fundamentally antidemocratic, fundamentally hostile to politics, fundamentally alien to the historical constitutional tradition.

LIBERAL SOCIAL MORALITY AND THE CONSTITUTION

The social morality approach in constitutional theory is sometimes described as fundamentally antiliberal, and indeed many of the communitarian theorists refuse description as liberal. But among the theorists who have adopted social morality accounts of constitutionalism are constitutionalists who are unashamedly liberal (and "liberal").[191] Liberalism, these writers insist, is not inconsistent with a "genuine form of identification" with community.[192] Professor Rogers Smith of Yale has attempted a thoroughgoing reconciliation of

190 See id. at 158–59.

191 The use of the word *liberal* both for the broad range of viewpoints that stem from the Enlightenment and for that specific brand of Enlightenment politics that is commonly called "liberal" in the contemporary United States is, as we have already noted, confusing. All of the theorists discussed in this chapter are liberal in the broader or fundamental sense, even those like Perry who believe they have rejected the Enlightenment; the theorists under consideration in this section define themselves explicitly both as (Enlightenment) liberals and as (contemporary American) "liberals."

192 Ronald Dworkin, "Liberal Community," 77 Calif. L.Rev. 479, 499 (1989). Dworkin, a distinguished legal philosopher, argues that liberals are not committed to rejecting the civic republican claim that "the lives of individual people and of their community are integrated and that the moral success of any one of their lives is an aspect of, and so is dependent on, the goodness of the community as a whole." Id. at 491. Liberals on the other hand necessarily reject the characteristic error of antiliberal communitarians, which is to anthropomorphize the "life" of a political community. That life, on the liberal view, is not "organic" but is constituted entirely by the "formal political acts of the community as a whole"; "citizens are understood to act together, as a collective, only in that structured way." Liberal communitarians will count their own lives enhanced or diminished by the moral successes and failures of those collective acts, and thus can truly be said to live in an "integrated" community. Id. at 500–501.

liberalism with a social morality interpretation of constitutionalism in his *Liberalism and American Constitutional Law*, published in 1985.[193] Smith follows a familiar path in tracing American constitutionalism's origins back to the early liberal thought of Locke and others, but he rejects the common description of those thinkers as Enlightenment foundationalists in search of neutral principles of morality. Early liberalism according to Smith was unabashedly non-neutral, committed explicitly to the pursuit of particular moral goods—"civil peace, mutual prosperity through economic growth, scientific progress, and rational liberty."[194] The liberal stress on legal and constitutional restraints on governmental power, which anti-liberal theorists regard as a demand for objectivity or neutrality in political decision making, was "qualified by its overriding concern to secure fundamental liberal ends effectively."[195]

The success of liberal thought and liberal institutions in shaping American culture has resulted in a general societal agreement on the moral worth of many of the liberal social goods, prosperity, growth, and progress. But the particular liberal good with which constitutionalism is most directly concerned, "rational liberty," is precisely that aspect of liberalism that contemporary theorists most often misunderstand. The liberal concept of rational liberty is based on a quite specific understanding of human nature as constituted by "basic deliberative capacities" and by the potential for "some measure of self-direction." On that basis, liberalism pursues "the preservation and enhancement of human capacities for understanding and reflective self-direction" as "the core of the liberal political and moral vision."[196] The telos of human life is "to enhance the experience of self-awareness and self-governance that is basic to our common sense of ourselves."[197]

Liberalism thus understood as a moral philosophy committed to certain normative goods is not antithetical to all forms of community. Our "personal experience of our selves as conscious, self-directing beings" is dependent (logically and practically) on the account of

193 Smith is a political theorist, not a lawyer, and the first part of the 1985 book is a brilliant analysis of early liberal thought. See Smith, *Liberalism*, 13–59.

194 Id. at 18.

195 Id. at 31.

196 Id. at 201, 200.

197 Id. at 202.

rational self-direction that is "perceived and expounded by the community at large." Constitutional democracy therefore is the most adequate embodiment of liberalism, since such a democracy institutionalizes the community's ability to "elicit prevailing social standards of what constitutes rational, deliberative conduct," while limiting community coercion to the enforcement only of those standards.[198] It is the liberal "emphasis on preserving our capacities for critical reflection, rather than any denial that moral personality" is shaped by the context of community, that marks the crucial difference between Smith's views and those of antiliberal theorists such as MacIntyre and Michael Sandel.[199]

From the beginning of the nineteenth century, Smith contends, the (genuinely) liberal interpretation of American political life and American constitutionalism has been challenged by two quite different competitors: romantic egalitarianism and democratic relativism. The romantic egalitarians, whose lineage Smith traces from Rousseau through Emerson and Thoreau, attacked liberalism as "narrow and ignoble," built on an impoverished account of human nature. The romantic critique of liberalism has led in a variety of affirmative directions; both an anarchistic exaltation of the individual and a social-egalitarian critique of capitalism are characteristic developments.[200] Democratic relativism, on the other hand, eschewed the theoretical and normative commitments of both liberalism and romantic egalitarianism in favor of a "pragmatic democratic appeal to evolving social values."[201] In the twentieth century, Smith argues, the Modern Theory and the rejection of *Lochner* were driven by a democratic-relativist belief that the decisions of the political process are normative, while many aspects of the jurisprudence of the Warren Court reflect romantic egalitarianism. The current crisis in constitutionalism stems in large part from the Burger Court's attempt to combine democratic relativism as a theory with significantly egalitarian and libertarian themes in legal doctrine.[202] Smith's answer to the crisis is to rediscover and refurbish the constitutional tradition's basic liberalism.

198 Id. at 213.
199 Id. at 296 n. 6.
200 Id. at 65.
201 Id. at 65.
202 See, e.g., id. at 114–15, 228–29.

Smith is concerned to distinguish sharply his liberal constitutional theory from the neo-Kantianism of Rawls and Dworkin. Neo-Kantianism, as Smith interprets it, rests on the twin propositions that society has "a moral obligation to show equal respect to all persons" and that as a result society must "be neutral toward all views of the good life that are consistent with justice."[203] This requirement of neo-Kantian politics, however, cannot be attained in practice. The notion of *equal respect* is "substantively vacuous" unless one fills it with the sort of moral content that the neutrality principle forbids. The idea of equal respect, in fact, may even be morally and psychologically harmful;[204] when liberal political institutions refuse "to define standards of moral worth concretely, the liberal market stands as the major alternative, ready to determine worthy attainments in measurable economic terms."[205] Neo-Kantian theory thus cannot prevent—indeed points the way toward—either a radical and illiberal egalitarianism or the legitimation of a society so "egoistic and materialistic" as to be morally reprehensible.[206]

According to Smith, liberalism organized around the principle of rational liberty reinstates "early liberalism's substantive purposes"[207] and thus escapes the problems of neo-Kantianism. Since it is based on the fundamental human experiences of consciousness and self-direction, the theory of rational liberty can deal with human beings as three-dimensional beings with characters rather than as the dimensionless centers of will to which the neo-Kantians reduce them.[208] Rational liberty theory replaces the vagueness of neo-Kantian equal respect, which is compatible with a variety of conflicting substantive moral positions,[209] with a substantive guide to moral evaluation: the "empirical question of whether, under the actual circumstances of a case, an action is judged likely to hamper or to promote the abilities of all involved to pursue their rational self-direction."[210] Because rational liberty allows the constitutionalist to

203 Id. at 185.
204 Id. at 185, 191.
205 Id. at 192.
206 Id. at 197.
207 Id. at 170.
208 Id. at 186–88.
209 Id. at 217.
210 Id. at 218.

make sense of "many deep-rooted American moral sentiments" that neo-Kantianism ignores or contradicts,[211] Smith's theory provides "practical guidance for the problems that perplex contemporary constitutional law."[212]

Translated into directly constitutional terms, Smith's theory identifies the core moral purpose of the Constitution as the promotion of rational liberty. This means that American constitutionalism is in no sense a "neutral" or "value-free" set of political rules; it is, rather, a forthright political attempt to impose liberal morality—based on rational liberty itself—insofar as that imposition is compatible with liberty.[213] Because it rests on the acknowledgment that individual judgments about rationality and self-direction depend on the community, rational-liberty constitutionalism "presumes that the legitimate form of decision making is through democratic processes."[214] Furthermore, because there "are few better indicators of social agreement on an institution's propriety than its constitutional enactment," institutions that are explicitly established by the constitutional text must be respected even if they do not seem in accordance with the moral principles of rational liberty.[215]

On the level of doctrine, the theory of rational liberty justifies the revival of the *preferred freedoms* approach to judicial review that enjoyed some popularity in the early 1940s but was abandoned

211 Id. at 170. See, for example, Smith's discussion of the neo-Kantian constitutionalism of David A. J. Richards. Smith criticizes Richards's version of equal respect on the ground that it so emphasizes "unbridled personal autonomy" that it endorses rights to suicide and pornography and affords no special moral or legal status to family relationships. Id. at 299 n. 32. Richards's constitutional theory thus is self-consciously opposed to many moral commitments that are widespread in contemporary American society. See generally Richards, *Foundations.*

212 Smith, *Liberalism,* 170–71.

213 Id. at 230, 250.

214 Id. at 236.

215 Id. at 250. (Smith includes under the label *institutions* what this essay has been calling "institutions, practices, doctrines" and "principles.") Smith does not think that in fact the American Constitution contains any institutions that deviate significantly from the requirements of rational liberty. The most obvious examples have been eliminated (e.g., slavery), or are, arguably or clearly, appropriate means toward rational-liberty ends (e.g., judicial review, senatorial equality). Id. at 249–51.

because its proponents did not develop an adequate explanation of it. Under Smith's preferred freedoms doctrine, courts should scrutinize closely legislation infringing "the liberties that can ordinarily be assumed to be integral to rational liberty."[216] Smith's preferred freedoms approach would give a special place to First Amendment freedoms because those freedoms are directly implicated in rational liberty.[217] Smith's theory would also generally endorse continued judicial support for the Warren Court's criminal procedure and reapportionment decisions because of their connections with rational liberty.[218] Furthermore, rational liberty theory clearly would legitimate substantive due process, the mode of argument at the core of the present debate, by providing it with substantive criteria of application. Smith's judges would rank the importance of asserted liberties according to two criteria: "whether the activities in question are directly essential to maintaining personal cognitive capacities" and "whether they are basic to the legitimate course [of life] a person has chosen." Liberties judged fundamental (meaning, directly related to rational liberty) would be protected against governmental invasion except upon a showing that "the capacities for rational self-direction of others would be too greatly endangered if a certain course is pursued."[219] While Smith does not apply his theory explicitly to *Eisenstadt*, it seems clear that he would hold the decision to be correct: a person's decision whether or not to bear a child is "integral to preserving and fulfilling personal capacities for rational self-direction."[220]

216 Id. at 238, 237.
217 Id. at 239–40.
218 Id. at 231–32.
219 Id. at 237.
220 Id. at 237. I think it unlikely that Smith would regard a counterargument based on the personhood of the fetus as persuasive. The primary moral obligation under his theory is to act "so as not to endanger significantly the preservation of [deliberative and self-directive] faculties in ourselves or others." Id. at 201. Such faculties are missing from "very young children," and the obligation not to harm them rests on "other social and personal obligations." Id. The overall structure of Smith's theory would make it anomalous for him to recognize the state's interest in enforcing the even more attentuated obligations that (may) exist toward the unborn as sufficiently compelling to justify overriding the pregnant woman's first-order rational liberty interest in freedom of choice. If this speculation is correct, it indicates one of the weak points in Smith's usually skillfully crafted reasoning:

Smith's theory of rational liberty is a clear and often illuminating application to constitutional law of some themes of classical liberalism. It is not, I think, a fully successful response to the epistemological crisis of American constitutionalism. Smith's theory rests on a foundationalist account of human nature that is vulnerable to most of the usual problems with such theories. It is reductionistic—like many other liberal theorists Smith has an overly rationalistic concept of personhood—and makes dogmatic assertions on the basis of contestable claims (for example, Smith's use of his view of human experience). The theory cannot avoid the problem common to human-nature arguments of being universal in pretension and parochial in reality. Rational liberty's description of human experience fits well one strand of American thought because liberals have played a major role in shaping the vocabulary with which Americans describe their experience.

Smith's attempt to escape these problems by invoking community standards fails. What he offers is actually a psychologistic description of how persons develop their opinions rather than a demonstration of any logical connection between the principles of rational liberty and the settings in which people learn them.[221] Smith's insistence that rational liberty theory avoids the problems of liberal individualism is limited to the point of emptiness; the theory permits "all associations"—but actually, only those which are "consistent with preserving the capacities for deliberative self-direction of all"—and authorizes the state "to override commitments to groups, associations, and corporate bodies" that interfere in the view of the state's officials with rational liberty.[222] The theory, in short, approves community so long as it is compatible with individualism.

Despite his association of rational liberty with the Modern Theory's recognition of the primacy of democratic decision making, Smith's theory puts few limits on the judicial displacement of democracy in the name of rational liberty. The express community checks

---

there are moral obligations that we ordinarily consider to be very weighty (e.g., responsibilities toward "very young children") that cannot be easily subsumed under the concept of rational liberty.

221 Id. at 212–13.

222 Id. at 223. Smith's theory in fact might be even more individualistic in practice than present law; Smith mentions "fundamentalist religions" as one possible object of state intervention. Id.

on the courts that Smith recognizes, the amendment process and Congress's power to alter jurisdiction,[223] have little practical importance.[224] The internal, intellectual framework Smith prescribes for constitutional adjudication would require the subordination of traditional legal argument to a rationalistic and quasi-philosophical inquiry sufficiently abstruse that Smith admits it might require "a division of labor among the bench, constitutional scholars, and the broader political community."[225] As he himself points out, Smith's constitutional theory resembles the moral-philosophical underpinnings of John Marshall's jurisprudence,[226] but it does so with respect to precisely those areas of Marshall Court thinking that are the most alien to twentieth-century democratic constitutionalism. Smith overcomes the constitutional tradition's crisis, as do so many of the other contemporary theorists, by downgrading in importance one of the tradition's central twentieth-century achievements—the recognition of the primacy of democracy.

POSTMODERN CONSTITUTIONALISM

The American constitutional tradition, like all MacIntyrean moral traditions, would have no substance, no historical reality, if it were not embodied in a community. As the tradition itself has changed over time, of course, so has its associated community. In the earliest years of the Republic, the constitutional community might be said to consist of the entire body of the white male gentry who were the rulers of the Republic. This (relatively) widespread and broad-based embodiment of the tradition supported a variety of practices. Congressional, presidential, and state-legislative interpretation, debate

223 Unlike the early Perry, *Rights*, 128–33, Smith regards Congress's majoritarian power over the courts' jurisdiction as subject to significant constitutional limitation. Smith, *Liberalism*, 230.

224 Only four Supreme Court decisions in two centuries have been overruled by amendment, and only on two occasions has Congress affected judicial decision making in particular cases by changing the jurisidictional statutes.

225 Id. at 230.

226 See Robert Faulkner, *The Jurisprudence of John Marshall* (Princeton: Princeton Univ. Press, 1968).

in newspapers and pamphlets, theoretical and belles-lettres[227] publications, and, of course, constitutional adjudication all flourished as the gentry as a whole engaged in reasoned (if often contentious) inquiry into constitutional matters.

As the last survivors of the founding generation died, it became apparent that both the de jure scope of constitutionalism as a discourse and the de facto scope of the constitutional community were narrowing. Constitutional discussion increasingly was seen not as the American polity's particular form of political discussion, but as a technical subject under the jurisdiction of the lawyers, and especially of the Supreme Court. Constitutional adjudication, and constitutional theory directed toward the interpretation of adjudication, eclipsed competing practices. The relationship of constitutional law and the legal community to the broader polity and its nonlegal political practices became less immediate. And so matters stood for well over a century.[228] The constitutional tradition developed within a community of generally elite lawyers applying their particular modes of common-law reasoning to argue over, evaluate, and make sense of "their" tradition. Community and tradition survived significant challenges by processes of deflection and absorption, and the tradition's mostly classical-liberal substance assimilated other, primarily democratic, themes.

The epistemological crisis that has openly besieged the constitutional tradition since *Eisenstadt v. Baird* is, in the first instance, a set of intellectual problems. What the tradition's inability to resolve these problems reveals, however, is not merely intellectual; it reflects the fracturing of the constitutional community.[229] Since the

227 I have in mind especially Justice James Wilson's 1790 *Lectures on Law*, which attempted to combine legal and constitutional theorizing with a literary appeal to the general reading public.

228 This summary omits the largely unsuccessful effort of the Reconstruction-era Radicals to revive congressional interpretation and to broaden constitutional discourse to include libertarian and egalitarian moral themes.

229 The social fact that the American legal profession no longer is a homogeneous, hierarchically arranged "community" is one of the two chief intellectual problems with Ronald Dworkin's jurisprudential theory. Dworkin's theory depends, anachronistically, upon the actual (*not* notional) existence of a community of lawyers sharing professional norms of argument and rationality. See Dworkin, *Law's Empire* (Cambridge, Mass.: Harvard Univ. Press, 1986). (The other major

early 1970s at the latest, lawyers have no longer found it possible to engage in constitutional adjudication as an unselfconscious professional activity or to make sense of the decisions of the Supreme Court by traditional means. The social sources of this breakdown in community are complex and not entirely clear. The vast expansion of the bar—no longer, even at elite levels, the exclusive preserve of prosperous white males—obviously has played a role in weakening the profession's shared social and intellectual assumptions. The arrival in the law schools of a generation of teachers politicized by Vietnam and convinced that law itself is intellectually uninteresting[230] plays its part. The very success of the practice of constitutional adjudication in achieving substantial social change increased enormously the external pressure on the practice. As the political stakes have risen, so has the desire of the politically active to shape and control constitutional decision making, or, from the point of view of tradition, to corrupt the institution supporting the practice of judicial review.

The institutional changes in constitutionalism have dramatically eroded the tradition's concept of constitutional virtue, leaving little or no shared agreement on what it would mean to succeed in realizing the internal goods of constitutional practices. In the 1960s Justice John Marshall Harlan II, a political "conservative" who opposed many of the Warren Court's innovative decisions, was almost universally praised by admirers of the Warren Court—and rightly so, for Harlan and the commentators shared traditional standards of reasoning and craft which Harlan admirably fulfilled. In the 1980s Justice Antonin Scalia, clearly one of the most intellectually capable justices

---

problem is that Dworkin cannot supply any link between his contextual, community-based account of legitimate legal argument and his egalitarian moral commitments except the dubious historical claim that the community, understood in its own best light, is egalitarian.)

230 See Francis A. Allen, "The Dolphin and the Peasant: Ill-Tempered, but Brief, Comments on Legal Scholarship," The Northwestern Reporter, No. 88 (Spring 1990), 8–14, discussing the assumption among some young academic lawyers that "even periodic concentration on basic legal materials is a formula for intellectual stultification." See also Robert Bork, *Tradition and Morality in Constitutional Law* (Washington: American Enterprise Institute, 1984), 2–3, on constitutional scholarship's vulnerability to intellectual capture by extralegal intellectual fashions.

since Harlan, receives little or no praise from any observers who do not share Scalia's particular form of "conservative" politics—and rightly so, for Scalia and the commentators lack any standards of evaluation except political ones, which are by definition not shared. The member of the present Court who most resembles Harlan in his adherence to the traditional craft standards, Justice John Paul Stevens, is almost universally seen as a maverick, not an exemplar.

While the constitutional community remained unfractured, constitutional theorists assumed and ignored its existence.[231] The current crisis has driven theorists to address explicitly the question of constitutional community and to reverse the early differentiation of constitutional from moral discussion. The theorists analyzed up to this point have, in one fashion or another, attempted to deny or overcome the fracturing of constitutional community and thereby to render cogent the concept of constitutionalism as a social morality. In this section I turn to constitutional theorists who accept what one of them calls "the modernist sensibility that our communities have shattered around us."[232] What does constitutional theory look like when done by theorists who accept both the necessity of social morality, and its absence?[233]

Professor Mark Tushnet of Georgetown University Law Center is perhaps the most prolific constitutional scholar of the generation that entered law teaching in the 1970s. In a veritable cascade of articles Tushnet has addressed virtually every issue in contemporary constitutional doctrine and theory, and he is a leading member of the Critical Legal Studies (CLS) movement.[234] *Red, White and Blue,*

231 Indeed, the tradition's combination of liberal substance and common-law traditionalism made it difficult for constitutional theorists to perceive the role of the community as long as liberalism was assumed to be antithetical to community.

232 Mark Tushnet, *Red, White and Blue* (Cambridge, Mass.: Harvard Univ. Press, 1988), 143.

233 Paul Kahn's elegant and important *Legitimacy and History* (New Haven: Yale Univ. Press, 1992) belongs in this discussion, but appeared too late for inclusion.

234 CLS is a supposedly radical alliance of law school teachers. In fact, it is divided into at least two major factions, one essentially Marxist and the other a repristination of the Legal Realism of the 1930s that pushes Realism's debunking of legal reasoning to its logical limit (Tushnet belongs to the Marxist faction). Feminist legal scholars and nonwhite academic lawyers often have a complex and

published in 1988, is Tushnet's major restatement to date of his views on constitutional theory.

Tushnet places his work in the context of constitutionalism's epistemological crisis, but he regards that crisis as itself but a version of contemporary Western society's overall crisis of legitimacy. "The crisis of [constitutional] theory is the form that the failure of liberal political theory has taken in constitutional law."[235] He therefore argues that it is necessary to address the crisis both on an intellectual or "logical" level, and in terms of its "sociological" meaning and manifestations.[236] *Red, White and Blue* proceeds along both of these tracks, although with much greater attention to the intellectual issues.[237]

The root intellectual source of the constitutional crisis, according to Tushnet, is that liberal constitutionalism is built on a paradox: "the liberal tradition makes constitutional theory both necessary and impossible."[238] Liberalism[239] "emphasize[s] the individuation of people acting in society"; it "stresses the self-interested motivations of individuals and treats the collective good as the aggregation of what individuals choose." The individualistic anthropology of liberalism inspires a political theory aimed at restraining the threat to the collectivity of individuals posed by their own antagonistic self-interests.[240] Without institutional checks on governmental power, that power might—indeed, inevitably would—be employed oppressively by the individuals wielding it, so liberal political arrangements have as their basic purpose the imposition of restraint on

---

ambivalent relationship to CLS, almost all of whose founders and leaders have been privileged white males. Tushnet recently has reviewed the history and location of CLS in the contemporary American legal academy. See Tushnet, "Critical Legal Studies: A Political History," 100 Yale L.J. 1535 (1991).

235 Tushnet, *Red, White and Blue*, 4.

236 Id. at viii.

237 The resemblances between Tushnet's approach and the MacIntyrean one adopted in this book are obvious.

238 Id. at 313.

239 Tushnet views liberalism and civic republicanism as "competing general frameworks for orienting thought about political life." Although both frameworks were operative in the Founding era, and republicanism has persisted in "dissenting and subordinate groups," Tushnet thinks that liberalism is overwhelmingly dominant in contemporary American constitutional thought. Id. at 5–6 and n. 13.

240 Id. at 4–6.

public power: "the aim of the Constitution is to prevent tyranny."[241] While liberalism therefore emphasizes the importance of spelling out as clearly as possible the scope and limits of governmental power, the liberal suspicion of human motivation makes liberals doubtful that any institution would long obey even the clearest definition of its own limitations. This doubt explains the ambivalence of liberalism toward parliamentary institutions. Liberals have agreed, almost universally, that elected legislatures are a necessary means for the aggregation and brokered implementation of individual preferences, but this functional justification itself makes liberals afraid of the legislature's capacity for the circumvention of its specified limits in the execution of legislative bargains.[242]

The great contribution to liberal theory of the United States has been its creation of a solution to the problem created by the necessity and untrustworthiness of legislatures. The solution is, of course, constitutional adjudication. American courts are seen as institutions empowered to compel legislators to act within their specified authority. This solution, unfortunately, immediately gives rise to another problem. Courts themselves are centers of governmental power; furthermore, federal courts are public institutions free even of the restraint imposed by the electoral process. How then to keep courts within *their* specified limits? The liberal and constitutional-tradition answer according to Tushnet is constitutional theory. The task of the constitutional theorist is to identify the criteria that will both allow courts to carry out their essential task of restraining legislatures and will restrain the judges themselves.[243] It is this function of constitutional theory, "the requirement that theory provide constraints on judges,"[244] that supplies Tushnet with his basic analytic approach to other theorists. Again and again, Tushnet insists that a constitutional theory is successful *only* if it constrains judicial decision making. "Neutral principles, like other theories, are supposed to *guarantee* that judges do not do whatever they want";[245] a constitutional theory based on American shared values fails because "it does not ade-

241 Id. at 179.
242 Id. at 213.
243 Id. at 146–47.
244 Id. at 112.
245 Id. at 54 (emphasis added).

quately constrain judicial discretion";[246] textualism "provides no constraint on the courts in choosing how to accommodate th[e] plurality of values" the text embodies.[247] It is, Tushnet writes, "a requirement" that "the risk of [judicial] tyranny be *eliminated*."[248] Tushnet's intellectual strategy throughout his book is to demonstrate that no existing or conceivable theory can eliminate judicial moral choice and thus that no theory can meet this requirement.

Tushnet, as mentioned earlier, pursues a second theme in *Red, White and Blue*, a "sociological approach to constitutional theory."[249] By this phrase, Tushnet means an approach similar to the "stereoscopic" social criticism of MacIntyre and Stout: Tushnet wants to pay attention to the external and institutional forces shaping constitutionalism as well as to its internal intellectual dynamic. The basic datum for the sociological approach is of course the location of the institution of constitutional adjudication within the American political system.

"In general and over the medium to long run, courts are part of a society's governing coalition."[250] In MacIntyre's terminology, constitutionalism can only be understood properly when one takes into account the impact of concern over external goods on the practice of constitutional adjudication. In so doing, however, Tushnet concludes that what the courts actually do in exercising judicial review is reflect the values of the politically dominant forces in American society.[251] But if that is so, then on social as well as theoretical grounds, constitutional adjudication cannot play the role liberalism designates for it.

The heart of *Red, White and Blue* is a series of chapters in which Tushnet examines and rejects, one after another, virtually all of the major constitutional theories propounded since 1980. Most of the theories Tushnet discusses are examples of what he calls *grand*

246 Id. at 135.

247 Id. at 66.

248 Id. at 185 (emphasis added).

249 Id. at 174 n. 97.

250 Id. at viii.

251 Although at one point Tushnet admits that "any of today's competing theories" probably would invalidate "Stalinism or apartheid," the apparent concession is empty, since neither Stalinism nor apartheid "is on the presently foreseeable political agenda," and if either were, Tushnet is confident that constitutional theory would adjust to accommodate them, Id. at 186 and n. 19.

theory, "comprehensive normative theories" that attempt to provide general, all-embracing justifications for judicial review in a democratic society. Tushnet notes that virtually all of the current grand theories have "a common structure," a critique of all other grand theories followed by "an assertedly defensible and therefore different" theory which turns out, upon analysis, to be little more than "a revived and purified version of an earlier grand theory." The result is "a wearying sameness" and sense of repetition.[252] However tiresome they may be, the grand theorists all are half-right; each of the contending theories is a failure, because none of them succeeds at what Tushnet has defined as the goal of constitutional theory, the elimination of judicial choice and discretion. None "guarantee[s] that judges do not do whatever they want."[253]

From the conclusion that no constitutional theory entirely "eliminate[s]" the exercise of judicial discretion, Tushnet draws a further inference: "in any interesting case any reasonably skilled lawyer can reach whatever result he or she wants."[254] This inference, which Tushnet seems to regard as inescapable, is contestable. It does not follow from the statement that judges are not totally constrained in decision making that they therefore are wholly unconstrained. Why then, does Tushnet make this logical error? The fundamental answer, I believe, is that Tushnet—like the other constitutional theorists—understands the processes of reasoning and argument in an Enlightenment, deeply rationalistic manner.[255] Arguments and actions are either right or wrong, within the applicable rule or outside it, logically demonstrable truths or mere matters of opinion. Tushnet basically does not accept the possibility of modes of rationality that afford standards for making and evaluating arguments but do not supply bright-line rules to "constrain" the arguers.

252 Id. at 1–3.

253 Id. at 54.

254 Id. at 52 (discussing neutral principles theories in particular). See also id. at 186.

255 Tushnet's remark that the idea of "practical reason is, if not entirely foreign to us, at least far enough removed from our way of thinking to require some effort to understand" (id. at 161) is revealing. Classical common-law reasoning, the sort of reasoning that became canonical for the constitutional tradition early in its history, *was* a form of practical reasoning. Tushnet's emphasis on its foreignness illustrates how alienated contemporary constitutionalists are from their own intellectual past.

Tushnet's rejection of non-Enlightenment forms of rationality becomes clear in his scattered remarks on common-law reasoning. Tushnet observes that the common law proceeds from individual decisions resolving particular conflicts.[256] This implies, according to Tushnet, that "[a]t the moment a decision is announced we cannot identify the principle it embodies . . . we learn what principle justified Case 1 only when a court in Case 2 tells us."[257] Therefore, he triumphantly concludes, "we lack *any* criteria for distinguishing between cases that depart from and those that conform to the principles of their precedents."[258]

Tushnet's argument is a mixture of truth and error. It is a gross overstatement to say that for a common lawyer the principle embodied in Case 1 is unknowable at the time Case 1 is decided, one that Tushnet makes because he is so completely (and so unconsciously) committed to a deductive style of argument as the only rational mode of discourse. Tushnet simply is assuming that principles of action *must* be logically complete in order to qualify as such: Case 2 could be said to "follow" Case 1 if and only if we could *deduce* the result in 2 from the principle in 1. But most of the forms of argument employed by common lawyers were not meant to follow the deductive model Tushnet is invoking. The "principle" embodied in Case 1 was understood to be indeterminate in its future implications because it took the following form: "in this situation, and in all analogous situations—where the cogency of the analogy is measured by the professional judgment of virtuous common lawyers—do x." Precisely because the set of relevant circumstances in Case 2—relevancy again measured by the informed practical judgment of the good common lawyer—could not be known in advance, one could not deduce the result in the later case at the time Case 1 was decided. Furthermore, one could not know, even in principle, whether in the interim

256 Common lawyers traditionally treated normative written instruments (statutes, wills, the Constitution) as, to a large extent, collections of such decisions. The Fourth Amendment, for example, was treated unselfconsciously as analogous to a judicial decision outlawing the specific, reprobated practice of using general warrants to enforce the royal customs laws (rather than as a general or abstract principle of "privacy"). Common-law constitutional argument then could address other problems (e.g., warrantless wiretapping to enforce the federal prohibition laws) by analogy.

257 Id. at 49.

258 Id. at 50.

between the cases the ongoing development of the legal discussion would have undercut or repudiated the reasoning on which Case 1 was decided. Whether Case 2, when decided, "followed" Case 1, erroneously misapplied the earlier decision, or made a rational judgment about modifying or rejecting Case 1, was a matter for the exercise of professional wisdom.[259] Tushnet is right, of course, that the common law's methods of discussion (the exercise of practical judgment, argument by analogy, and so on) did not satisfy the demands of a system of deductive logic, but they were not meant to do so, and their "failure" to link cases and "principles" by syllogistic reasoning did not mean that most common lawyers, most of the time, could not agree over the relationship of Cases 1 and 2.

Tushnet gives as an example of the inadequacy of common-law reasoning the use of precedent in *Griswold v. Connecticut*, the original contraceptives decision. Justice Douglas's opinion in *Griswold* invoked two *Lochner*-era decisions (*Pierce* and *Meyer*) as support for the Court's decision that the Constitution forbade criminal punishment of a married couple for using contraceptives. *Pierce* and *Meyer* had invalidated statutes forbidding, respectively, parochial school education and the teaching of certain foreign languages in all schools. Tushnet points out that these precedents could be read as embodying either a "principle about freedom of inquiry" inapplicable to *Griswold* or a "principle of privacy" supporting Douglas's argument. Because either reading is possible, Tushnet concludes, Douglas's invocation of the cases is meaningless.[260]

Tushnet's criticism of Douglas misconstrues Douglas's argument which, as discussed above, was a poorly written but perfectly traditional constitutional argument. Douglas cited *Pierce* and *Meyer* as First Amendment cases—in other words, he accepted the reading that Tushnet claims renders the cases inapplicable—but went on to argue that those decisions, along with other decisions and constitutional provisions, showed the propriety of the Court not giving deference to legislation that, in the Court's practical judgment, struck too close to the heart of the family. Douglas never claimed that the earlier cases, or their "principles," compelled the result in *Gris-*

259 See Postema, in Goldstein, *Precedent*, 15–23; Evans, in id. at 43–46.
260 Tushnet, *Red, White and Blue*, 50.

wold in a deductive or syllogistic sense. His argument, in classical common-law fashion, was of another type: he was inviting the reader to apply shared, professionally shaped standards of reasoning to judge the propriety, in the circumstances of *Griswold*, of taking action similar to that the Court took in the circumstances of, among other cases, *Pierce* and *Meyer*. Even at the time of *Griswold*'s decision, when the constitutional tradition's common-law tradition of argument was beginning to fray, Douglas's use of *Pierce* and *Meyer* was comprehensible. Few lawyers at the time doubted that *Griswold* was a rational extension of those decisions; the debate was over the *legitimacy* of "following" rather than repudiating them.

My response to Tushnet's attack on the rationality of common-law argument rests explicitly, of course, on the existence of a professional community which makes sense of arguments through shared and "well-developed techniques of legal reasoning."[261] It was the shared standards of that community that rendered *Pierce* and *Meyer* problematic after 1937, and that made Douglas's argument *both* comprehensible and problematic in 1965. Tushnet, Enlightenment liberal that he is, regards the socially embedded nature of common-law reasoning as a fatal vice. Reasoning that depends on community and tradition for its intelligibility loses its status of reasoning for Tushnet. Discussing other situations where it seems implausible to argue that norms must be capable of deductive application, Tushnet writes that "we know something about the rule to follow only because we are familiar with the social practices [in which the rule is embedded]. That is, the answer does not follow from a rule that can be uniquely identified without specifying something about the substantive practices." This carries the implication—a damning one according to Tushnet—that such reasoning makes sense only "by reference to an established institutional setting" and is accepted "as a matter of contingent fact" by participants in those institutions.[262] Classical common lawyers, and their American constitutional-tradition heirs, did not act on any different assumptions. It is Tushnet's allegiance to the Enlightenment that makes him dismissive of common-law reasoning because of its contingency. Tushnet's critique demonstrates

261 Id. at 51.
262 Id. at 55–57.

his liberal presuppositions, not the emptiness of tradition- and community-dependent modes of reasoning.[263]

Tushnet's intellectual critique of contemporary constitutional thought finds common ground among the various theories in their inability to eliminate judicial discretion. His "sociological analysis" identifies what all of the theories, in Tushnet's opinion, are really about: "grand theory's primary function is to explain why the existing system of constitutional law deserves our rational respect." Regardless of the "conservative," centrist, or center-left political complexion of the theory, it always turns out to accept "the premise that at the core of the system things are basically all right."[264] The theorists all act as apologists for the courts. The courts' institutional role as part of government and the characteristics of the social group to which theorists and judges belong make both courts and theorists unsurprising supporters of the status quo, sometimes intermixed with a mild dollop of reformism.[265]

Tushnet's wholesale demolition of contemporary constitutional theory raises for him the questions of what has happened to American constitutionalism and what is to be done with (or about) it. At first glance, Tushnet appears to offer a single answer for both questions: the decline and revival of civic republicanism. The original republican tradition, which Tushnet defines much as do the neorepublicans,[266] played a vital role in the American founding. The Founders married republican assumptions about community, deliberation, and virtue to liberal concerns for individual liberty and developed what may have been at first a coherent system of government. They relied, for example, on civic virtue to enable the judges to impose liberal limitations on legislators without themselves succumbing to

263 At one point, Tushnet seems to recognize that his dislike for classical common-law and constitutional reasoning ultimately reflects his moral objections to the elitism of the constitutional tradition and not to its lack of internal rationality. Id. at 56–57.

264 Id. at 3. In discussing Perry's view of judges as the prophets of the American civil-religious community, for example, Tushnet criticizes the remarkably unprophetic message Perry wants the judges to proclaim. "Another objection is that Perry's religious vision is so conventional—everything converges on the left-liberal wing of the Democratic Party." Id. at 144 n. 125.

265 Id. at 184.

266 Id. at 5–6.

the temptation to act in self-interested or wayward manners.[267] But the republicanism of the Founding era was undermined by the inexorable historical forces of urbanization, mass politics, and above all by the market: republicanism is now nothing more than a remote memory or tradition of rhetorical protest.[268] To revitalize it would require, far more than the academic articulation of neorepublican theories, "large transformations in our present social arrangements."[269]

The disappearance of republicanism, both sociologically and intellectually, leaves the political system the founders built on republican and liberal assumptions fundamentally undercut. "The framers thought of the government they were creating as an integral system of [liberal] grants and limitations, set in a society connected by civic virtue. The Congress that exists when the limits are conceded to be indeterminate, or when civic virtue has been lost, is not the Congress that the Framers created, even though it has the prescribed two houses and the like."[270] The current crisis in constitutionalism, according to Tushnet, is only the final, irrevocable realization that American constitutionalism died long ago.

In the postmodern world in which the Constitution stands revealed as a chimera, Tushnet at first seems to recommend the recreation of republicanism. "The task of constitutional theory ought no longer to be to rationalize the real in one way or another. It should be to contribute to a political movement that may begin to bring about a society in which civic virtue may flourish."[271] But Tushnet's sociological perspective leads him to conclude that the result of such a movement would be to eliminate further need for constitutional theory or law. If American society changed sufficiently to enable civic virtue to flourish, the newly public-regarding political process "would therefore rarely generate the sort of legislation that republican judges would want to correct."[272] But Tushnet himself is not, finally, a

267 Id. at 15, 17.

268 Id. at 13.

269 Id. at 166.

270 Id. at 44 n. 69.

271 Id. at 187. See also id. at 128, 166–67, 314–17.

272 Id. at 167. "[I]t is not clear that the [republican] commonwealth would have a Constitution or constitutional theories of the sort we have examined." Id. at 317. A footnote to the discussion in which the latter statement occurs cites

neorepublican; he neither expects nor seriously seeks a republican revival. This is due in part to Tushnet's pessimism about republicanism's chances.[273] Fundamentally, however, Tushnet believes that the republican commitment to community is as flawed as liberal individualism.

> The republican tradition emphasizes experiences of love and connectedness that the liberal tradition places in the background; it places in the background experiences of anger, threat, and autonomy that the liberal tradition emphasizes. . . . Human experience consists of connectedness and autonomy, love and hate, toleration of others and anger at their differences from an ever-changing "us." Neither the liberal tradition nor the republican one can accommodate the aspects of experience that the other takes as central.[274]

Tushnet, who avows himself a "socialist,"[275] is a postmodernist (and an individualist) first: "Critique is all there is."[276]

Few contemporary writers on constitutional matters are less likely to be associated with one another than Mark Tushnet and Robert H. Bork, President Reagan's defeated nominee to the Supreme Court. Tushnet is a prominent academic leftist; Bork's appointment to the Court stemmed from his perceived "conservative" politics. But in their attitude toward American constitutionalism, Tushnet and Bork agree far more than they disagree. Bork, like Tushnet, is a constitutional postmodernist, a proponent of social morality who no longer believes in the possibility of political community. In comparison with the liberal premises and postmodernist conclusions they share, the two men's intellectual disagreements are mere in-house squabbles.[277]

Bork enjoyed a distinguished career as a law professor at Yale and

MacIntyre's *After Virtue* as "broadly consistent with the approach taken here." Id. at 317 n. 10.

273 See, e.g., id. at 314.

274 Id. at 317–18.

275 Id. at 146 n. 130.

276 Id. at 318.

277 To say this is not to ignore the great human importance of many of the substantive political issues on which Tushnet and Bork disagree. Think, for example, of the death penalty, which Bork would enforce and Tushnet would invalidate.

as a public servant (as solicitor general of the United States, 1973–77)[278] before being appointed to a federal court of appeals in 1982. Bork's stature as a lawyer and his highly vocal criticisms of Supreme Court activism led most observers to predict further promotion, and in 1987 Reagan nominated Bork to become a Supreme Court justice. After extensive hearings and a vigorous public campaign against Bork, the Senate rejected the nomination.[279] Bork soon resigned from the bench, and in 1990 published *The Tempting of America*, a book-length statement of his constitutional views and of his confirmation ordeal.

Bork agrees with the common observation that American constitutionalism is in crisis; like Tushnet, Bork sees the constitutional dilemma as part of a much larger cultural crisis. For Bork, this larger crisis takes the form of "the politicization of the culture at large."[280] Throughout American institutional life the partisan struggle for raw political power has infiltrated and attempted to subvert or replace whatever internal goods the institutions and their practices embodied.[281] Bork is not always clear about the sources of this assault by politics on all other cultural forms. At times he suggests that what is happening is a manifestation of a general pattern of cultural disintegration,[282] but his more usual claim is that the politicization of

278 The solicitor general is the fourth-ranking official in the Department of Justice; the Office of the Solicitor General is responsible for formulating and arguing the legal views of the federal government in cases before the Supreme Court. The Office has long enjoyed a high reputation for professionalism. Lincoln Caplan's book *The Tenth Justice* (New York: Random House, 1987) chronicles the history of the Office and of the adherence of the solicitors general to the internal goods of the constitutional tradition. According to Caplan, that history was interrupted by the Reagan administration's successful effort to corrupt the Office.

279 The struggle over Bork's nomination was marked by the spread of considerable disinformation by some of his opponents, some of whom attributed to Bork views, and even judicial decisions, with which he had not associated himself. Bork's supporters, in turn, seriously inflated Bork's renown as a constitutionalist. Apart from one significant article published over fifteen years before his nomination (see Bork, "Neutral Principles and Some First Amendment Problems," 47 Ind.L.J. 1 [1971]), Bork's constitutional writing was confined almost entirely to popular lectures and magazine interviews. His academic reputation rested on his scholarship in the law of antitrust.

280 Bork, *Tempting*, 2.

281 Id. at 1.

282 Id. at 10.

culture is a conscious campaign on the part of a particular, "powerful American subculture."[283] This subculture, which Bork calls "the intellectual or knowledge class," or "the American left," is a radically egalitarian and libertarian minority of the populace with its firmest centers of power in the universities and the "liberal press."[284] This intellectual class is deeply hostile "to the attitudes of middle-class, bourgeois culture," and it has striven to take over the law as part of its struggle "to achieve the hegemony of the left-liberal culture."[285] Its legal program is a bizarre mixture, demanding, "simultaneously, governmental coercion in the service of [radical egalitarian] moral values, and individual freedom from law in the service of [a hedonistic and individualistic] moral relativism."[286] The effects on law of the intellectual class's campaign of politicization have been disastrous; according to Bork, the law rapidly "is losing its integrity as a discipline."[287]

Bork's account of the purpose of the Constitution and constitutional theory is essentially identical to that of Tushnet. The Constitution was designed to "preserv[e] our liberties" by defining and limiting governmental power. In turn, the federal judiciary's "great office is to preserve the constitutional design" by limiting the president and Congress to their designated functions. But this, of course, presents the familiar problem, "who is to protect us from the power of judges? How are we to be guarded from our guardians?"[288] Judges no less than presidents and legislators are subject to the allure of self-interested or partisan overreaching. "Either the Constitution and statutes are law, which means that their principles are known and *control* judges, or they are malleable texts that judges may rewrite to see that particular groups or political causes win."[289]

The crucial role of "guarding the guardians," Bork agrees with Tushnet, belongs to constitutional theory.[290] Theory must do so by

283 Id. at 241.

284 Id. at 8, 109.

285 Id. at 245.

286 Id. at 244.

287 Id. at 262. See also id. at 345–55, for a specific discussion of the effects on constitutional law.

288 Id. at 405.

289 Id. at 2.

290 "The functions assigned the Court impose a need for constitutional theory." Id. at 140.

explaining what renders a judge's power to override democratic choices legitimate.[291] To be successful, a constitutional theory must constrain judicial discretion and "in doing that, confine the judge's power over us." Theories which cannot point out "the limit of the judge's legitimate authority" are not "worthy of consideration."[292]

Tushnet and Bork disagree over the origins of the requirement that constitutional theory eliminate judicial discretion as the criterion of its success. Tushnet credits the founders, or at least the logic of their liberalism, with the requirement, but Bork bases his insistence on the constraint criterion on a profound scepticism about the meaningfulness of public moral argument in the contemporary United States. *The Tempting of America* is replete with dismissive references to moral arguments as expressions of "modern sensibility," "mood," or "emotion"; statements of preferred "gratifications"; processes of "personal choice" or "personal desire." Moral arguments that antisodomy laws are oppressive and that laws forbidding rape or cruelty to animals are just are pointless attempts to use "moral facts" (which do not exist) or subjective expressions of "outrage" as the bases for accepting (or rejecting) such laws. The real basis for accepting or rejecting any law, according to Bork, is strictly positivist: the decision of the majority of the polity, expressed through its formal methods of lawmaking.[293]

Moral arguments, for Bork, are appeals to our emotions, not our minds. No one has a rationally convincing argument to persuade anyone else that "regardless of law or our own moral sense" a given activity must be permitted or forbidden on moral grounds.[294] Nonetheless, "all law is based upon moral judgments";[295] the consequence is that all legitimate public moral judgments are reached by the aggregation of preferences, and there is no rational basis for moral objection to majoritarian moral decisions.[296] The Constitution's lim-

291 Id. at 78.

292 Id. at 141.

293 Id. at 121–25. Legislators of course have no shared morality on which to legislate and must make their choices on the basis of preference-utilitarianism. See id. at 80–81.

294 Id. at 204. By "moral sense," Bork simply means "what I happen to prefer."

295 Id. at 122.

296 Bork does not address the question of what reason (if any) a dissenter has to obey such law, other than fear of public coercion.

itations on majoritarian choice prove the rule, since they owe their authority to prior, supramajoritarian choices.

Bork has been criticized for concealing a radical moral relativism or skepticism within a "conservative" veneer, and in *The Tempting of America* he occasionally takes the opportunity to deny the accusation. In doing so, Bork cites approvingly the work of a variety of clearly nonrelativist and nonskeptical ethicists, including MacIntyre. But his denials, however sincere as a statement of "private" moral belief, do not affect the fact that his constitutional theory rests the case for democracy and a constrained judicial role squarely on a rigorous and unremitting insistence on emotivism as the only intelligible and the only legitimate public account of moral discussion.

The purpose of constitutional theory, then, is to identify limitations on constitutional adjudication that will rule out as illegitimate any attempt by judges at "legislating policy in the name of the Constitution."[297] Like Tushnet, Bork evaluates a variety of past and present theories and finds them all wanting. In each case, the theory permits or even encourages judges to exercise their own discretion as to what is right, just, or constitutional.[298] "Every one of the revisionist[299] theories we have examined has involved major moral choices. At some point, [each involves] the creation of new constitutional rights or the abandonment of specified rights [and thus] requires the judge to make a major moral choice." In making such choices, the judge "is at once adrift in an uncertain sea of moral argument," a sea which for Bork has no nonsubjective markers at all.[300]

Bork rejects as unworkable any attempt simply to do without a conscious theory; in order to decide any controversy a judge must apply theoretical concepts to make sense of the facts and point to a

297 Id. at 101.

298 For example, theories that expect judges to evaluate the "justice" of legislation are empty since justice is a purely subjective notion. Id. at 35. Footnote four of *Carolene Products* was "nothing more" than an announcement "that the Justices will read into the Constitution their own subjective sympathies and social preferences." Id. at 61.

299 For Bork, a revisionist theory is any theory but his own. He justifies what he means to be a derisory term on the basis of his claim that his theory is *the* original theory of constitutional interpretation. That claim has not fared well as an historical assertion. See, e.g., Suzanna Sherry, Book Review, 84 Nw. L. Rev. 1215 (1990).

300 Bork, *Tempting*, 251–52.

legal conclusion. Indeed, one of the problems Bork sees at present is that the current judiciary tends to be largely unaware of the implicit theories influencing its decisions.[301] "Too often the judge is not conscious of the organizing principles that guide him, which means that he is likely to be led to a decision by sentiment rather than reason."[302] For Bork, who again resembles Tushnet in his Enlightenment presuppositions about rationality, a decision cannot be reasoned unless it can be broken down into axiomatic premises from which the conclusions flow by deductive logic. The notion of tradition-dependent practical reasoning is as alien to Bork as to Tushnet.

Bork parts company with Tushnet over the success of originalism (or interpretivism) as a constitutional theory. For Tushnet, originalism is merely one more failed candidate; for Bork it is the one theory that can fulfill the constraint criterion and thus is the one legitimate theory. Originalism, for Bork, rests on a general theory of law. "When we speak of 'law,' we ordinarily refer to a rule that we have no right to change except through prescribed procedures. That statement assumes that the rule has a meaning independent of our own desires." Since Bork is a good postmodernist, he knows that words and concepts have no intrinsic meanings,[303] and thus the meaning of a rule stated in language must itself come from outside the rule. For the originalist, the authoritative meaning is "the meaning understood at the time of the law's enactment."[304]

Once the original meaning of a law is determined (through historical investigation presumably), the judge must undertake the task of "finding the proper level of generality" at which to understand the principle embodied in the text. If the judge states the principle at too high a level of generality, he or she "transforms" its meaning.[305] Bork gives as an example the equal protection clause of the Fourteenth Amendment. Suppose for the sake of argument that the amendment

301 Id. at 241–42.

302 Id. at 136.

303 See, e.g., id. at 35 ("justice" has no meaning in itself).

304 Id. at 143, 144. Bork is careful to disavow interest in the private intentions of the lawmakers; what matters to the originalist is "what the public of that time would have understood the words to mean." Id. at 144. (As a logical matter, Bork's formulation of originalism suffers from an infinite regress problem, since the only sources of "what the public of that time would have understood" are other words.)

305 Id. at 148.

originally was "intended to guarantee that blacks should be treated by law no worse than whites, but that it is unclear whether whites were intended to be protected from discrimination. On such evidence, the judge should protect only blacks from discrimination [because] the next higher level of generality above black equality, which is racial equality, is not shown to be a constitutional principle."[306]

On the other hand, the originalist judge should not simply confine the application of legal provisions to those specific applications that the lawmakers actually had in mind. The task of the judge, and especially of the judge deciding a constitutional case, is "to discern how the framers' values, defined in the context of the world they knew, apply to the world we know." The existence of social change requires "the evolution of [judicial] doctrine to maintain the vigor of an existing principle."[307] Bork illustrates his point by discussing *Brown v. Board of Education*. Bork assumes that the Fourteenth Amendment originally was meant to guarantee blacks equality before the law, but that it was also originally believed that such equality and de jure racial segregation were compatible. By 1954, however, it was apparent that "segregation rarely if ever produced equality" and that a case-by-case process of invalidating individually proven instances of unfair treatment "would never produce the equality the Constitution promised." The Court therefore faced a painful decision, to jettison segregation as a whole or to deny equality. "Either choice would violate one aspect of the original understanding"; the Court correctly chose to discard the original assumption that segregation would remain legal in order to honor the main historical purpose of the amendment.[308]

Bork's formulation of originalism seems clearly to violate the constraint criterion that he claims the theory fulfills. Each of the

306 Id. at 149. Bork sometimes refers to the originalist judge's sources of argument as including the text as well as history. His equal protection clause example demonstrates that in his view textual argument is wholly subordinate to historical. Bork concedes that the text of the clause "being general, applies to all persons," but he takes it as too obvious to require explication that historical evidence of a narrower purpose automatically would overrule the implications of the text. Id.

307 Id. at 168–69.

308 Id. at 81–82.

crucial moments in originalist judging that Bork describes requires (or can require) the exercise of the very judicial discretion and choice that are the great threat to constitutional legitimacy according to Bork (and Tushnet). As Bork formally acknowledges, determining the original meaning of constitutional provisions is no simple or mechanical activity; as his *Brown* example shows, the very act of determining what among a variety of historical goals was a provision's main purpose and what were its subsidiary or secondary assumptions involves complex and morally charged acts of judgment.[309] The crucial act of determining what the "proper" level of generality is for applying a provision even more clearly requires the exercise of judgment and choice. In practice,[310] Bork's originalism turns out to be little more than a strong recommendation that the Court return to the New Deal rejection of the legitimacy of substantive due process, and also be a bit slower to overturn legislation challenged by legitimate arguments.

Despite their obvious disagreement over originalism's success in fulfilling the constraint criterion, the parallels between the views of Tushnet and Bork are striking. Primarily, of course, they agree on

309 Bork fails even to acknowledge the further problems that arise when the historical evidence indicates that different groups of lawmakers intended different meanings, all of them possible linguistically, for the same text, or that the text was a deliberate compromise the exact meaning of which the lawmakers themselves did not even try to resolve.

310 Bork's summary descriptions of his originalism usually sound as if they would sharply curtail constitutional adjudication. His discussions of substantive constitutional issues, however, sometimes seem to identify him as a thoroughly mainstream and nonrevolutionary constitutionalist who rejects substantive due process as a mode of argument (a rejection he shares with respected constitutional scholars such as Ely). For example, Bork accepts the extension of the equal protection clause to nonracial ethnic groups, despite his belief that historically the clause concerned black equality, because the extension "seems within the general intention [??] of the clause, and . . . raises no question about courts making political and cultural choices [!!]." Id. at 329–30. Bork also asserts that the general language of the clause imposes a requirement that all statutory distinctions, of whatever sort, be reasonable. Id. at 150. Equal protection "rationality review" is, historically, the twin of substantive due process, and intellectually the two doctrines are very similar, facts Bork does not discuss. See also Bork's approval of Marshall's decisions (id. at 21), his defense of the original reapportionment decision (id. at 85–87), and his justification of the vast extension of the free speech clause (id. at 167–68, 334), all positions often assailed as contrary to original meaning.

the purpose of constitutional theory—to constrain judges from exercising significant choice and discretion. Constitutional theory, as they see it, is concerned with an aberration in the American democratic system, and they both reject the attempt of some other theorists to abandon or redefine the American commitment to democracy. With the explicit formulation of the constraint criterion as the core of constitutional theory, theory has completed a total transformation from its historical function. The original purpose of theory in the constitutional tradition was to render intelligible the conclusions of constitutional adjudication and thereby to indicate larger themes, identify issues that had been settled, and examine questions that remained or had become open.[311] Nineteenth-century theorists were interested in discovering how to engage in constitutional discussion more rationally. The introduction of Modern Theory around 1900 put the question of reconciling constitutional adjudication with the primacy of democracy at the top of the theoretical agenda, but Modern Theory constitutionalists still couched their theoretical work in affirmative terms of describing how to reach "good" constitutional conclusions—conclusions justifiable within the tradition, including the tradition's democratic commitments. The current epistemological crisis has rendered this affirmative vision of constitutional theory naive or even incomprehensible to many contemporary theorists. The constraint criterion, in contrast, continues to make sense of theory—as a means of keeping judges from cheating. The cost is that constitutionalism is transformed into a discourse of self-suspicion, practiced by a "community" that assumes its central practice is empty (or nearly so) of affirmative content. Constitutional theory according to Tushnet and Bork is the equivalent of a philosophy of science that defined its crucial and indeed almost only purpose as the prevention of the falsification of data.

Tushnet and Bork also share a set of Enlightenment presuppositions about the nature of rationality as deductive, manipulative, and purely formal. For both men, reasonableness is solely a matter of logical derivation or utilitarian means-ends fitness. They thus represent the posthumous triumph of eighteenth-century rationalism over the tradition-dependent common-law modes of argument that the

311 See generally Elizabeth K. Bauer, *Commentaries on the Constitution, 1790–1860* (New York: Columbia Univ. Press, 1952).

constitutional tradition historically employed. Those modes of argument were, of course, simply a peculiar version of pre-Enlightenment culture's general belief in *recta ratio*, a "right reason" capable of rational inquiry into ends as well as means. A crucial factor in the constitutional tradition's crisis is the collapse within the constitutional community of "faith in right reason and . . . the subsequent restriction of reason to mean simply ratiocination, logic."[312] Tushnet and Bork share an inability to understand reason in any other way.[313] This inability should not be ascribed to any intellectual failing on their part; rather, they simply are clearer about their presuppositions than many of their contemporaries. It was modernity that "effectively abolished from our active vocabulary the concept of 'right' reason";[314] the constitutional community's fracturing in the contemporary period has now undone that community's successful resistance to modernity on this issue.[315]

Tushnet and Bork come to almost identical analyses of the role of "community" and social morality in contemporary constitutionalism. Both repeatedly note that the theorists they critique, no matter how different their approaches, seem invariably to come to substantive conclusions that (as Tushnet wittily puts it) lie somewhere between saying that "the Constitution requires the implementation of the platform of the 1964 Democratic Party [and that it requires] implementation of the 1972 Democratic platform."[316] Tushnet and Bork agree, furthermore, on a sociological explanation for this fact: contemporary constitutional theory, in Tushnet's words, is in practice an attempt "to explain why the values of a particular elite ought to be imposed on people who are not part of the elite."[317] Both agree,

312 Joan S. Bennett, *Reviving Liberty* (Cambridge, Mass.: Harvard Univ. Press, 1989), 11.

313 "The thought which modernity, whether conservative or radical, rejects is that there may be traditional modes of social, cultural and intellectual life which are as such inaccessible to it." MacIntyre (1988), 387.

314 Bennett, *Reviving Liberty*, 222 n. 14; See also 114.

315 Parallels from the religious sphere are obvious. Various Christian communities, for example, often were able to preserve pre-Enlightenment concepts and modes of reasoning until twentieth-century social changes loosened the cohesion of the community.

316 Tushnet, *Red, White and Blue*, 3.

317 Id. at 313.

finally, that the elite in question is neither representative nor morally attractive.[318]

That a leading socialist CLS professor and a "conservative" Republican judge have so much in common at the most fundamental intellectual level tells us something very important about American constitutionalism. In this chapter, I have discussed the efforts of contemporary theorists to resolve the tradition's crisis by an explicit redefinition of constitutionalism as the social morality of the American community. Tushnet and Bork are social morality theorists too, of a sort; they both want to reject liberal individualism and to recognize the role of the community in forming morality.[319] But they are both postmodern communitarians, believing in its necessity while recognizing its absence. Like most proponents of "cultural revolt in the modern world," Tushnet and Bork direct much of their energy to "[u]nmasking the unacknowledged motives of arbitrary will and desire which sustain the moral myths" of their "particular moral predecessors."[320] But Tushnet and Bork, more clearly than any other contemporary constitutional theorists, have carried this activity of unmasking through to its logical conclusion. For them even their own constitutional "theories" are acknowledgments that in a world without community there is nothing but the exercise of arbitrary will. Tushnet's endless critique and Bork's emotivist legislature are all that is left.

THE END OF THE TRADITION

The failure of the social morality approach in constitutional theory—or its postmodern consummation in the antitheories of Tushnet and Bork—raises the serious possibility that the constitutional tradition

318 See, e.g., id. at 184; Bork, *Tempting*, 241–42. Tushnet and Bork seem to assume that they themselves have not fallen into the trap of social determinism, even though they both clearly are members of what Bork calls "the information class."

319 See, e.g., Bork, *Tempting*, 55 (discussing importance of "consensus"); Tushnet, *Red, White and Blue*, 158 ("constitutional theory requires a theory of community").

320 MacIntyre (1984), 72.

cannot surmount its current crisis. Contemporary theorists all assume that it is not possible to rely any longer on the modes of reasoning and concepts of professional virtue that animated the community of elite lawyers that once was, in all but name, *the* community of American constitutionalism. This assumption about the social realities of American society is correct. But the theorists' various attempts to identify an alternative concept of community are unconvincing, and it is the most socially realistic of them, Tushnet and Bork, who have given up the hope for community that inspires the entire effort. All that remains is to surrrender the notion of constitutionalism. A recent book by Sanford Levinson, a political theorist and lawyer at the University of Texas at Austin, takes that final step.[321]

Levinson's *Constitutional Faith* is not in form a constitutional theory at all; it is instead a series of meditations on American civil religion, law, and morality and the relationship of these themes to the various institutional aspects of the constitutional system. Like Tushnet, Levinson is an avowed postmodernist.[322] He notes that he has been classed as a nihilist because he has "drunk deeply at the well of those branches of modern thought most skeptical of concepts like truth, neutrality, or disinterestedness."[323] For Levinson, a defining characteristic of "our modernity" is its inculcation of the "ability to adopt ironic postures" toward talk of community, attachment and commitment.[324]

Levinson recognizes that the very notion of the Constitution is deeply problematic in a postmodernist world, and that this poses a serious cultural problem for late twentieth-century American society (and for the liberal West generally). "The 'death of constitutionalism' may be the central event of our time, just as the 'death of God' was that of the last century (and for much the same reason)."[325] Levinson, in appropriately postmodernist fashion, never conclusively resolves

321 Levinson, *Constitutional Faith* (Princeton: Princeton Univ. Press, 1988).

322 See, e.g., id. at 6–7, 22, 61. Levinson himself uses the term *modernist/modernism* where I refer to *postmodernist/ism*.

323 Id. at 175.

324 Id. at 110. For Levinson, the "true patron saint of modernity" is Pontius Pilate, the archetypal detached and ironic individualist. Id. at 171.

325 Id. at 52.

the question of whether constitutionalism has died even though his book is deeply concerned with that problem.

Levinson's most basic theme in *Constitutional Faith* is a search for community. "To try to discover what bonds us (or could bond us) into a coherent political community, especially after the triumph of a distinctly (post)modernist sense of the contingencies of our culture and the fragility of any community memberships is the core of this book."[326] Levinson sees no easy answers to such questions for a society increasingly shaped by the "skeptical ethos of late twentieth-century modernism,"[327] and his interest in constitutionalism is motivated in part by the observation that in the United States "much of our disputation is in some sense organized around constitutional categories."[328] If, as it does, constitutional law provides "a public vocabulary" that most Americans in fact employ in political argument, it is at least possible that constitutionalism may serve in some fashion to "bond us" into community. This hypothesis Levinson terms *constitutional faith*.

Levinson recognizes that law generally, and constitutional law in particular, cannot hang in intellectual midair: they depend on "the 'common ground' of [a community's] social and political life."[329] He dismisses a MacIntyrean analysis of law as a social practice as meaningless; the standards of legal argument necessarily are too indeterminate to allow a distinction between good and bad arguments and there is no shared distinction between goods internal to a constitutional tradition from those external to it.[330] He therefore turns to a "linkage of law and morality" that would make "submission to the Constitution" not only a means to order "but also the condition of a social order worthy of respect." But, he notes wistfully, the concepts of a shared morality and a common good "have barely, if at all, survived" the arrival of postmodernity. The more carefully one has absorbed the lessons of postmodern thought, the less one can even imagine a (morally attractive) "common . . . moral order" that could serve as the underpinning for a law worthy of respect.[331] While "a

326 Id. at 6–7.
327 Id. at 108.
328 Id. at 27.
329 Id. at 120.
330 Id. at 177.
331 Id. at 60–62.

nonmoralized law is unworthy of faith," "a joinder of law and morality" is "perhaps incomprehensible."[332] Indeed, Levinson's postmodernism remains thoroughly liberal in its individualism: "Law, even as bounded by the Constitution, is a series of outcomes of a bargaining process among atomistic beings."[333]

Levinson rejects the possibility of rendering law communally rational by finding a socially stronger community. He is contemptuous of any notion that "a priesthood of lawyers" might play that role,[334] while dismissing as absurd any effort to answer his primary question ("what, if anything" makes America a community) by a circular invocation of a national community.[335] Even the notion of American civil religion, which clearly intrigues Levinson, is ultimately rejected.[336]

Constitutional Faith is not, and is not intended to be, a systematic examination of the various possible means of construing constitutionalism as the basis of American community, but Levinson leaves the reader with the clear impression that none of the suggestions he considers are successful. Postmodern thought's "brutal washing in what Holmes called 'cynical acid' "[337] has stripped the postmodernist of the ability to make the necessary affirmations of faith in law, common morality, community, or civil religion. What then is left?

Levinson's first point is that the dissolution of the constitutional tradition does not of its own accord affect the continued existence of constitutional institutions. "Law is stripped of any moral anchoring becoming instead the product of specific political institutions enjoying power under the Constitution."[338] For the foreseeable future attorneys will continue to cite "the Constitution," judges will continue to make decisions in its name, and other officials will continue ordinarily to enforce or obey those decisions. Constitutionalism may be dead but people will continue to be harmed or saved from harm by magistrates invoking its ghost.

332 Id. at 74.

333 Id. at 70.

334 Id. at 38, 47, 174. As this book argues above, this has been the implicit traditional answer to the necessity for an "interpretive community."

335 Id. at 119–20.

336 Id. at 179.

337 Id. at 171.

338 Id. at 64–65.

Because the constitutional institutions carry on, it is still possible to do good (or evil) through "constitutional" argument—assuming the postmodernist has criteria for identifying good and evil. "I do indeed believe that law, especially constitutional law matters . . . at least some decisions made in the name of the Constitution . . . have important consequences for the lives of others."[339] Discussing the 1943 case of *Schneiderman v. United States*,[340] Levinson ultimately concludes that in *Schneiderman* the Court trivialized the idea of the Constitution by denying to it "any necessary content." But in writing this, Levinson does not mean to be criticizing the Court for failing to see something that Levinson the postmodernist knows is not there.[341] Instead, he praises the decision for upholding "the value of protecting human dignity."[342] Of course, this value, and any others pursued or achieved through constitutional adjudication, must be derived from outside "constitutional law," for the latter is devoid of independent content.[343] Levinson's "definition of a meritorious result is ultimately external, based on moral or political views rather than on" anything internal to constitutionalism.[344]

Levinson's final judgment on American constitutionalism, perhaps surprisingly, is not entirely negative or cynical. Indeed, he does finally "profess at least a limited constitutional faith," but he does so in a postmodernist idiom. The Constitution's emptiness, which spells its death, is also its promise, for its infinite malleability "allows one to grapple with every important political issue imaginable." "There is nothing that is unsayable in the language of the Constitution, even if some things will sound strange and 'off-the-wall.'" There is, of course, no postmodernist means of ruling ungrammatical political evil spoken in constitutional terms, but neither are there limits to the political goods that can be enunciated. Levinson's postmodernist

339 Id. at 168. Levinson's moral seriousness on this point contrasts sharply with Tushnet's explicit retreat to the pleasures of intellectual critique (Tushnet, *Red, White and Blue*, 318) and with Bork's call for a constitutional "posture of moral abstention" (Bork, *Tempting*, 259).

340 320 U.S. 119 (1943).

341 If anything, Levinson finds *Schneiderman* interesting because it seems such a remarkable adumbration of postmodernism.

342 Levinson, *Constitutional Faith*, 148, 142, 150.

343 See id. at 177.

344 Id. at 170.

constitutional faith can be no more, and is no less, than "a commitment to taking political conversation seriously."[345] Or, more darkly, postmodernist constitutional faith is "a means of fending off the end of conversation itself."[346]

345 Id. at 191–93. Levinson, in the end, is not all that far from Bobbitt. The difference is that the latter accepts the tradition's historic self-confidence in the disciplined nature of constitutional conversation.

346 Id. at 7.

Chapter Four

A THEOLOGICAL RESPONSE TO AMERICAN CONSTITUTIONALISM

As Stanley Hauerwas has insisted, the "primary subject of Christian ethics in America has been America."[1] From the time of the Social Gospel, through the era of Christian realism, to the successive decades of "liberal" and "conservative" social activism, the relationship between Christian commitments and American politics[2] has dominated American Christian ethical discussion. Several factors no doubt have contributed to this fact: the historical connections between secular American public institutions and ecclesial forms,[3] "culture christianity,"[4] American civil religion with its deliberate cooptation of biblical imagery,[5] the role Christians historically have played in American political and social change.[6] Clearly, however, the framework of most such Christian-American ethics is what contemporary theologians often call the Constantinian paradigm, the assimilation of Christian social thought and action to the supposed constraints of political realism.[7] Constantinians typically have re-

1 Hauerwas, *Christian Existence*, 177.

2 By "politics" I mean here the activities of the polity in the widest sense, i.e., not only explicit governmental actions, but also the supposedly "private," market-oriented structures that in fact rule much of contemporary American life.

3 See, e.g., Rossiter, *Six Characters*.

4 See Julian N. Hartt, *A Christian Critique of American Culture* (1967).

5 See Russell E. Richey and Donald G. Jones, eds., *American Civil Religion* (New York: Harper and Row, 1974).

6 See, e.g., Dorothy Sterling, *Ahead of Her Time: Abby Kelley and the Politics of Antislavery* (New York: W. W. Norton, 1991). I cite Sterling's biography of Kelley, a nineteenth-century Quaker actively involved in the antislavery movement, to indicate that it is not the assumption or conclusion of this book that political activity undertaken in this polity in the name of Christ necessarily is theologically or ethically mistaken. The anti-Constantinian theological premises from which I am working require not that Christians absolve themselves of concern for civil society, but that they act on "the concrete social meaning of their loyalty to Jesus Christ." Yoder, *Priestly Kingdom*, 91.

7 See Yoder, *Priestly Kingdom*, 135–47; Hauerwas, *Christian Existence*, 180–84.

garded the "civil government [as] the main bearer of historical movement," and the imagined ethical agent to be employed in social thought as either the sovereign or "Everyman."[8] Both assumptions have been especially congenial to many American Christians, for they dovetail with American political mythology (Washington, Jefferson, Lincoln, and so on) as well as with the typical American rhetoric of popular sovereignty. The result, which is somewhat ironic given the stringency of the formal constitutional separation of church and state, has been a strong tendency to see in the American political system a precursor or embodiment of the kingdom of God.[9] The influence of the Constantinian paradigm in constitutional thought can be seen in the work of an avowedly Christian theorist such as Michael Perry; it probably also is present in the willingness of many secular constitutionalists to accept the "decisions" of "the American people" as fundamental ethical norms.

The purpose of this book has been to describe and evaluate American constitutionalism from a Christian perspective that is self-consciously anti-Constantinian. The arguments against Constantinianism have not been rehearsed, but rather assumed. In this concluding chapter, I shall explore the implications for Christian social thought of the account of constitutionalism developed in chapters 2 and 3. My primary interest is in exploring the appropriate theological and ethical response of Christians living in this republic to the republic's constitutionalism. Put in another way, my hope to illuminate some of the ways in which Christians may respond faithfully to the demands, pretensions, and opportunities that our particular Caesar, the American constitutional order, presents.

The fracturing of community and the crisis of discussion that have overtaken American constitutionalism might spell, for some other type of MacIntyrean tradition, a swift collapse or supersession by a competitor. Constitutionalism, however, is unlikely to do either in the foreseeable future, precisely because it has not been, unlike, say, chess, a more-or-less self-contained tradition in which those interested participated and which other people could ignore. Instead, the constitutional tradition has served as the means by which the constitutional elite and its social allies dominated the American social

8 Yoder, *Priestly Kingdom*, 138–39.

9 See Hauerwas, *Against the Nations*, 122–31.

order, as the fundamental criteria by which the polity directed its use of violence, and as a primary rhetoric of legitimation for both order and polity. The demise of chess as a living tradition would not of necessity be of great consequence to those not involved in it; the death of constitutionalism unavoidably affects the lives of all who live in the United States.

The constitutional community and the rational debate may die, but the institutions still live. Even if, as this investigation suggests, constitutional discourse is increasingly incoherent rationally, it retains enormous cultural force, and its employment by courts—one of the ruling institutions of this society—means that the link between the language of constitutionalism and the exercise of state power remains as salient as ever. Stripped of the channeling that the tradition's moral inquiries provided, the American polity's employment of violence is increasingly wayward, increasingly brutal.[10] This assertion can be substantiated by a brief foray into recent constitutional caselaw.

The decisions of the Supreme Court since the mid-1970s, as a body of law, share certain important characteristics. Most important for this book, the Court's willingness to restrain the government's use of violence has become ever more attenuated. This development is

10 Leftist lawyers sometimes deny that Anglo-American law has provided even the modest channeling function for state violence that I ascribe to it. See, e.g., Morton Horwitz, "The Rule of Law: An Unqualified Human Good?," 86 Yale L.J. 561 (1977). This denial seems to me based on a demonstrably untrue account of history and is, I think, a product of a perceived political need to reject the possibility that anything of human value has come from traditional Western political arrangements. See, for example, the great Marxist historian E. P. Thompson's *Whigs and Hunters* (New York: Pantheon, 1975), the object of Harvard law professor Morton Horwitz's scathing attack just cited, which richly documents the role of eighteenth-century English legal process in mitigating to some extent the brutality of the Black Acts, a collection of particularly bloody and class-biased statutes. Unlike such secular leftists, Christians should have no need to deny the existence of some human good in the institution of law. The fact that the law only mitigated state violence and class oppression rather than eliminating them is unsurprising from a theological perspective, and the Christian understanding of community makes even the partial shielding of some persons from suffering and oppression a matter for rejoicing. Christian theology, in short, provides an intellectual and moral basis for a social criticism of American (or Western) law and politics that is both more radical and more truthful than that based upon secular leftist ideologies. See Hauerwas, *Christian Existence*, 199–217.

perhaps clearest in the area of constitutional criminal procedure, where an increasingly aggressive "conservative" majority has converted most procedural constraints on police violence and other forms of coercion into reviews of the "reasonability" of the officials' conduct that legitimate all but the most egregious forms of misconduct.[11] The Court's near-eagerness to uphold state power in dealing with crime is exemplified by its death penalty jurisprudence, which combines an insistence that capital sentences be imposed "rationally" through the use of balance-sheets of "aggravating" and "mitigating" factors,[12] with a process for postconviction review that arguably provides fewer safeguards for persons sentenced to die than for those who receive prison sentences.[13]

The Supreme Court's case law since the constitutional tradition entered crisis is also marked by increasing signs of intellectual incoherence. The justices have abandoned any effort at deliberation and consensus; the Court's decision-making process apparently now consists of the announcement of positions determined without any perceived need for discussion. Particular constitutional positions are defended by an automatic rejection of any argument remotely in tension with them. The "liberal" justices, for example, moved from striking down limitations on the availability of contraceptives for unmarried adults, to *Roe v. Wade*, to a blanket rejection of any impediments to the abortion right recognized in *Roe*, to a solemn constitutionalization of the "right to die."[14]

This book's philosophical-history interpretation of American constitutionalism has arrived at the conclusion that constitutionalism is beset by a fundamental contradiction. Both in its historical origins

11 See, e.g., Ross v. Oklahoma, 487 U.S. 81, 90 (1988) (upholding state rule because it is not "arbitrary or irrational").

12 On the incoherence of this strand of the Court's decisions, see Charles Black, *Capital Punishment: The Inevitability of Caprice and Mistake*, 2d ed. (New York: W. W. Norton, 1981).

13 See Robert Weisberg, "Deregulating Death," 1983 Sup.Ct.Rev. 305.

14 Justices Brennan and Marshall, both of whom are now retired, never rejected a serious "privacy" substantive due process claim presented on full review in the period from 1972 to 1991. The fact that the right to die case, *Cruzan v. Director* (496 U.S. 261 [1990]), unanimously assumed the existence of such a right highlights the lack of any deep or principled intellectual disagreement between "liberal" and "conservative" justices on the central moral commitment of constitutionalism: the "protection" of the atomistic individual from moral involvement with anyone other than the omnipresent state.

and in its contemporary self-description, the constitutional tradition has as its purpose the creation of a sphere in which reason guides the social and political relationships of human beings—in the language of the tradition itself, a realm of "ordered liberty." The liberty of which constitutionalism has spoken has never been Christian freedom, and so the degeneration of the tradition's internal rationality is not of itself of grave importance to Christians.[15] But the inability of the constitutional tradition to overcome its present crisis demands a response from people who have no intrinsic interest in the tradition's well-being because constitutionalism is the most fundamental mode by which the American republic attempts to channel and mitigate the violence of the state and (since the state attempts to enforce a monopoly on violence by violence) the society. The increasingly obvious incoherence of constitutional discussion makes clearer what was always the case, that the peace of constitutionalism is a false "peace"; in addition, and in part because of this, the epistemological crisis of constitutionalism is rapidly undermining the capacity of constitutionalism to enforce even the orderliness of the coercive society.

The norm of Christian social ethics is the obligation to see and speak truthfully. Because of that obligation, Christians ought not to take the easy paths of blanket denunciation or of uncritical acceptance in confronting American constitutionalism. The church[16] "must be a community where the truth is lived and spoken. The story that forms the church is . . . a reality-making claim that tells us the

15 Milbank's remark in passing that "freedom of the will in itself is not the goal" for Christian social thought and praxis (Milbank, *Social Theory*, 418) implicitly captures the fundamental difference between Christian ethical commitments and American constitutionalism. Constitutionalism's Enlightenment assumptions, increasingly dominant as the constitutional tradition decays, identify its goal precisely as the protection of the "freedom of the will" of the individual. From a Christian perspective, constitutionalism's simultaneous commitment to the imposition of "order" by force renders it self-contradictory and self-defeating. See Roberto M. Unger, *Knowledge and Politics* (New York: Free Press, 1975), 83–100.

16 Talk about the church is inherently ambiguous, and particularly so in the American context, where references to the community of the church can be as vacuous as invocations of the American community. Fortunately, for present purposes these difficulties need not be resolved. In this book, all that I shall mean by use of the word is "that set of Christian communities that actively seek to live out Christianity in a non-Constantinian manner."

truth about the world and ourselves."[17] Christian analyses of political structures and forms of thought must be shaped fundamentally by "New Testament realism about the nature of governmental power,"[18] and not by Constantinian assumptions about the compatibility of Christ and Caesar. Christian truthfulness, on the other hand, should not be defensive: Christians have no stake in denying the goodness of Caesar's acts when the latter are, in Christian terms, good.[19] Chapters 2 and 3 have been an attempt to describe truthfully the nature of American constitutionalism.

In attempting to accomplish the goal of truthful description, the book has employed a nontheological set of concepts: Alasdair MacIntyre's social theory of tradition, practice, institution, and virtue. Chapter 1 discussed at length the suitability of MacIntyre's theory for a social-critical or philosophical analysis of constitutionalism. It is necessary now to consider the propriety of using MacIntyre's theory in a theological analysis. The objection to doing so is obvious: employment of such a methodology threatens to hold theological analysis hostage to the nontheological commitments of the theory.[20] If the theological task in social criticism is "to exploit the considerable

17 Hauerwas, *Christian Existence*, 102.

18 Yoder, *Priestly Kingdom*, 153.

19 The tendency to demonize the American polity which mars some Christian social criticism (see, e.g., the writings of William Stringfellow) is perhaps an exaggerated reaction to American Constantinianism and suffers from many of the same problems (only in a mirror-image form). Stringfellow, for example, equated the American Republic with the Great Harlot of Babylon in a manner reminiscent of the "conservative" identification of the United States with the "city on the hill." See Stringfellow, *An Ethic for Christians and Other Aliens in a Strange Land* (Waco, Tex.: Word Books, 1973), 32–34.

20 The fact that MacIntyre was a Christian when he wrote *Whose Justice? Which Rationality?* (see MacIntyre [1988], 10–11) does not answer the objection by itself. As chapter 1 argues, MacIntyre's theory remained basically unchanged between *After Virtue* (written before MacIntyre's reconversion to Christianity) and *Whose Justice? Which Rationality?* More importantly, MacIntyre's purposes in formulating his social theory were not fundamentally Christian or theological in nature. The Thomistic moral tradition for whose rational superiority MacIntyre argues in the later book *is* explicitly Christian, but its social presuppositions arguably are Constantinian and thus incompatible with the perspective adopted in this essay.

Milbank makes a similar point about the essentially contingent and even fortuitous nature of the fact that the tradition from which MacIntyre criticizes modern liberalism is Christian. Milbank, *Social Theory*, 327.

resources embodied in particular Christian convictions,"[21] extensive use of a nontheological social theory might appear self-defeating.[22]

This objection, although powerful, should not be considered finally persuasive. The injunction to "keep theological ethics theological,"[23] in order to be effective, must govern the purposes and basic assumptions of Christian theological writing; it is not a prohibition on the use of nontheological methods and discourses, and indeed could not be. (The heedless subservience of much of American fundamentalist Christianity to nineteenth-century secular ideology demonstrates the inevitable result of attempting to think theologically in an intellectual vacuum.[24]) An authentically theological approach to social criticism does not require the avoidance of all nontheological methods any more than a theological critique of cosmology must eschew quantum mechanics. Theology by itself does not generate all of the tools necessary to engage in many theological tasks.[25] In the pursuit of Christian truthfulness, the theologian legitimately can employ nontheological methods and theories—so long as they remain tools, the servant rather than the master of the investigation.

The decision to employ the social theory of MacIntyre rather than, say, that of Anthony Giddens,[26] was not random, of course, but

21 Hauerwas, *Against the Nations*, 44.

22 See Milbank, *Social Theory*, 389, on the theological necessity of seeking "one's fundamental principles of *critique* within the Christian 'text.'"

23 Hauerwas, *Against the Nations*, 23–29.

24 See George Marsden, *Fundamentalism and American Culture* (New York: Oxford Univ. Press, 1980).

25 "It is impossible to do all of our politics from political theology alone." John A. Coleman, *An American Strategic Theology* (New York: Paulist Press, 1983), 293.

26 See Giddens, *The Nation-State and Violence*. A theological social criticism of American constitutionalism employing Giddens's social theory would yield, I expect, a portrait complementary to that drawn in this book of its subject. The stress on the institutional role of the federal courts—and thus of constitutional adjudication—in the maintenance of the national government's surveillance and control of the society probably would be greater, and the attention paid to intellectual developments considerably less. The advantage of MacIntyre over Giddens from a theological perspective is that the "stereoscopic" character of MacIntyre's theory permits more direct consideration of the interplay between the social consequences of institutional arrangements and the intellectual arguments concerning those arrangements. Giddens's emphasis on state violence certainly is not *mistaken*, however, and for other theological purposes his social theory well might be an appropriate tool.

depended largely upon two distinct characteristics of MacIntyre's work. MacIntyre's "stereoscopic" approach seems ideally suited to the analysis of a social phenomenon that involves both intellectual argument and the institutional exercise of power. MacIntyre's theory, furthermore, is fundamentally compatible with the presuppositions discussed below of non-Constantinian Christian social criticism. MacIntyre's careful distinctions between practices and institutions, and internal and external goods, further the theological goal of interpreting constitutionalism truthfully.

John Howard Yoder has argued persuasively for the need to start from a "Gospel" or "New Testament realism about the nature of governmental power" in engaging in theological social ethics. Yoder's realism distinguishes three separate levels of social reality that must be considered in examining political matters theologically.[27] "One level is the fact of dominion. It is simply there, independent of and prior to any process of evaluation." The "facticity of dominion," the reality of the coercive exercise of power by society's rulers, is a given, according to Yoder.[28] Christians never find themselves in a situation where dominion is not present,[29] nor do they ever find that "it is in our power to state the rules of the [political] game,"[30] so that dominion could be eliminated.

Dominion in Yoder's sense certainly is a central characteristic of American constitutionalism. Constitutional questions are, by definition, controversies over the (potential) exercise of state power and the primary institutional embodiments of constitutionalism, the

27 The fusion of these levels, according to Yoder, is one of the primary intellectual errors of Constantinianism and is, like all true intellectual errors, ethically significant. Yoder, *Priestly Kingdom*, 157.

28 Id.

29 There are interesting side issues, both theoretical and empirical, here. Is the facticity of dominion an inescapable element of (fallen) human life, or could there be a *political* community without dominion? Are the anthropological reports of noncoercive societies examples of the absence of dominion? See Michael Taylor, *Anarchy and Cooperation* (Cambridge: Cambridge Univ. Press, 1987). For present purposes these issues need not be resolved; whatever else American constitutionalism may be, it incontrovertibly exemplifies what Yoder calls dominion. Indeed, one of the primary purposes of the Constitution of 1787 was to empower the federal government to exercise coercive force on individuals as well as states. See *The Federalist* No. 15 (A. Hamilton), 93–96.

30 Yoder, *Priestly Kingdom*, 169.

courts, rest on "the appeal to force as ultimate authority."[31] The coercive and ultimately violent character of constitutional law is easily overlooked because almost all of its forms are those of decorous argument and reasoned deliberation. "The violence of judges and officials of a posited constitutional order is generally understood to be implicit in the practice of law and government. Violence is so intrinsic to the activity, so taken for granted, that it need not be mentioned."[32] Indeed, much of the point of legal ritual and procedure is directed at "denying or making invisible the violence [law] inflicts."[33] But violence *always* lies behind the arguments and the reasoning.

The violence of American constitutional law runs throughout the various modes in which that law might be said to exist. The practice of constitutional adjudication eventuates in judicial decisions that are by definition invocations of coercion. All judicial decisions are, directly or by implication, orders to state officials to act, if necessary by employing deadly force,[34] even when the decision takes the form of prohibiting official action.[35] The primacy of dominion in American constitutional thought thus is reflected in the constitutional-law doctrine that citizens must obey even a patently erroneous or unconstitutional court order or be liable to punishment.[36]

Constitutionalism is, however, unlike some other areas of law,

31 John Howard Yoder, *The Christian Witness to the State* (Newton, Kans.: Faith and Life Press, 1964), 12.

32 Cover, "Violence and the Word," 1610 n. 22.

33 Sarat and Kearns, in Sarat and Kearns, *Fate of Law*, 209. Milner Ball's theological analysis of American legal process is marred by his use of the metaphor of theater for the act of judging. See Ball, *The Promise of American Law* (Athens: Univ. of Georgia Press, 1981), 29–94. That metaphor obscures the most ethically significant feature of the process—people are hurt, sometimes killed, through and as a result of the judges' actions. Ball thinks the American courthouse can be usefully analogized to Greek theater; the better analogy might be to the Roman amphitheater.

34 "The judicial word is a mandate for the deeds of others." Cover, "Violence and the Word," 1611.

35 Official disobedience to a judicial order renders the disobedient official liable to coercion or punishment by other officials, at the court's direction. The possibility that no official with coercive force at his or her disposal would act to enforce the will of the court has been almost wholly theoretical in American history. In any case, that possibility in no way changes the total permeation of American constitutionalism by state power.

36 See Walker v. Birmingham, 388 U.S. 307 (1967).

directly concerned with the regulation of violence. This point was unmistakably clear in the early years of the constitutional tradition, when most important issues revolved around federalism—questions about the relationship between the coercive power of the federal nation-state and that of its constituent states. Arguing the first great federal constitutional case before the Supreme Court in 1793, Attorney General Edmund Randolph warned that constitutionalism was ultimately dependent on "a distant glimpse of the federal arm uplifted"; the "peace and concord among the states" that were "two of the great ends of the constitution" could be achieved in Randolph's opinion only by a clear recognition of the Supreme Court's authority to subject acts of state power to judicial examination, and to support its decisions with whatever coercion was necessary.[37] Randolph's intention, of course, was to contrast the lawless war of all against all with constitutionalism's promise to fulfill "the Enlightenment ideal of holding acts of power up to the critical light of reason."[38] But, as Randolph candidly if reluctantly admitted, that ideal itself was itself only the penultimate step in a legal progression that culminates in theory or in practice in the use of force, by the nation-state, against whoever would dare defy its decrees. A few years later, James Madison defined coercion as essential to the definition of constitutional adjudication. Madison distinguished the Virginia legislature's resolutions denouncing the 1798 Sedition Act as unconstitutional from judicial judgments on constitutional matters by defining the legislature's formal resolutions as "expressions of opinion, unaccompanied with any other effect than what they may produce on opinion, by exciting reflection." "The expositions of the judiciary," on the other hand, "are carried into immediate effect by force."[39]

Contemporary American constitutionalism seldom involves even the remotest possibility that armed officials of disagreeing governmental bodies might come to blows.[40] Most hotly disputed constitu-

37 Chisholm v. Georgia, 2 U.S. (2 Dall.) at 424.

38 Robin West, "Disciplines, Subjectivity, and Law," in Sarat & Kearns, *Fate of Law*, 119.

39 Virginia Report of 1800, in Powell, *Languages*, 145.

40 Such possibilities are only a few years in the past, however. Explicit violent confrontation between state and federal actors was a recurrent threat in the 1950s and early 1960s during the initial stages of enforcing *Brown v. Board of Education*.

estions in the present era concern someone's rights, a con-ricans typically associate with notions of stability and order an with the control of violence.[41] The association is, how-sleading: *all* assertions (and denials) of constitutional right ions of power and implicit invocations of the courts' power to ence to enforce obedience. No matter how benign the right, t announcing it and the officials who are pledged to enforce it cising dominion.

second level of social reality which a New Testament realism zes is the existence of what Yoder calls the *language of legit-*: "there is the level of moral rhetoric used by the bearers of to legitimize themselves. This legitimation language comes e fact of dominion."[42] Rulers invariably[43] seek to justify their se of dominion with the claim that their rule is morally legiti-and socially beneficent. The language of legitimation is, Yoder , always conceptually distinct from the dominion it justifies.[44] are social realities, but one exists as the coercion of human s by other human beings on the physical, economic, verbal, piritual planes while the other exists only as verbal explanation. r also implies that the legitimating rhetoric is always (partly) the rulers invariably deliver less than they promise and the uage of legitimation is to that extent misleading or a lie. This is, aps, especially likely to be true of relatively benign political ems, which often have extraordinarily inflated pretensions.

The act—rather, announcement—of legitimation is in any event ondary to the dominion it legitimates. "It remains the nature of civil order itself that its coercive control is prior to any justifica-ns or qualifications thereof."[45] This is true, Yoder asserts, even of lightenment-influenced political systems, which usually "clai[m]

41 Criminal procedure rights, most of which are constitutional in origin, do al unmistakably with the control of state violence against individuals.

42 Yoder, *Priestly Kingdom*, 157.

43 Yoder acknowledges the theoretical possibility of "the shameless tyrant" ho "would admit he is doing us no good." This "is not a very threatening real ossibility since most rulers do claim beneficence." Id. at 169. For present urposes, the question is of no importance, since American constitutionalism nakes very strong claims about its beneficent nature,

44 Id. at 159.

45 Id.

directly concerned with the regulati
unmistakably clear in the early years
when most important issues revolved
about the relationship between the c
nation-state and that of its constituent
federal constitutional case before the
torney General Edmund Randolph wa
was ultimately dependent on "a distant
uplifted"; the "peace and concord among
of the great ends of the constitution" coulc
opinion only by a clear recognition of the
to subject acts of state power to judicial ex
its decisions with whatever coercion was
intention, of course, was to contrast the lav
with constitutionalism's promise to fulfill "t
of holding acts of power up to the critical lig
Randolph candidly if reluctantly admitted, tl
only the penultimate step in a legal progress
theory or in practice in the use of force, by th
whoever would dare defy its decrees. A few ye
son defined coercion as essential to the defini
adjudication. Madison distinguished the Virgini
tions denouncing the 1798 Sedition Act as ur
judicial judgments on constitutional matters by
ture's formal resolutions as "expressions of opini
with any other effect than what they may produ
exciting reflection." "The expositions of the judic
hand, "are carried into immediate effect by force."

Contemporary American constitutionalism seld
the remotest possibility that armed officials of disa
mental bodies might come to blows.[40] Most hotly di

37 Chisholm v. Georgia, 2 U.S. (2 Dall.) at 424.

38 Robin West, "Disciplines, Subjectivity, and Law," in
Fate of Law, 119.

39 Virginia Report of 1800, in Powell, *Languages*, 145.

40 Such possibilities are only a few years in the past, ho
violent confrontation between state and federal actors was a rec
the 1950s and early 1960s during the initial stages of enforcing *Bro
Education*.

tional qu
cept Am
rather th
ever, mi
are exer
use viol
the cou
are exe
The
recogn
imatio
power
after t
exerci
mate
insist
Both
being
and s
Yode
false
lang
per
syst

sec
the
tio
E

d

to reverse the sequence, deriving the fact of dominion from a process of legitimation."[46] But this claim is unfounded, for the alleged legitimating origin of Enlightenment polities is a myth. "Those views hold that there is some such thing out there as a *demos*, which is capable of ruling, and that if the *demos* were to rule we would be well governed. There is no such animal."[47]

Yoder's concept of the language of legitimation certainly applies to American constitutionalism. Indeed, constitutional doctrine (with regard to specific decisions) and constitutional theory (with regard to the system as a whole) are in large part precisely that—justifications for the exercise of dominion by the courts. The Constitution of 1787 begins with a powerful assertion of the legitimacy of the system of dominion it is about to describe, combining an Enlightenment reference to the supposed origin of constitutional power ("We the People of the United States . . . do ordain and establish this Constitution") with the age-old claim that its dominion is good for its subjects ("in order to form a more perfect Union, establish justice," and so on). As discussed above, contemporary constitutional theory is marked by its tendency to confuse this justificatory rhetoric with the reality of coercive power in the United States: to legitimate their constitutional views, the theorists frequently invoke a national community or consensus that they assume into existence. James Rorty long ago denounced the "democratic dogma expressed in the phrase 'We the People.' We have never had in this country any such identity of interest as is implied in that first person plural."[48] Nonetheless, the social morality turn in constitutional theory has actually increased the already high volume of American popular sovereignty talk. The theorists who are the most clear-sighted about the difference between that talk and the social realities of power distribution in this society, Tushnet, Bork, and Levinson, are the ones who have, in part or in whole, given up on constitutionalism as anything other than talk.

American constitutionalism comprehends a second, quite distinct language of legitimation, the language of rights. Rights talk is of course directly derived from Enlightenment liberal individualism:

46 Id. at 157.
47 Id. at 168.
48 Rorty, *Where Life is Better* (New York: Reynal & Hitchcock, 1936), 169.

its legitimating function in the American system is to reassure Americans that their rulers fundamentally respect and protect that individualism.[49] The notion of a constitutional right indeed is, in form and sometimes in substance, a limitation on some form of governmental coercion. But rights talk, and the political scheme of liberty it creates and defines, is analytically dependent upon the existence of a judicial system authorized to order the employment of force in order to implement judicial rights decisions.[50] "The very essence of civil liberty certainly consists in the right of every individual to claim the protection of the laws, whenever he receives an injury."[51] Constitutional rights talk legitimates the American polity not by appealing to shared, substantive moral commitments,[52] but by extolling its "liberal . . . regulation of power by power."[53] Yoder, furthermore, points out that this limiting character of rights talk is not different in kind from the effect of all languages of legitimation, each of which provides some means for criticizing the exercise of dominion.[54] The legal subordination of rights to obedience to judicial dominion, noted above, is a telling indication of the true role of the rhetoric of rights.[55]

Another feature of American constitutionalism indicates a complexity of the relationship between dominion and legitimation that Yoder does not seem fully to have explored. The self-justificatory

49 There seems little reason to doubt that the successful mobilization of public opinion against Robert Bork's nomination to the Supreme Court was due in large measure to the creation of a perception that Bork was unconcerned with safeguarding the individual rights of Americans—in other words, their claim to put their individual interests first.

50 Even as a formal matter, Anglo-American students of jurisprudence have usually identified the existence of a remedy—some recognized mode by which a court can exercise coercive force—as logically interdependent with the recognition of a right.

51 Marbury v. Madison, 5 U.S. 137, 163 (1803) (Marshall, CJ).

52 Indeed, a polity legitimated by its protection of liberal rights is, as Augustine regarded the Roman Empire, intentionally "vacuous at its core." Williams, "Politics and the Soul," 61.

53 Milbank, *Social Theory*, 290.

54 See Yoder, *Priestly Kingdom*, 159, 169.

55 As Tushnet and Bork both point out, furthermore, every judicial protection of a constitutional right involves the assertion of judicial power against other governmental actors and in defiance of majoritarian politics. The judicial enforcement of rights is a mode of exercising dominion, whatever the rhetoric of rights talk may assert.

rhetorics of popular sovereignty and individual rights that constitutionalists employ are not, in fact, merely tools for explaining or defending the exercise of power; they are themselves, in their articulation by the courts, a form of the exercise of power. As the late Robert M. Cover argued several years ago, one of the primary functions of American[56] courts is "jurispathic": by declaring the "imperial" *nomos* of the nation, judges (attempt to) kill or destroy the contrary *nomoi* of subnational, ethnic, and religious groups. A system of constitutional rights, grounded upon the basis of the will of the people, is necessarily intolerant, even in its enforcement of liberal tolerance. Cover's analysis supports MacIntyre's claim that a liberal society must fall back on "the assertive use of ultimate principles to close moral debate."[57] Despite some contemporary theorists' fascination with the notion of deliberation, the constitutional decisions of the courts are more likely to have the effect of ending serious moral discussion than of furthering it.

The final level of discussion that Yoder identifies is "the differentness of the disciples," "the ethic of Jesus and his followers, who take their signals from somewhere else [than the secular realities of dominion and ruler self-justification]."[58] One basic point here is the anti-Constantinian one: the Christian ethic must not be confused either with the facticity of dominion or with any of the rhetorics used to legitimate it. This prohibition carries with it an affirmation as well. Christian social criticism rightly measures secular political arrangements by "the Kingdom as [a] social ethic,"[59] and not (as the so-called Christian realists thought) by assuming the conceptual priority of secular assumptions.[60] "[T]here can only be a distinguishable Christian social theory because there is also a distinguishable Christian mode of action, a definite practice. . . . The theory, therefore, is first and foremost an *ecclesiology*."[61] The remainder of this conclusion is an attempt to indicate what ought to be said about the constitutional-

56 Cover clearly intended his argument to be general in nature. See Cover, "Nomos and Narrative," 97 Harv.L.Rev. 4 (1983).

57 MacIntyre (1984), 35.

58 Yoder, *Priestly Kingdom*, 157.

59 Id. at 80–101.

60 See id. at 164 (referring to "the children of Troeltsch and Niebuhr, for whom the pagan definitions are semantically prior").

61 Milbank, *Social Theory*, 381.

ism that the book has described from the perspective of "the ethic of Jesus."

The most important particular conclusion the book's analysis reaches about American constitutionalism is that it is a MacIntyrean tradition of rational inquiry that has entered into an epistemological crisis it is unlikely to overcome. American constitutionalism for much of its history explored (mainly) liberal moral principles through the use of tradition-dependent (common-law) modes of reasoning. The tradition recognized practices (constitutional adjudication and constitutional theory) with well-defined internal goods that demanded the exercise of intellectual and moral virtues. The tradition was embodied in a community of elite lawyers, judges, and scholars who functioned, as de Tocqueville observed long ago, as a sort of aristocracy. This community shared a rich culture of moral and social commitments, standards of rational argument and professional craft, and historical exemplars of virtue. As with any living tradition, constitutionalism lived through serious debate over its meaning and implications—think for example of the early twentieth-century criticisms of *Lochner*. As with any living tradition, the intellectual struggles were a vital factor in institutional and social change: one of the major reasons *Lochner*'s "conservative" pro-property doctrine became discredited among the "conservative" and propertied elite lawyers of the community was the growing conviction that Holmes and the Modern Theorists had the better of the argument.

The constitutional community now has fractured irreparably. Its breaking is the result of a confluence of factors—general social change including the "democratization of moral agency,"[62] the vast expansion of the bar and its consequent loss of shared understandings, and the rise of the administrative state. The traditional relationship between common lawyers (including American constitutional lawyers) and administrative bureaucracies was one of suspicion. Much of the common law's historical development in the early modern period resulted from the common lawyers' struggle to impose their standards of justification—and, of course, their own political power—on institutions such as Star Chamber and the ecclesiastical courts that were protobureaucratic in nature. American lawyers continued this insistence that bureaucrats, with their administrative

62 MacIntyre (1984), 32.

discretion and utilitarian forms of reasoning, be subject to the courts, with their nonutilitarian modes of justification.[63]

In the twentieth century, this effort at imposing law on bureaucracy was gradually subverted from within. The subversion began with the reaction to *Lochner*, which was, as noted above, a perfectly traditional exercise of judicial reason. Part of the post-1937 constitutional consensus was the recognition of large areas of governmental activity as the domain of administrative means/ends calculations, with legal reasoning serving only to police the administrators' subordination to democratically selected ends and constitutionally mandated limits. This recognition was not intended as a judicial withdrawal from oversight of the bureaucrats: the post–World War II Administrative Procedure Act, which codified the general understanding, was meant to confirm the continuing role of the courts. In fact, however, the act has ultimately become the vehicle by which bureaucratic utilitarianism has supplanted most of what remained of judicial supervision. The act's transformation is the doctrinal reflection of a fundamental change in the nature of the bar. More and more lawyers are, or have been, bureaucrats themselves, and have accepted as the "central task" of the lawyer "the rationality of adjusting means to ends in the most economical and efficient way."[64] The ongoing conversion of legal discourse generally into the utilitarian calculus of the bureaucrat, a conversion now lauded by lawyers politically opposed to public choice and economic-efficiency theories of policy,[65] renders any return to the moral discourse of the constitutional tradition virtually impossible.[66]

The fracturing of the constitutional community, and the accompanying crisis of constitutionalism as an intellectual tradition, are not disasters in themselves for Christians. The community was a narrow

63 See generally Nelson, *Roots of American Bureaucracy*.

64 MacIntyre (1984), 86.

65 See Bruce Ackerman, *Reconstructing American Law* (New Haven: Yale Univ. Press, 1984).

66 This is not meant to imply that Christians have any reason to work for such a return. While contemporary utilitarian modes of legal and constitutional argument probably are more remote formally from appropriate Christian modes of moral discussion than was the moral discourse of John Madison and John Marshall, the latter was substantively non-Christian.

Yoder has pointed out the tendency of utilitarian thinking to drive out other, more complex forms of moral discourse. See Yoder *Priestly Kingdom*, 140.

professional oligarchy that exploited its political power to protect its own socioeconomic interests. The moral content of the tradition was largely liberal and individualistic in nature; the Social Darwinism of the *Lochner* era was as natural a development of the constitutional tradition as it was repugnant to the Christian commitment to the weak and outcast. It is a mistake, therefore, to regard the rehabilitation of constitutionalism as an obvious Christian objective.

The mistake is found in several forms. Some Christian social critics, John Neuhaus for example, seem to understand the constitutional crisis itself as the result of American law's loss of its implicitly Christian moral underpinning.[67] But American law never was Christian in the requisite sense; Neuhaus and others have confused the legitimating language of American politics (an aspect of which is the biblically derived rhetoric of civil religion) with the moral reality of the coercive rules of law enforced by American courts.

Judge John Noonan has proposed a variant of this perspective. Without endorsing Neuhaus's romanticized picture of American legal history, Noonan interprets American law as open to treatment by judges who are so inclined as a means of achieving personalized and compassionate justice rather than the detached arbitration of others' rights that is the professional ideal of the judge's role.[68] Noonan's viewpoint shares with Neuhaus's a fundamentally Constantinian approach to law: both men attempt to work out a Christian appraisal of American law by assuming the perspective of the lawgiver and asking what the best form of it would be.[69] Like all forms of Constantinian social thought, this commits a double-barrel error, simultaneously accepting as normative the coercive nature of the state while overstating egregiously the significance of having individual Christians exercise the state's power.

A far more pernicious error is that of Christian constitutionalists such as Michael Perry. Perry's theory effectively collapses Christian ethics into contemporary constitutionalism, and by doing so gives an ersatz Christian blessing to the atomistic individualism of contemporary constitutional law. Theories such as Perry's are nakedly Con-

67 See John Neuhaus, *The Naked Public Square* (Grand Rapids, Mich.: W. B. Eerdmans, 1984).

68 See, e.g., John Noonan, *Persons and Masks of the Law* (New York: Farrar, Straus and Giroux, 1976).

69 See Yoder, *Priestly Kingdom*, 154.

stantinian, and they pose a serious threat to the ability of the church to engage in authentic Christian social criticism by their cooptation of the language of prophecy and (faith-)community. American constitutionalism's intellectual collapse threatens even the weak and wayward constraints the tradition has placed on state violence in our society. Attempts to revive Constantinianism obscure the growing violence of the system and thus are fundamentally misleading. Christians cannot adopt the language of constitutionalism and remain faithful to their own social vision, but neither should they simply ignore the state of constitutionalism, for (like all legitimating languages) it can be used as "the instrument of our critical and constructive communication with" our rulers.[70] But which constitutional language should we use to communicate when the rulers themselves seem unsure which they speak?

Perhaps the fundamental characteristic of the contemporary constitutional crisis is that constitutionalists seem to have lost the ability to reconcile constitutionalism's twin rhetorics of justification, popular sovereignty, and rights talk. The problem of reconciliation, which has been prominent since the creation of Modern Theory at the end of the nineteenth century, was negotiable as long as most people were willing to accept the autonomy and rationality of constitutional discourse. Granting that assumption allowed constitutionalists to explain constitutional adjudication as the enforcement of generally shared traditions (Holmes's view, for example), the interpretation of rules adopted by democratic supramajorities (Justice Black and the legal process school of the 1950s and 1960s), or the perfection of the democratic process (Stone's footnote four as well as many Warren Court decisions). In the 1970s, however, the support for the assumption largely evaporated. Constitutional theory since then, as we have seen, has been a long effort to put democracy and an active judicial role in moral-political policy-making back together again, while the Court lurches from decision to decision with no obvious rationale other than the specific substantive preferences of a majority of the justices. What should be the Christian response to the struggle between deference to legislative decision and the exercise of judicial choice?

In attempting to answer this question, we must decide whether

70 Id. at 158.

any normative significance should be attached to the fact that legislative decisions in the American political system are democratic, or (more precisely) the majoritarian decisions of representative bodies elected through majoritarian processes. If not, there would seem to be no reason not to adopt a completely casuistical approach, arguing for judicial invalidation when and only when the substantive outcome of judicial intervention seems morally preferrable to the outcome of the legislative process.

Most American Christians probably assume that democracy is the preferrable, or even only acceptable, form of government from a Christian standpoint. This widespread assumption is supported by two main forms of argument, one we may call pessimistic and the other optimistic. The canonical proponent of the pessimistic or "Augustinian" justification for democracy was Reinhold Niebuhr. Niebuhr summarized "Augustinian democracy" in a famous aphorism: "Man's capacity for justice makes democracy possible, but man's inclination to injustice makes democracy necessary."[71] Augustinians such as Niebuhr lay great emphasis on human sinfulness, which in their opinion renders all actual social relationships flawed and potentially coercive in nature; at the same time they emphasize the absoluteness of the Gospel ethic of love which, they insist, requires the renunciation of power. The result, particularly in Niebuhr, is a dialectic between an unavoidable realism of social and political life and the unattainable but essential idealism of Christianity. Christian political life therefore must be lived on the razor's edge between a complete surrender to sinful power and the wholesale abandonment of any hope for "effectiveness." "Goodness, armed with power, is corrupted; and pure love without power is destroyed."[72] Democracy is the form of political life most acceptable to Christian commitments because it fears the worst of its rulers and provides means for removing them from power.

Augustinian political thought does not seem an appropriate basis on which to proceed in our inquiry because it contradicts the in-

71 Reinhold Niebuhr, *The Children of Light and the Children of Darkness* (New York: Charles Scribner's Sons, 1944), xiii.

72 Reinhold Niebuhr, *Beyond Tragedy* (New York: Charles Scribner's Sons, 1938), 185.

quiry's non-Constantinian starting point.[73] The Augustinians are deeply Constantinian in their presuppositions, their acceptance of secular standards of political effectiveness and success, their exaltation of pragmatic "responsibility" as the primary political virtue. An Augustinian, we may assume, would almost automatically adopt the viewpoint of most contemporary constitutional theorists: assuming we can state the "rules of the game,"[74] what mix of majoritarian and judicial policy-making will best achieve the optimal realistic mix of governmental actions based on "unselfishness mixed with self-interest."[75] The answers to such Constantinian questions, in all likelihood, would closely resemble theories such as Perry's, and be subject to similar criticisms.

The optimistic version of the argument for democracy is well represented in Glenn Tinder's recent book *The Political Meaning of Christianity*.[76] Tinder rejects the relativistic conclusion that modern American Christians favor democracy because they live in one; despite his admiration for Niebuhr's criticisms of liberal optimism,[77] Tinder believes Christians should support democracy because it is the only political system that is positively linked with Christian moral commitments. Christian belief in what Tinder calls the "exaltation of the individual"[78] and in the ethical primacy of *agape* "make[s] it impossible to regard democracy as merely one among several equally legitimate political forms."[79] Christian moral commitments demand equality as a standard of political conduct. "No natural, social, or even moral differences justify exceptions to this rule."[80] Democracy, therefore, is the only legitimate form of government from a Christian

73 As I will discuss below, the usual Augustinian approach may not be that which is most faithful to the actual views of the historical Augustine.

74 Yoder, *Priestly Kingdom*, 169.

75 Id. at 100.

76 Glenn Tinder, *The Political Meaning of Christianity* (Baton Rouge: Louisiana State Univ. Press, 1989).

77 Id. at 157.

78 Tinder's use of this term is strongly reminiscent of pre–World War I "liberal Christian" formulae about the "infinite value of each human soul." See, e.g., Adolf von Harnack, *What Is Christianity?*, 2d ed., trans. Thomas B. Saunders (New York: G. P. Putnam's Sons, 1901).

79 Tinder, *Political Meaning*, 178.

80 Id. at 32.

standpoint because "[i]t is the only political form based on the idea of equality. It prescribes equality of power."[81]

Tinder's association of democracy with a Christian egalitarian commitment is not wholly dissimilar to the view of democracy that will be developed below, but the power of his perspective as a means of responding to American constitutionalism is vitiated by a curious ambivalence in his discussion of equality.[82] Tinder argues that the political ideal of justice, when informed by Christian commitments, demands a "radical"[83] standard of equality: "The first principle of justice is equality. This is clearly implied by the concept of the exalted individual."[84] Immediately upon making this ringing pronouncement, however, Tinder deradicalizes it by reintroducing worldly, "pragmatic" considerations that concepts such as *agape* and "the equal and transcendent dignity inherent in mere humanity" might be expected to rule out of the discussion. It would be "not only unjust but subversive of any sound set of values" to deny recognition to the "more intelligent, more virtuous, more gifted, [and] more highly disciplined." "The pursuit of justice is consequently subject to irreconcilable demands."[85] If this sounds like vintage Niebuhr, that impression is sealed by Tinder's discussion of democracy. After identifying democracy as the only legitimate system because of its egalitarianism, Tinder immediately adds a typically Augustinian qualifier that converts (apparent) ethical obligation into a mere unattainable limit case: "Needless to say, there cannot be equality of power; if there was, there would be no government. But the ideal can be approached."[86] Tinder's optimistic argument for democracy simply collapses into the Augustinian pessimistic view. Like Niebuhr's, therefore, Tinder's support for democracy provides no critical stance from which to construct a Christian response to the democracy-

81 Id. at 178.

82 If this were a full-scale examination of Tinder's theological presuppositions, the fundamental point at which I would want to criticize his work is the notion of the "exaltation of the individual," which seems to be a theologized form of liberal individualism.

83 Id. at 32.

84 Id. at 62.

85 Id.

86 Id. at 178.

versus-judicial review struggle within contemporary constitutionalism.

A more useful starting point for our response lies in a third, and quite distinct, argument for democracy. In an essay on "The Christian Case for Democracy,"[87] Yoder has presented a twofold justification for (a kind of) Christian support for democracy. The more basic side of the argument, which he calls the "negative case for democracy,"[88] rests on the legitimating function of democratic rhetoric in modern Western democracies. As in all societies, Christians can use the language of legitimation to communicate with and criticize those who rule society. But the efficacy of this language is relatively greater in modern democracies than in most other polities. As Yoder observes, Western liberal democracy makes strong self-justificatory claims about its grounding in the people as a political community; this "language of justification and therefore of critique" thus is available as a means by which democracy's "subjects may [seek] to mitigate its oppressiveness." This does not entail any romantic, unrealistic notions about the correspondence between the rhetoric of democracy and the reality of dominion: "I do not therefore believe that I am governing myself or that 'we' as 'the people' are governing ourselves. We are still governed by an elite, most of whose decisions are not submitted to the people for approval."[89]

Yoder's discussion of the "strength" of democratic justification-rhetoric is abbreviated, and as it stands it is not entirely convincing. The Marxist language of legitimation of the former Eastern bloc countries, for example, combined democratic themes as fulsome as those of the Western republics with egalitarian assertions a good deal stronger. On the basis of Yoder's express argument, one might have expected that justification rhetoric to be socially more potent than that of the West, and yet that appears not to have been the case. An additional element needs to be added (or brought out) to render the

87 Yoder, *Priestly Kingdom*, 151–71.

88 Id. at 166.

89 Id. at 158–59. Yoder's assertion that "[o]f all the forms of oligarchy, democracy is the least oppressive" is an empirical claim for which he provides no support. The bare existence of a strong rhetoric of legitimation, without more, does not *prove* that that rhetoric is being used successfully to mitigate oppression.

argument successful. The democratic language of the Western democracies stands in some factual relationship to the actual processes of acquiring power in those countries. A great deal of the actual exercise of dominion is conducted by persons who are vulnerable, directly or indirectly, to removal by majoritarian electoral means. However sporadic in occurrence and partial in effect, the exercise of the franchise (which in virtually all Western democracies is theoretically open to essentially all adult citizens) sometimes does change not just persons but policies. Western nation-states with their "punctualist"[90] electoral systems are not in any literal sense "democracies," but there is sufficient connection between rhetoric and reality to give the language of democracy great social force. In such systems, Yoder's argument seems to have some force.

The "negative case for democracy" can be expanded somewhat by considering a (perhaps surprisingly) complementary argument, Rowan Williams's account of the historical Augustine's understanding of politics. As Williams reads the *City of God*, Augustine was not arguing for a radical separation of the political and the spiritual, either in an individualist direction or in anticipation of the paradoxes of Niebuhrian "realism." Augustine, instead, was seeking to show that "the spiritual is the *authentically* political . . . he is engaged in a *redefinition* of the public itself, designed to show that it is life outside the Christian community which fails to be truly public, authentically political."[91] Pagan society, despite its pretensions, is in fact the sphere of political vice, not political virtue, because it is incapable even in theory of satisfying the Ciceronic definition of a commonwealth as "an assemblage associated by a common acknowledgment of law, and by a community of interests."[92] The "law" such societies acknowledge is the external imposition of order by force; while it "can in certain circumstances save a society from total dissolution [it] is also potentially a murderous and divisive force [that] consistently subvert[s] true common life."[93] The political arrangements of the

90 I have borrowed Yoder's phrase for "the predilection within ethics to consider primarily those decisions which are made at one time and place." Id. at 35.

91 Williams, "Politics and the Soul," 58.

92 Augustine, *The City of God* II.21, trans. Marcus Dods (Chicago: Encyclopedia Britannica, 1952), 161–62.

93 Williams, "Politics and the Soul," 62.

classical world all were attempts "to create an *ersatz* unity in a fundamentally fragmented and disordered group": Williams points out that Augustine regards the ideals of classical politics and their supposed antithesis, "the tyrannies of the Orient," as points on a single continuum.[94]

The failure of classical Athens and imperial Rome to satisfy Cicero's definition and their own pretensions is not according to Augustine merely contingent. It is instead the product of their (necessary) inability to acknowledge that which is the true "community of interests" of human beings, the communal shaping of human life as oriented toward God. "A social practice which impedes human beings from offering themselves to God in fact denies that central impulse in human nature which Augustine defined as the unquenchable desire for God and his truth. . . . In short, while [a pagan state] may be empirically an intelligibly unified body, it is constantly undermining its own communal character, since its common goals are not and cannot be those abiding values which answer to the truest human needs."[95] Only the Christian community is capable of acknowledging the true law of human well-being and building its common life around the true interests of human beings.

Despite the radical nature of his critique of pagan politics, Augustine's thought does not lead to the conclusion that there are, theologically, *no* differences among various political arrangements. Augustine's thought was in intention anti-Constantinian even if his practical political judgments did not always reflect perfectly that intention.[96] The "empirical state" is "always characterized by the exercise of coercive power" in the pursuit of goals that are at best negative.[97] But those goals, as long as they are understood to be the

94 Id. at 65, 59–60.

95 Id. at 59–60.

96 From the perspective of this book, Augustine's acceptance of the role of coercion in the pre-eschatological city of God is deeply problematic because it is unclear that Augustine recognized the unavoidable problems that *all* coercion poses for the Christian norm of true community. Id. at 63. See Milbank, *Social Theory*, 417–22, discussing the problem of coercion in Augustine's thought.

97 Williams, "Politics and the Soul," 63. The "classical republic is shut out from *ordo* and *lex aeterna*; it is built on disorder, in that what should restrain passion is itself replaced by a passion. . . . [The means employed] can assist the unity of a society only negatively, as we have seen, by restraining tyranny." Id. at 61.

negative ones of avoiding tyranny, mitigating oppression, and restraining violence,[98] are appropriate "within the inescapable constraints of fallen finitude."[99] It was precisely the pagan emperors' claim to provide true justice and true peace that rendered their rule wholly vicious: Augustine located the greatness of the Christian emperor Theodosius I in the humility of his pretensions.[100] An empirical state aware of the limited nature of its possible purposes can be a sphere of "negative order." A wise ruler properly aware of his "alarming task of discerning the point at which what he is defending has ceased to be defensible because the means of defence beyond this point undermine the real justice in the state" can justifiably act to preserve the imperfect justice and order of such a state.[101]

Augustine's theological argument for recognizing some possible empirical states as provisionally—pre-eschatologically[102]—justifiable, as "negative" spheres of imperfect order and justice, comple-

98 In acting to maintain civil peace and independence, "what it seems [the wise ruler] must beware of is supposing that what he is defending is the city of God." Id. at 66.

99 Id. at 63.

100 Id. at 64–65.

101 Id. at 66. Augustine's, and Williams's, discussion explicitly concerns the conditions under which an earthly ruler is justified in engaging in defensive war against an external foe. There would not seem to be any difference in principle, however, between the use of violence to defend the order of the state from external attack and its use to defend the internal order of the state against domestic turmoil.

102 My point here is not simply that no empirical state can be identified with the church or, in Augustine's image, the city of God. Augustine's theological and anthropological assumptions led him to "postpone" to the Eschaton the true, noncoercive community that is God's will for humans. See Williams, "Politics and the Soul," 63. That postponement is, I suspect, one of the aspects of Augustine's thought that provides a genuine basis for Constantinian and Niebuhrian interpretations of his political views. More important, such a postponement is an implicit denial of the church's eschatological nature as "substantive peace . . . actually performed [as well as] ideally imagined." John Milbank, "'Postmodern Critical Augustinianism': A Short *Summa* in Forty Two Responses to Unasked Questions," 7 Modern Theology 225, 229 (1991). Christian commitments, understood from the non-Constantinian perspective this book assumes, entail not only a sharper critique of empirical political arrangements, but also a richer social hope, than Constantinians and Niebuhrians can sustain. See Milbank, *Social Theory*, 228, describing "true community" as "what 'Church' should be all about."

ments and expands Yoder's "negative case for democracy." Yoder identifies the availability of a relatively strong rhetoric of legitimation as a theological basis for preferring democracy to other political arrangements. Augustine suggests that Yoder's judgment is necessarily an empirical one, not the logical product of the presence of democratic language in a political system. Where democratic rhetoric is directed toward describing the limited purposes and powers of the state, Augustine might say, it can serve as a powerful tool by means of which the subjects of the state can criticize their rulers' actions, and indeed by which the rulers themselves can be brought to see their authority as limited and provisional. But, Augustine might continue, if the language of democracy acts to identify the actions of the state as "the will of the People," that language and the political arrangements it legitimates will be *less* desirable from a Christian perspective than a more honest and less pretentious oligarchy.

Augustine's argument suggests a second correction to Yoder's negative case. Democracy, as understood in the modern liberal West, necessarily involves notions of political change, however superficial, and is typically praised for its openness to revision and correction. To the extent that democratic language reminds rulers and ruled of the impermanence and lack of absolute value of existing political and social arrangements, both in rhetoric and in the political reality of electoral change, it *can* help to avoid what Augustine perceived as the fundamental source of political viciousness in pagan polities, their "elevation to supreme status of a material or worldly interest capable of masquerading as spiritual."[103] "It is the awkwardness and provisionality, the endlessly *revisable* character (morally speaking) of our social and political relationships, that, in the Augustinian world, keeps us faithful to the insight of humility."[104] Yoder's "negative case for democracy" can be made when (and only when) democracy provides a language of criticism *and* a means for making evident the provisional and revisable nature of the political order.

The "more hopeful case for democracy" can be made properly only in situations where "their numbers, or their virtues, or their

103 Williams, "Politics and the Soul," 61.
104 Id. at 69.

friends, or their good luck should give to Christians a chance for positive model building. . . . This is the vision of the Christian cultic commonwealth as a model for the civil commonwealth." (What Yoder has primarily in mind is the free church vision of a community of faith in which "all should be free to speak and all should listen critically.")[105] In such situations, Christians may be able to move beyond democracy as a tool for reducing the injustice of elected oligarchs to urging on the general society "the open conversation of the church under the Word" as "a paradigm for government." As with the negative case, Yoder's "positive" argument is carefully distinguished from romantic or Enlightenment presuppositions about the nature of political life. The point of providing models for free discussion is not that Christians should expect the polity to become a true dialogical community; non-Constantinian ecclesiastical communities are essentially different from the fundamentally coercive polities of even the most benign democracies. Nor does the positive case rest on a Holmesian market metaphor (the truth will prevail in a free marketplace of ideas) or on liberal assumptions about the value of self-expression, or on notions of representation-reenforcement. The primary Christian motivation for modeling dialogical community is the Christian concern for those who have no voice, the victim and the alien. "So the irreducible bulwark of social freedom is the dignity of dissent; the ability of the outsider, the other, the critic to speak and be heard. This is not majority rule; it is minority leverage. . . . The crucial need is not to believe that 'we, the people' are ruling ourselves. It is to commit ourselves to defending *their* right to be heard."[106] At its narrowest, this "theologically mandatory vesting of the right of dissent"[107] enhances the ability of Christians and others, in Hauerwas's words, to see "that secular society [is not] more unjust than it already has a tendency to be."[108] At its best, such a Christian modeling of dialogical community may lead to a situation where "faith communities, and . . . other voluntary associations and household structures [may] pursue their own ends without any more central management, by the *demos* or anyone else, than the peace of

105 Yoder, *Priestly Kingdom*, 166.
106 Id. at 167.
107 Id. at 168.
108 Hauerwas, *Christian Existence*, 185.

the total community demands."[109] The ultimate goal of the positive case for democracy thus is actually to *reduce* the sphere in which the coercive power of the democratic process holds sway by strengthening the voices of disagreement and dissent that can challenge the exercise of dominion.[110]

Yoder's two cases for democracy provide the basis for several conclusions about the appropriate Christian response to the current dilemma of constitutional thought. First and most important, there can be no general principle, based on Christian commitments, for deciding in the abstract the proper balance between majoritarian and judicial decision making. A New Testament realism about the nature of political activity in this society will puncture the pretensions of elected officials to represent the will of the people as much as it unveils the emptiness of judicial claims to be humble servants of the people's Constitution. Majoritarian electoral processes and constitutional adjudication are both means by which relatively small political elites make policy decisions backed up by the threat of coercion. Augustine's perception of the need for political humility can be better met, in different circumstances, by either majoritarian or judicial decision making.

This conclusion might lead to a further one, that the Christian attitude to the constitutional struggle between majoritarian and judicial power ought to be entirely ad hoc and a posteriori: wait and see which institution provides the more acceptable answer. This sort of opportunism, however, ignores the fact that individual political decisions do not have only individual political consequences. *Roe v. Wade* did not just prohibit state legislatures from enacting a variety of abortion regulations, it also galvanized popular political movements, polarized (and sometimes paralyzed) legislative bodies, broke down the deeply embedded resistance of many constitutionalists to substantive due process as a rationale for judicial decision, and so on. Judicial deference to evil legislation tends to reenforce the social and

109 Yoder, *Priestly Kingdom*, 167.

110 Actually, as Hauerwas reminds us, even the most successful democratization of a polity would reduce only the ordinary exercise of coercive power, and not the polity's ultimate claim to absolute authority: "democratic societies and states, no less than totalitarian ones, reserve the right to command our consciences." Hauerwas, *Against the Nations*, 127.

political strength of those supporting the legislation[111] while repeated judicial intervention tends to undermine confidence in ordinary politics and draw still more policy issues into the courts.

The indeterminate systemic consequences of individual decisions render the strategy of "ad-hockery"[112] a dangerous one at best. A superficially more attractive Christian response would be one of strong support for judicial policy-making in the name of the Constitution (essentially the position adopted by many of the theorists discussed in chapter 3). Given there are no real theological reasons, based on the negative case for democracy, for preferring majoritarian over judicial decisions, one might argue that as a practical matter judges are more likely to make acceptable decisions than are legislators. The age-old pliability of elected officials in the face of public opinion, and the New Age technological means of manipulating that public opinion, make it difficult to put much credit in the willingness or ability of legislators and executive officials to listen to dissident or abberant voices. Federal judges at least are insulated from popular pressure and professionally socialized to listen to both sides of a dispute.

This argument contains a grain of truth (which will be discussed below), but despite its popularity among constitutional theorists it is unpersuasive in Christian theological terms. The argument is, in the first place, fundamentally unrealistic in what Tushnet calls "sociological" terms. Judges, and especially federal judges, belong overwhelmingly to an educated upper-middle class not notable for its responsiveness to Christian commitments.[113] The result of expanding the current judicial role in policy-making would probably be to accelerate the atomization of American society, both because of the acute individualism of the contemporary American legal elite and because the courts' mode of operation enhances the social value of

111 Think, for example, of the dismal history of the post-Reconstruction Supreme Court and legal racism.

112 See Patrick S. Atiyah, *The Rise and Fall of Freedom of Contract* (Oxford: Oxford Univ. Press, 1971), 114.

113 To say this is not to question the sincere Christian beliefs of some judges, but only to observe that the education and professionalization of most judges is a powerful socializing force in favor of privatizing whatever religious beliefs they hold and shaping their judicial behavior to conform to the deeply secularized and intensely individualistic values of their social class.

describing a political or moral position as based on constitutional rights, which are individual by definition. One need not romanticize the openness of American legislatures to Christian and other deviant voices to question the wisdom of narrowing drastically the range of persons able to make policy.

The negative case for democracy, as Yoder states it, does not seem clearly to call for Christians to respond to the constitutional crisis either by supporting or opposing judicial activism. The corrections Augustine provides, however, point at least marginally in the direction of a theological preference for majoritarian decision making. The actual range of electorally viable political positions in the United States is, of course, with few exceptions quite small. But the rhetoric of electoral politics—and on occasion the outcomes—are quite the opposite. American electoral politics loudly proclaims its own corrigibility, its openness to revision by the citizens' exercise of the vote and by the politicians' responsiveness to public opinion. However superficial the reality, the language of American democracy is a pervasive reminder of "the endlessly *revisable* character . . . of our social and political relationships,"[114] a reminder, as Augustine saw, that is of theological value. American constitutional rhetoric, in contrast, is a language of permanence, of settled decision, of absolute political value. Matters subject to judicial decision in the name of the Constitution are, by definition, beyond ordinary revision, perhaps beyond legitimate revision altogether.[115]

The positive case—the argument that democracy may be relatively justifiable in theological terms because of its relative openness in some situations to voices of dissent—provides additional and somewhat more definite elements for a Christian response to the question of majoritarian versus judicial policy-making. There are specific areas of contemporary American constitutional doctrine that are supportive in a fairly direct way of the ability of the weak, the victimized, and the outsider to make their voices heard, and that (to some degree) act to interrupt the growing violence of the political system. The judicial protection of racial, religious, and other distinct

114 Williams, "Politics and the Soul," 69.

115 One of the most striking elements of the debate over whether to overturn the Supreme Court's flag-burning decision (Texas v. Johnson, 491 U.S. 397 [1989]) by constitutional amendment was the constant argument by the amendment's critics that it was literally unthinkable to revise the First Amendment.

minorities ("discrete and insular minorities" in the language of footnote four) against exclusionary uses of the political process and the specifically political-process aspects of the Court's free expression jurisprudence, seem valuable in Christian terms as means of opening or keeping open the avenues of minority leverage. To say this is not to suggest a determinate Christian answer to specific questions, affirmative action for example. The argument is instead that while there are theological reasons for generally preferring majoritarian over judicial decision making in this society (the negative case for democracy), the positive case for democracy identifies certain areas of governmental action in which judicial decisions are preferrable to majoritarian ones because American judges are somewhat more likely, on the whole, to heed, or at least provide a voice for, minority voices.

There is a third area of contemporary constitutional law that, on the theological grounds just invoked, would appear to be an appropriate one for judicial activism. The concept of procedural due process requires the judicial enforcement of "ideals of governmental *reliability* and *regularity*."[116] Due process doctrine requires governmental decision-makers to act through procedures that permit affected persons to present their views in an efficacious manner and attempts to limit the ability of decision-makers to act on the basis of bias or unguided discretion. Due process "norms reduce the helplessness of individuals and groups by limiting their dependence on distant and inaccessible centers of implacable authority."[117] By doing so, procedural due process compels governmental institutions to pay some heed to the legitimation language of the political system, and thus interferes with the tendency of all state institutions, and especially bureaucratic ones, to seek limitless power.[118] For these reasons, procedural due process meets the theological rationale for supporting judicial activism. Furthermore, as with political free speech and (at least the core of) equal protection for racial and other distinct minorities, procedural due process continues to enjoy wide intellectual acceptance even in the expanded and fractured legal community. (Contemporary American legal education is, both in

116 Laurence Tribe, *American Constitutional Law*, 2d ed. (Westbury, N.Y.: Foundation Press, 1988), 629.

117 Id. at 631.

118 See Hauerwas, *Against the Nations*, 126.

form and content, a socialization into due process ideals.)[119] It is, in short, not unrealistic to hope that in these areas of constitutional doctrine, Christians can identify "a chance for positive model building."[120]

The identification of discrete areas of constitutional doctrine in which theological argument supports judicial nondeference to majoritarian decisions does not of course amount to a constitutional theory. Like the preferred freedoms jurisprudence of the 1940s, the argument just outlined is, from a viewpoint within the constitutional system, a series of exceptions to a general rule of judicial deference. What theological reason, if any, supports such a general rule? The argument (based on the positive case for democracy) has two steps. First, Christians should respond to the current constitutional crisis by joining others calling for renewed judicial deference for a distinctively theological reason; majoritarian processes in the United States, at least when policed by the limited judicial activism just discussed, increase minority leverage by increasing the variety of forums and the variety of decisionmakers available to hear and respond to deviant or weak voices (including the deviant voices of Christian communities). By doing so, those majoritarian processes serve the right of dissent that Christian experience and reflection has shown to be theologically mandated. This does not imply that at times (perhaps often) the results of majoritarian decision making will not be oppressive, but majoritarian decision making does not differ

119 See Stevens, *Law School*, 264–79.

120 Yoder, *Priestly Kingdom*, 166. There are many issues in which churches could model and Christians could argue for an improved judicial responsiveness to the voices of the outsiders in these doctrinal areas. Judicial free speech doctrine, for example, has become confused as a result of the contrary influences of a political rationale for free speech (similar to the theological one advocated here) and romantic-liberal views of freedom of expression as a necessary element in individual self-fulfillment. Defenders of the latter often argue that no reasoned lines can be drawn between forms of expression. Christian experience and reflection on the nature of dialogical community might serve to indicate where those lines may fall. Or, to give another example, in recent years the Supreme Court has tended to limit the scope of procedural due process by defining in a narrowly positivistic way those individual interests the state must respect. Christian experience and reflection might help to break due process doctrine out of the positivistic paradigm of rights and redefine its concern as affording voice and consideration to those who experience harm or alienation from the actions of the polity.

from any other form of political structure in that respect. Second, Christians should support an appropriately bounded rule of deference to majoritarianism because courts, and particularly the Supreme Court, are centralizing and homogenizing agents of social change under present conditions. As an empirical matter, it seems arguable that such agents are already overly plentiful in contemporary society.[121] If families, religious communities, and other social structures mediating between the individual and the nation-state are to have space in which "to pursue their own ends without any more central management" than necessary,[122] the hostility of the contemporary Court toward such structures must be curbed.[123]

Christian commitments, construed in a non-Constantinian manner, lead to a relatively austere view of American constitutionalism. The tradition of rational inquiry that enlivened constitutional institutions for much of the Republic's history seems fatally stricken. Bits and pieces of constitutional rhetoric remain viable means of communicating the Christian concern for the voices of the other and the victim to the judicial holders of governmental power. In general, however, it appears that Christian commitments are more likely to be met by the majoritarian political processes (as unlikely as that often is). There is no Christian constitutionalism; Caesar remains Caesar.

121 At other points in history a contrary Christian judgment may have been appropriate. During the period of massive resistance to *Brown v. Board of Education*, for example, it probably was appropriate to stress judicial freedom and authority.

122 Yoder, *Priestly Kingdom*, 167,

123 See Employment Div. v. Smith, 494 U.S. 872 (1990) (which upheld against First Amendment challenge a state's denial of unemployment benefits to members of a Native American religious community because of their use of peyote in the community's rituals).

INDEX

H. Jefferson Powell is Professor of Law and Divinity at Duke University and Special Counsel to the Attorney General of North Carolina. He has previously published *Languages of Power: A Source Book of Early American Constitutional History* as well as articles in law reviews and theological journals.